Knowledge
and
Politics

Knowledge
and
Politics

Case Studies in the Relationship Between Epistemology and Political Philosophy

edited by

Marcelo Dascal and **Ora Gruengard**
Tel Aviv University

WESTVIEW PRESS
Boulder, San Francisco, & London

Copyright © 1989 by Westview Press, Inc.

Published in 1989 in the United States of America by Westview Press, Inc., 5500 Central Avenue, Boulder, Colorado 80301, and in the United Kingdom by Westview Press, Inc., 13 Brunswick Centre, London WC1N 1AF, England

Library of Congress Cataloging-in-Publication Data
Knowledge and politics / edited by Marcelo Dascal and Ora Gruengard.
    p. cm.
  Bibliography: p.
  Includes index.
  ISBN 0-8133-0455-5
  1. Political science. 2. Knowledge, Theory of. I. Dascal,
Marcelo. II. Gruengard, Ora.
JA74.K56 1989
320—dc19   88-31223
                                                                  CIP

Printed and bound in the United States of America

∞ The paper used in this publication meets the requirements of the American National
   Standard for Permanence of Paper for Printed Library Materials Z39.48-1984.

10   9   8   7   6   5   4   3   2   1

Contents

PART FOUR
THE REVISION OF EPISTEMOLOGY

PART FIVE
THE METHODOLOGISTS

PART SIX
THE ANTIMETHODOLOGISTS

PART SEVEN
THE REBELS

Acknowledgments

Hagit Dascal faithfully and professionally prepared the various versions of the coded typescript of the book. Spencer Carr and the Westview Press staff have provided sympathy, encouragement, and expertise for accomplishing the task. Our students at Tel Aviv University were exposed to our joint and separate seminars touching on the topics of this book, and their enthusiasm and criticism were an invaluable stimulus for the crystallization of the project. We thank all of them as well as the authors of the chapters for their patient cooperation throughout the lengthy process of preparation of this book.

Marcelo Dascal
Ora Gruengard

Introduction

Marcelo Dascal and Ora Gruengard

Many philosophers have put forth both a theory of knowledge and a political philosophy. The studies in this book address the work of a sample of these thinkers, past and present. Each chapter undertakes to clarify— and eventually criticize—the kind of connection, if any, obtaining between a philosopher's epistemology and his political philosophy.

In one way or another, the underlying issue in each case is this: Given that a philosopher has expressly put forth certain doctrines in epistemology and political philosophy, how does the adoption of one such doctrine in one field *rationally* constrain in any way the kind(s) of doctrines that are adopted by him in the other? For instance, is there an identifiable rational connection leading from Russell's views on the conditions of human knowledge to his claims about the conditions of human freedom, as has been argued by Noam Chomsky? Does Paul Feyerabend's "methodological anarchism" in the philosophy of science commit him to the adoption of anarchism (or of what he calls democratic relativism) as a political position? Or is the former perhaps required by the latter? Does "methodological individualism"—the requirement that the "behavior" of social complexes such as groups and institutions be solely explained in terms of the behavior of individuals—entail political individualism, or vice versa? To what extent is Popper's critical rationalism indeed an overall framework covering his views both on science and on politics?

Each chapter deals with questions of this kind and related ones, mainly from the assumed perspective of the philosopher on whom it is focused, and takes into account his own conception of the connection—if any— between his epistemology and his political philosophy. As a whole, however, the collection goes beyond the individual cases. As a sample of case studies it helps to reveal recurrent patterns of connection and enables us to analyze their significance in a way that is less dependent on the biases of a single philosopher or interpreter. Furthermore, the analysis and comparison of the kinds of philosophical reasoning that purport to establish—or to discover— systematic connections between theories that belong to *prima facie* unrelated disciplines may shed some light on the meta-philosophical issues of the

1

nature of philosophical reasoning and of the coherence that holds together philosophical systems.

This introductory chapter is devoted mainly to the implications of the findings of the case studies for these general and meta-philosophical questions. Anticipating our conclusions, we might say that the present sample shows that the level at which the connections between theoretical options in the two domains are brought into sharpest focus is neither the level of sheer logical necessity nor that of mere historical or otherwise merely circumstantial contingency. It is, rather, an intermediary level, for which we employ the term "strategy."

The bulk of this introduction elaborates upon this approach and illustrates connective strategies in the cases studied in this book as well as in other well-known examples. But first, we wish to explain why we characterize our interest in this inquiry and its results as a search for "rational connections," and to discuss the considerations that have led us to select this particular set of case studies.

A Non-Reductionistic Approach

Traditional answers to the question about the relationship between epistemological and political doctrines are of two kinds, which correspond to different conceptions of the history of ideas. They focus either on connections of a structural/logical or of a genetic/causal nature. Neither of these approaches excludes the other. Because they emphasize different connections, what is usually found in the literature are studies which combine, in various proportions, both. What turns out to fit better the case studies here assembled, however, is a third *kind* of approach, not reducible to a combination of the former two, though sharing some features with each of them. The search for the rationale of the connection between philosophical positions, marked by the use of terms such as "reasonable" and "rational," indicates what it shares with the first approach. The emphasis on the specificity of the problems with which each philosopher is trying to cope, which puts a premium on a "token-token" rather than "type-type" analysis and fully acknowledges the historicity of the criteria of reasonableness, points to its similarity with the second approach.

Other approaches usually rest content with highlighting thematic similarities or dissimilarities between doctrines, disciplines, and authors, and with the ability to explain them in terms of logical and genetic relationships. Our analysis of the case studies purports to show that such relationships can be further clarified by considering the variety of *argumentative* environments within which both authors and their interpreters establish, justify, or simply rely upon them. Argumentation lies, of course, at the core of the philosophical game and it is via the critical assessment of arguments that the rationality of philosophical theories and systems is usually judged. Yet as the present studies reveal, it is not just a matter of logical inferences. This is why the question of whether there are rational connections between a philosopher's epistemological and political theories cannot be construed as a matter of purely logical relations between these theories *qua* articulated bodies of conceptual constructs. It rather involves a more complex relationship whose terms are the thinker's "problem-situation," the tacit criteria of rationality he or she takes for granted, his or her presuppositions, and the explicit theories he or she puts forth. Such a relationship cannot be elucidated by focusing exclusively on the question whether and how *the theories* are connected. One must rather stress such questions as: Does giving one's assent to a certain theory in one domain determine or otherwise constrain— by one's standards of rationality—one's theoretical options in the other? What is the connection—if any—between the problems in epistemology and political philosophy that the philosopher's respective theories are sup- posed to solve? Does the success of a solution in one of them function as an argument for proposing a similar solution in the other?

Obviously, in an inquiry of this sort, the explicit statements of the philosopher about the connections of the two theories he holds must be taken into account. But interpreters of the philosopher's positions can and should go beyond his explicit statements about those connections. After all, philosophical reasoning, despite the philosophers' claim to self-awareness, is only partially explicit, like the reasoning of ordinary humans. Sometimes philosophers knowingly avoid giving reasons which are relevant but im- permissible according to their putative methodology. They may even give methodologically acceptable reasons which are only excuses for choices actually motivated by other considerations. Sometimes they are not fully aware of their own reasons, biases, and problem-situations. As it is often the case with other mortals, interpreters may find in their statements, both the "official" ones and those expressed off the record, links that the philosophers themselves have never paid attention to: a recurrent structure, a pervasive model, a frequent metaphor, a consistent use of the same rule, and so forth. We believe that interpretations which take these possibilities into account are relevant to the understanding of a philosopher's positions, perhaps even more relevant than the philosopher's explicit arguments and self-perception of his considerations and method of reasoning. Interpretations such as these are particularly important in the case of reasoning which links two apparently separate domains, since the philosophers themselves may deny the connection. They are perhaps even more important when one of the domains is a battlefield of conflicting norms and interests, as politics often is, while the other is at least seemingly neutral, as epistemology aspires to be.

Licensing the interpreters to go beyond the philosopher's own perception of the connections between his theories paves the way either to the discovery of (possibly hidden) internal *reasons* for a philosopher's holding his two theories or to the explanation of their being in the same package in *causal* terms, e.g., by reference to some external connection (such as the fact that both theories symbolically fulfill the same unconscious wish, serve the same class interests, have their origin in the same authority). Though in our invitation to the contributors we did not exclude the latter possibility, nor the option of "no connection," all of the authors of the studies in this book undertake to explain the philosophers' particular choice of epistemological and political theories as *inherently* connected. Contributors generally applied the so-called principle of charity, assuming, further, that each philosopher's package of positions was somehow supported by reasoning and argumentation, rather than being merely the product of arbitrary circumstances. As could be expected, some of them maintain that a given philosopher's reasons are not convincing or even are defective. None, however, explains this flaw by resorting to unconscious motives or to considerations such as political opportunism or mere lip service paid to some authority (an allegation previously leveled against some of the philosophers here discussed). Perhaps this reflects some bias in our invitation's formulation of the exploratory questions to be addressed in each study. More probably, it reflects the currently prevailing norms of philosophical interpretation. Be that as it may, such a result certainly reflects the belief of at least fourteen contemporary philosophers of different backgrounds, positions, and styles that major epistemological and political doctrines can—and perhaps should—be connected "rationally."

But it also shows that there is ample variation and flexibility in the understanding of what counts as a "rational connection" between theories. Indeed, the interpretations here offered differ considerably from the standard ones. Differing conceptions of epistemology and politics, as well as a corresponding diversity of links between them are revealed. A variety of criteria for what counts as a reason or a rational connection emerges, which turns out to be much richer than anything one can find in textbooks and monographs devoted to these thinkers. Moreover, the variety of problems these philosophers are here shown to have been trying to cope with proves to be richer than anything we had envisaged when we undertook this project. And yet, as we try to show below, these results can be usefully analyzed in terms of a small number of argumentative strategies.

The Sample

A few comments on the way this volume was put together are now in order. We have selected as topics for the chapters of this book the work of a number of major philosophers who have contributed both to epistemology and to political philosophy. We invited several colleagues, some of them well known for their scholarly interpretations of the works of the selected philosophers, to write a chapter. Each scholar was requested to analyze the connection, if any, between the epistemological and political views of one or more of the selected thinkers. Our guidelines did not specify which data, besides the key relevant texts, should be taken into account. We suggested that the thinkers' political activities, though not our primary concern, might be taken into account, if necessary, only insofar as they were deemed to spell out the philosopher's political theory. No attempt was made to impose a unified approach. Each commentator was left free to rely upon his or her own conception of what are 'epistemology', 'political philosophy', and 'rational connection'. Indeed, in order to somehow prevent bias in favor of a given approach, we deliberately chose interpreters representing different points of view and styles of analysis; contributors even differed in their attitude—critical or sympathetic—toward the views of the philosopher they discuss.

Inevitably, however, there was some bias. Accessibility and familiarity led us to focus our attention on the Western philosophical heritage. Preference for theories which do not rely on divine assistance or a ready-made realm of Ideas, independent of human reasoning, induced us to concentrate on modern philosophy (with the exception of Aristotle), leaving aside philosophers who accept either revelation or some forms of intellectual intuition as a source of knowledge and norms. And, since we were interested in the strategies linking two *different* domains, our sample includes mainly philosophers for whom epistemology and politics are at least *prima facie* separate fields. Finally, limitations of space have forced us to reduce the size of the sample to fourteen case studies, namely: Aristotle, Hobbes, Hume, A. Smith, Condorcet, Hegel, J. S. Mill, Marx, Nietzsche, Neurath, Heidegger, Foucault, Habermas, and Feyerabend. The omission of Spinoza, Locke, Kant, Rousseau, Dewey, Popper, Nozick, Rawls, and others is not due to our underestimation of the relevance of their contributions for the present study, but rather to the lack of space.

Among those philosophers to whom a chapter in this anthology could not be devoted, some are indirectly represented via the reaction to their views by others. This is the case, for instance, of Locke (via the criticism of Nietzsche and Foucault) and of Kant (via the reaction to his views by Hegel). The thinking of other philosophers played an instrumental role in motivating this project. In this regard, we should mention Popper's attempt to connect his epistemological and political views through the principle of rational criticism: under closer scrutiny the apparently seamless connection lost much of its tightness. This incited us to probe deeper into the nature of such connections in Popper's as well as in other cases. Though no chapter is devoted to Popper, his strategy is discussed in some detail in this introduction.

The inclusion of Smith, Condorcet, and Heidegger needs justification, since their celebrity is due neither to their epistemologies nor to their political theories. Smith, who is known as the founder of economics, is an interesting case for two reasons. His political reasoning and conclusions are different from those of Hume, though their epistemologies are quite similar. They are also quite different from the liberal laissez-faire ideology, with which his name is sometimes wrongly associated: the latter applies to politics a principle Smith himself invokes only in economics, namely the blissful "invisible hand." Condorcet, who is known as a political activist and victim of the French Revolution, combined epistemological fallibilism with a resilient political optimism, which he did not give up even in the turmoil of the revolution: his unshakable belief in the possibility of solving political and social problems scientifically was grounded in his faith in his probabilistic conception of science in general, and of the social sciences in particular. In this respect, Condorcet too stands in opposition to Hume.

Whereas Smith and Condorcet represent lesser known variants of the frequent fallibilism-*cum*-liberalism package, Heidegger, *qua* supporter—be it only momentarily, as some of his defenders claim—of the Nazi movement, is perhaps the representative of a one-member class (as far as famous philosophers are concerned). Even though he did not develop a full-fledged political theory and was in fact a critic of traditional epistemology, his case is of interest here for several reasons. First, his political views and activities in Nazi Germany remain a source of deep embarrassment for those who admire his thought, and who see in it an expression of humanism and anti-authoritarianism: are these two strands connected, and if so, how? Second, Heidegger's case raises the question of whether the rejection of traditional epistemology is, as such, conducive to or compatible with right-wing totalitarianism. In this respect his case contrasts significantly with that of Nietzsche. The latter was more aggressively "deconstructionist" than Heidegger, and yet—despite claims to the contrary by some interpreters—never supported political views which resemble Nazi ideas and ideals. It also contrasts with the case of Feyerabend, another anti-epistemologist. The latter rejects traditional epistemology for utterly different reasons and favors opposite political ideals, and yet is ready to admit—in the name of both his (anti-)methodological and his political views—something that Heidegger never did, namely the legitimacy of an opponent's perspective. Whereas Feyerabend goes as far as to admit that racist ideologies such as anti-Semitism (which he opposes) might be as reasonable as his own preferred humanism, if viewed from a perspective which is no less "legitimate" than his own liberal outlook, Heidegger can hardly be credited with a similar attitude toward his own beliefs.

No doubt issues that are considered by some philosophers as real and important are judged by others as trivial, and sometimes as pseudo-problems. It is therefore inevitable that different commentators on the same philosopher tell different stories about the connections, their rationale, and the problem-situations that brought them about. Since our purpose was not to determine the "correct" interpretation, nor to offer our own alternative, we discuss in what follows the individual cases as they are interpreted in the studies here assembled. It should also be stressed that it has not been our purpose to pass judgment on the rationality of the philosophers' arguments and on the moral acceptability of the political positions attributed to them.[1]

Strategies of Connection

The cases studied here exemplify various ways of linking epistemology with political theory. None of these ways, however, consists of purely deductive inferences. In no case can one rightly claim that accepting one theory while rejecting the other involves inconsistency. Indeed, each theory in either field is compatible with more than one theory in the other field. But one should not hastily conclude that there is no rational connection between the philosopher's theories in a broader sense. For the assumption that one theory is true, or at least reasonable, can serve as a rationale for the acceptance of the other as a reasonable theory, as well as for the rejection of theories which are inconsistent with the former—at least from the perspective of the theories' author. By a "rationale" we mean a reasonable though defeasible argument. This term is intended to suggest that the linkage relies on additional assumptions that are not part of either theory; if such assumptions are denied, or supplemented by others that change their implications, the argument might be defeated. By saying "at least from the perspective of the theories' author" we do not, however, claim that if the philosopher's presuppositions are accepted the connection becomes strictly inferential. His perspective does not consist only of propositions to which he would be ready to give his assent. It also includes the problems with which he tried to cope and the goals that their solutions are to serve. Hence, accepting one theory while assuming that the other is right, or accepting both theories by the same rule, should be regarded as a reasonable solution, though not necessarily the only possible one, to the problems with which the thinker tries to cope.

Two examples may clarify this point. From the perspective of the Scottish skeptics the lack of any objectively valid criterion for the correctness of rules in either epistemology or politics was a serious problem. Hume believed that consistent rules in scientific as well as in political matters are practically indispensable, and he wanted their choice to be rational. He decided, according to Don Herzog's interpretation (Chapter 3), to solve the problem in both fields by employing a single principle: adopt the rules that people are naturally inclined to use, for these rules, which depend on the mind's tendency to make associations, are both simple and universally acceptable. Smith, on the other hand, was intrigued, as Sergio Cremaschi suggests (Chapter 4), by the gap, in both domains, between the rationalistic values and the empirical data. Smith wanted to bridge those unattainable ideals and the inclinations of the human mind. He decided to apply to politics a solution which follows the example he believed Newton had set for science, namely, to postulate an intermediate domain—"nature"—which is indeed determined by laws, but laws that are only probable and approximate, lying between the necessary laws of rational reality and the contingent content of human experience. He thus postulated the existence of "natural sentiments" in the social realm, and based his theory of justice on the rules that govern this nature, rather than on the mind's inclinations.

These examples show that the linkage of epistemology and politics can be a strategic move, rather than an attempt to form a comprehensive theory which includes both. Such a move is, however, reasonable only because there are prior possible links between these fields. In Hume's case, the natural tendencies of the mind which leave their impact in both; in Smith's case, the assumption that the political, no less than the physical, is a domain which can be studied scientifically. Nevertheless, the *actual* adoption of such possible links can be viewed as strategically motivated, though the philosophers whose theories we discussed above did not necessarily think in strategic terms.

"Strategy," as the term is nowadays used in both psychology and the philosophy of science, describes quite adequately reasonings that are not reducible to strictly logical inferences, but rather are guided by some heuristics, of which the reasoner himself is not always fully aware. Adoption of the strategic approach in the case of the philosophers discussed in this book has several advantages. It permits the discovery of a kind of coherence in the philosophical enterprise as a whole, despite the variety of approaches and styles of both the philosophers and their commentators. In particular, it solves the problem of the diversity of their conceptions of "epistemology," "politics," and "rational connection." It allows, further, a reduction of the great variety of connections the commentators have created or found to a small number of strategies. It justifies, finally, viewing the cases studied here as a sample from which something concerning the nature of philosophical reasoning in general can be learned.

We distinguish between two broad kinds of strategies: the "hard" ones, which tie the two domains to each other within some sort of a system; and the "soft" ones, which just establish some link between them. The hard strategies do not necessarily imply more logical rigor than the soft ones, though the links they seek to establish are presented as more direct, systematic, and inferential than those based on the latter kind of strategy. Within each kind two sorts of recurrent strategies have been identified: the "common core" and the "subordination" strategies (both hard), and the "mediating domain" and the "analogy" strategies (both soft). Several versions of each of these strategies can be further distinguished. We shall describe and illustrate each kind of strategy in the following sections, mainly through examples from the present collection. It will become apparent that the same philosopher often employs more than one of these strategies, since none is, in itself, sufficiently effective. Nor is the list exhaustive, presumably not even for the present sample. We only highlight some salient strategies and invite the reader to look for additional ones.

The Common Core Strategy

The common core strategy connects the two domains via a core common to both, as their shared source, basic feature, function, precondition, or the like. Hobbes, for example, found two common features. The first is a characteristic which is common, according to his view, to all existing things— the *conatus*, or the drive for self-preservation (and self-enhancement). The other is specific to humans, namely the knowledge of causes and effects, which is, according to Hobbes, the only possible kind of knowledge. Physical knowledge is not only the most eminent example of knowledge, but also the most basic one, since Hobbes's materialism maintains that all genuine knowledge is reducible to physics (as conceived by him). The *conatus* motivates both the wish to know (since knowledge is power) and behavior. Ethics, and therefore also politics, is, just like physics, a matter of knowledge—the ability to infer rightly effects from causes (including actions), and causes from effects. As being good is nothing but being appetitive, and being bad is equivalent to being aversive, moral knowledge is the knowledge about which actions have appetitive results and which lead to aversive ones. Given that the *conatus* is common to all humans, there is also a common good and a common bad. Political knowledge is the knowledge of their causes. It involves, like any knowledge, logical inferences. But while everybody has, in the modern idiom, the competence for such inferences, most people perform poorly when either a long chain of deductions is needed or an immediate good is more salient than a greater but remote one. Given that in the state of nature everyone is endangered, peace is a very salient common good, and that is why everybody is capable of seeing the advantage of the social contract, i.e., of the investment of individuals' powers in the hands of the sovereign. Most people, however, are not able to infer the right means for peace maintenance, and that is why they should accept the absolute authority of the intellectually superior sovereign. The conventionalism of Hobbes—the sovereign determines which religion, for instance, is true—is consistent with this view, for divergence of beliefs causes controversies and wars.

This theory is, or seems to be, consistent, but it has also an argumentative function, and this is why we treat this quite coherent theory as a strategy. Let us examine more closely Hobbes's argumentation. Hobbes believes that his materialism justifies the claim that all knowledge is reducible to physics, whose laws govern cognitive as well as emotional processes, and therefore also determine what is politically appropriate. It is this reductionism which supports his claim that there is only one kind of knowledge. Hobbes, however, does not need such a reductionism in order to support his political claims. The validity of the consideration which should lead people to adopt the Hobbesian political formula does not depend on the question of whether there is any physical explanation to the fact that they perform such a consideration. Moreover, the claim that human wishes are physically determined is irrelevant to the sovereign's policies. The sovereign's ability to make complex inferences about politically relevant causes and effects does not depend on his knowledge of their physical basis. In fact, Hobbes's sovereign is supposed to know even less than the future Skinnerian psychologist: the latter will know the environmental conditions which mold behavioral patterns and will thus be able to control behavior, whereas the former is supposed to know only which conditions prevent conflicts, and he is only able to enforce rules.

The reduction to physics is, however, useful because it can help Hobbes to support his political solution, which is not the only possible solution to the political problem he tries to solve, and certainly not the most appetitive: if all true knowledge is reducible to physics then every belief which cannot be translated into physical terms is the result of either an invalid inference or an intentional inducement by the powerful of a false belief. When common values and ideals are involved, the second alternative is more plausible and useful. It permits one to claim that any opposition to the proposed solution on the grounds that it violates some allegedly inalienable rights or natural laws actually relies on beliefs which have been induced by some powerful authority for its own interests. Inducement of beliefs by the Hobbesean sovereign is preferable, for he will do it for the common interest, and with better knowledge of the appropriate means. Seen from this perspective Hobbes is closer to Skinner than to the legal positivists. Skinner uses the same reductive strategy when he claims that people consider freedom and dignity as values only because of prior conditioning. His wise king, the psychologist, will condition them more knowingly and more efficiently, and for more general interests. But he will do it without relying upon slogans which are irreducible to behavioristic language (and would therefore be invalid), while the Hobbesean sovereign (though not the philosopher) cannot avoid appeal to non-physical terminology.

The common core strategy is not always reductive, however. Aristotle, for whom the common core is the human soul, is insistently anti-reductionist. He disagrees with the Platonic reduction of all knowledge to theoretical *epistēmē* as well as to the reduction of all forms of social organization to that of the state. He also denies Plato's claim that there is only one kind and one source of good, and rejects his thesis that the knowledge of the good, regarding any object, is epistemic. Aristotle believes that the knowledge of temporal, changeable matters is necessarily doxastic (a matter of opinion), though he maintains that some opinions are better than others: in technical issues, the opinion of the person who excels in *technē*, and in moral and political matters, the opinion of the one who excels in *phronēsis*. He therefore rejects the Platonic ideal of a state governed by a philosopher who excels in *sophia*—a state in which each person is assigned to a class and a role according to his or her epistemic competence (or incompetence). By making the human soul, rather than *epistēmē*, the common core of both his ideas about knowledge (he did not have an epistemology in the modern sense, which is narrowly concerned with questions of validity) and his political theory, Aristotle is able to find support for an alternative political theory. The rational part of the soul, which is specific to humans, is responsible, on the one hand, for all kinds of knowledge, and, on the other, for the human ability to choose a course of action according to an opinion about the good. It is also responsible for the human capacity to speak, *logos*, the capacity which enables them to form a state. The state, unlike the social units of which it is composed—economic organizations (villages) that are composed of biologic units (families)—is thus specific to humans. Though it too is formed to provide for vital needs, its end is not just life, but the good life. People have different opinions about the good life and the means to achieve it, and this should be taken into account in the good state. But Aristotle is neither an individualist nor a relativist; for him good is the perfection of the characteristic which differentiates the species of a given individual from other species. The *differentia specifica* of humans is the rational part of the soul, and the good of the state, i.e., its product, should also involve rationality. Though it is not the arena of the highest function of this part—i.e., theoretical knowledge (whose perfection is the virtue of the best man, and preoccupation with it is the best life)—the state is nevertheless an arena of rationality. It is the practical *phronēsis*, the capacity to choose reasonably and prudently, to form good arguments and persuade, which is to be perfected in the good state. The good statesman is the one who excels in this capacity, and the citizens of the good state are all virtual statesmen. They elect as temporary ruler the one who has convinced them with his ideas about the common good, and each citizen has the chance to persuade and to be elected in the next election.

This theory too is quite coherent, though its parts are not tied together as tightly as in Hobbes's case. But it can also be seen as a strategy: Aristotle is as anti-democratic as Plato, for he too wants to exclude the *demos* from political activity. But he does not share Plato's conception of knowledge, and therefore cannot apply the Platonic epistemic criteria for exclusion. So Aristotle uses a common core, namely his own theory of the human soul, in order to rank people according to the degree of perfection of the various functions, hierarchically ordered, of its rational part. This enables him to invent the notion of "a slave by nature," who may have *technē* but lacks *phronēsis* and therefore needs a master to tell him what to do; and he assigns to such slaves the chores assigned by Plato to the epistemically incompetent class. It also enables him to exclude the Platonic philosopher from the political sphere, as someone who should prefer a contemplative life. Yet Aristotle shares the Platonic ideal of a moral, just state governed by the wise. As his conception of knowledge does not allow him to connect *sophia* with practical issues, he establishes in the rational part of the soul a sub-part whose function is related to virtues as divergent as prudence and eloquence. His ethical principle of the middle way allows him to argue that prudence is morally relevant; his rhetorical and logical theories are supposed to teach how to distinguish good eloquence from demagoguery. His conception of justice as distributive, finally, can support the idea of the distribution of political power among the wise citizens.

Aristotle certainly wants to improve the Greek model of the polis-state, but he accepts its basic structure. He does not want to dissolve the kinship groups and the existing economic frames as Plato had suggested, so he argues that these were pre-political, indeed pre-human, "necessary for life," forms of social organization. The state, which is superimposed on them, should accept them as given. The linkage of knowledge with politics through the common core of the human rational soul (an idea which was, perhaps, inspired by the analogy Plato drew between the soul and the state), and the integration of different virtues in a single category of practical knowledge, allow him to combine his preferences—as well as his objections to many of Plato's ideas—with the ideals he had inherited from him.

The examples of Hobbes and Aristotle both show that the common core strategy enables the establishment of a multiplicity of ties that link the two domains together, and the number perhaps compensates for the looseness. It best serves philosophers who try to integrate their ideas in various domains into a comprehensive theory. Such philosophers employ this strategy, each with his own idea of a common core, encompassing conceptions of knowledge and society, cognitive and political ideals. Hume chooses the human mind. Hegel focuses on the Spirit with its dialectical logic. Heidegger prefers a basic form of relatedness to the world. Habermas votes for rational discourse. For Nietzsche, a reductionist who is midway between idealism and materialism, the common core is the will to power. Their argumentative styles are at variance, and they differ widely not only in the degree of logical power, but also in their conception of logic. Furthermore, none of them uses this strategy in a flawless way, and all of them employ at least one additional strategy. In some cases this other strategy is even more salient than the common core one.

The Subordination Strategy

This strategy subordinates one domain to the other by making an interest of the latter the aim that actually dominates the considerations in the former. It can work in both directions. For some, the political arena is seen as a place where the aim of advancing knowledge should be served, and they construct their political arguments with this aim in mind, each according to his preferred epistemological conception. For Condorcet, the aim is enabling the discovery of propositions endowed with a high degree of probability; for Mill, almost like Popper, it is creating optimal occasions for the discovery of errors; for Feyerabend, preventing the enforcement of dogmatic beliefs; and for Habermas, political institutions that create favorable conditions for the development of certain cognitive competences—notably those connected with rational discourse—are desirable.

For others, knowledge and the theory of knowledge are both seen as serving political interests, so that the direction of subordination is reversed. This is the case with the Marxist interpreters of non-Marxist theories, as well as with Nietzsche and Foucault. This line of argument is often considered as a reason for adopting an anti-epistemological attitude, i.e., for claiming that since epistemology is at any rate biased by political considerations, it cannot fulfill its own promise of providing a neutral and objective conception of what knowledge is, and should therefore be discarded as a worthwhile human endeavor. On this view, the "subordination" of epistemology to politics amounts in fact to the death of epistemology. Nietzsche, Foucault, Feyerabend, and the recent work of Richard Rorty all illustrate variations on this theme. But it need not be so. One might rather stress that precisely because the value of knowledge lies in its being a means to achieve political ends, epistemology should be raised to one of our highest priorities. Moreover, its aim should be to provide a method of knowing as objective and unbiased (by political considerations, among others) as possible, for otherwise its instrumental value itself would be severely undermined. This is the conclusion that Bacon, for one, draws from his acknowledgment (much before Hobbes and Nietzsche) of the fact that knowledge is power.

The choice of a particular direction does not, therefore, determine how the subordination strategy will be used. This is why we describe it as a *strategy* in the first place. In fact, the subordinating relation, in all the cases here analyzed, can hardly be conceived in terms of a single, well-defined, deductive chain. Marx is a case in point. Though it is widely assumed that Marx somehow paved the way for taking into account the influence of political and other "external" factors on any conception of what is knowledge, the interpretation of Marx's own position is still a matter of intense debate. Some argue that his account of ideology applies to *all* theories, including itself (as well as Marx's other theories). Some maintain that despite this self-reference, the Marxian theories are objectively valid, for they are the ideology of the class whose revolution will create the classless society, and which, on Marx's analysis, is on its way to become an almost universal class; and according to the epistemological tradition that Marx inherited from Hegel, universal consensus and objective validity are the same thing. Some hold that according to Marx only some aspects of epistemology can be mobilized for a political cause, an approach represented in the present volume by Gideon Freudenthal's analysis of Neurath's ideas (Chapter 10). Some view Marx as criticizing others' epistemological errors while accepting the basic ideas of the traditional epistemology. In this vein, Robert Paul Wolff's study (Chapter 8) presents Marx as actually holding a position that many Marxists would discard as "idealistic." Some, finally, suggest that, despite Marx's own claims to the contrary, his approach is well within a tradition that conceives epistemology as a politically neutral domain—a view reflected in Chapter 9, by Jon Elster.

Mill's approach is a salient example of the opposite direction, namely of the subordination of politics to epistemology. Two moral principles, which are not always compatible, seem to dominate his political liberalism: individualism and utilitarianism. When they are in conflict, he appeals to a further principle, that of "better knowledge," even if the price is inconsistency in his political recommendations. Thus, for example, he argues for non-interventionism because nobody knows better than the individual himself what is good for him. But on another occasion he supports intervention in favor of the poor by means of regulations, reform, and education. The rationale here is utilitarian, with elitist and paternalist overtones: only and all people who have tasted moral or spiritual pleasures know that they are—objectively [sic]—more pleasant than other pleasures; hence the rich as well as the poor should be happier if the former have less wealth and the latter some more. Mill's bias in favor of knowledge also leads him to recommend that the people's representatives be more enlightened than the general public. This bias does not follow only from the belief that knowledge is important for happiness. For him knowledge, a higher pleasure, is also an independent aim, which justifies political preferences. Freedom of thought and speech, encouragement of the expression of opposed views in public forums, and open debates are all supported by the claim that they enable society as a whole to discover errors and to argue better for non-falsified beliefs. One may argue that the connection Mill establishes between his fallibilistic conception of knowledge and the political aim to advance knowledge leads him to forget that in politics what is at issue is often a conflict of interests or values rather than falsifiable beliefs. But this is an objection which Mill can answer with the help of his objective utilitarianism, according to which interests and values rather than a last court of appeals can occasionally be shown to be wrong on utilitarian grounds. On similar grounds he can also reply to the objection that the suffering of the person whose opinion is publicly criticized and falsified is not necessarily compensated by the increment of truth, for, on Mill's theory, intellectual pleasures are (objectively) superior to those derived from honor. Yet, despite its elasticity, Mill's strategy does not help him to resolve all the conflicts between his various ideals. In fact, it cannot, for Mill is an individualist who believes that freedom of thought should be respected even when it leads to errors and suffering.

We call the subordination of politics to epistemic aims a strategy, and not simply a claim to the effect that the state should above all foster knowledge, because the philosophers who use such a strategy do not make, and would not give their assent to, such a claim. In the case of conflict between the epistemic and the other ideals these philosophers cherish, they would tend to prefer the latter, but try to support their preference as if knowledge were the issue. Individualism is a political ideal often defended in this way, sometimes clumsily and not without conflict, not only in Mill's case. It sneaks into Feyerabend's argument for "epistemological anarchism." It is less apparent in Popper's theory of the open society, but as Popper's use of this version of the subordinating strategy is an outstanding example thereof, it is worthwhile to analyze his case.

Popper tries to argue for liberal individualism in the most parsimonious way, i.e., with the help of the smallest possible number of non-justified principles. So he adds to the principle of minimization of human suffering only one principle, the one which his epistemology demands: critical rationalism, i.e., to behave in a way which creates the best chance for the detection and elimination of false beliefs. What helps him to make this principle provide support for individualism is the fact that other political individualists have already found ways to defend their political position by means of epistemological arguments. Thus, Kant formulates the categorical imperative in three, allegedly equivalent, ways. One of them states a formal condition: the criterion for the right rule of conduct is its capacity to be a general, natural law (i.e., a law in the ideal state, where everybody obeys the laws, just as every natural object behaves according to the laws of physics). Another formulation specifies that the criterion for the right rule is that its application is possible even if everybody follows it. In other words, the laws of the ideal state should not bring about the annihilation of that state. This condition is the equivalent of the principle of Reason, according to which the physical laws are such that Nature is not self-destructive. Kant creates thereby a strong connection between practical (ethical and therefore also political) and pure (epistemological) Reason. The third version explains that the essence of the right rule is an unconditioned respect for the individual.

It is the availability of this type of argumentation linking epistemological principles to political individualism that forms the background that lends plausibility to Popper's strategy. But the reliance upon such a background is not without problems. For example, Popper applies a combination of the first two versions of the Kantian principle (thereby accepting the third) in order to defend his "rule of restricted tolerance," i.e., the view that the freedom of speech of those who preach against the open society can and should be curtailed. But this rule, which should help to bypass some difficulties inherent in individualism, clashes with other key tenets of Popper's epistemology. First, it clashes with fallibilism: not only the suppressed opinions might turn out to be true (as Mill pointed out), but also the criteria employed by those that suppress them might be wrong. Second, it does not fit Popper's anti-essentialism: treating the existence of any society—even the ideal open society—as a goal which should be protected no matter how commits the essentialist mistake of attributing some sort of existence and privilege to collectives over individuals. For similar reasons, the rule in question also clashes with Popper's principle of methodological individualism.

Popper's other political uses of the epistemological principle of methodological individualism further illustrate the kind of compromises his strategy forces him to adopt. This principle was originally used by Von Mises and Hayek with the explicit purpose of discarding political holism as an ideology based on theories that are methodologically invalid. But Popper does not apply this principle more critically than his predecessors, as he perhaps should, nor does he check whether the individualist political ideologies he favors are based on a more valid methodology than their rivals. By the adoption of the principle of methodological individualism, Popper purports to bypass the issue of holistic political ideals, and thus to avoid the need to deal with politics in its own, non-epistemic, terms. A case in point is his argument against revolutions. He favors "piecemeal social engineering" (i.e., gradual reforms) for two reasons: through the implementation of small changes based on methodologically valid theories, governments minimize possible suffering and provide the only occasion to falsify those theories. But the methodologically valid social theories Popper has in mind always take into account only a small number of aspects of the social reality. They do not allow one to predict whether a small change in some respect is also *politically* a small change: no economic theory (i.e., a classical theory, which is for Von Mises and Hayek, and therefore also for Popper, the paradigm of a valid social science) could have predicted that a tax on tea would ignite the American Revolution. No serious scientist, moreover, would try to falsify predictions about the effect of any given operation without having some experimental, or at least statistical, control over intervening, allegedly theoretically irrelevant, factors.

Popper is compelled to use invalid arguments because his dominant strategy does not allow him to support openly political individualism—a preference which is the true reason for his fear of "the enemies of the open society" as well as of revolutions. Whereas Mill uses this strategy because his utilitarian principle leads him to believe that politics is involved mainly with knowledge, Popper uses it because his epistemological principle does not let him commit himself in his philosophical writings to political principles. His problem is to show that though philosophy should, as the logical positivists claim, deal only with epistemological criteria, it still can say something important about politics.

While the Achilles heel of the subordination of politics to epistemology is the possible inconsistency of the epistemic aim with non-epistemic ideals, the weakness of the subordination of epistemology to politics lies in its not permitting the open admission of an implicit commitment to epistemic values. Nietzsche, unlike Marx, has indeed immunized himself against the charge of self-reference: he would simply admit it. According to his perspectivistic epistemology people believe in theories that enhance their power, or seem to enhance it. Nietzsche believes that his theory reinforces his attack against the traditional epistemology, the existing political system, and the prevailing values and ideals. He maintains that there is a connection between representational epistemology and representational democracy. Locke, their alleged inventor, used for both—Nietzsche argues—the same inadequate model. But the model is wrong, and the troublesome dichotomies upon which it relies (e.g., subject vs. object) are invalid. Knowledge does not represent the world, just as the representatives in democratic institutions do not represent the people. They are merely powerful and power-seeking individuals, representing nothing but their own interests and dominating the weak multitudes.

Nietzsche's theory of Man is quite similar to that of Hobbes, although Nietzsche describes human beings as organisms rather than physical objects, and rejects Hobbes's theory of knowledge. Whereas Hobbes distinguished between the wise sovereign and the not-too-wise multitudes, Nietzsche distinguishes between the few, who are courageous enough to admit to themselves and others their will to power and determination to live according to their own rules and aspirations (the "masters"), and the many, who have no courage to do so (the "slaves"). The latter live in self-deception and hypocrisy and are afraid of each other. They are the ones who might find an illusory refuge in social contracts, egalitarian ideologies, altruistic life-hating religions and ethics, and a metaphysical comfort in the dogma that their beliefs represent reality. But actually they believe in knowledge because knowledge is power, and they pretend to know because it makes them, socially, more powerful. The masters, who live fully and creatively in a value-free manner, should be the elite leading the multitudes toward authenticity in an anarchic society. It is clear that Nietzsche uses his theory of knowledge in order to deconstruct the prevailing dogmas and values; in this sense the self-reference of the theory indeed does not harm it. It is also clear why Nietzsche connects the prevailing epistemology with democracy: whatever the other similarities between them, they are similar in being part of the tradition that he rejects *in toto*. It is, finally, clear which of his interests are served by claiming that the search for knowledge, which can be satisfied by subjective illusions as long as it seems to work, is motivated by a will to power: in a society that believes in objective, instrumental knowledge, those who seem to know better have actual power even if their beliefs have no objective validity. Yet there is a flaw in this method. If Nietzsche were consistent he would discard not only prophets, priests, philosophers, and some sciences; he would also discard the biological theory upon which he purports to base his perspectivistic epistemology, the theory of Man as an organism, as well as the insightful psychological analyses of the slave mentality, and the ideal of the "noble beast." He does not discard them, however; for to do so and still argue for his theory would be self-refuting. It is bad rhetoric to tell people to shed their illusions and to accept the speaker's illusions instead, even if the speaker tries to assure them that if they are brave enough his illusions will give them power. It is therefore understandable why Nietzsche often prefers a prophetic style or the use of elusive aphorisms to more conventional ways of argumentation. But this does not overcome the difficulty. He cannot argue like Hobbes and Skinner by discarding the prevailing beliefs and values in the name of an "objective science." His strategy permits him neither to deny nor to affirm the theory in which he believes—though he wants *us* to believe in it because he really thinks that it is *objectively* true that it can enhance, independently of *his* personal interests, *our* power to will ourselves to be more authentic humans than we actually are.

Mutatis mutandis, Foucault and some other deconstructionists are in the same boat. But Nietzsche has a further difficulty, irrespective of his desire to improve humanity: his perspectivism perhaps does not require universal criteria of validity; but even the claim that people believe in any theory that seems to give them power presupposes at least some intra-perspectival criteria for choice among theories. If one is acquainted with more than one theory and consequently has to choose the best one as a guide for action, one should be able to compare their forces, and distinguish between that which *is* and that which perhaps only *seems to be* more reinforcing from one's perspective. Although the capacity to do this may enhance one's power, the distinction itself is not a matter of power but of truth. Nietzsche cannot afford the answer that people do not make more or less rational and consistent choices, or that any theory one happens to believe in enhances one's power thanks to this belief—for the price for Nietzsche would be to give up his biological conception of man as an organism that strives to survive in a non-idealistic reality. This difficulty can be generalized. Whoever claims that people stick to their theories because of some motivational rather than cognitive factor has to assume, if the alleged factor is to work consistently, that they have some cognitive criteria for the validity of the distinctions

they make between those theories that are, and those that are not, moti-
vationally adequate.

The Intermediate Domain Strategy

In the cases discussed in this volume the intermediate domain is some
kind of social or behavioral science. *Prima facie* such a science is a natural
candidate for this role, for it is connected, on the one hand, to the epistemology
that validates its constructs and methods, and, on the other, to the facts of
human action that politics has to deal with. But, given that the predominant
tradition in modern epistemology has taken physics as the model of science,
the question of whether a meaningful social study can or should be "scientific"
has caused endless debates. Some argue that it can and should, others claim
that it can but should not, still others maintain that it cannot and should
not pretend to be scientific. Some, however, claim that it can be systematic
and indeed scientific—though not according to the prevailing conception of
science, which should be changed or supplemented by a special methodology
for the human sciences. Few, but influential, philosophers go further and
demand a total revision of the theory of knowledge so as to make room
for an adequate idea of a social science, i.e., one that fits the special
characteristics of the social domain. Such a step inverts the relationship
between epistemology and science, or rather the relationship that should
obtain between them according to traditional methodological conceptions.

We shall discuss here two cases. In one of them, Condorcet's, it is
presupposed that epistemology should be revised to fit certain developments
in mathematics (Chapter 5). The revised epistemology should then allow
for the constitution of a scientific social science. In the other case, Freudenthal's
analysis of Neurath's ideas (Chapter 10), it is presupposed that epistemology
should be revised to fit what seems to be the adequate social science. Both
cases show that the relationship between a social science and politics is
equally problematic. Granted that politics should take the social facts into
account, how should it do it? Should it accept them as inevitable, i.e., as
part of a necessary process? Should it say that contingent facts and existing
trends can be changed by actions inspired by ideals? Should it try to assess
the statistical probability of the success of such changes on the basis of
empirically discovered social laws? Should social science be seen as a research
that reveals the true ideals and values of the people, to which political
ideals should ultimately conform?

The "this is an is/ought problem" formula, which might be invoked to
discard the above questions, is too simplistic, and covers only part of the
relevant issues. It fits a naïve empiricistic perspective, which maintains that
all empirical data are contingent as well as ethically and politically neutral,
and that there is only one possible representation of those data, which is,
of course, true. This perspective is not shared by some of the philosophers
and by most of the commentators in the present book. Both Condorcet and
Freudenthal think that the social data are not value-free, though their reasons
are entirely different. The former wants politics to adapt to the values that

are found by a science that is legitimized by the new epistemology; the latter claims that—in the case of Neurath—it is epistemology which is adapted to politics through the mediation of social science.

According to the empiricist creed, science should deal only with perceptual data and look for strict regularities which can be expressed in mathematical formulas, while mathematics itself is, just like ethics, a non-empirical domain of analytic truths. The political domain, which involves both irregularity and ethics, cannot therefore be the subject matter of science in the strict sense. Condorcet rejects this conception for reasons that, to his mind, obliterate the difference between the natural and the political domains. Inspired by the new mathematical theory of probability, he points to the fact that even in mathematical matters our reasoning is not always reliable, and argues that from this point of view even analytic truths should be regarded as generalizations from empirical facts (the conclusions people often arrive at on the basis of their human experience), which must be dealt with in probabilistic terms. Mathematics is therefore an empirical science whose methods can be applied to other empirical sciences, including ethics. Just as mathematicians learn to distinguish between the essential and the accidental characteristics of, say, triangles, students of human phenomena can learn empirically, by probabilistic methods, to distinguish between essential and accidental features of humans. They can, further, make generalizations about human behavior; the truth of these generalizations will be only probable, but such is the case in the natural sciences as well. A political science, whose possibility has thus been demonstrated, will be able to guide political decisions, whose ultimate aim is to enhance human happiness. Condorcet hopes that the future findings of this science will help to resolve many political controversies. What is specific, however, to the strategy with which we deal here is not the patience to wait for the empirical findings, but rather the immediate inferences from the epistemological features of this science to its expected findings, and the application of these a priori findings in political argumentation. Condorcet has, for instance, inferred in this way that the right to freedom is an essential characteristic of humans, whereas the color of their skin is only an accidental one. He also somehow infers from experience that humans suffer not only when their own essential rights are violated but also when they learn about the suffering of others for similar reasons. On these grounds he concludes that black slavery in the colonies should be abolished.

While Condorcet's epistemological proof of the possibility to discover empirically natural rights is rather idiosyncratic, his strategy is not. Hume, proceeding on the assumption that social science should be exclusively concerned with the empirical investigation of human behavior and has nothing to do with essential features, reaches—following the same strategy— the opposite conclusion concerning black slavery. For, unlike Condorcet, he does not assume the possibility of unlimited generalization or strict regularity in the social domain. Consequently, any social study—as well as the recommendations drawn from it—should be comparative and differential.

This program allows him to put forth the following argument opposing the abolition of black slavery: since behaviorally the difference between the blacks and us (the whites) is so great, it can be predicted that our sympathy (the source of moral feelings and rules), which does not extend at present to these unreasonable and unchangeable beings, will never extend to them; so, since we, reasonable and benevolent persons, do not suffer from their slavery, there is no reason for abolishing it. Similarly, though without traces of racism, Skinner bases his political utopia, *Walden II*, on the findings (extant as well as expected) of a behaviorist psychology, which he believes to be the only methodologically valid framework for the study of human behavior. Some ethologists and sociobiologists follow the same prophetic route, albeit with different empirical theories and political views. In a sense they are all following Plato, who tried to apply philosophical knowledge to political affairs while he still had only a blueprint for achieving that knowledge, i.e., knowledge of the world of Ideas—the world that the philosopher should know in order to have the comprehensive understanding, the *synopsis*, which is necessary for the correct solution of political problems.

A more interesting, and more complex, version of the intermediate domain strategy works in the opposite direction: the existing social sciences are discarded on the grounds that they inadequately represent social reality because they are based on a wrong epistemology. The alternative epistemology justifies the constructs and methods of an alternative, more adequate, social science. The new epistemology, however, is not based only on logical considerations and on the examination of supposedly basic contents of consciousness. It is adapted to the alternative science by an intricate analysis of the logic of concepts that are supposedly embedded in the pre-scientific cognition of social phenomena and/or in the social phenomena themselves. The findings—actual or expected—of the alternative science are then applied to politics, supported by a claim to epistemological validity. This is, of course, an implicitly circular argumentation, for the pre-scientific concepts that the philosopher picks up for analysis, as well as his idea of the adequate science, already reflect his political preferences. Hegel, Marx, and to some extent Habermas follow this route, and they would be the last to deny it, since their epistemologies do not sustain the "is/ought" distinction, and they maintain that every epistemology reflects social conceptions and political ideals. (They would not like, however, the arbitrariness implied by "picks up.") But the extent to which these philosophers have intentionally devised their epistemologies and social theories as political tools is a matter of debate. What is beyond debate is that some Marxists, following Marx, often claim that their political opponents (in particular those who can benefit from already knowing the Marxian theory) intentionally use such a strategy.

The analysis of Neurath's ideas by Freudenthal illustrates this version of the intermediate domain strategy. On this analysis, Neurath, a logical positivist, maintains a peculiar view of the relationship between epistemology, science, and politics. For him epistemology is reduced to an anti-psychologistic methodology of science, i.e., to a system of rules which is totally independent of the specific contents of science, and completely value-free. Neurath has contributed to the positivistic camp its physicalistic turn: the demand that all the observation sentences in a scientific theory be formulated in terms of the perceivable physical characteristics of the studied objects. Whereas most of the logical positivists are interested in physics and mathematics, and do not really get involved in politics, Neurath has a program for a methodologically adequate social science and political action. He maintains that social science should study the behavior of the human organism in its reactions to the perceivable environment and in its linguistic communication with other humans. Politically, he is a social democrat, and he believes that the lot of the working class can be improved by a redistribution of income, unaccompanied by socialization of capital and abolition of the state, for a socialist government can achieve redistribution by means of laws and regulations. Such a solution, if not unrealizable, cannot have, according to non-revisionist Marxists, a durable effect. Neurath, adopting Bernstein's influential revisionist interpretation, rejects these claims. He contends that his own conception of a biologically based social science, upon which political action should be based, is true to the spirit of Marx's materialism. Since the economists of the Austrian school had previously rejected Marx's analysis as logically invalid, and some former Marxists had claimed that its conclusions were not necessary, it would seem natural to describe Neurath's position, with regard to the Marxists' political claims and their conception of the social sciences, as a direct consequence of his philosophy of science. Freudenthal, however, argues that the determination of Neurath's ideas took place in the opposite direction. A logical positivistic conception of science, he argues, does not *require* a physicalistic interpretation. But if the presuppositions that support physicalism are denied, the non-revisionist interpretation of Marx's theory will have to be considered as methodologically valid. Physicalism fits well the atomistic conception of man that underlies Neurath's idea for a social science. This atomism, in turn, fits well the individualistic conception of society, which goes together with Neurath's political preferences. Yet an individualistic conception of society is not *per se* more valid than a holistic one, and the latter, which is presupposed by Marxism, does more justice to everyday social notions. It seems therefore reasonable to surmise that it is Neurath's individualistic bias that leads him to the atomistic conception and to the idea of a behavioristic social science. His physicalism is the way by which he adapts, for the sake of consistency, his epistemology to this idea: perception of the physical aspects of other humans and of the sentences they utter are all there is in the social experience of his non-social man.

It should be noted that there are versions of extreme behaviorism which have been developed without their authors intending to refute Marxism, whereas the individualism of the methodological individualists, who argued that Marxism was methodologically invalid, is utterly non-behavioristic. Physicalism, moreover, is not only incompatible with any theory that tries to take into account human intentionality. It was abandoned by the positivists themselves because it is too restrictive even for physics. Besides, it is debatable whether Marxism is indeed methodologically holist. Elster, for one, claims in Chapter 9 that Marxism is not inherently holistic, though it is compatible, just like any methodologically individualist theory, with political holism. Finally, though liberals tend to be individualists, not all individualists are liberal—to wit, Hobbes.

Yet there is a point in Freudenthal's argument which goes beyond the issue of atomism and Neurath. The argument reveals a sort of underdetermination of epistemological theories which renders them adaptable to various preconceptions, and useful for multiple political purposes, through the addition of some further constraint. Physicalism is one such constraint. That behaviorism may also function as such a constraint is illustrated by the case of Skinner, another atomist who is not a liberal. Certain brands of rationalism—notably those that assume some fairly elaborate innate endowment of the mind—may function as another constraint of this sort. Thus, Chomsky, despite the fact that his views in epistemology and politics are the opposite of Skinner's, provides yet another instance of this version of the intermediate domain strategy. He argues from his scientific theory (of language and mind) against competing theories and the (empiricist) epistemology that legitimizes them, proposes to replace the latter with another (rationalist) epistemology, and contends that his findings about the fundamental capabilities of the human mind (e.g., creativity) unequivocally support a political ideal that should ensure everybody's "natural right" to the free exercise of these capabilities. Epistemologically, Chomsky is quite close to Popper, and politically his libertarianism might be seen as a radicalization of Popper's notion of an "open society." But Chomsky's strategy should be distinguished from Popper's: Popper also criticizes the epistemologies of his political opponents and consequently their social theories; but he rejects explicitly only those political statements (by his opponents) that are presented as descriptions or predictions of inevitable historical events, which he considers to be mere unscientific "prophesies," and his own epistemological revision is neither motivated by the need for a new social scientific theory nor provides the basis for such a theory.

Another version of the present strategy accepts the prevailing epistemology as a partial theory, which adequately applies only to physical phenomena, and only when the latter are related to in an instrumental way. The attempt to apply it to human individuals and societies is seen as the cause of social evils. A supplementary, or more basic, epistemology is then proposed, and it is claimed that it not only redeems the theoretical understanding of human phenomena from wrong methodology, but also prepares the ground for a blissful social, cultural, and political change. Often the theory that replaces the prevailing epistemology is not considered by the author as an "epistemology," for he sees the latter as concerned exclusively with conceptual knowledge, while he is interested in characterizing another form of knowledge, be it based on "intuition" (Bergson), "understanding" (Dilthey), "sympathy" (Scheler), or the practical knowledge that is involved with "Being-in-the-world" (Heidegger). For such philosophers, the relation "state/citizen" is too abstract, and their political ideals, although most often non-anarchistic, are expressed by invoking the notion of a "community." This variant is common especially among German philosophers, often with a nationalistic flavor (the young Marx is, of course, an exception). Heidegger represents this group in the present book, though most of its members would not agree with his political conclusions—and behavior.

The Analogy Strategy

"Analogy" is a term that covers a variety of relationships between two fields, A and B. The least stringent form of an analogical connection is some kind of isomorphism without any factor that is common to both fields: [A]:R(x,y,...) = [B]:R(z,r,...). At the other extreme, the analogical connection is based on an isomorphism of relations between factors that are all common to both domains: [A]:R(x,y,...) = [B]:R(x,y,...). All the philosophers in the present book use at least one form of analogical inference; the most frequent and salient is an intermediate form in which one factor is common or seems to be so: [A]:R(x,y,...) = [B]:R(x,z,...). Though common factors appear in all the preceding strategies, their role here is singled out because of the overall analogical structure of the reasoning within which they are embedded.

Sometimes the similarity of factors is based only on a verbal family resemblance. Since the list of terms that are frequently used in both fields is quite long (e.g., subject, rational, Reason, rule, law, norm, consensus, conflict, determination, perception, private, representation, and, more recently, revolution), the use of this rhetorically effective device is to be expected. It is even more so if terms that are borrowed from one of the domains and used in the other (such as autonomy or authority), and those which are taken from a third field and applied in both (such as power or force), are added to the list. It is therefore possible that the two domains are connected only through frozen metaphors, as are the cases, if Harry Redner is right (Chapter 13), of Nietzsche and Foucault. However, it is also possible, as argued by Nietzsche and Heidegger (as well as by some linguists, see Lakoff and Johnson 1980), that the use of common terms actually involves the use of a common model of relationships, whose origin and/or outcome originates in or leads to a deeper conceptual connection between the fields, and consequently also to a link between the practical decisions in both. Nietzsche, for example, accuses not only Locke, but also all the ensuing liberals, of employing an inadequate model of representation (as a sign represents an object) in both epistemology and politics.

Sometimes, however, a common model is claimed to be at work even though the terms are not common to both domains. Thus Marx accuses Hegel, according to Wolff's interpretation (Chapter 8), of performing the same logically absurd "inversion" of the correct role and status of subject and predicate (or concrete and abstract) in epistemology and in politics. That is, Hegel would have maintained that the fruit is more real than the apple or pear, just as the state is more real than the individual citizen. Marx also contends that this error is typical of bourgeois society, which actually lives according to it. For it takes the "abstract labor" (the quantity of labor time which is relevant for the calculation of market values) as more real than the concrete, qualitatively specific, creative work of individuals. Hegel, in turn, applies the same kind of argument to Kant. He argues that Kant has erroneously applied the "subject/object" dichotomy in both fields, which led him to claim that human Reason can neither reach cognitively the Thing-in-itself nor realize practically an objective Kingdom-of-Ends, i.e., a moral state.

These analogies, like all analogies, create a connection only between some aspects of the relevant domains; the connection becomes loose when attention is paid to other aspects. Thus, Hegel applies a whole series of dichotomies to the theories of both nature and human history, and to the realities they respectively describe: universal-particular, necessary-contingent, rational-arbitrary. He does not, however, use in history (and politics) the same notion of rationality as in his theory of nature, when he claims, following Kant, that in the former the rational is morally desirable. It is also questionable whether the analogy Hegel discloses in Kant is indeed there. For Kant actually says that pure Reason reaches the inter-subjective Nature, while practical Reason—the moral intention—is not to be judged by its actual social, intersubjective, consequences. Similarly, one might object to the analogy Marx draws between abstract labor/concrete labor and state/individuals, for the former is the relation which exists between a category and its instances, whereas the latter is the relation of a whole to its parts. For the same reason, one might argue against Heidegger that the analogical inferences he draws from the "authentic" attitude of an individual toward other individuals to the desirable attitude of our (German) nation toward other nations and that of our (academic) circle toward other circles (the peasants) are not convincing, because "authenticity" seems to apply to the individual *Dasein* but not to groups; and even if it did, the ideology of the groups with which Heidegger chooses to identify himself, and to whose leaders he gives his assent, does not aspire for a kind of relation with other groups which resembles what Heidegger himself takes to be desirable between individuals. One can also argue against Hume, as Smith does, that following the natural tendencies of the mind is a good rule in science but it is a source of trouble in politics. Smith himself chooses a more cautious way, which is why his use of analogy is more complex, as we shall presently see.

Often the common factor that serves as the fulcrum of the analogical connection is assumed to be good for progress (and "progress" is itself assumed to be good). Hence "progress strategy" is, perhaps, an appropriate name for this use of analogy. The basic structure of the argument is simple. The philosopher has two assumptions. The first is that progress is desirable both in knowledge and in politics. The second is based on analogical inference: if there is a feature that is common to both domains and there is a factor that affects it in a certain way in one of them, then this factor will affect that feature in a similar way in the other domain. The philosopher then finds a factor which affects a feature that is common to both fields in a way that is good for progress in one of them, and infers that it should be valuable in the other as well. He therefore argues that that factor should be introduced and/or nurtured in the latter domain, and sometimes implies that this should be the main consideration in that field.

Thus, according to Cremaschi (Chapter 4), Smith believes that the introduction of Nature between the rational ideal and the empirical tendencies of the mind has helped to overcome the crisis in epistemology, and thus has put science on the way of gradual progress. Smith therefore hopes that the introduction of the natural sentiments between unachievable ideals and emotional tendencies will help to overcome the crisis in ethics and politics; the discovery and practical application of the rules of this social nature— Smith believes—will contribute to progress in these fields. He therefore dedicates himself to the study of various sectors of the social life, such as political economy and law. According to this interpretation, the founder of the allegedly most scientific social science—economics—did it not because he believed in the objective validity of science, but because he believed in the utility of compromise. Science can suggest how to achieve compromise in a way that is appropriate to the respective sector. Thus, science suggested to Smith that the free and unencumbered operation of natural tendencies, which is good for national wealth, may be bad in the realm of justice—a lesson many of Smith's followers in economics have forgotten.

Other philosophers resort to the progress strategy less cautiously. Mill, the truth lover, believes that the freedom of thought and speech encouraged by public debate helps to discover and eliminate errors in science, and thereby advances it towards true knowledge. He infers that it should have the same effect in politics. Yet, a cynical Hobbesean could suggest the possibility that in politics such a freedom brings about more conflict than truth; a relativist might wonder what objective truths Mill seeks in politics; and a non-utilitarian would ask whether knowledge of such truths is more important than other values.

Heidegger claims that the "crisis in the sciences" and the "crisis in society" are both caused by the same factor, namely "the forgetfulness of Being." He believes that a return to metaphysics (as he proposes to do it) will resolve both problems by bringing about a new form of unity in each of these domains, and will open a new way for improvement. But while he has some definite idea about a new kind of unity in the national sphere, an idea which follows from his analysis of "being-with" (others) in the world, his analysis of the "Being-in-the-world," which perhaps could help to overcome the "as if" skeptical attitude, has nothing to contribute to the basic problems that intrigue contemporary scientists, such as the logical impossibility of determining the truth value of every theorem in mathematics, the so-called uncertainty principle, and the failure to find a unified field theory in physics. His cure for the troubles of the human sciences is to replace their methods with hermeneutics and to replace their pretense of predicting the behavior of individuals with a readiness to understand their cultural worlds—a solution which replaces the old troubles by new difficulties.

Feyerabend, the arch-enemy of unity in the sciences, who is interested in a return to a metaphysics of a different kind and for entirely different reasons, thinks that disobedience to the authority of experts is the factor of progress in science, for it gives a chance to new conceptions and alternative theories which may succeed where the conventional approaches fail. He therefore argues for an "epistemological anarchy" in public life in general, on the grounds that people have enough good sense to decide in public affairs without reliance on experts, who are always eager to defend their own dogmas. But, as Alastair Hannay points out (Chapter 11), there is a variety of other relevant political considerations that might require policies inconsistent with the one proposed by Feyerabend. We might add that "anarchic" behavior is not the only factor of progress in science itself, and that its interaction with other factors should not be ignored.

Condorcet, finally, believes that statistics helps the sciences by teaching them, for example, that the larger the sample, the better it represents (*ceteris paribus*) the population. He infers by analogy that a decision of the majority in politics is better than any decision taken by an individual. But it is not clear what the majority is supposed to do: To represent more adequately the population's interests or opinions? To reach a better "average" (moderate? compromising?) decision or a more correct one?

All these examples show that this strategy is often employed without due attention to the need to define a criterion for progress in the domain to which the analogical inference leads, and to the need to check whether the relevant factor is always beneficial in the domain from which the analogy is drawn. Moreover, it is often overlooked that the effect of the relevant factor on the common feature—if indeed it is the same feature—is not always equally desirable in both domains, as Popper was well aware when he recommended daring, risky (in terms of potential falsifiability) theories in science, and cautious and modest reforms in politics.

Strategies and History

As the cases analyzed here show, there is no systematic connection between the brands of theories that a philosopher favors and the types of linking strategies he employs. Nor did we find restrictions on the combinations of strategies used, though each different strategy can be singled out. This "combinatory freedom" is apparent in the now fashionable deconstructionist attitude. Its prevalent mode, in philosophy, is that of a total disenchantment with epistemology, with the consequent demand that this discipline simply cease to exist (see, for instance, Rorty 1979). But the reasons for this opting out of epistemology as well as the ways in which it is (or is not) linked to political attitudes vary widely. For some (e.g., Derrida), who seem to follow the analogy strategy, opting out of epistemology should go hand in hand with opting out of (conventional) political thought (and action). For others (e.g., Heidegger), who seem to rely on the subordination strategy, it is the prevalence of the epistemic mode of relating to the world that is responsible for the crisis in Western culture in general and for the now firmly established 'non-authentic' modes of relating to oneself, other persons, society, and history: this way of relating to the world should be reversed by appropriate political changes. It should be recalled, however, that other philosophers—like Nietzsche and some existentialists—who also call attention to the distorting effect of overestimating the epistemic/theoretical perspective, share with Heidegger neither his political diagnosis nor his therapeutic prescription. Some pragmatists (e.g., Dewey, Rorty), who also think that the perspective of traditional epistemology is wrong, couple their critique instead with faith in the democratic ideals and institutions (see, for instance, Rorty 1983), and hope that in freeing ourselves from foundationalism, we are paving the way for non-pretentiously improving those institutions and fulfilling those ideals. It might be argued that anti-foundationalism functions, for them, as the common, good-for-progress factor through which both their (anti-)epistemological stance and their political views are linked.

Criticism may range from the identification of relatively specific problems and connections of certain epistemologies and political philosophies to a more general dissatisfaction with the nature of the enterprises called epistemology and political philosophy. In its most holistic form, which sees both domains as deeply intertwined, "failures" can no longer be ascribed atomistically to this or that component. Rather, it is the whole system formed by epistemology-cum-politics that is to be blamed. This is the line of criticism taken by Roberto Mangabeira Unger (1975). He argues that epistemological and political conceptions within what he dubs the liberal paradigm are intertwined in a network of multiple interrelations in such a way that they staunchly support each other. As a consequence, any criticism that is directed at only one of the components is doomed to failure, for, by relying upon the other component of the system, such criticism in fact ends up by supporting the whole structure. Only *total* criticism, which completely steps out of the paradigm, can be effective. This, however, is extremely difficult to achieve, Unger acknowledges, since the liberal paradigm comprises, according to him, practically all thinkers from Hobbes to Popper, including, among others, Marx. Furthermore, this paradigm has so shaped our language and conceptual tools (including the notion of "criticism" itself) that stepping out of the paradigm means fashioning an entirely different way of thinking and speaking. It this this Protean task that Unger undertakes in his recent trilogy (1987), which we cannot discuss here. Unger's over-inclusive notion of a liberal paradigm and his description of the relationships between epistemology and politics in strictly logical terms do not detract from the fact that his analyses reveal many of the tacit links between these two domains. It is precisely the subtlety and variety of such links—we submit—that calls for a treatment in terms of the *strategies* that we have attempted to single out here.

All the strategies here discussed establish connections by highlighting some aspects and ignoring others. The extent to which the linkage is tight depends on the type of relations and the number of links. The extent to which such ties can be untied depends, however, on the relevance the author, critic, or interpreter assigns to the highlighted aspects for the specific problems he or she is attempting to solve, as well as on the presuppositions he or she takes for granted. The connection established by Mill, for example, would find a great measure of agreement among those who share Popper's opinions. For they too think that the advance of knowledge should be a political ideal, and share with Mill the consequentialist and individualist ideas. If they look for weak logical points in his argument they will do it for the sake of parsimony. On the other hand, Marx, or a Marxist, who does not treat the advance of knowledge as a major political ideal, but rather puts a premium on equality and justice, would disagree not only with Mill's political solution, but would try to find and attack as many of the weak links as he or she can, in an attempt to prove that Mill's, like any other liberalism, is an absurd theory. The weak points in Hobbes's linkage are different for those, like Jean Hampton, who assent to the idea of a social contract but disagree with Hobbes's absolutism (Chapter 2), than for those who maintain, as Wolff does, that no contract can give a *de jure* legitimation to any authority (Chapter 8). These weak points are also different from those that would attract the attention of the Hegelians, who believe that the state's end is not only to maintain peace, and who reject the social contract idea because such a contract constitutes only "formal" relationships, and not really social ones.

The above remarks are part and parcel of the awareness of the historicity of theory construction and deconstruction, generally accepted in the last quarter of the twentieth century. The political and epistemological doctrines discussed as well as the discussants' tools can no longer be viewed as ahistorical objects. Though theories seek to transcend the contingencies of their creation, they are nevertheless concrete products of human activity performed in given historical circumstances. Similarly, the interpretation of the "meaning" of a theory and the assessment of its rational links with another theory are activities performed in a definite historical context. Consequently, if the search for "rational connections" aims at disclosing definitive, necessary relations between the once-and-for-all fixed meanings of theories, it is doomed to failure. In some contexts, assent to a theory of a given type in one of the two domains should commit one to accept a theory of a specific type in the other; but in other contexts this need not be so. Consequently, looking for type-type connections between theories is not enough. In addition to overlooking the historicity of the theories and criteria of assessment, such an endeavor is perforce conducted at a level of abstraction in which the theories are stripped of their specific contents. As a result, indeterminacy becomes the rule: any number of theories in one domain are "rationally connectable" with a given type in the other. As opposed to this, attention to specifc *cases*, i.e., to token-token relations, leads to a gain in specificity, which renders the non-necessary connection less arbitrary and allows the discovery of interesting, albeit not easily generalizable, rational connections in the form of the strategies here described.

Yet, we would like to stress that the acknowledgment of the undeniable fact that theories and interrelations between theories cannot be appropriately discussed in an abstract, ahistorical manner should not push one straight into the arms of purely genetic explanations. As already said, we think that, in understanding philosophical theories, the search for reasons takes precedence over the search for causes. What the awareness of historicity requires us to bear in mind is, rather, the fact that the "order of reasons" is not necessarily a matter of purely internal conceptual constraints and that the very notions of "reason" and "order" may be much looser than their strictly logical counterparts, and may vary historically. Nor does historicity necessarily imply incommensurability and parochialism. Within a given historical period, all domains of inquiry and culture may be governed by the same set of underlying assumptions—what Foucault (1966) called the *epistémé* of an era, and others, its *Zeitgeist*. Those that posit such an all-embracing unity *within* a period, often hasten to posit unsurmountable discontinuities *across* periods. Others, more congruently, accept incommensurability as the rule, both horizontally and vertically (e.g., Rorty 1979). They argue that each practice, in each period, has its own parochial 'form of life,' its vocabulary and set of standards, none of which are comparable with or connected to those of other practices in terms of a non-parochial set of rational criteria. Our enterprise is in fact opposed to all of these sweeping generalizations. All we presuppose is the possibility of *local* commensurability both within and across historical periods. Such a commensurability certainly manifests itself in the recurrence of the strategies we have been able to identify. The reader will be able to find in the case studies here assembled other parallelisms that bear testimony to the fruitfulness of such a minimalist, but powerful, presupposition.

To be sure, there is hardly a link that philosophers establish between different domains that is logically undefeasible. Our point is, however, that it is an error to look only or even mainly for strictly logical consistency, and wrong to claim that there is no connection or coherence at all because logical connections are not found. Philosophical reasoning, like reasoning in other domains, cannot and should not be reduced to its narrowly conceived logical dimension. The appropriate questions to ask are whether the connection has a good rationale and is relevant to the problem it is to solve. It should, moreover, be realized that there is no "perspective-free" answer to such questions.

The question of whether a philosopher discovers connections in an abstract realm of ideas, expresses in conceptual form the inarticulate ideas that are embedded in his culture, or makes artificial connections because he is bewitched, as Wittgenstein would say, by language, can be bypassed. We suggest, instead, that a philosopher who addresses problems that are considered relevant at his time, and whose reasoning is convincing, *creates* new connections. He or she thereby changes the very conceptions of the fields he or she deals with. Whoever looks for logical connections between "epistemology" and "politics" that are defined once and for all fails to recognize the dynamic nature of philosophical concepts—or any significant concepts, for that matter.

The strategies we have described are certainly not the only ones that can be found in philosophical reasoning. We believe that further research from the "strategic" perspective here adopted can create more awareness of the nature of philosophical thinking and contribute to a non-dogmatic approach to the conventional fragmentation of philosophy into separate disciplines. It can also lead to a more realistic assessment of the nature of the "systematicity" of philosophical systems. What holds them together is certainly not a set of purely logical bonds. Admirable achievements of the human mind as these systems undoubtedly are, the minds that have engendered them are, still, all too human. And yet, the bonds are not entirely arbitrary nor merely extrinsic, for they are constrained at least by requirements of persuasive reasonableness.

Acknowledgments

We benefited from comments by Sergio Cremaschi, Gideon Freudenthal, and an anonymous referee on earlier versions of this chapter.

Notes

1. In particular, we would like to point out that no *philosophical* analysis of Heidegger's thought can clear him from his *personal* responsibility for endorsing and actively pursuing Nazi policies, a responsibility he never openly admitted. We remain both astonished and deeply unsatisfied by his later explanations (e.g., in Heidegger 1976, a posthumously published interview) as well as by the fact that he never publicly condemned Nazism.

References

Chomsky, Noam. 1972. *Problems of Knowledge and Freedom*. London: Fontana/Collins.
Foucault, Michel. 1966. *Les Mots et les Choses*. Paris: Presses Universitaires de France.
Hayek, F. A. 1952. *The Counter-Revolution of Science: Studies in the Abuse of Reason*. Glencoe, Ill.: The Free Press.
Heidegger, Martin. 1976. Nur noch ein Gott kann uns retten (an interview conducted on September 23, 1966). *Der Spiegel* 23: 193–219.
Lakoff, George, and Mark Johnson. 1980. *Metaphors We Live By*. Chicago: The University of Chicago Press.
Mises, Ludwig von. 1951. *Theory and History*. New Haven, Conn.: Yale University Press.
Popper, Karl. 1966. *The Open Society and Its Enemies*, 2 volumes. London: Routledge and Kegan Paul.
Rorty, Richard. 1979. *Philosophy and the Mirror of Nature*. Princeton: Princeton University Press.
———. 1983. Postmodernist bourgeois liberalism. *The Journal of Philosophy* 90: 583–589.

Skinner, B. F. 1972. *Beyond Freedom and Dignity.* New York: Bantam/Vintage.
Unger, Roberto M. 1975. *Knowledge and Politics.* New York: The Free Press and London: Collier MacMillan.
_____. 1987. *Politics: A Work in Constructive Social Theory,* 3 volumes. Cambridge: Cambridge University Press.

1

The Political Animal's Knowledge According to Aristotle

Jean-Louis Labarrière

In raising the issue of the political animal's knowledge,[1] I propose to discuss a double question: that of the knowledge required in order to be a political animal, i.e., a psychological question, and that of the status of such a knowledge, i.e., an epistemological question. The issues raised in this connection both by Aristotle and by his interpreters—recent or ancient— are in fact at least of two levels. The first series of questions addresses the differences that Aristotle establishes between various kinds of political animals, since, it is worth recalling, the political quality is not reserved exclusively to humans. Since these questions rely upon psychological and physiological criteria that differentiate between man and animal, they require one to inquire whether the meaning of the property 'political animal' is the same for humans and for certain animals.

Aristotle's arguments lead to the characterization of the *homo politicus* as an ethical animal on the grounds that he possesses *logos*. They imply, therefore, a second series of questions, having to do with that which is characteristic (*idion*) of humans. These are rather epistemological questions, since they amount to inquiring what is, for humans, the status of political knowledge; in other words, the formidable question of the existence of a political science (*epistēmē*. Even though here too Aristotle relies upon his theory of knowledge and psychology, it seems that he also makes use of another kind of argument—political in nature—having to do with the issue of the best possible and desirable political regime.

Having thus set up the problems I want to deal with, I will proceed as follows: first, I will briefly analyze what Aristotle understands by a 'political animal', by investigating the kind of knowledge required in order to be one, as well as the way of life called 'political'; second, I will discuss more specifically the status of such knowledge in humans, beginning from that which distinguishes humans from animals, and asking whether ethics or politics can be called sciences in Aristotle's sense; finally, following Aristotle himself, I will conclude by examining the conditions that define the best regime.

Political Animals

There are many who have been and still are guilty of misinterpreting Aristotle's thought by excessively simplifying it: among them, Hegel and Marx. According to such a traditional reading, Aristotle would have been the first to establish that man is a political animal by nature and by excellence, since only he has—as a proper characteristic—the *logos*, by virtue of which he, unlike the other animals, is a rational animal; and also because the *polis*, also characteristic only of humans, exists by nature and is prior to its members. Such a difference between man and the other animals is so much stressed that many contemporary philosophers criticize Aristotle precisely on that count.

Yet this interpretation does not easily fit the texts, since one cannot rest one's case merely on such a way of reading the well known passages of *Politics* I, 2, 1252a24–53a38, or VII, 13, 1332b1–8 (cf. Arendt 1958). To be sure, Aristotle seeks to demonstrate that man is a political animal by nature, in that opening chapter of *Politics*. Similarly, there is no doubt that he undertakes to do so by appealing to biological and historical arguments: the theory of the first necessary couplings—those of male and female and of master and slave; and the chronological succession of family, village and *polis*. Also, it is beyond doubt that such arguments are supported by the thesis of the logical priority of the whole over its parts (Hegel and Marx will recall this in their attacks on the historicist school). But this interpretation does not imply that only man is a political animal. First of all, let us notice that such a demonstration seeks to solve not only a problem posed in the earlier tradition (e.g., the debate between Plato and the Sophists on the opposition between that which is 'by nature' *kata physin*, and that which is 'by convention' *kata nomon*), but also a problem that Aristotle himself had to face, in his double opposition both to Plato and to the Sophists. The existence 'by nature' and not only by convention of the *polis* and, consequently, the ascription to man of the property of political animal 'by nature' is in fact a delicate question that he tries to solve in *Pol.* I,2 through the reaffirmation of his teleology.

Two brief passages of the *Nicomachean Ethics* will underline the problematic character of this issue of 'by nature':

> Every form of friendship, then, involves association [*koinōnia*], as has been said [= 1159b29–32]. One might, however, mark off from the rest both the friendship of kindred and that of comrades. Those of fellow citizens, fellow tribesmen, fellow voyagers, and the like are more like mere friendships of association; for they seem to rest on a sort of compact [*kath'homologian tina*]. (*E.N.*, VIII, 12, 1161b11–15)[2]

This is why the city looks less natural than the family:

> Between other kinsmen friendly relations are found in due proportion. Between man and wife friendship seems to exist by nature; for man is naturally inclined to form couples—even more than to form cities, inasmuch as the household is earlier and more necessary than the city, and reproduction is more common to man with the animals. (*E.N.*, VIII, 12, 1162a15–19)

Before getting to the core of the problem, namely, the difference between man and animal, I would like to observe that the inversion of the two types of priority (according to necessity and according to finality) shows that things are more subtle than they might seem to be. For if the private link, family-like or economical, is prior (because of necessity) to the public, political link—which in turn is logically prior by virtue of finality—then it follows that the vital order is not the same as the political order. This is in fact the meaning of the priority according to finality assigned to the *eu zēn*, the good life, over the mere living, *zēn*, or even of the living together, *suzēn*. There cannot be a political community unless, beyond the private interests, there is something really shared. In other words, although according to the order of necessity a community of needs constitutes indeed the basis of the political community, it cannot be equated with the latter, since the "former" only exists in order to lead to the "latter." Hence the difficulty in understanding the meaning of the term *koinōnia*, translated on different occasions either by "association" or by "community," because it covers both the sharing of needs and interests upon which is grounded the reciprocity and the equality of exchanges, and the sharing of the good life, characteristic of the human political community insofar as it is a city, which, in turn, stems—as we shall see—from a free choice (*pro-hairesis*, *Pol.*, III, 9, 1280a31–34 and 1280b38–1281a4), rather than just from material necessity.

Tradition has also excessively simplified matters regarding the difference between man and animal. When in *Pol.*, I, 2, 1253a7–19 Aristotle appeals to the *logos* in order to differentiate the human political animal from its non-human counterpart, he is not in fact appealing to reason in the modern, Cartesian sense of the term, any more than he is denying to animals the political quality. Let us recall, first, in order to avoid ambiguity, that Aristotle, in the *Historia Animalium*, does not hesitate to qualify certain animals as political, a fact that shows—no doubt—that even though his "biology" is anthropocentric, one cannot hasten to accuse him of an exclusive anthropocentrism with respect to the political quality. Eventually, he can afford not to restrict this quality to humans—a fact that shows that it is not necessarily dependent upon the *logos*—by virtue of his theory of science, namely of his psychology and biology. This is an important epistemological point, since, if the political quality is not deducible from 'reason,' then one must ask what is its foundation, and whether it is applied to humans and animals in the same sense.

The *Historia Animalium*, I, 1 specifies the nature and the extent of such a quality. After presenting "the following differences [which] are manifest in their modes of living and in their actions [*diaphorai kata tous bious kai tas praxeis*]" (487b33–34), Aristotle proceeds to distinguish between gregarious animals, *agelaia*, and solitary ones, *monadika*, and points out, without further explanation, that man belongs to both categories (488a1–13). Perhaps this is an allusion to the savage men mentioned in *De Partibus Animalium* (I, 3, 643b5) or to those "bad men without a *polis*" (*Pol.*, I, 2, 1253a3–5 and 25–29), or even to the human ability to lead a contemplative, rather than a political life. At any rate, the text becomes extremely complex, since in a quite ambiguous sentence (which has been, for this reason, often contested or corrected) Aristotle (488a2) distinguishes two species within each of these kinds: the *politika*, political (and not 'social'), and the *sporadika*, sporadical, dispersed. Unfortunately, since he is concerned with the distinction between *monadika* and *agelaia*, and within the latter, between those who are only *agelaia* from those who are *politika*, Aristotle does not say a word about the *agelaia-sporadika*, the *monadika-politika*, and the *monadika-sporadika*. Thus, though man might doubtless represent the second of these classes, interpretation can only be conjectural (cf. Mulgan 1974: 438–439).

Be that as it may, what is important to establish for our purposes is that the political, as opposed to the merely gregarious, animals do not content themselves with living in bands, but are characterized as being "such as have some one common object in view" (488a8–9). Aristotle mentions a few species of them: men, bees, wasps, ants, cranes. Then he observes that some of these political species, such as the bees, "submit to a ruler," a chief, *hegemona*, whereas ants and many others, which he calls *anarcha*, are "subject to no rule." The political quality, therefore, is not reserved to humans alone, and, furthermore, it differs from the mere gregarious character, so much so that one can even speak—referring to certain species of animals— of a *quasi-polis* grounded on shared work, i.e., on a division of labor, as illustrated by the description of the life of the bees (*H.A.*, IX, 40).[3]

Even though the *logos* is the foundation for the difference between human and animal, it is not the natural foundation of the human political quality since, for that purpose, biology is enough. What it provides the foundation for is, *de facto* as well as *de jure*, the political superiority of man over animal, i.e., man's *characteristic* political quality, rather than his political quality *tout court*. Aristotle is quite explicit on this matter. In the same chapter of *Politics* (I,2, 1253a7–18) he writes, not that humans are political animals to the exclusion of the other animals, but that they are *mallon*, "more of a political animal than any other gregarious animal." It seems that here one must read "gregarious" in the broad sense, including the political species, since the bee, a political and not merely a gregarious animal according to the *H.A.*, is the only animal mentioned. Man's superiority derives from his being endowed with *logos*, speech, and not only with *phōnē*, voice:

Whereas mere voice is but an indication [*sēmeion*] of pleasure and pain, and is therefore found in other animals (for their nature attains to the perception of pleasure and pain and the intimation of them to one another, and no further), the power of speech is intended to set forth the expedient and the inexpedient, and therefore likewise the just and the unjust. (1253a10–15)[4]

We are now at the heart of my first point. The question raised is that of the superiority of human political knowledge over animal political knowledge: the *logos* produces a "take-off" within the domain of *aisthēsis*, sense-perception, in that it goes beyond the stage of simple knowledge of pleasure and pain and of its communication, reaching the realm of the ethical. The latter, to be sure, is grounded on the economic, but goes beyond it, and the whole movement of thought here described is possible—as I will show—only through a variety of rhetorical means. Since I am concerned here only with the status of such a political knowledge, I will not elaborate upon the opposition between the good life, *eu zēn*, and living—*zēn*—or living together, *suzēn*. Yet, I should point out the fact that, although Aristotle, in this passage of *Politics*, relates man's political character to the *logos* and that of the animal to the *phōnē*, he does not thereby imply that political animals necessarily have *phōnē* (the bee, for one, is mute). Furthermore, the same passage suggests two important theses directly relevant to our topic: man is more political than other animals because, being a "rhetorician," he becomes ethical; and political animals have an *aisthēsis* more developed than that of other animals, i.e., some of them have *phōnē*, which, for Aristotle, means a perfection vis-à-vis the Good (*De Anima*, II,8, 420b13–421a6; III, 13, 435b19–25).

The above hypothesis could be supported by the following statement, establishing—within the realm of sense perception—a hierarchy between animals:

> Some animals, like plants, simply procreate their own species at definite seasons; other animals busy themselves also in procuring food for their young, and after they are reared quit them and have no further dealings with them; other animals are more intelligent [*sunetōtera*] and endowed with memory [*mnēmēs*], and they live with their offspring for a longer period and on a more social footing [*politikōteron*: more political]. (*H.A.*, VIII, 1, 588b30–589a2)

Thus, "intelligence" and "memory" apparently make some animals more political than others, a fact no doubt to be related to the theory of knowledge developed by Aristotle in the first chapter of *Metaphysics* and in the last of *Posterior Analytics*.

Beginning with *aisthēsis*, the lowest degree of knowledge—but still knowledge since it is the power of discrimination (*to kritikon*), Aristotle establishes a hierarchy, leaving several kinds of animals *en route*, to reach finally man, alone to have the *logos*. Thus, though all animals have sense-perception, only a few are endowed with memory—being thus more intelligent, and among these some possess hearing (and on occasion voice)—thus becoming more apt to learn and to teach (*De Sensu*, 1, 437a1–17; *H.A.*, IV, 536a21 and IX, 1, 608a17–21; *P.A.*, II, 660b1). Endowed with *phantasia*, "imagination," and memory, certain animals participate somewhat in experience and habituation (*Pol.*, VII, 12, 1332b3–4), but none of them is able to achieve what man alone can do, namely to build up a *single* notion out of the repetition of experiences and memories, which is precisely the ability that allows him to develop both art and science. What animals lack is this "conception," *hypolēpsis* (*E.N.*, VII, 3, 1137b3–5), which collects the multiplicity into a unity. That is the reason for the careful distinction (in *De Anima*, III, 3 and 11) between *phantasia* and both *hypolēpsis* and *doxa* (belief, opinion).

The human take-off is therefore based on a psychological theory of knowledge that denies *doxa* to animals, and it is to this theory that the difference between *phōnē* and *logos* at the beginning of *Politics* refers. But one must note that it is because such a theory of knowledge is itself based upon psycho-physiology and biology (cf. Pellegrin 1982 and Romeyer Dherbey 1983), and not—as in Plato—upon mathematics, that Aristotle does not deny to animals (at least to some of them) the political quality. Let us also point out, concluding this argument, that he even links the development of certain faculties in animals to their "family feeling," and he does not hesitate to speak of friendship between animals, based on pleasure and utility (*E.E.*, VII, 1236b6–11; 1239b18–22; 1254a11–15). By the same token, the properly human friendship—the one that constitutes the supreme political bond—is specified as being based on virtue. That is—so it seems—the effect of the *logos*. It remains to be seen what is the kind of knowledge that it affords to its owners.

Science, Ethics, and Politics

The present question cannot be reduced to the question of whether it is possible for *Ethics* and *Politics* to be sciences in Aristotle's sense. The question must also be extended to asking whether it is desirable that they be. We shall see that this has to do both with the opposition between Aristotle and Plato (cf. Nussbaum 1980) and with our way of managing the Aristotelian heritage.

In order to clarify the status of political knowledge in humans, as well as its political and epistemological consequences, one must first delineate more carefully what is characteristic (*idion*) to man, namely the fact that he alone (*monon*) is endowed with *logos*. The *hypolēpsis*, that "supposal" (Hamlyn 1968: 130) out of which opinion, prudence, science, and art are born, generates the difference between human and animal knowledge, by opening for man the possibility of being ethical, which in turn transforms man's political quality. Briefly stated, for Aristotle what characterizes ethical knowledge and action is precisely the opinion—*doxa*—which accompanies and regulates our actions, thus going beyond the stage of biological reflexes or reactions typical of animal behavior. The psycho-physiology that has been our guide so far thus tends to leave the ground of biology and emerge into a "moral psychology," into education and culture. Endowed with the *logos*, humans have the ability to persuade and be persuaded to such an extent that, apparently, every ethical conception they have must be preceded by some persuasion (Fortenbaugh 1975: 63–70).

In this sense, it is not by accident that that which is manifested by the *logos* in *Politics*, I, 2, namely "the expedient and the inexpedient, and therefore the just and the unjust," can be directly related to the oratorical genres defined in *Rhetoric*, I, 3: deliberative speech (*symbouleutikon*), characteristic of the political orator that advises pro or contra what is useful or harmful for the city; forensic speech (*dikanikon*), which deals with what is just and unjust—in the juridical and judicial senses, not in the legislative sense, which belongs to deliberative speech; and finally epideictic speech (*epideiktikon*), which criticizes or praises with regard to the ugly and the beautiful. All of these kinds of speech have to do with opinions, i.e., with that which makes the difference between man and animal. Broadening a little the scope of a definition given in *Rhet.*, I, 6, 1363a7–8, one might say that all of these kinds of speech are aimed at the good, i.e., "that which most people seek after, and which is obviously an object of contention." What characterizes man, therefore, is mediation and argumentation, so much so that the desires that distinguish him from animals may be called reasoned, since they are consecutive to *hypolēpsis* and persuasion (*Rhet.*, I, 11, 1370a17–27).

Let us turn now to the epistemological consequences of this point, regarding the *Politics* and the *Ethics*. From *Posterior Analytics*, I, 33, we know that science and opinion differ in that the object of the former, since it cannot be other than it is, is necessary, whereas the object of the latter, which can be other than it is, is contingent. Hence, there should only be science of that which is necessary and unchangeable. Yet in *Metaphysics*, VI, 1, Aristotle divides science—*epistēmē*—into productive (*poiētikē*) practical (*praktikē*) and theoretical (*theōrētikē*) and the latter into mathematical, physical, and theological science. It would thus seem that one could speak of the "sciences of the contingent," the one "productive," namely *technē* (art), having its aim outside of itself, i.e., in production and in the product; and the other, "practical," having its end in itself, in the agent and his action. But would this way of speaking be rigorous? I don't think so.

Let us observe, first, that beyond this well-known difference between *praxis* and *poiēsis*, these two "sciences" are both opposed to the theoretical sciences whose aim is knowledge in itself, since both of them belong to the domain of "doing." Furthermore, even though *praxis* and *poiēsis* differ in the way described above, one must not forget that insofar as *praxis* is concerned, virtue is not to be found in the intention (a concept which is, by the way, foreign to Aristotle and to the whole Greek intellectual world), but rather in the tangible, accomplished action (Romeyer Dherbey 1983: 259–262). Both the *Eudemian Ethics* (I, 5, 1216b1–26) and the *Nichomachean Ethics* (I, 3, 1095a5–6; II, 2, 1103b26–9) contrast theoretical and productive sciences on the grounds that in the latter (both in *praxis* and *poiēsis*) the end is other than science and knowledge. In fact, *praxis* is not concerned with knowing what is virtue alone, but rather with producing it: what one desires, says Aristotle, is not to know what is courage or justice, but to be courageous or just.

Before proceeding, it is worth noting that the problem here raised is of extreme importance: it is in fact the problem of the inefficacy of the theoretical sciences in the practical domain, i.e., in modern terms, the impossibility of deriving prescriptive statements from descriptive ones (cf. Lyotard 1983). In this sense, even if *Ethics* and *Politics* could be sciences—which remains to be demonstrated—this would be of no help with respect to the practical inefficacy of science as such (*E.N.*, VI, 7, 1141a28–b8; *E.E.*, I, 8, 1217b24–25). I will try to show in what follows that if there were a political science in the strong, narrow sense of the term "science," then this would pose serious political problems from an Aristotelian point of view.

But before getting to these final questions, let me first try to specify further the nature and status of ethical and political knowledge. Aristotle himself stresses that "if we are to speak exactly and not follow mere similarities" (*E.N.*, VI, 3, 1129b18–19) (as when we speak about a practical or "poietic" science), there is science only of that which cannot be other than it is, from which it follows that contingency is excluded from the domain of science. Neither *technē*, which controls *poiēsis*, nor *phronēsis*— the practical wisdom or prudence that rules over *praxis*—can be called sciences, except metaphorically (*E.N.*, VI, 3–5). That is the reason why one cannot demand either from the *Ethics* or from the *Politics* the same rigor as that of the scientific treatises (*E.N.*, I, 3, 1094b12ff.; *E.E.*, I, 8, 1218a16ff., where the difference between ethics and mathematics, and the opposition to the Platonic theory of numbers are clearly presented). Their objects are of a different nature, not fit for that kind of rigor, so much so that in these domains one cannot begin with *a priori* definitions, but only with opinions and examples, since all men have in principle (though not necessarily in fact, since they must also, for that purpose, be reasonable and knowledgeable) a say in public affairs (*E.E.*, I, 6, 1216b26–17a16).

What underlies this reasoning is in fact Aristotle's fundamental opposition to Plato. By arguing that there is no Idea of the Good, nor any Idea *tout court* in the Platonic sense, Aristotle is defending in ethics a thesis that is more pragmatic than scientific. It amounts to the claim that the good strived for is the good achievable by man, i.e., the practical good, the one that appears to us to be good, whether it really be so or not; a human good that can be other than it is or appears to be, and that consequently is open to deliberation and debate. If such a good belonged to the realm of science, it would not be open to deliberation, since one deliberates and calculates only about what can be otherwise and about what is feasible (*E.N.*, VI, 1, 1139a9–15; 5, 1140a31ff.; 12 and 13). Here too Aristotle's argumentation rests upon a psychology—now human and moral rather than biological— which, in defining what is characteristic of man, is far apart from Plato's. Not only does it redefine the "parts" of the soul, but it also stresses that, for ethics, it is irrelevant whether such a division be real or only logical (*E.N.*, I, 13, 1102a30–33 and b24–25; *E.E.*, II, 1, 1219b33). On this, as on many other issues, Aristotle no longer shares his teacher's views.

Since Aristotle points out that "the student of politics must know somehow the facts about the soul" (*E.N.*, I, 13, 1102a18–19), I will briefly recall that division, in order to make precise the status of political knowledge, a knowledge that includes ethics, since politics is "the most authoritative art and that which is most truly the master art" (*E.N.*, I, 2, 1094a26ff.). Putting together the statements found in the *Eudemian* (II, 1) and in the *Nichomachean Ethics* (I, 13 and VI, 2), we may say that moral psychology performs the following divisions: the soul is divided into two major parts, the one rational or logical and the other irrational or alogical (*logos/alogos*). The latter in turn splits up in a nutritive (*to thrēptikon*) or vegetative (*to phytikon*) part, regulating the basic vital functions and hence to be neglected here, since it is common to all living beings, including plants, and a desiderative (*to orektikon*) part, also called *to ēthikon*, the moral part (*E.N.*, VI, 13, 1144b15) and *to pathētikon*, the passionate part (*Pol.*, I, 5, 1254b8). Aristotle sets aside the "sensitive or perceptive part" (*to aisthētikon*) too, on the grounds that, being shared by men and animals, it is not the principle of any action. On the other hand, he divides the desiderative or desiring part, i.e., the desire, *orexis*, in three sub-parts: appetite (*epithymia*), spirit (*thymos*), and wish (*boulēsis*). Yet this last part of desire, *boulēsis*, is no longer really alogical, since it "obeys" the *logos*. Hence, the logical part itself must be subdivided into a component that obeys the *logos* and a component that possesses the *logos*. Clearly Aristotle is in fact questioning both the bipartition of the soul into *logos* and *alogos* and the well-known Platonic trichotomy *epithymia/ thymos/logos* (*Rep.*, IV, 12–15, 436a–441c). Now, what should be of utmost interest to us here is the further subdivision of that logical part possessing the *logos* into a scientific (*to epistēmonikon*) and a calculative (*to logistikon*) part, also called deliberative (*bouleutikon*) or opiniative (*doxastikon*), "the part of us which forms opinions" (*E.N.*, VI, 13, 1144b14). The characteristic virtue of the former is *sophia*, the philosophical or theoretical wisdom that has to do with unchangeable and necessary objects, whereas that of the latter is *phronēsis*, the practical wisdom that has do with deliberations about contingent, human things. If we allow ourselves an extreme anachronism, this amounts to a distinction between theoretical and practical reason, but even sharper than the distinction in Kant since, here, theoretical reason is declared to be totally incompetent vis-à-vis the striving for the practical good, and cannot therefore postulate even one single practical idea, not even as a regulative one (*De An.*, III, 9, 432b27–28).

Phronēsis, the ethical-political virtue, is by no means a science (*epistēmē*), as is made clear by Aristotle's moral psychology. Furthermore, far from being articulated with *sophia*, it is rather connected with the ethical virtues of the desiderative part, which it regulates, and from which it receives its movement. In this sense, even though *praxis* differs from *poiēsis*, *phronēsis* seems to be closer to *technē* (which is why people may wrongly take the one for the other) than to *sophia* and *epistēmē*, since both *phronēsis* and *technē* stem from the same logical part of the soul, namely the calculative one, that which deliberates and which stands in opposition to the scientific part. To all these theoretical reasons for excluding practice from the domain of science, one should add a further, pragmatic and scientific reason: *phronēsis*, in dealing with the human things that are capable of deliberation, has in fact to do mainly with particular rather than universal things, which are not objects of science, but of *aisthēsis*, sense-perception (*E.N.*, VI, 8, 1142a23–30; *An. Post.*, I, 31).

This may justify Aristotle's claim (*Pol.*, I, 2) that the *logos* manifests man's characteristic sense-perception of good and evil. The *phronēsis* has as its object precisely this *aisthēsis* that distinguishes man from animal, the latter being unable to go beyond the sense-perception of pleasure and pain. Now, as you will recall, this good and this evil are practical and, because human desire strives for them, they depend upon opinion and deliberation, and not upon science. Human action, in order to be both human and action, cannot be a mere immediate reaction: it requires the mediation of decision and choice (*pro-hairesis*), resulting from deliberation about the means to achieve the ends proposed by desire, as well as—to some extent—about the ends themselves, since some desires should be rejected. What is characteristic of the human political animal is thus further specified: its *polis* comes into existence for the purpose of the good life (*eu zēn*) and not only of life (*zēn*), because it is achieved through *pro-hairesis*. Consequently, only humans can reach happiness (*eudaimōnia* or "human flourishing" according to Cooper 1975: 89–143), which derives from *pro-hairesis*, a fact that modifies considerably the nature of their community, since, even though friendship is the supreme bond, human friendship should also be grounded on virtue—the only kind of friendship actually based on *pro-hairesis* (*E.E.*, VII, 1236b1–6).

Toward a Deliberative Politics

It is *pro-hairesis*[5] that singles out the human political animal: both his actions and his community—the *polis*—exist only in view of achieving happiness. It is not only a matter of what one does willingly or voluntarily (i.e., *de plein gré*),[6] since animals, though lacking *pro-hairesis*, perform their movements voluntarily (*E.N.*, II, 2, 1111b6–10). Such a notion, based on a moral and human psychology, qualifies in important ways the human political sense as well as the nature of the human community, thus allowing for, on the one hand, a critique of certain political analyses, and, on the other, a justification of Aristotle's political preferences.

We already know that *phronēsis*, the practical wisdom—the ethico-political virtue *par excellence*—cannot be a science. Even if it could become scientific—a possibility which is excluded by the psychology of the two *Ethics*—that would not be desirable, since science is incompetent regarding the striving for the practical good, the only pertinent one in this context. But such a *phronēsis* makes sense only because man is endowed with *pro-hairesis*. This, however, is true only of the free man. The slave, even though he is a man insofar as he "apprehends" the *logos* (*Pol.* I, 5, 1254b20–24; 13, 1260a12; III, 9, 1280a32–34), is not free, since his existence and his "reason" exist only for the sake of his master. The latter, liberated from a "for-the-sake-of" existence, can exercise at leisure the *pro-hairesis* to which the slave, by fact and by nature, has no access. Though he is a man, the slave remains closer to the other domestic animals, since there is no *polis* as such without *pro-hairesis*.

It is not without importance, however, to observe that in the two *Ethics* (*E.E.*, II, 6–11; *E.N.*, III, 1–5) this notion is discussed in the books devoted to the moral virtues—"excellence of character," i.e., to those belonging to the desiderative part of the soul, which is different in man and animal. Since in man the desire must obey the *logos*, it is fully justified to return to *pro-hairesis* in the *Nichomachean Ethics*, VI, 2 (= *E.E.*, V, 2), i.e., at the beginning of the investigation of the intellectual virtues, which stem from the sub-part of the logical part of the soul named *to logistikon*, calculative. Thus, besides the fact that the theoretical intellect is inefficient, the practical intellect can only act accompanied by desire, from which it receives its impulse, even though it must regulate such desire.

Aristotle's originality lies in the fact that his practical thought allows him to deduce conclusions regarding good politics, since, remaining all along at the practical level, his argument does not have to bridge a gap—which is what would happen were he to move from science to morality.[7] Such a deduction, however, may become circular because political analyses are likely to influence moral psychology just as much as the converse, since the model of ethical action is isomorphic with that of political decision. Yet, the force of such a circle—if indeed it occurs—lies in its marking the barrier between the theoretical and practical domains. These deductions are performed through the use of the notion of "conformity with nature" (*kata physin*), but such a nature is already quite political. In fact, while the first necessary bonds are formed with the purpose of living (*zēn*), under the pressure of necessity (*Pol.*, I, 2, 1252a26–b5), the *polis*, on the contrary, is established in view of the *good life*, under the law of *pro-hairesis* (*Pol.*, III, 9, 1280a25–1281a4). Now, if "[the *polis*] is a community of families and aggregations of families in well-being, for the sake of a perfect and self-sufficing life" (*Pol.*, III, 9, ibid.), and if "the will to live together is friendship" (ibid.), then virtue must be sought by politicians, since only in that way will man be truly himself.

Let us note, before proceeding, that the introduction of *pro-hairesis* in the human political sphere suppresses the historical and biological basis of Aristotelian politics, since *pro-hairesis* is at variance with strict natural necessity. Yet, to some extent, politics remains connected with biology, through the mediation of psychology, which, however, being human and moral, is no longer biological *strictu sensu*. That is what permits such a give-and-take between politics and psychology, of which the analysis of the different types of authority (*archē*) in terms of their psychological foundations is but an example. It remains to be seen how such an analysis leads to a political theory, insofar as it provides the ammunition for a critique both of Plato's politics and of its mask—sophistic rhetoric.

The whole of Aristotle's analysis—especially in books III to VI of the *Politics*—amounts in fact to an argument against despotism (*archē despotikē*) which is identified by the fact that it treats free men as slaves. As a consequence, a despotic regime manages the city's affairs for the sake of the "masters," rather than for the sake of the common interest (*to koinon sympheron*), i.e., of the *res publica*, regardless of whether these masters be one (tyranny), a few but mainly rich (oligarchy), or many but poor (democracy). Tyranny, oligarchy, and democracy are all of them despotisms—to be sure, more or less harmful—insofar as they are deviations from the correct, "republican" constitutions, motivated by the common interest of the whole city, namely monarchy (or kingship), aristocracy, and that nameless regime that is in fact the best one, the "polity" (*politeia*, constitution, is the name shared by all constitutions). These are States of Law, where law rather than passions and private interests rule. Tyranny, oligarchy, and democracy are not only despotisms *de facto*, which typically suppress the right of free men to speak their minds, thus treating them as slaves, but also—and mainly— *de jure*. For, more essentially, despotism's characteristic is that it ignores the political level *as such*, because, like Plato, it does not distinguish between the different types of authority: it mixes up the authority of the master over his slaves—of a despotic kind—with the political authority, within which free and equal men, having in common a common thing—the *res publica*, are, in turn, governors and governed.

Such a political fault denounced by Aristotle already in the first lines of the *Politics* (I, 1, 1252a7–18)[8] is coupled with a serious psychological blunder (*Pol.*, I, 5, 1254b2–9): while one can admit that the soul commands the body with the authority of a master, the same cannot be said about the authority of its logical over its alogical part, here called "affective" (*pathētikon*). It is rather in a political way, like a monarch, that the calculative part controls the desiderative one—which means, in spite of the comparison with monarchy, that these two parts are, in turn, governing and governed.[9] We have the model of this connection in practical action, where the intellect is powerless without the desire, while the latter obeys the *logos*. In politics, therefore, the process of practical action should be respected (the latter having, in turn, its model in the process of making "good" political decisions), namely to create the conditions required for deliberation to be able to occur, so as to enable preferential choice to follow. In this, Aristotle is frontally opposed both to Plato's psychology and to his politics, whose "despotism of reason" finally disintegrates the city by transforming it into an excessively unified body, subjected to the philosopher-king who rules absolutely and undividedly by virtue of his alleged possession of political science, which he has because, having a golden soul, he is master by nature.[10]

Against this, Aristotle—in full harmony with his method in the practical disciplines—highlights the virtues of the multitude vis-à-vis the knowledge of the experts or "technocrats" (*Pol.*, III, 11). The latter should not go beyond their function, which is to advise. Nor should they monopolize power by controlling all decisions, because their competence does not grant them property rights over the common, public thing. As advisers, they have no right to suppress the citizens' freedom of speech in the name of some hypothetical "science of the State." Their lot is similar to that of the makers of rudders: it is the pilot that steers the course of the vessel, because, in using the rudders, he knows more about them than the maker himself, who must content himself with advising the pilot, letting the latter benefit from his particular competence. Similarly in politics: it is the free and equal citizens, users of the public thing, that should jointly govern, because they are more familiar with it than the experts in common interest. Yet such a multitude cannot judge appropriately unless it is organized, assembled. It is because it is collective that the multitude's virtue can be superior to that of the experts, and it cannot be such unless it results from the debates that take place in the people's assembly. The latter should meet at the center of the city, where the common things, about which all the citizens have the right to say something—precisely because they are common, are to be found. The good politics, the "republican" one, distinguishes itself from despotism—whether "cynical" or "scientific"—in that it is *deliberative*. It grants free men, the users of the public thing, full use of the weapons— beginning with the *logos* (*Pol.*, I, 2, 1253a33–38)—with which nature has endowed them, so that they become virtuous and prudent.

Let us conclude by stressing that *deliberative politics* corresponds to the political superiority of man over animal, since it is the politics of the *logos*. This is the reason for Aristotle's interest in rhetoric, for what is characteristic of man is his ability to defend himself by means of his *logos*, rather than by means of his body (*Rhet.*, I, 1, 1355a38–b7). Still, one should make good usage of it, rather than reducing politics to rhetoric—a move that characterizes sophistry and demagogy. Every citizen, though he need not be a great political orator, must at least be a good listener, i.e., a good judge, because it is to him and his fellow voters or rather decision-makers that all discourse on public matters is addressed. Being deliberative, politics will either be argumentative or vanish, thus dissolving the *polis* into some vague association of masters and slaves, prone to fall prey to despotism.

Notes

1. "Knowledge" is here taken in its most general sense, rather than in its narrow, technical sense of "scientific knowledge." The term *epistēmē* will thus be translated by "science" rather than by "knowledge," which will be reserved for the "faculty of discrimination," the ability to draw differences and use them, i.e., both the result and the nature of the critical function (*to kritikon*).

2. All the quotations from Aristotle are from the *Complete Works of Aristotle*, The Revised Oxford Translation, ed. by Jonathan Barnes, 2 vols., Princeton: Princeton University Press, 1984 (Bollingen Series 71–2). The following abbreviations are used: *An. Post* for *Analytica Posteriora*; *De An.* for *De Anima*; *E.E.* for *Eudemian Ethics*; *E.N.* for *Nicomachean Ethics*; *H.A.* for *Historia Animalium*; *Pol.* for *Politics*; *Rhet.* for *Rhetoric*.

3. On this issue, see Mulgan (1974: 438–445), who has ably distinguished three different—though related—senses of the term "political animal," namely: (a) an *exclusive* sense, referring to the human need for *polis* as opposed to other social institutions; (b) an *inclusive* sense, referring to the human need for *polis*, including other social institutions; and (c) a *metaphorical* sense, referring to the need, common to man and some other animals, of sharing a collective activity with other members of the same species. Senses (a) and (b) are connected by the notion of *polis*, while

senses (b) and (c) are linked by the idea of a collective activity, in contrast to solitary activities.

4. On the *logos* and its distinction from *phōnē*, see Aubenque (1972: 94–134), J. L. Ackrill (1963: 113–128), and Labarrière (1984, 1985).

5. The usual translation—"choice"—is unsatisfactory. This is why I deliberately employ this term in its Greek form. One should notice its neatly political connotations: *hairesis* is the action of grasping, of choosing something, rather than (*pro*) another, as a result of a deliberation (*E.N.*, III, 3, 1113a7–9; *E.E.*, II, 10, 1226b6–10). See Aubenque (1963: 119–143), as well as Gauthier and Jolif (1970, II, 1: 189–212).

6. *Hekousios* does not cover the same ground as the modern concept of "will." It refers, rather, to actions performed without any constraint that, in turn, are not opposed to those performed necessarily or automatically. For Aristotle includes the movements of animals among the *hekousioi* movements (accomplished voluntarily), although they are performed mechanically and necessarily whenever there is no obstruction to them. See Vernant (1972: 43–74), Gauthier and Jolif (1970, II, 1: 168–189), and Furley (1978: 165–179).

7. See *Posterior Analytics*, I, 7–12, and *Nichomachean Ethics*, VI, 2.

8. See also *Pol.*, I, 3, 7, 12–13; III, 4, 1277a33-b16; and III, 6, 1278b30–79a21.

9. Besides the fact that the calculative part deliberates—so it seems—less about the ends than about the means, since the ends are posited by the desire, we should notice that for the calculative part to govern like a monarch is also to depart from tyrannical rule, because the king is subject to the laws and to the common interest.

10. It is in *Pol.*, II, 1–6 that Aristotle develops most extensively his critique of Plato's political views.

References

Ackrill, John L. 1963. *Aristotle's Categories and De Interpretatione*. Oxford: Oxford University Press.

Arendt, Hannah. 1958. *The Human Condition*. Chicago: Chicago University Press.

Aubenque, Pierre. 1962. *Le Problème de l'Etre chez Aristote*, 3rd ed. (1972). Paris: Presses Universitaires de France.

————. 1963. *La Prudence chez Aristote*. Paris: Presses Universitaires de France.

Cooper, John M. 1975. *Reason and Human Good in Aristotle*. Cambridge, Mass.: Harvard University Press.

Fortenbaugh, William W. 1975. *Aristotle on Emotion*. London: Duckworth.

Furley, David J. 1978. Self movers. In G.E.R. Lloyd and G.E.L. Owen (eds.), *Aristotle on Mind and the Senses. Proceedings of the Seventh Symposium Aristotelicum*. Cambridge: Cambridge University Press, pp. 165–179.

Gauthier, René Antoine, and Jean Yves Jolif. 1970. *Aristote. L'Ethique à Nicomaque*. Louvain: Publications Universitaires, and Paris: Béatrice-Nauwelaerts.

Hamlyn, David W. 1968. *Aristotle's De Anima Books II, III*. Oxford: Oxford University Press.

Labarrière, Jean-Louis. 1984. Imagination humaine et imagination animale chez Aristote. *Phronēsis* 29: 17–49.

————. 1985. Neutralité du signe et neutralité du symbole chez Aristote. *Exercices de la Patience* 6: 135–144.

Lyotard, Jean-François. 1983. *Le Différend*. Paris: Les Editions de Minuit.

Mulgan, Richard G. 1974. Aristotle's doctrine that man is a political animal. *Hermès* 102: 438–445.

Nussbaum, Martha Craven. 1980. Shame, separateness, and political unity: Aristotle's criticism of Plato. In Amélie Oksenberg Rorty (ed.), *Essays on Aristotle's Ethics.* Berkeley: University of California Press, pp. 395–435.

Pellegrin, Pierre. 1982. *La Classification des Animaux chez Aristote. Statut de la Biologie et Unité de l'Aristotélisme.* Paris: Les Belles Lettres.

Romeyer Dherbey, Gilbert. 1983. *Les Choses Mêmes. La Pensée du Réel chez Aristote.* Lausanne: L'Age d'Homme.

Vernant, Jean-Pierre. 1972. Ebauches de la volonté dans la tragédie Grecque. In *Psychologie Comparative et Art, Hommage à I. Meyerson.* Reprinted in J.P. Vernant and P. Vidal-Naquet (eds.), *Mythe et Tragédie en Grèce Ancienne.* Paris: Maspéro (1981), pp. 41–74.

2

Hobbes's Science of Moral Philosophy

Jean Hampton

In all of his political writings Thomas Hobbes maintains that it was *bad reasoning* that had plunged England and other European societies into chaos during the seventeenth century, so that the only effective cure for this disorder was to give members of these societies a sound, rational argument for the correct political structure of the state as rigorous as any of Euclid's geometric proofs.[1] Starting from certain metaphysical premises, in particular materialism, nominalism (or at least a tendency toward it),[2] and a conception of human beings that is radically individualist, Hobbes believes that it is possible, using the correct physical facts about us, to derive true ethical and political conclusions. In his masterpiece *Leviathan* he presents a chart describing the relationships of the different sciences, and in it he represents ethics as simply a branch of psychology, which is itself a branch of physics (Lev, 9, 41). A philosopher who could say such a thing clearly has an unusually "scientific" understanding of ethical and political knowledge, which down through the centuries some readers have found refreshingly direct and demystifying, and others have found shockingly crude and misdirected. In this chapter I want to explore Hobbes's rather complicated position on the nature and possibility of moral knowledge, showing how he uses this position to justify the institution of a sovereign. It is a position that allows him to affirm the existence of moral facts, but also leads him to despair of these facts becoming widely known or held. Curiously, modern liberals with political positions that are virtually antithetical to those of Hobbes have used Hobbesian-like skepticism about the possibility of attaining moral knowledge to justify severe limits on state authority and power. Hence this chapter concludes by offering an argument warning those who would resist Hobbes's political conclusions to beware of defending their anti-Hobbesian positions by appealing to Hobbesian views about how little most people can or do know about moral matters.

Hobbes's Science of Moral Philosophy

There appear to be maddening inconsistencies and confusions throughout Hobbes's writings on the nature of science and scientific methodology that probably rest, in the end, on an equivocation about the nature of truth.[3] But his predominant view of science rests on a correspondence theory of truth, and it is important for us to understand this view so that we can correctly understand his stand on the possibility of moral and political knowledge. An incautious reading of *Leviathan* might lead one to think that Hobbes is a moral conventionalist, who denies that there is such a thing as genuine moral or political knowledge. I shall now argue that this reading is false, and that much of *Leviathan* is an attempt to develop what Hobbes himself calls the "Science of Moral Philosophy."

Much historical work has yet to be done to learn how Hobbes was affected by the skeptical views of the men with whom he frequently discussed philosophy during his sojourns in Paris, among them Mersenne, Gassendi, and Descartes (Popkin 1982, 133–48). In the skeptical environment of seventeenth-century Paris, these and other thinkers questioned the extent to which we had criteria for determining what was true, and their questioning involved not only the kind of radical doubt characteristic of Cartesian methodology but also more quotidian worries about positions that seemed far less well founded than the existence of the external world, including Aristotelian physics (attacked, for example, by Mersenne and Charron) and the idea that there is an established and objective body of moral truths. Several thinkers, among them François de La Mothe Le Vayer, followed Michel de Montaigne in putting forward skeptical positions on the existence of moral truths that made use of the fact that men in different cultures and times had disagreed dramatically on questions of what was right and wrong.[4]

Nonetheless, these skeptics' intentions were not merely destructive. Descartes was concerned with sweeping away all that could be doubted in order to find a foundation on which to build true theories of the world. Likewise, Hobbes was concerned in all of his writings with sweeping away the cobwebs of false and outmoded theories—particularly what he called the "filth and fraud" in Greek philosophy (De Corp, EW i, Epistle Dedicatory [ep. ded.], ix)—in order to make room for science (or philosophy, for he uses these words interchangeably). In the Epistle Dedicatory to *De Corpore*, he celebrated Copernicus, Galileo, and Harvey as men who established new doctrines of knowledge in modern times, and he perceived himself to be one of this small company of scientists whose use of reason was helping us to achieve *certainty* (that is his word [De Corp, EW i, ep. ded., viii–ix]) in our knowledge of the world. Indeed, when reading *Leviathan* or *De Corpore*, one is often struck by Hobbes's supreme confidence that human beings can ascertain the truth about the world through the use of reason, and it is partly this confidence that drives his own encyclopedic project. That confidence, however, is sometimes shaken. As will be noted later, a kind of skeptical despair occasionally creeps into *Leviathan* that causes him to wonder if any sense can be made of the confusing and chaotic world in which we live. But generally Hobbes maintains what seems an almost naïve faith in the power of human reason to penetrate the mysteries of the world, a faith that was certainly pervasive among many intellectuals of his day.

How is it that modern thinkers are to attain knowledge of the world? According to Hobbes, the key to its penetration is the proper use of reason:

> Every man brought Philosophy, that is, Natural Reason, into the world with him; for all men can reason to some degree, and concerning some things: but where there is need of a long series of reasons, there most men wander out of the way, and fall into error for want of method, as it were for want of sowing and planting, that is, of improving their reason. (De Corp, EW i, I, 1, 1, 1)

But what is right reason? Hobbes seeks to define it in *Leviathan*. He starts in Chapter 3 simply by defining mental activity or thinking, which he claims is always regulated "by some desire or designe" (Lev, 3, 4, 9): "From Desire, ariseth the Thought of some means we have seen produce the like of that which we ayme at; and from the thought of that, the thought of means to that mean; and so continually, till we come to some beginning within our own power" (Lev, 3, 4, 9). Hobbes goes on to explain that there are two kinds of "regulated" means-end thinking: One involves going from the effect or the goal to the cause or way of producing it, a form of thinking that both animals and humans can do; the second involves going from the cause or the means to all the effects or goals that can be produced by it, something that only humans can do (Lev, 3, 5, 9).

Next, Hobbes goes on in the same chapter to define "prudence" as the ability to determine what effects will be brought about by one's actions.[5] But what is important for our purposes is that in Chapter 5 he distinguishes between prudence and genuine reasoning by saying that, although both involve cause-and-effect chains of thinking, reasoning involves the use of language, whereas mere prudential thought does not. So reason is barely, but nonetheless importantly, distinguishable from mere prudence because reason is

> not gotten by experience onely; as Prudence is; but attayned by Industry; first in apt imposing of Names; and Secondly by getting good and orderly Method in proceeding from the Elements, which are Names, to Assertions made by Connexion of one of them to another; and so to Syllogismes, which are the Connexions of one Assertion to another, till we come to a knowledge of all the Consequences of names appertaining to the subject in hand; and that is it, men call SCIENCE. (Lev, 5, 17, 21)

But what is the "apt imposing of Names," and why is it so important?

One point Hobbes is certainly trying to make is that a language user has the capacity to reason syllogistically and thus to arrive at conclusions that are "logically necessary"—i.e., necessary in the sense that they are logical implications, and that are true provided that the premises of the syllogism are true. If two names are copulated in a proposition, and the second name is copulated with a third name in another proposition, then the first and third names can be copulated in a third proposition that is true provided the first and second propositions are true. Hence, a scientist is a person who reasons logically about the world after rightly naming and defining the world around him: *"a demonstration is a syllogism, or series of syllogisms, derived and continued, from the definitions of names, to the last conclusion.* And from hence it may be understood, that all true ratiocination, which taketh its beginning from true principles, produceth science, and is true demonstration" (De Corp, EW i, I, 6, 16, 86).

However, not only does Hobbes perceive science as a discipline that follows a logical method to yield logically necessary truths, he also sees it as having a certain *content*, in which necessity of a very different and *causal* sort is made manifest. The official Hobbesian definition of "Philosophy" or "Science" goes as follows: "PHILOSOPHY is such knowledge of effects or appearances, as we acquire by true ratiocination from the knowledge we have first of their causes or generations" (De Corp, EW i, I, 1, 2, 3). Similarly, Hobbes insists in *Leviathan* that "Science is the knowledge of Consequences" (Lev, 5, 17, 21). In other words, science seeks to know about a world that is experienced by us as filled with change—objects move, they degenerate or generate, and they affect one another in many ways. Hobbes argues in *De Corpore* that the foundation of such a world can be revealed to us "without method," for the causes of such changes "are manifest of themselves, or (as they say commonly) known to nature"—and he contends that the cause of all change is *motion* (De Corp, EW i, I, 6, 5, 69). Hence, the first principles of science must explain and reveal the causal connection of objects in the world by appeal to certain *laws of motion*, one of which Hobbes is prepared to state, namely, Galileo's law of inertia (De Corp, EW i, II, 9, 7, 124–125; see also I, 6, 6, 70–73).

Moreover, when Hobbes speaks of the causal connection of objects that follow these laws of motion, he characterizes this connection as *necessary*:

> And seeing a necessary cause is defined to be that, which being supposed, the effect cannot but follow; this also may be collected, that whatsoever effect is produced at any time, the same is produced by a necessary cause. For whatsoever is produced, in as much as it is produced, had an entire cause, that is, had all those things, which being supposed, it cannot be understood but that the effect follows; that is, it had a necessary cause. (De Corp, EW i, II, 9, 5, 123)

This necessary connection between causes and their effects is clearly not logical; indeed, it is inexplicable unless we believe with Hobbes that such necessity is simply "manifest" in experience. Hume's attack on this notion of causal necessity fairly leaps from the pages of *Leviathan* and *De Corpore*, and yet Hobbes himself was too committed to the concept of causal necessity even to question the notion in any of his works.

Note that the picture of science that emerges from these passages is one that presupposes the correspondence theory of truth. A true scientific proposition is one that corresponds to the way the world is. In science, objects are correctly described, and causal connections are correctly drawn and are derivable from first principles that we *know* describe the world because they are, in Hobbes's words, "self-evident" or "manifest."

After setting out his conception of science in *Leviathan* and *De Corpore*, Hobbes goes on to explain in both works the purpose of science. It is his view that we do not engage in this descriptive project solely or even primarily because we value the acquisition of truth about the world for its own sake. Instead, reminiscent of Bacon,[6] he believes that true scientific descriptions of causes and effects are valuable to us because they are useful to us. "The *end* or *scope* of philosophy is, that we may make use to our benefit of effects formerly seen . . . *for the commodity of human life*" (De Corp, EW i, I, 1, 6, 7; emphasis added). And a bit later he insists with Baconian fervor: "The end of knowledge is power . . . the scope of all speculation is the performing of some action or thing to be done" (De Corp, EW i, I, 1, 6, 7). Thus, science, for Hobbes, has a prescriptive role as well as a descriptive role. It not only describes the world but also directs us in efficacious ways of behavior based on the information it has about the structure and operation of the world. If we want to shoot a cannonball to destroy our enemy in battle, or if we want to change our body chemistry to cure a disease, science tells us what to do by giving us the causal information we need to achieve these aims.

Having seen how Hobbes understands the nature of science, we are now in a position to appreciate how significant it is that he calls his body of ethical and political views a "science" at the end of Chapter 15 of *Leviathan*. After completing his definition of nineteen moral laws of nature, the second of which contains the directive to institute an absolute sovereign, he maintains that "the science of them is the true and onely moral philosophy" (Lev, 15, 40, 79). Because science previously had been defined as "knowledge of consequences," is he saying that these nineteen laws give us causal knowledge about the world?

Indeed he is, as he goes on to explain. After repeating his subjectivist definitions of 'good' and 'evil' from Chapter 6 (where the former is defined as that which we desire and the latter is defined as that toward which we feel aversion), he says: "For Morral Philosophy is nothing else but the Science of what is *Good*, and *Evill*, in the conversation, and Society of mankind. *Good* and *Evill*, are names that signifie our Appetites, and Aversions; which in different tempers, customes, and doctrines of men, are different" (Lev, 15, 40, 79). At this point, Hobbes's moral philosophy sounds like little more than an anthropological study—it certainly would appear to be a wholly descriptive rather than a prescriptive enterprise. But this is a premature conclusion. He goes on to note that although men differ greatly in what they desire, "all men agree on this, that Peace is Good" (Lev, 15, 40, 80). In *De Homine*, Hobbes calls this type of good (i.e., one that all human beings want and that they can all share) a "common good."[7] But Hobbes also distinguishes between two sorts of desired goods: real and apparent. The former is what a person would desire if he had true beliefs as well as a rightly functioning reason and desire-formation system in his body; the latter is what a person actually desires given the beliefs that he has and the physiological state he is in. Therefore, when Hobbes speaks about moral philosophy as the science of what is good in the conversation of mankind, he is not being completely clear. He is not interested merely in what people actually seek, given their desires, as means to achieving those desires; he is also interested in what they *should* seek as means to achieving them (i.e., the correct or most effective way to realize the object they are pursuing). Peace is, in his eyes, a "real" common good insofar as it actually does lead to the furtherance of what people desire most—their self-preservation. Moreover, he also believes that peace is actually perceived by all men as a good—the apparent and the real coincide in this case. But what is not so manifest to all men is that if peace is good, then also "the way, or means of Peace, which (as I have shewed before) are *Justice, Gratitude, Modesty, Equity, Mercy,* & the rest of the Laws of Nature, are good; that is to say *Morall Vertues*; and their contrarie *Vices,* Evill" (Lev, 15, 40, 80). The laws of nature assert a causal connection between these cooperative forms of behavior and self-preservation: these forms of behavior effect peace, although he specifies later on that they do so only in circumstances where others are also willing to perform these actions, and peace in turn helps to effect longer life.

So, when Hobbes calls his laws of nature "Conclusions, or Theoremes concerning what conduceth to the conservation and defence of [people]" (Lev, 15, 41, 80), he is saying that they are statements of causal connection between a common desired object and certain cooperative actions. Moral science, just like any other science, gives us causal knowledge about the world, and it is useful to us in the same way as any other science; that is, it supplies us with the causal information (in this case, about how to attain peace) that we need in order to get what we want. They are what Kant would call hypothetical imperatives,[8] of the following form: "If one wants x, one ought to do y, where x is peace, a common instrumental goal desirable insofar as it is necessary for self-preservation, and y is the action which, when performed in conjunction with others' performance of the same action, will help to effect the achievement of peace." Moreover, Hobbes perceives his role to be one that any good scientist plays, that is, the role of giving people the causal information they lack so that they can achieve what they desire:

> The utility of moral and civil philosophy is to be estimated, not so much by the commodities we have by knowing these sciences, as by the calamities we receive from not knowing them. Now, all such calamities as may be avoided by human industry, arise from war, but chiefly from civil war; for from this

proceed slaughter, solitude, and the want of all things. But the cause of war is not that men are willing to have it; for the will has nothing for object but good, at least that which seemeth good. Nor is it from this, that men know not that the effects of war are evil; for who is there that thinks not poverty and loss of life to be great evils? The cause, therefore, of civil war is, that men know not the causes neither of war nor peace, there being but few in the world that have learned those duties which unite and keep men in peace, that is to say, that have learned the rules of civil life sufficiently. Now, the knowledge of these rules is moral philosophy. (De Corp, EW i, I, 1, 7, 8)

In other words, Hobbes perceives his theorizing to be valuable because the people of his day, although eager to further their lives and live in peace, do not know how to achieve this goal, and thus end up performing actions that result in war rather than peace. Hobbes's argument in *Leviathan* is meant to demonstrate the truth of a certain critical piece of causal information, that is, that the institution of an absolute sovereign is necessary for peace.

I have attempted to show, in this section, that Hobbes regards ethics and physics as methodologically identical. But as I have already noted, he also believes that there is a substantive connection between the two. The former, he maintains, is a branch of the latter. Insofar as we are entirely material beings, he argues that we can be exhaustively described in physical terms by a complete and correct physical theory.[9] However, because no such theory was available to his readers, Hobbes says in his introduction to *Leviathan* that political philosophy must start with what is known about human beings from everyday observations of them. These observations are sufficient, he thinks, to give us enough accurate knowledge about our desires and our (war-prone) nature to yield moral and political imperatives that are both true and also applicable to us, given our actual desires. But he hopes that these conclusions can one day be derived from knowledge of the physical operation of the human machine, and his own discussions of human physiology in his various works are in pursuit of such knowledge.

Hobbes's View of the Advantages of His Approach to Ethics

Aristotelians and Kantians will find Hobbes's physicalist approach to ethics not only wrong but objectionable. Nonetheless, if we stop for a moment to take stock of the virtues of Hobbes's "moral science," we can appreciate why Hobbes himself regarded it as an intellectual achievement equal to those produced by Galileo, Harvey, Kepler, and Copernicus.

First, Hobbes's moral science has a way of accounting for why the moral laws of nature are true. The traditional moral theorist claimed to issue moral commands that were objectively true; yet such a theorist always found it difficult to explain how this was so, sometimes doing so only by postulating strange moral objects or strange moral properties that had prescriptive powers. However, Hobbes's explanation of the truth of moral laws is easy and straightforward; the moral laws are true to the extent that they state correctly what actions will effect longer life. They are true in the same way as any conditional cause-and-effect proposition in a physical science is true. Indeed, Hobbes can even regard himself as a "moral objectivist" of sorts, because he has shown that moral propositions can be understood to be objectively true and necessary if they are interpreted as assertions of a causal connection between certain actions and a desired common goal. Of course, this is not the sort of objectivity a Kantian or Aristotelian wants, particularly because Hobbes's objectively true moral prescriptions can move someone to act only if that person happens (contingently) to desire that common goal. But for Hobbes this is the only kind of objective truth that *any* proposition, including moral and political propositions, can have. The attraction of this approach to moral objectivity has persisted to the present day.[10] Indeed, what this shows is that we should beware of the terms 'subjective' and 'objective' in moral theory, because they do not necessarily mark the right distinctions. Hobbes is a subjectivist in the sense that he defines value as subjective preference. For him, there is no objective good or right, but only, as he puts it, what is "good for someone or other" (DH, XI, 4, 47). But he is an ethical objectivist in the sense that his moral propositions are statements of causal connections that purport to be true. Because the phrase 'ethical objectivism' has traditionally been used to describe deontological moral theories such as those espoused by Kant, I will continue to call Hobbes an ethical subjectivist in virtue of his subjectivist theory of value. But the reader should note that Hobbes is a value-subjectivist who nonetheless seeks to espouse objective moral principles.

Second, Hobbes not only explains how moral propositions are true but also why they have prescriptive power. One of the most disturbing questions plaguing the moral deontologist is the following: Why should I act morally? But Hobbes maintains that the answer to this question is simple: One should do the moral thing because it will advance one's self-interest (and avoid such behavior when it will not). It is an explanation that, in his view, far outstrips previous explanations of the prescriptivity of moral behavior, for example, the account offered by Aristotle:

> The Writers of Morall Philosophie, though they acknowledge the same Vertues and Vices; Yet not seeing wherein consisted their Goodnesse; *nor that they come to be praised, as the meanes of peaceable, sociable, and comfortable living;* place them in a mediocrity of passions: as if not the Cause, but the Quantity of a gift, made Liberality. (Lev, 15, 40, 80; emphasis added)

So Hobbes believes that his self-interested deduction of the virtues both preserves and explains the prescriptivity of moral commands. We ought to act morally in the same way that we ought to take our medicine when we are sick; both actions are necessary causes of desired effects.

This passage also reveals a third feature of Hobbes's moral science which he sees as a virtue. He believes his science explains why human beings have been perennially pleased by and promotive of more or less the same cooperative actions, whether their cultural background is Athens of the fourth century B.C. or seventeenth-century England. Moral philosophers "acknowledge the same Vertues and Vices" because of their causal connection with peace (see also DC, EW ii, 3, 32, 48–9). This explanation is, in Hobbes's eyes, far more sensible than the Aristotelian explanation, which maintains that these virtues are valued insofar as they represent (as he puts it in the passage quoted above) a "mediocrity of passions." Hobbes indeed believes that there is such a thing as "too much virtue"—being virtuous when others are prone to prey upon one is something he condemns rather than praises. But he also believes that his moral science will offer the correct account of the limits of virtuous action.

Finally, Hobbes values the fact that in his moral science all of the terms are defined so that they refer. Throughout *Leviathan* Hobbes seizes on traditional moral words and phrases, such as 'good', 'right', and 'law of nature', draining them of their traditional objectivist meaning and then infusing them with subjectivist meanings of his own. Hobbes is not merely announcing his subjectivism in these passages, but also showing how moral terms must be defined so that they can refer to determinate objects. In a passage already quoted, Hobbes insists that scientific reasoning must presuppose the "apt imposing of Names" (Lev, 5, 17, 21); otherwise, assertions will be false. In *De Corpore*, Hobbes explains that one way in which we err when we reason is to use names that denote only phantasms (De Corp, EW i, I, 5, 4, 59), and he counsels that the way to detect false propositions is to resolve terms in these propositions into their definitions so as to determine whether or not the terms actually refer. Clearly, he believes that moral objectivists such as Aristotle use moral terms, such as "summum bonum," that do not refer.[11]

So what does one do with these words? Mackie has suggested in his own defense of ethical subjectivism that we retain these moral words and their objectivist meanings and allow the making of false moral assertions, using them so long as such assertions are useful.[12] Hobbes does not even consider the possibility that an entire body of discourse that is judged to be false can have any value in our search for knowledge and power. However, he opposes the junking of moral discourse entirely. His project in *Leviathan* is to keep moral discourse by changing the reference of moral terms so that they refer. For example, 'good' no longer refers to the nonexistent summum bonum but to the collection of objects desired by a particular person in a particular place and time. Therefore, the unwary reader who does not appreciate the radical revisionist project under way in the early chapters of *Leviathan* will substantially misunderstand in the rest of the book not only the Hobbesian ethical position but also the Hobbesian argument for absolute sovereignty that presupposes that position.

Hobbes's Moral Skepticism and the Need for a Sovereign

I have presented Hobbes's view of science as an enterprise concerned with deriving causal propositions from first principles of motion that are true insofar as they correspond with the world. But intermixed with this view is a rather different picture of scientific methodology resting on a conventionalist account of truth. There is a side to Hobbes that seems to have given up on the prospect of attaining true representations of the world, and instead believes that we can only construct a science based on first principles that are "made" true by convention. This conventionalist side of Hobbes is noted and discussed by McNeilly (1969, ch. 3 and 4) and by Watkins (1965, sect. 28). It is his "dark" side, the side of him which is worried and pessimistic about the chances of coming up with "certain" knowledge of the world.

One might think that it is this skeptical, conventionalist tendency which explains Hobbes's tendencies toward both legal and moral positivism in *Leviathan*, i.e., the views that law and morality are only what a ruler stipulates and commands.[13] Consider that the subjective definition of 'good' in Chapter 6 (Lev, 6, 7, 24) of *Leviathan* as "whatever a person desires" can be read as a way of saying that there is no "natural" definition of these terms that all men can accept. And the sovereign is frequently presented as necessary in order to define not only laws but also moral truths that do not exist naturally, as when Hobbes says that "the makers of civil laws, are not only declarers but also makers of justice and injustice."[14] Indeed, Hobbes defines his own project in *De Cive* as demonstrating "that there are no authentical doctrines concerning right and wrong, good and evil, besides the constituted laws in each realm and government" (DC, EW ii, pref., xiii). And this demonstration certainly seems to presuppose showing that there are no *natural* doctrines of right and wrong, good and evil, capable of being discerned (e.g., by reason) and accepted by human beings inside or outside a civil society.

But what about the laws of nature? Aren't they supposed to be natural doctrines of right and wrong? Why couldn't they serve as ready-made moral rules which a government should use in declaring law in order to realize peace in a society? It is precisely because these laws of nature are supposed to constitute a moral *science* that we cannot take Hobbes to have been a straightforward conventionalist about moral knowledge. We need a more complicated explanation of his conviction that the sovereign must stipulate what counts as moral behavior than the explanation that he held a simple-minded moral skepticism, since it is clear he did not hold such a view.

A search through the pages of *Leviathan* reveals a better, more sophisticated explanation for his legal and moral positivism. It is not that Hobbes was skeptical about the existence of genuine moral knowledge, but rather that he was skeptical about the idea that large numbers of human beings could attain such knowledge. The precise details of the causal connections between various forms of cooperative behavior and self-advantage are, according to Hobbes, hard to see, so that many people will insist, mistakenly, that it is rational for them to behave uncooperatively, even aggressively toward their fellows. *Leviathan* contains passages that suggest three reasons for Hobbes's pessimistic assessment of how widespread moral knowledge could ever be.[15]

First, in his discussion of the causes of conflict in the state of nature in Chapter 13 of *Leviathan* he suggests that people are too shortsighted to appreciate the advantages of cooperation, seizing the short-term benefits of aggression without realizing that doing so means forgoing the greater benefits that come from contract keeping, respect for property, and so forth. Second, he argues that human beings are glory seekers, intent on proving themselves superior to their fellows, and thus inclined to war with them when others question what they take to be (or wish to be) their sense of their own excellence. This kind of glory-induced conflict is irrational insofar as it means risking harm or death. Hobbes need not argue that every human being is inclined toward this irrationality or toward the shortsighted stupidity that prevents them from seeing the advantages from cooperation. He need only argue that there is a significant number of such people, so that those rational individuals who will not risk self-preservation for glory and who can see the rationality of cooperation will nonetheless find that they cannot risk cooperation with a population too many of which may be these dangerous folk. As Hobbes puts it, "he that should be modest, and tractable, and performe all he promises, in such time, and place, where no man els should do so, should but make himself a prey to others, and procure his own certain ruine, contrary to the ground of the Lawes of Nature, which tend to Natures preservation" (Lev, 15, 36, 79).

But third, even among these rational and intelligent human beings, cooperation would prove difficult because the *details* of peace-producing cooperative behavior tend to be either hard to know or else hard to agree on. Consider, for example, Hobbes's ninth law of nature on equity, which contains only the vaguest prescriptions about how private property ought to be apportioned. Human beings are notorious for being unable to agree with one another on a peace-producing way to divide goods among people, or indeed on *any* distribution of goods. And in general Hobbes argues that access to the precise details of the laws of nature is difficult because self-interest can overpower and distort the reasoning ability of even the most rational and intellegent human beings:

> The unwritten Law of Nature, though it be easy to such, as without partiality, and passion, make use of their naturall reason [to interpret], and therefore leave the violators thereof without excuse; yet considering there be few, perhaps none, that in some cases are not blinded by self love, or some other passion, it is now become of all Laws the most obscure; and has consequently the greatest need of able Interpreters. (Lev, 26, 21, 143)

So in virtue of what Hobbes takes to be an inevitable and irremediable ignorance of large numbers of human beings about moral matters, warfare would exist were there no government to control human behavior.

Because so many human beings cannot attain moral knowledge or develop workable cooperative practices, Hobbes believes that peace is only attainable if an absolute sovereign is empowered. And one of the sovereign's roles is to develop (using sanctions) cooperative practices and "objective" meanings for moral words which the larger community is incapable of arriving at by genuinely objective reflection on what actions and policies will further the cause of peace and (thereby) their own self-interest. The "measure of Good and Evill actions is the Civill Law" (Lev, 29, 6, 68; see also Lev, 29, 7, 68–9). The sovereign's civil laws define "Good, Evill, Lawfull and Unlawfull" (Lev, 18, 10, 91) and the "Rules of Propriety (or *Meum* and *Tuum*)" (Lev, 18, 10, 91, and 24, 5, 127). Moreover, the word 'justice' is not a word to which people are able to give any objective moral content naturally; rather, "Laws are the Rules of Just, and Unjust; nothing being reputed Unjust that is not contrary to some law" (Lev, 26, 4, 137). Indeed, for the sake of peace, Hobbes maintains that the sovereign is given the power to determine answers to all issues, not just moral ones: "it is annexed to the Soveraignty, to be Judge of what Opinions and Doctrines are averse, and what conducing to Peace" (Lev, 19, 9, 91).

So, although Hobbes admits that there are objective facts of the matter about how people who desire self-preservation ought to behave toward one another in a community in order to attain a life-preserving peace, he also insists that access to these facts is difficult for us less-than-reliable, biased and glory-prone human reasoners. Hence, if people desire to resolve their disputes, they must "by their own accord, set up, for right Reason, the Reason of some Arbitrator, or Judge, to whose sentence they will both stand, or their controversie must either come to blowes, or be undecided, for what of, a right Reason, constituted by Nature" (Lev, 5, 3, 19; see also DC, EW ii, 12, 1, 149–51 and 14, 17, 195–7). And the institution of a sovereign is essentially the establishment of a judge whose reason will substitute for the "universal reason" (i.e., the shared, correct interpretation of the laws of nature) which does not exist in our world. Throughout his political writings, Hobbes challenges his opponents to answer the question "Who shall judge?" in all of those situations where there is disagreement giving rise to conflict. And he maintains that to give any answer other than "an absolute sovereign" is to invite political and social anarchy.

However, this Hobbesian skepticism about the possibility of large numbers of human beings coming to know the precise nature of the causal connections between peace-promoting cooperative action and self-interest seems dangerous if pushed too far. Isn't the argument for the institution of the sovereign one that relies on a causal connection between the attainment of peace given this widespread moral disagreement and the creation of a ruler with absolute power? *Leviathan* presents, after all, an elaborate argument in defense of the second law of nature, commanding people to institute a sovereign in order to attain peace. The truth of this law is not conventional; rather, it is true because it describes correctly the causal connection between peace and actions bringing about the sovereign's institution. And this causal connection is supposed to be important to us insofar as (almost) all of us agree that peace is desirable. So if there could be no moral truths outside of those conventionally established, Hobbes's project in *Leviathan* would be impossible. The considerable moral chaos about which he worries would be complete and irremediable, because the ultimate peace producer, the sovereign, could not be instituted. It is Hobbes's deepest faith that he can show a *necessary causal connection* between at least one cooperative project (i.e., the institution of the sovereign) and peace. As John Dewey has remarked, "Hobbes is in the somewhat paradoxical opinion of holding that while all order proceeds from the unquestioned authority of the sovereign, the permanent and settled institution of sovereignty itself depends upon a recognition of the scientific truths of morals and politics as set forth by him" (Dewey 1974: 23). But if people could learn and accept the truth of *this* prescription for peace, why couldn't they come to know of others? Hobbes walks a tightrope in *Leviathan*, trying to show that human reason is too weak to enable men to govern themselves but relying on human reason to show it.

Hence, faith in the ability of human reason to discern a true causal connection between a certain kind of political institution and human self-interest is critical to Hobbes's project of justifying the state in *Leviathan*. But the idea that this is effectively the *only* moral knowledge that could become widespread in a human community is critical to Hobbes's argument that a ruler requires absolute power in order to achieve peace. So there are two kinds of moral facts relevant to political matters which Hobbes considers that we can know: first, that the state is necessary and desirable for peace; and second, that other moral knowledge is largely unattainable for most of mankind, so that our state must be ruled by an absolute sovereign.

Can this seemingly paradoxical position succeed? Not as it stands; I have argued elsewhere that Hobbes's argument can only be made valid if its conclusion is the establishment not of an absolute sovereign but rather of a ruler whose power, although considerable, is nonetheless neither absolute nor permanent. By giving a rational argument for preferring political society over a state of nature (which is taken to establish at least *this* moral fact), Hobbes also gives subjects rational standards for criticizing—and even rebelling against—rulers or political arrangements that do not live up to these standards. My argument to this effect is long and complex; therefore, I cannot present it in detail here.[16] But its outlines are easy to see. If a subject knows that her state is justified because it has certain desirable consequences and if she can determine the extent to which her political society is realizing those consequences, then in concert with others she will not only be able but also justified in effecting political change if doing so is a way of securing more fully and effectively those desirable consequences.

There are times in Chapter 21 when Hobbes comes very close to saying this: "When . . . our refusal to obey, frustrates the End for which the Soveraignty was ordained; then there is no Liberty to refuse: otherwise there is" (Lev, 21, 15, 112); and "The obligation of Subjects to the Soveraign, is understood to last as long, and no longer than [sic] the power lasteth, by which he is able to protect them. . . . The end of Obedience is Protection" (Lev, 21, 21, 114; and DC, EW ii, 6, 74–5). But such overt support for disobedience and rebellion is generally something that he renounces. To admit that the answer to the question "Who shall judge whether the ruler should continue in power?" is "The people" is to admit that the sovereign's rule is not permanent, and therefore, because he does not have jurisdiction over whether or not he will remain in power, that he is also not an absolute ruler. Hobbes seems to believe that arguing for a ruler whose power was defined by and derivable from the people would be to encourage exactly the kind of dissension and civil war which was tearing Europe apart in his day. Yet Hobbes cannot escape the fact that by building his justification of the state on morally relevant facts which he thinks that subjects can and should know, he justifies the idea that not only the creation of the state, but also its continued maintenance, is a function of the subjects' knowledge and political support. Hobbes's theoretical dilemma teaches us the following lesson: to offer an argument purporting to establish that political society is justified and why it is justified is to promulgate (what one takes to be) facts about political matters that, if commonly known, can become the justification for political change—perhaps even change that is violently accomplished.

Moral Skepticism and Liberalism

The preceding section shows the way in which skepticism about the chances of large numbers of people attaining moral knowledge is critical to Hobbes's political argument. However, modern liberals have also made use of skeptical positions on the ability of human beings to attain moral or religious knowledge in order to justify their anti-Hobbesian political conclusions. In his paper "Non-neutral Principles" Gerald Dworkin (1974) notes the way in which some liberals argue for freedom of speech and religion and other sorts of restraints on government power by appeal to the problematic epistemic status of certain of our beliefs. For example, it seems quite impossible that any human being could ever come to *know* which religion, if any, is the true one. Dworkin contends that Rawls is one of a number of liberals who argue that when the epistemic warrant of a belief or practice is problematic, the government must refrain from using its coercive powers to enforce the belief or practice. As Dworkin puts the position: "While it may be biased to put one's interests and desires in a favored position, it is not biased to give preference to the truth or the highly probable. It is only where the views put forward are all on the same epistemological plane that giving preference to some may be arbitrary" (Dworkin 1974: 504). In a sense, the answer which these liberals give to Hobbes's "Who shall judge" question when there is a disagreement over some hard-to-resolve issue is "No political official—let each citizen decide for himself." Liberalism is thus presented as the political principle which advocates *neutrality* between competing and controversial moral, religious, artistic or scientific beliefs. And this political neutrality is supposed to be a consequence of what I will call the "Proof Principle," which states that it is a necessary (but probably not sufficient) condition on the use of political force that one have a high degree of proof that the proposition one is enforcing is true (and not merely believed to be true by many).

On reflection this principle for the use of political force obviously cannot be right. No one could argue that any human society now or in the past has been or is presently in possession of an argument which establishes beyond reasonable doubt that a certain system of property distribution is correct, and yet a government is surely reasonable (and even required) to enforce *some* principle of property distribution, on the grounds that there will be inevitable conflict if it does not. More generally a liberal who is advocating the Proof Principle is forgetting that when disagreement over a certain issue or belief exists, conflict can ensue which is dangerous to the peace of the community. And it seems morally irresponsible to remove political officials from arbitrating disputed issues in areas where not enough epistemic warrant exists for any of the proposed parties when the disputes are threatening to effect, or actually precipitating, violence.

Hobbes maintains that it is, at the very least, a sufficient condition for the use of political force that it be required to secure peace. Since there is, in his view, virtually no area of human thought or endeavor in which disagreement is not possible among biased, glory-prone, and sometimes stupid human beings, this means that a political system must be instituted which has the capability of interfering and enforcing beliefs in *any* area of human life in order to resolve violence-producing disagreements: "it is annexed to the Soveraignty, to be Judge of what Opinions and Doctrines are averse, and what conducing to Peace" (Lev, 18, 9, 91). A ruler with this kind of power is not yet one whose power is absolute or permanent, and as I noted, Hobbes's contention that a ruler must have these two features is problematic. Nonetheless it is already a power which is vastly more than liberals would want a ruler to hold.

But what about the epistemic warrant for Hobbes's second law of nature, justifying the institution of a sovereign? Why should it be plausible that people can come to have knowledge of this law, but not of other propositions in moral or natural science? Hobbes would reply that it is easy even for slow-witted and glory-prone people to see that a state of war is bad for their health, and he wrote *Leviathan* with a great deal of faith that his argument for instituting a sovereign was clear enough that even these sorts of people would understand and accept it in virtue of their overwhelming commitment to furthering their self-preservation.

A liberal could always contest this by maintaining that Hobbes's proof was either wrong, or difficult to understand, or both (in which case, would any kind of persuasive argument in political philosophy be possible?). But suppose a liberal were to grant, for the sake of argument, the clarity and force of Hobbes's proof of this conclusion: it would seem this critic could insist that it must only be a *conditional* argument to the effect that "*if* people are unable to refrain from coming to blows about a disputed issue, then the government must interfere in the dispute and enforce some resolution of the issue; otherwise Hobbes has given it no warrant for interfering."

According to such a critic, if people in a community "behave themselves" and agree to disagree amicably, government intrusion into that disputed area cannot be justified if peace is what legitimates political power. To put it succinctly, Hobbes's argument would be taken to justify only the following conclusion: *the price of political liberty is rational self-restraint,* or alternatively, *the cost of unrestrained exploitation and aggression toward others is government regulation.*

I have argued that this is exactly what Hobbes's argument *must* be taken to justify, despite his enthusiasm for a seemingly more powerful and interventionist government (see Hampton 1986, chapter 8.2–8.5). But why isn't this principle one that liberals could endorse? Surely a liberal would not want to argue that government control of certain "private" areas of our lives is *always* off-bounds even in situations where disputes in these areas are causing violence.

Perhaps some liberals would so argue. I suspect, however, that the majority would agree that *any* area could become the affair of government if the peace of the community required it. Nonetheless, even this majority would insist that the state should follow a policy of toleration to resolve conflicts when appropriate (where, for example, such a policy would not be appropriate as a way of resolving property disputes) and in areas held to be "private" or "a matter of individual conscience" (e.g., religious affiliation). For example, suppose a community experienced religious conflict between two groups, one of which comprised 90 percent of the population and the other of which comprised 10 percent. A liberal would argue that any interference by the government in this conflict should be with the view toward protecting each group's ability to worship as it chose, and thus to promote each group's tolerance of the other. But Hobbes would argue that whether or not this policy should be adopted by the government would depend entirely on whether or not peace could be promoted most effectively by it; if long-term security could be purchased by siding with the 90 percent and outlawing the minority's religion, Hobbes would believe the government should pursue this intolerant policy.

What this example shows is that the *telos* of peace may, but need not, justify a political policy of enforcing toleration, because peace may be better achieved by intolerant policies. Liberals who would argue that government intrusion into certain private areas must always be with the aim of coercing the disputants to tolerate each other's views must therefore provide an argument for their position which does not invoke simply the goal of peace or the problematic epistemic status of many of the beliefs held in these "private" areas, for, as we have seen, these two precepts are effectively used by Hobbes to justify in certain circumstances decidedly unliberal political policies, which oppose (for the sake of peace) the tolerance of disparate viewpoints. The traditional liberal talk of the importance of respecting "individual autonomy" and "the individual's right to decide matters of conscience" is presumably meant to suggest a liberal's response to the Hobbesian argument, where the importance of autonomy and individual rights would be thought to justify the state in risking or permitting a certain amount of violence as it implements policies of toleration aimed at resolving disputes. However, no liberal political theorist, in my view, has developed to any degree of precision an argument showing how and when the goal of peace and the value of autonomy jointly permit tolerant policies.[17]

The idea that liberalism presupposes such an argument shows something which at least some liberals do not wish to believe; namely, that theirs is a substantive moral and political conclusion which presupposes beliefs about what is valuable in and about human beings which a community, in its use of political force, must respect. If this is right, liberalism is a moral and political conclusion that relies on what the liberal takes to be true moral beliefs. It is, I suspect, rather embarrassing for a liberal to be caught taking a stand on what counts as genuine moral knowledge since liberalism advocates tolerance of a variety of positions on moral and religious matters. Rawls expresses the embarrassment nicely in a recent article: if liberalism, he says, has to depend on a commitment to moral values such as autonomy, it becomes just "another sectarian doctrine" (Rawls, 1985, 246). And in his recent work Rawls (1985; 1987; 1988) has tried to develop a way of understanding liberalism such that it is an entirely neutral, non-metaphysical doctrine. But I have argued (Hampton 1989) that his way of doing so makes the liberal policy of toleration—contrary to what Rawls says—little more than a *modus vivendi* for contemporary Western pluralist societies. Hobbes would certainly argue that it constitutes an inferior *modus vivendi* (one inclined to break down too quickly) for these societies.

The only way for one to insist on tolerance in the face of Hobbesian arguments showing that intolerant policies better ensure long-term peace is to justify tolerance on other, moral grounds. And this means that the liberal theory one develops is no longer neutral. Such a liberalism is "non-neutral" in the sense that it presupposes substantive beliefs about what is morally true regarding the treatment of human beings, while it advocates a political policy toward conflicts in some (but not all) areas that is "neutral" in the sense that it promotes the toleration of the disputants' views and practices for the sake of these substantive moral beliefs. And note that these beliefs generate reasons for action that are not directly connected with (and may even conflict with) the attainment of peace. Those who advocate intolerance in this liberal society will therefore be branded as "wrong" and, if they persist in intolerant practices, they will be coerced by the government into respecting the tolerance they find so repulsive. Indeed, even if proofs were developed which showed with a high degree of probability that a certain position in one of these private areas were correct (suppose, for example, a proof were developed for the proposition that God existed), a liberal should still insist that a government could not legitimately coerce any individual into accepting the results of the proof. After all, those choices which are *solely* a matter of individual conscience remain so, no matter how much epistemic warrant exists for a particular choice.

Hobbes's political position isn't neutral either. But he never claims that it is. Instead he advances an argument to establish his political conclusions which relies heavily on the problematic epistemic status of the majority of our beliefs but which claims to have a high degree of epistemic warrant itself. So liberals who would invoke Hobbesian-like epistemological skepticism to advance the principle of toleration by arguing that the state cannot enforce what it does not have substantial epistemic warrant for, are misguidedly using a premise that advances their enemy's cause. I have argued, first, that the Proof Principle, "No interference without substantive epistemic warrant," fails to justify state interference in certain areas where liberals would clearly want such interference to secure peace; and second, that if the principle is modified to become "Interfere in disputed areas only to secure peace," it fails to require that the state only enforce policies of toleration, in particular when such policies are not the best way to realize long-term peace. If liberals were to argue against anti-liberal Hobbesian political conclusions, they should do the work of providing a substantive argument of their own for a principle which would justify state action even in areas where there is little epistemic warrant for the principles it proposes, and which justifies enforcing toleration even when doing so may risk future discord. They should not cover up, by appeal to a skepticism that only *appears* congenial to the liberal cause, the fact that there is a high degree of commitment on their part to the truth of the moral principle that human beings ought not to be politically coerced in certain private areas of their lives.[18]

Notes

1. See EW vii, p. 184 and DC, EW ii, Preface, xiii–xiv. In this paper I have used the following system of referencing Hobbes's works (which will appear in the body of the text). For *Leviathan* I have referred to the pagination in the 1651 edition, also given in the Macpherson and Oxford editions of the book, and to help readers use other editions, I have included chapter number and number of the paragraph in which the passage appeared. Citations will take the following form: (*Lev*, chapter number, number of paragraph in chapter, page number in 1651 edition). *De Cive:* I have used the edition in Molesworth's *The English Works of Thomas Hobbes* (1840): (DC, EW ii, chapter number, section number, page number). *Elements of Law:* I have used Frederick Tönnies' edition (1928): (EL, part number, section number, page number). *De Homine:* Bernard Gert's edition has been used in his *Man and Citizen* (1968): (DH, chapter number, section number, page number). *De Corpore:* the edition has been taken from Molesworth's *The English Works:* (De Corp, EW i, part number, chapter number, section number, page number). All references to other works by Hobbes will be to the editions of those works in Molesworth's *The English Works of Thomas Hobbes.*

2. See Watkins' discussion of Hobbes's nominalist tendencies (1965: 143–160).

3. However, I believe at least some of the confusion surrounding Hobbes's philosophy of science is generated by us rather than by him. Were we to read Hobbes's views on science in the context of the philosophy of science of his day, we would have a much better understanding of his position. For example, he occasionally shows signs of espousing the hypothetico-deductive model of scientific methodology (see McNeilly's discussion [1969: 61–71]); yet, insofar as Hobbes's use of the word 'hypothesis' is taken as evidence for this espousal, we should be sure that Hobbes was not using the word in its Aristotelian sense to mean a "statement that posits the existence or

inexistence of something." (See Roberto Torretti [1978: 5ff.] for a discussion of the terminology of Aristotelian and Euclidean science.) For if he were, then the methodology he espouses would have to be understood to be Aristotelian, not hypothetico-deductive as we understand that phrase. Other passages in *De Corpore* also suggest that Hobbes was influenced by the Cartesian scientists of his day. We await a definitive study on this aspect of Hobbes's thought.

4. See La Mothe Le Vayer (1669: 115–20) and Montaigne (1922: 147).

5. Given that this would seem to involve the second kind of regulated thought (going from causes to effects), which only humans have, it is strange to see Hobbes maintaining that animals as well as humans have prudence.

6. Hobbes was Bacon's secretary as a young man and had philosophical discussions with him (Aubrey 1898: 331).

7. Economists today say that this sort of good is in "perfect joint supply."

8. Watkins (1965: 75–99) also invokes Kant's phrase to describe Hobbes's laws.

9. In Hampton (1986: 11–13), I discuss in more precise terms the kind of reductionist project Hobbes believes is possible.

10. David Gauthier (1986) has presented a moral theory in which moral propositions are true insofar as they give correct causal information about how to effect desired goals.

11. Hobbes would likely agree with John Mackie (1977, ch. 9) that apart from anything else, they are too "queer" to exist.

12. This appears to be Mackie's position in *Ethics*, Part 1 (1977); however, in Part 3, Chapters 5 and 9, he appears to be in favor of modifying at least some moral discourse fairly substantially.

13. Watkins (1965, sect. 29) generally appears to take this line.

14. See *Lev*, 42, 107, 306; quoted by Watkins 1965: 154; see also *Lev*, 18, 9, 91; 26, 4, 137; 29, 6, 168; and 42, 78, 295.

15. I discuss the first two reasons at length in Chapter 3 and the third in Chapter 4 of Hampton (1986).

16. See Hampton (1986), especially Chapters 7 and 8.

17. Certainly not Mill, who unequivocally embraces the "Hobbesian" principle of liberty stated above. Mill argues in *On Liberty* that "despotism is a legitimate mode of government in dealing with barbarians, provided the end be their improvement and the means justified by actually effecting that end. Liberty, as a principle, has no application to any state of things anterior to the time when mankind have become capable of being improved by free and equal discussion" (1965: 14).

18. Much of this final section was inspired in reaction to Thomas Nagel's intriguing article (Nagel 1987) in which he explores the idea that liberalism is in some sense neutral.

References

Aubrey, J. 1898. *Brief Lives*, ed. by Andrew Clark. Oxford: Clarendon Press.

Dewey, John. 1974. The motivation of Hobbes's political philosophy. In Ralph Ross, H. Schneider and T. Waldman (eds.), *Thomas Hobbes in Our Time*. Minneapolis: University of Minnesota Press, pp. 8–30.

Dworkin, Gerald. 1974. Non-neutral moral principles. *Journal of Philosophy* 71: 491–506.

Gauthier, David. 1986. *Morals by Agreement*. Oxford: Clarendon Press.

Hampton, Jean. 1986. *Hobbes and the Social Contract Tradition*. Cambridge: Cambridge University Press.

_____. 1989. Can political philosophy be done without metaphysics? *Ethics* (Summer, 1989).

Hobbes, Thomas. 1968. *Man and Citizen,* ed. by Bernard Gert. Atlantic Highlands, N.J.: Humanities Press.

_____. 1928. *Elements of Law,* ed. by Frederick Tönnies. Cambridge: Cambridge University Press.

_____. 1940. *The English Works of Thomas Hobbes,* ed. by W. Molesworth. London: John Bohn.

_____. 1968. *Leviathan,* ed. by C. B. Macpherson. Harmondsworth: Penguin.

La Mothe Le Vayer, François de. 1669. Discours pour montrer que les doutes. . . . In *Oeuvres de François de La Mothe Le Vayer.* Paris: L. Billaine.

Mackie, John. 1977. *Ethics: Inventing Right and Wrong.* New York: Penguin.

McNeilly, F. 1969. *The Anatomy of Leviathan.* New York: St. Martin's Press.

Mill, J.S. 1965. *On Liberty,* ed. by Currin Shields. Indianapolis: Bobbs-Merrill.

Montaigne, Michel de. 1922. Apologie de Raimond Sebond. In *Les Essais de Michel de Montaigne,* ed. by Pierre Villey. Paris: F. Alcan.

Nagel, Thomas. 1987. Moral conflict and political legitimacy. *Philosophy and Public Affairs* 16: 215–240.

Popkin, Richard. 1982. Hobbes and scepticism. In *History and Philosophy in the Making,* ed. by R. Popkin. St. Louis: Washington University Press.

Rawls, John. 1971. *A Theory of Justice.* Cambridge, Mass.: Harvard University Press.

_____. 1985. Justice as fairness: political not metaphysical. *Philosophy and Public Affairs* 14: 223–251.

_____. 1987. The idea of an overlapping consensus. *Oxford Journal for Legal Studies* 1: 1–25.

_____. 1988. The priority of right and ideas of the good. *Philosophy and Public Affairs* 17:

Torretti, Roberto. 1978. *Philosophy of Geometry from Riemann to Poincaré.* Dordrecht: Reidel.

Watkins, J. W. N. 1965. *Hobbes's System of Ideas.* London: Hutchinson.

3

David Hume: Crusading Empiricist, Skeptical Liberal

Don Herzog

Visiting Hume on his deathbed, Katherine Mure received an inscribed copy of his *History*. "'O David,' said she, 'that's a book you may weel be proud o; but before ye dee, ye should burn a' your wee bookies.'" The "wee bookies," of course, were Hume's philosophical writings, notoriously offensive to the religiously orthodox. Here for once, if Hume's devoted biographer is right, the normally sunny Hume was irritated: "David replied with some vehemence, half offended, half in joke, 'What for should I burn a' my wee bookies?'" (Mossner 1980: 601f.).

We still place Hume's skeptical epistemology at the center of his philosophy, and rightly so: Hume precedes Kant in making the epistemological turn. Its consequences for theology no longer seem devastating. But still some divide between that epistemology and his politics beckons. How could Hume's ruminations on imagining a shade of blue you've never seen influence his account of Britain's tendency to become a republic? What road might lead from Hume's discussion of the infinite divisibility of mathematical points to his scornful rejection of England's allegedly timeless ancient constitution? Is the man who worries away at personal identity even distantly related to the man who presumes to shed a generous tear for the Earl of Strafford? That Hume's philosophy is profound no one will question. But his political theory, while less well known, is itself profound, far more than a cursory addition to his philosophy. Indeed, Hayek is willing to credit Hume with "probably the only comprehensive statement of the legal and political philosophy which later became known as liberalism" (Hayek 1966: 340).

I mean to argue that there are ties between Hume's epistemology and his political theory. But they are not so strong as some have suggested; nor are they where scholars have looked. Briefly, Hume's commitment to finding fundamental laws of human nature does not yield any ideological identification of England's middle classes with the essence of humanity. And Hume is in fact quite sensitive to the decisive effects of shifting social context. Hume's habits of the mind, though, do play a role in his political theory. More important, Hume's insistence on bowing to experience has much to do with the tenor of his political thought. Or so, at any rate, I shall argue. I shall comment too, in passing, on the (in)famous gap between "is" and "ought" that is for many the sum and substance of Hume's ethics.

Hume's Epistemology

First we need a characterization of Hume's epistemology. It is tempting to read Hume through the lens of later developments in philosophy. So, for example, we can enlist Hume as the intellectual grandfather of the young A. J. Ayer, bonded by a sometimes caustic skepticism. Since we have no idea of substance, Hume argues, we should simply discard the debate over the materiality of the soul as so much meaningless gibberish. Hume can scornfully indict the "scholastic way of talking, rather than thinking," occasionally deflate all moral talk to emotive posturing, and draw up limits to knowledge.[1] Or for that matter, counterintuitive though it sounds, we might enlist Hume as a Kantian.[2] Though his vocabulary makes it hard for him to say so, he is terribly interested in the way our mental habits structure our knowledge and can even say that human nature would go to ruin without those habits (*Treatise:* 225).

That Hume lends himself as readily as he does to both readings should invite caution. Here I would suggest that we begin with another reading of Hume, one consecrated now and begun in Hume's own lifetime by Beattie. That is Hume the fiendish skeptic, the destroyer of old systems and sphinx of future philosophy.[3]

There are two notable conceptual sources of Hume's skepticism. First is the copy theory of ideas. Like Locke, Hume holds that all our knowledge of the world arises from sense impressions. Our senses receive a vivid impression of a mountain, say, and thus furnish us with the idea of "mountain." The idea is nothing but a fainter image of the original impression. We can juggle our ideas about and combine them in new ways. But the mind, a reproducing mechanism, can operate only on materials flowing from original impressions. From the opening pages of the *Treatise*, Hume is quite sure that all our ideas do in fact arise this way.[4] The skeptical upshot is clear enough: Hume can always point at some alleged idea and demand from what impressions it might have proceeded. If no response is forthcoming, Hume will quickly decide the idea is nonsense. The copy theory drives Hume to some very odd claims indeed, as when he claims that we believe history because it invariably strikes us more vividly than fiction does, or when he argues that someone desiring 1,000 pounds has 1,000 separate desires (*Treatise:* 98, 625f., 141, 22, 25, 72; *Enquiry:* 48). We might prefer then that Hume reconsider the copy theory itself, instead of summarily discarding all the notions it cannot accommodate. But on that score he will not budge.

The second source lies in Hume's account of what sort of knowledge we can have. Hume accepts what we would now call an analytic/synthetic dichotomy: subjects like geometry admit of certain demonstration, while matters of fact are always contingent (*Enquiry:* 25, 35), and so typically are paired to what Hume calls probabilities. But Hume somehow squeezes in a third epistemic category, proofs, which he characterizes as "such arguments from experience as leave no room for doubt or opposition" (*Enquiry:* 56n; *Treatise:* 124). Hume can claim to have proved the copy theory, and to have proved we cannot be justified in thinking anything is a miracle (*Enquiry:* 62, 114f.). Within the world of the analytic/synthetic dichotomy, it seems there could be no proofs. But he does wield his notion of proof as another potent skeptical weapon, finding it easy to show that many beliefs cannot be supported by proof. Readers desiring certainty will find these arguments compelling.

Hume has still more skeptical tricks up his sleeve. But as Norman Kemp Smith argues in a landmark study, Hume's philosophy is not just a corrosive battery of skeptical arguments.[5] Hume has constructive arguments to offer. If reason is powerless, he thinks, still nature or custom gives us beliefs. So Hume zeroes in on human nature, which he hopes will serve as "the only solid foundation" for knowledge (*Treatise:* xvi). Given the principles of human nature, the mental habits that choreograph our flood of impressions, Hume thinks we can better understand human knowledge in all areas. It is true, then, that Hume launches a skeptical attack against causation, arguing that we can know nothing about necessity in the external world and have no clear idea of power. But Hume also argues that the mind's habit of association explains our belief in causation. Given the constant conjunction of two events, he holds, we always come to think of the second on thinking of the first, and we wrongly project the apparent necessity of the mind's leap onto the world. That is the normal structure of Hume's arguments: witheringly skeptical attacks on some idea clear the ground for an account of how human nature leads us to it. We may be able to find no rational justification for our beliefs in causation or induction; we may be hard pressed to say anything coherent about personal identity or power. But we can identify the crucial role custom or nature plays, the mechanisms by which human nature leads us back to those odd beliefs. We cannot cling to our skepticism outside the study, but it can yield increased illumination about the nature of our knowledge.

A bit artificially, then, we can emphasize two motifs in Hume's epistemology. First is the copy theory of ideas; second is the appeal to human nature. What, if any, are the political uses of these motifs?

Constancy and Variation: Human Nature in Social Context

It surely cannot be the case that given just this much epistemology, we can predict Hume's politics, or predict at least what his politics would be if he were wholly coherent. If we are inclined to make the deductive

connections between empiricism and liberalism very tight, we should remember that Kant was a liberal too. But suppose we move away from
thinking about uniquely determined deductive implications. Suppose we
take up the question as one of what we might call elective affinities. Granted,
many political theories might come next; but which one should we expect?
What politics seems best to fit this conceptual world, even if there are other
possibilities?

We are often told that liberals are insensitive to, or even wholly unaware
of, society. Liberals are supposed to picture a world of individual monads
who happen to meet in the same place. Hume's epistemology might seem
to provide the perfect fuel for this view. Hume can have no clear idea of
society, since after all he has never had a vivid impression of society.
Individuals, on the other hand, are medium-sized physical objects, just the
sort of thing Hume appeals to in offering examples of how the copy theory
is supposed to work. At the same time, Hume's insistence on discovering
the constant principles of human nature is further evidence that he is
sociologically and culturally naïve. Only someone oblivious to social variation
could so blithely insist on such principles; or so it might seem.

So it did seem, at any rate, to Carl Becker. In a mischievous study of
the Enlightenment, Becker sets out to demonstrate deep continuities between
the *philosophes* and the medieval Christians they congratulated themselves
on rejecting wholesale. All the Enlightenment talk of experience, Becker
suggests, is a sham: "the philosopher-historians possess the idea of the just
and the unjust, they have their 'universal principles' and their 'man in
general' well in hand before they start out to explore the field of human
experience" (Becker 1932: 104f.). Hume has already invested his own
Enlightenment prejudices in the human nature he proudly claims to be
empirically studying. Not surprisingly, Becker chose an appropriate snippet
of Hume for giving such an impression. But it will be useful to quote the
passage in full:

> Mankind are so much the same, in all times and places, that history informs
> us of nothing new or strange in this particular. Its chief use is only to discover
> the constant and universal principles of human nature, by showing men in
> all varieties of circumstances and situations, and furnishing us with materials
> from which we may form our observations and become acquainted with the
> regular springs of human action and behaviour. These records of wars, intrigues,
> factions, and revolutions, are so many collections of experiments, by which
> the political or moral philosopher fixes the principles of his science, in the
> same manner as the physician or natural philosopher becomes acquainted with
> the nature of plants, minerals, and other external objects, by the experiments
> which he forms concerning them.[6]

Sometimes too the regular springs seem not to vary in different societies.
Hume seems, for example, to take it for granted that people are generally
stupid.[7] That claim he casts as an observation about an apparently invariant
human nature.

Here as elsewhere, Becker's line is plausible. Despite criticisms, his reading of the Enlightenment and of Hume has been taken up and extended.[8] But Becker profits greatly from quickly skating over an enormous amount of textual material, and it is still skating, even if performed with remarkable grace and agility. Hume is not always so confident about his science of human nature as Becker suggests. He can write, for example, "that the world is too young to fix many general truths in politics, which will remain true to the latest posterity" ("Of Civil Liberty," *Essays:* 89). And he can suggest that we cannot find instructive lessons in very different societies (*History,* II: 566f.). But we can rebut Becker's case without noting Hume's demurrers. Here I mean to take the bull by the horns. Properly understood, Hume's science of human nature has room for both sweeping social variation and constant principles. Also, Hume sometimes casts his science as actually requiring the decisive impact of social institutions.

The point is simple enough: a few regular principles can account for spectacularly varying outcomes. (Hume is not the Newton of the human sciences for nothing.) Instead of certain traits of human nature recurring constantly, the same underlying mechanisms may in different contexts yield different traits. The constancy lies in the causal mechanisms, not in the observed results. But we are more likely to see the point clearly in the context of physical sciences. Suppose we are marveling at the great variety of motion we see in the world: objects rolling, objects falling, objects colliding, some slowly, some quickly, some for a long time, some briefly. Suppose that I then say there are a few constant and universal traits of physical bodies that explain their behavior. You are hardly likely to accuse me of ignoring the rolling objects, or the speedy ones, and riveting my gaze on falling objects alone. Instead you will assent: whether it is classical mechanics, or some later version, we assume there are some basic causal laws that account for the variations.

Hume's science of human nature has the same form. There is variation, and Hume is hardly unaware of it. Any reader of his writings comes away with fairly vivid conceptions of Danish marauders in early England, Puritan religious fanatics, bellicose ancients, four different philosophical temperaments, and more. Hume may like to describe the causation of human action as though it were simply on a par with the movement of billiard balls, as when he likens the efforts of an artificer handling dead matter to a politician directing living agents (*Enquiry:* 86). But that commitment, whether right or wrong, is incidental here. With human beings too, we ask for explanations when we find interesting differences. Those explanations may or may not take the form of causal laws. Whatever form they take, though, we want to find some explanations capable of economically organizing and illuminating our multifarious "data." The claim that there are constant and universal principles of human nature may be taken simply as a resolution that there should be such explanations, or that we should try to look for them. The Rhine and the Rhone may flow in different directions, but still there should be an appropriate general account of why rivers flow the way they do ("A

Dialogue," *Enquiries:* 333). Hume might still seem naïve. Why is it a science of human nature, not a science of society? Isn't there something ruthlessly psychological about his focus, something guaranteed to make him miss social institutions? No; in fact, it is the preeminent importance of social institutions that makes a science of human nature possible in the first place. Social facts, far from vanishing in Hume's account, become central. Birds may nest alike everywhere, thanks to instinct, but "Men, in different times and places, frame their houses differently: Here we perceive the influence of reason and custom" (*Morals:* 202). If different men behaved differently because they had different natures, Hume, writing before the advent of genetics, could say nothing more. But politics, Hume holds, can be studied scientifically because we can isolate the effects of different social institutions on a human nature presumed to be uniform. "So great is the force of laws, and of particular forms of government, and so little dependence have they on the humours and tempers of men, that consequences almost as general and certain may sometimes be deduced from them, as any which the mathematical sciences afford us" ("That Politics May Be Reduced to a Science," *Essays:* 14). Indeed Hume is at least as sensitive to social context as Montesquieu, and he departs from Montesquieu in insisting that "moral causes," those working "on the mind as motives or reasons" ("Of National Characters," *Essays:* 202), matter more than anything else in shaping human behavior.

Becker, then, is wrong in holding that Hume finds his own liberal Enlightenment human nature wherever he looks. There may be constant and universal principles of human nature, but Hume does not use them to solve political problems. Those traits of human nature Hume does think persist pretty much in all societies actually *cause* political problems. So Hume's theory of justice is the solution to a problem posed by moderate scarcity and constrained benevolence.[9] Perhaps the best place here to see how human nature works in Hume's political theory lies in his case for the separation of powers.

"It is, therefore, a just *political* maxim, *that every man must be supposed a knave*": another of Hume's apparent generalizations about human nature, one inviting laments about liberals' embracing a meanly egoistic account of man.[10] But the continuation is crucial: "though, at the same time, it appears somewhat strange, that a maxim should be true in *politics* which is false in *fact*" ("Of the Independency of Parliament," *Essays:* 42). (True prescriptively—it's prudent to think this way in politics—though false descriptively. Politics is a science—experience matters—but experience may suggest adopting counterfactual beliefs to cut our losses.) Taken as private individuals, men may be fairly honest; they may be driven by a concern for the regard of others. But politics is a distinct context, and the distinction makes a difference. The concrete social settings of political life create incentives for individual action. So, for instance, men can learn assiduously to cultivate the regard of others of their own party. At the same time, Parliament can move to further its interest as a body. The reader of Hume's *History* will be aware that unattractive political goals may be viewed by many, even those pursuing them, as exalted. Since in politics such tendencies may be teased out of the multifaceted potential of human nature, we would be prudent to design institutions to thwart them. Happily, England has institutions that do the job: "The crown has so many offices at its disposal" that it can offset any excess tendencies toward the aggrandizing of power in the Commons, by buying off individual members with lucrative jobs ("Of the Independency of Parliament," *Essays:* 45). Writers like Bolingbroke, seeing here corruption and dependence, may despair. But the corruption Walpole excelled at manipulating is politically beneficial.[11]

Hume, then, is well aware of the place social institutions play in human affairs. If they don't fit comfortably into his copy theory of ideas, neither does much of anything else. That theory cannot accommodate all sorts of perfectly respectable claims to knowledge, and Hume drops it when he turns to politics. Nor does Hume ideologically cast his own preferred vision of humanity—the mildly skeptical, sober, secular, moderate man—as the essence of human nature. Cromwell and Pascal are instantiations of human nature, too. Hume never even flirts with Locke's game of demoting his enemies to subhuman status. We ought not, then, follow Becker and seek ties between Hume's epistemology and his political theory here. Where else might we turn?

The Role of Mental Habits

We will do better to turn to Hume's account of the habits of our mind.[12] The copy theory provides a poor account of the origins of our mental states. Nevertheless, Hume may still have illuminating things to say about what our minds do, once furnished by experience. Custom and nature, the mental operations Hume detects by observation, play a crucial role in Hume's epistemology. It turns out that they also play a role in Hume's political theory, though they can provide nothing like the royal road from epistemology to politics Becker tried to pave.

Let me begin by recalling Hume's characterization of possible projects in ethics. An author might proceed as an anatomist of morals, a detached observer striving to frame purely descriptive accounts on such issues as what structure our moral beliefs have, what their causal origins are, or what role they play in social life. Or an author might proceed as a painter, a committed actor portraying the life of morality in the most favorable light. Hume does cast himself as an anatomist.[13] At the same time, though, his descriptive theories provide the resources to take up the paintbrush and commend the life of morality (*Treatise:* 619f.; *Morals:* 278ff.). Once he shows, for example, that justice allows us to reap the fruits of long-term cooperation impossible in its absence, he can commend justice. This sort of tie between "is" and "ought" should not be surprising. That Hume fails to provide a knock-down argument against an egoistic skeptic prepared to play free-rider should not be surprising either.

In Hume's political theory, we find the same pattern. Certain propensities of the human mind explain the political judgments people make; given that explanatory account, we can then endorse those judgments. Here too there is no reason to be surprised at this sort of tie between "is" and "ought." We can reconstruct Hume's argument without any trace of an officially illicit deduction.[14] By the same token, we can also see why that much ballyhooed deductive tie isn't all that important. Here I consider Hume's accounts of how we get property rights and what makes kings legitimate.

Hume does not want to say that property rights are somehow out there, objectively existing in a certain pattern whether we know it or not. He wants to deny there are any such moral relations, and some of his most trenchantly skeptical arguments are leveled against theorists like Samuel Clarke and William Wollaston who defended their existence. It hardly follows, though, that property is a matter of mere personal preference. There may be no objective moral facts for people to respond to in their discussion of property rights. But as a detached observer, Hume finds that their judgments do not fluctuate whimsically. Instead they are clearly structured, and four principles—occupation, prescription, accession, and succession—fit the data of actual judgments people make.[15]

Occupation, or first succession, is generally conceded to give a property right. Why? Hume does not follow Locke and adopt a moral theory urging that one gains the right by mixing labor with unowned things. He finds it easy to criticize that theory; but more important, he wants to be an anatomist, and distance himself from the question of whether our ascriptions are right or wrong. On Hume's account, men realize that property is essential to peace and cooperation, and are happy to adopt a rule so easily applied. And the rule is so easily applied, in turn, because of a mental habit: "the first possession always engages the attention most."

Mental habits play a role in the other principles, too. When right of first possession becomes obscure, we turn to prescription, or long possession. Nor is the turn just an occasional and unfortunate necessity: "Any considerable space of time sets objects at such a distance, that they seem, in a manner, to lose their reality, and have as little influence on the mind, as if they had never been in being." The great mental principle of association by resemblance enters when Hume turns to accession: "Where objects are connected together in the imagination, they are apt to be put on the same footing, and are commonly suppos'd to be endow'd with the same qualities." So if I own a tree, I own the fruit that falls from it, and even the currently nonexistent fruit that will grow on it. The thought of the tree naturally leads to the thought of the fruit. Succession too depends partly on the association of ideas. We may grant children the property of their deceased parent because we believe the parent would have done so. But there is more: when we ask who should own what the deceased owned, "the person's children naturally present themselves to the mind; and being already connected to those possessions by means of their deceas'd parent, we are apt to connect them still farther by the relation of property."

The vagaries of the mind may cause some problems here, as when we forget a long-standing original claim because its remove in time makes it less vivid. Nevertheless, the constructive role played by the mind is far more notable. The mind assigns rights that are not "out there" in any way. Before explaining how Hume moves on to endorse the mind's assignments, I want quickly to sketch his account of the legitimacy of kings.

Which kings rule legitimately? That query might seem to demand a first-order moral theory, one identifying to whom we ought to give our allegiance. But Hume again takes up his detached stance. He asks, as a matter of fact, which kings do we think rule legitimately? Here again, Hume would deny that legitimacy is objective in any interesting way. Yet again, it hardly follows that our judgments are irreducibly chaotic. Hume once again discerns an underlying structure to the ascriptions of legitimacy people make. Five principles—long possession, present possession, conquest, succession, and positive law—provide a structure for popular judgments (*Treatise:* 556ff.). Here too, our mental habits help the explanation along. When we think of the father, we are led naturally to think of the son; if we have already invested the father with legitimacy, we are then likely to pass it along to the son.

Our mental habits, along with other considerations Hume enlists in his account, may point in conflicting directions. Some aspirants to the throne may be able to plead present possession; others may plead succession; and so on. What then? "When these titles are mingled and oppos'd in different degrees, they often occasion perplexity; and are less capable of solution from the arguments of lawyers and philosophers, than from the swords of the soldiery" (*Treatise:* 562). No prefabricated natural harmony ensures that our mental propensities will issue in happy political consequences.

Some patrons—and, for that matter, some critics—of the is/ought or fact/value gap will seize on such admissions. Hume may be able to tell a story about how we in fact do make our judgments about property and legitimacy; but can he do any more? His theory may have explanatory or even predictive value, but can it yield any normative consequences? Yes; having completed the work of the anatomist, Hume finds it quite easy to take up the paintbrush.

The crucial point in each case is the same. What matters is that we converge on some solution to the problem of assigning the right, not precisely to whom we assign it. As Hume puts it in discussing the legitimacy of rulers, "The interest of a nation requires, that the succession to the crown shou'd be fix'd one way or the other; but 'tis the same thing to its interest in what way it be fix'd" (*Treatise:* 560). People do consistently make certain judgments. They do not view those judgments as Hume does, as exhibiting an interesting quirk of their mental habits. Instead they view themselves as saying who has the right in question.[16] Given that they make certain judgments consistently, given that those judgments do typically allow us to converge on a requisite solution to a pressing social problem, it makes perfectly good sense to endorse those judgments. So Hume can effortlessly move from a stance external to the institution of property, saying only "people do use principles like accession in deciding on property rights," to an internal stance. As a participant within the institution, he can say in his own voice, "accession gives a right in property."

There is no mysterious leap here from is to ought. If we spelled out every step of the argument, we would find a major premise qualifying as an "ought" statement. Yet the major premise in each case—that we ought to have some scheme of social cooperation, or that we ought to avoid civil war by agreeing on some ruler—is hardly problematic. It would take a Pyrrhonian skeptic to doubt either one. So we may accept the structure of Hume's arguments on property and legitimacy as perfectly sound.

I do not say, of course, that these actual arguments are sound. There is plenty to say about the limits of Hume's discussion, and some will be troubled by the conservative cast his theory takes.[17] But such objections can be voiced and pursued without anyone's ever trying to figure out how to build a deductive bridge over the is/ought gap. So that gap, which some have put at the center of Hume's thought, has little role in his constructive thought.

Political Theories and Experience

I have argued so far that Hume's devotion to seeking out constant principles of human nature is not politically charged in the way Becker thought it was. I have argued too that Hume's habits of the mind do have some political implications, though they are rather more piecemeal and incidental than the sweeping connections Becker hoped to find. Are there no general points to make about Hume's epistemology and political theory? Must we rest content with the ancillary role the habits of the mind play in property rights and legitimacy?

There is a general point to make, an important one at that. What passes under the unhappily vague name of Hume's "naturalism" explains why he takes the general approach to politics he does. It explains too why there can be no essential ties between his epistemology and his political theory. The "naturalism" in question is not of course any teleology; Hume rejects final causes out of hand,[18] and he casts justice as a way of thwarting tendencies in human nature, not helping it perfect itself. Ayer neatly captures the spirit of the relevant naturalism in referring to Hume's "insistence that every branch of science be anchored in experience" (Ayer 1980: 96). For good reason Hume's *Treatise* is subtitled, "An Attempt to introduce the experimental Method of Reasoning into Moral Subjects." Hume wants to do away with what he scornfully calls hypotheses, or aimless speculations— note again the echoes of Newton—and instead develop theories out of experience.

That descriptive theories must be based on experience is a commonplace. But the point applies every bit as much to normative ones, and I think we should follow Hume in rejecting normative views that claim to be *a priori* or transcendent. Political theories based on experience will be contingent and tentative. If things change, as they always might, our political views will appropriately change with them. There are some things Hume thinks will never change: he thinks, for example, that moderate scarcity and confined generosity are simply the human condition, and so can say, rather shamelessly boosting his own theory, "The interest, on which justice is founded, is the greatest imaginable, and extends to all times and places. It cannot possibly be serv'd by any other invention" (*Treatise:* 620). But in the *History* Hume knows full well that there have been societies without his unique solution of justice, and even commends their different arrangements as suiting their different contexts.[19] And in any case one can always imagine scenarios that would force us to alter or even discard the central place scarcity and confined generosity have in our thinking. They may be relatively well entrenched in our current account of human society, but they are hardly immune to revision.

I have elsewhere considered the empirical slant Hume's political theory takes in his *History of England* (Herzog 1985). Here I shall consider Hume's case for freedom of the press.[20] Once again we find Hume moving from an explanatory theory to a prescription. He begins by noticing an empirical quirk: only Great Britain enjoys the "peculiar privilege" of "extreme liberty." Why? Because Britain's form of government is peculiarly mixed, "neither wholly monarchical, nor wholly republican." Paradoxically, absolute monarchs are likely to give their subjects great freedom, Hume thinks, since they have nothing to worry about. (Hardly the most plausible view of the matter!) And republics like Holland give magistrates great discretion, which must curtail individual liberty. In Britain, however,

> it is apprehended that arbitrary power would steal in upon us, were we not careful to prevent its progress, and were there not an easy method of conveying the alarm from one end of the kingdom to the other. The spirit of the people must frequently be roused, in order to curb the ambition of the court; and the dread of rousing this spirit must be employed to prevent that ambition. Nothing so effectual to this purpose as the liberty of the press.

Freedom of the press is thus "essential to the support of our mixed government," so we need not worry about *"whether this liberty be advantageous or prejudicial."* Here Hume allows himself an ironic thrust at Whig theorists of the ancient constitution, a mode of analysis he holds is utterly silly: "there being nothing of greater importance in every state than the preservation of the ancient constitution, especially if it be a free one." The British, Hume believes, have good reason to value British government, as it ensures the rule of law and so individual liberty. If that government is a complex balance, liable to be restructured by too much poking around, the British should beware seizing on some apparently offensive institution and changing it. The unintended consequences of such action might be politically appalling.

That this argument is open to objection goes without saying. But it is essential to my point that it should be. It relies on a host of empirical suppositions: that British government is a delicate, complex balance; that liberty of the press does help the republican side of the balance; that changing the balance would probably worsen matters; and so on. (Hume's emphasis on the uncertain effects of change may seem offensively conservative, though it should be refreshing to find such a conservative argument being made for freedom of the press, not rank, hierarchy, and privilege.) These empirical suppositions are open to criticism and revision in the light of further experience and investigation. So Hume's liberalism cannot be woven into the very fabric of his epistemology. Liberalism emerges as the best political option in the world as Hume knows it, but that world and our knowledge of it are always changing.

Hume adds another defense of freedom of the press, one less tied to contingent facts about Britain and so more stable. With a touch of Enlightenment fiendishness, he notes that in fact only ecclesiastical governments need to fear the consequences of public discussion. In all others, not just Britain, freedom of the press would seem to be harmless. "A man reads a book or pamphlet alone and coolly," so we need not fear the dread consequences that followed "the harangues of the popular demagogues of Athens and Tribunes of Rome." Publicity may also alert the magistrate to sources of popular discontent, allowing him to defuse it. This case is perhaps less contextual than that flowing from his analysis of British government, but it too is empirical. It is an empirical discovery, Hume declares, "that the *people* are no such dangerous monsters as they have been represented, and that it is in every respect better to guide them like rational creatures than to lead or drive them like brute beasts." This case too, then, is contingent, though not so dramatically as the other. Though Hume glides over these issues, we could show that there are particular social circumstances in which freedom of the press or the people are not dangerous. In other circumstances, Hume's case collapses.

Far from being a weakness of consequentialist approaches to political theory, the contingency of Hume's political views is a strength. We are capable of learning more about political problems and possibilities, capable too of responding to new circumstances. As the world shows no signs of grinding to a dreary halt, it would take a curious doctrinaire to embrace timeless political principles. Given the broad outlines of his epistemology, Hume's defense of liberalism properly takes on a slightly diffident tone. Despite his confidence in his principles, there is always the intimation that in other circumstances things would properly be different. What else should we expect from a devoted experimentalist?

Notes

1. *Treatise:* 234, 243, 469; *Enquiry:* 12. The claim in *Enquiry:* 21 might well be Ayer in *Language, Truth, and Logic* discussing the verificationist principle of meaning.

2. The point is made by Stroud (1977), and particularly by Wolff (1960).

3. For two prominent adherents of this view after Beattie, note John Stuart Mill (1982)—Mill is mostly concerned to indict Hume's *History* as romantic nonsense,

plagiarized to boot, but he does begin by sneering at Hume's epistemology—and T.H. Green (1964).

4. Generally Hume writes with confidence that is simply extraordinary for a skeptic: note for example *Treatise:* 4, 101, 102, 118, 164, 178, 332, 347, 486, 575, and the Abstract (in *Treatise:* 654). But he does apologize for this stylistic indulgence (*Treatise:* 273f.).

5. Smith (1941). Norton (1982) attempts, I think unsuccessfully, to qualify Smith's views.

6. *Enquiry:* 83f. For a good discussion of this passage and its place in Hume's thought, see Forbes (1975: 113ff.). Becker quotes the first sentence and the first part of the next, without using an ellipsis.

7. "Of Public Credit" (*Essays:* 369). Note also *Religion:* 49f. and "Of the Protestant Succession" (*Essays:* 492).

8. For a critical treatment, see Gay (1964). For a more intensive reading of Hume and the Enlightenment very much in Becker's vein, see Spragens (1981).

9. The best account of that theory is Mackie (1980: 76ff.).

10. George Will misreads the passage in this way: see his "complaint against the modern world" (p. 167) (Will 1983: 34).

11. Hume doesn't mention Bolingbroke and Walpole, though they are the obvious referent in his alluding to "the invidious appellations of *corruption* and *dependence.*" For the contemporary debate over corruption, see Kramnick (1968). Despite the occasional placing of Hume in the tradition of civic humanism, I think Forbes is right: "Hume has virtually no affinities with the Machiavellian moralists and corruption mongers of his age" (Forbes 1975: 225).

12. Just this tack is taken by Miller (1981), who pursues this strand of Hume's thought much more intensively than I can here.

13. *Treatise:* 620f.; *Morals:* 177; Hume to Francis Hutcheson, 17 sep 1739 (*Letters,* I: 32f.).

14. Here I follow the orthodox reading of Hume's famous passage on "is" and "ought" (*Treatise:* 469f.). For a sampling of the oppressively large literature on this passage see Hudson (1969).

15. *Treatise:* 505ff. I draw the conclusion that follows from these pages.

16. Here I attribute to Hume an error theory of the sort developed by Mackie (1977).

17. See here Wolin (1954).

18. *Treatise:* 171; Hume to Hutcheson, 17 sep 1739 (*Letters,* I: 33).

19. *History,* I: 116; note too *History,* II: 476.

20. "Of the Liberty of the Press" (*Essays:* 8–12). The following discussion and quotations are all from this essay.

References

Ayer, Alfred J. 1980. *Hume.* New York: Hill & Wang.

Becker, Carl. 1932. *The Heavenly City of the Eighteenth-Century Philosophers.* New Haven, Conn.: Yale University Press.

Chappell, Vere C. (ed.). 1966. *Hume.* Garden City, NY: Doubleday Anchor.

Forbes, Duncan. 1975. *Hume's Philosophical Politics.* Cambridge: Cambridge University Press.

Gay, Peter. 1964. Carl Becker's Heavenly City Revisited. In *The Party of Humanity.* New York: Knopf.

Green, T.H. 1964. Introduction. In Hume, *A Treatise of Human Nature*, eds. T.H. Green and T.H. Grose. Aalen: Scientia Verlag.

Hayek, F.A. 1966. The Legal and Political Philosophy of David Hume. In Chappell (1966).

Herzog, Don. 1985. *Without Foundations: Justification in Political Theory*. Ithaca, NY: Cornell University·Press.

Hudson, W.D. 1969. *The Is-Ought Problem*. New York: St. Martin's.

Hume, David. [*Enquiries*]. *Enquiries concerning Human Understanding and concerning the Principles of Morals*, ed. L.A. Selby-Bigge, 3d ed. rev. by P.H. Nidditch. Oxford: Clarendon Press, 1978.

————. [*Enquiry*]. *An Enquiry concerning Human Understanding*. In *Enquiries*.

————. [*Essays*]. *Essays: Moral, Political and Literary*. Oxford: Oxford University Press, 1974.

————. [*History*]. *History of England*, new ed., 6 vols. Boston: Little, Brown, 1872.

————. [*Letters*]. *The Letters of David Hume*, ed. J.Y.T. Grieg, 2 vols. Oxford: Clarendon Press, 1969.

————. [*Morals*]. *An Enquiry concerning the Principles of Morals*. In *Enquiries*.

————. [*Religion*]. *Natural History of Religion and Dialogues concerning Natural Religion*, eds. A. Wayne Colver and John Valdimir Price. Oxford: Clarendon Press, 1976.

————. [*Treatise*]. *A Treatise of Human Nature*, ed. L.A. Selby-Bigge, 2d ed. rev. by P.H. Nidditch. Oxford: Clarendon Press, 1980.

Kramnick, Isaac. 1968. *Bolingbroke and His Circle*. Cambridge, Mass.: Harvard University Press.

Mackie, J.L. 1977. *Ethics*. Harmondsworth: Penguin.

————. 1980. *Hume's Moral Theory*. London: Routledge & Kegan Paul.

Mill, John Stuart. 1982. Brodie's History of the British Empire. In *Essays on England, Ireland, and the Empire*, ed. John M. Robson. Toronto: University of Toronto Press (Collected Works of John Stuart Mill, vol. 6).

Miller, David. 1981. *Philosophy and Ideology in Hume's Political Thought*. Oxford: Clarendon Press.

Mossner, Ernest Campbell. 1980. *The Life of David Hume*, 2d ed. Oxford: Clarendon Press.

Norton, David Fate. 1982. *David Hume: Common-Sense Moralist, Sceptical Metaphysician*. Princeton: Princeton University Press.

Smith, Norman Kemp. 1941. *The Philosophy of David Hume*. London: Macmillan.

Spragens, Thomas A., Jr. 1981. *The Irony of Liberal Reason*. Chicago: University of Chicago Press.

Stroud, Barry. 1977. *Hume*. London: Routledge & Kegan Paul.

Will, George. 1983. *Statecraft as Soulcraft*. New York: Simon and Schuster.

Wolff, Robert Paul. 1960. Hume's Theory of Mental Activity. *Philosophical Review* 69: 289–310 (reprinted in Chappell 1966).

Wolin, Sheldon. 1954. Hume and Conservatism. *American Political Science Review* 48: 999–1016.

4

Adam Smith: Skeptical Newtonianism, Disenchanted Republicanism, and the Birth of Social Science

Sergio Cremaschi

Ethics, Economics, Politics, and History of Science in the Works of Adam Smith

The prevailing image of the work of Adam Smith has for a long time been that of a blend of Deism, Natural Law philosophy, and mechanistic science, a deductivistic and aprioristic metaphysics of society. *Das Adam Smith Problem* originated within this framework: it was the problem of the difficult cohabitation of two different metaphysics of man, one based on the principle of self-love and the other based on the opposing principle of benevolence (Raphael and Macfie 1976: 20–25). In the 1930s and 1940s a rescue operation took place: Adam Smith's economic work, to begin with, and later on his ethical work too, were held to be free from dogmatic metaphysical implications; for the puzzling words "nature" and "natural" a graceful translation was found in the words "ordinary" and "average" (WN I.vii.3), and his ethical theory was twisted into a value-free sociology of ethical behavior (Viner 1927; Bitterman 1940; Campbell 1971; for an overview see Lindgren 1973: 1–3).

Only after the full "empiricization" of Adam Smith had been carried out, some attention was paid to his writings in the area of philosophy of science, and it was suggested that the possible influence of his philosophy of science on his economic theory deserved to be explored (Becker 1961; Thompson 1965; Lindgren 1973: ch. 1). These first attempts were the victims of a high degree of anachronism and Smith was dressed up as a follower of Hempel, Popper, or Peter Winch. The rediscovery of Smith's epistemological writings was nonetheless laudable, and some other contributions were able to place these writings within their appropriate context, that is, within the several trends of eighteenth-century Newtonianism (Moscovici 1956; Skinner 1974; Megill 1975).

The next step was to develop a balanced reconstruction of the relationship between Smith's version of Newtonian methodology and his political economy, viewed against the background of the wider Humean project of a Newtonian science of human nature (Cremaschi 1981; Cremaschi 1982; Hetherington 1983; Cremaschi 1984). The main theses put forth in these contributions are as follows: (1) the central feature of the epistemological background of *The Wealth of Nations* is the Newtonian thesis of the 'intermediate' character of the principles of the theory, between the phenomena and the principles of reality in itself; (2) political economy becomes a comparatively autonomous discipline, precisely because of this intermediate character of its principles; (3) even if its principles are no longer identical with the principles of Natural Law, political economy is still inherently part of the wider body of a "moral science" along with ethics and natural jurisprudence; the difference between it and the seventeenth-century attitude lies in the fact that the "science of natural law" or "moral science" ceases to be a unitary deductive system.

Within the framework of these theses, it may prove useful to reexamine Smith's political economy alongside of his political theory. A parallel development in Smith's scholarship during the past decade has destroyed the myth of the "liberal" Smith, proponent of a theory of the minimal state (Winch 1978: 6 ff.). The discovery of a new set of notes from his *Lectures on Jurisprudence* has contributed much to a fuller appreciation of what his projected "history and theory of law and government" was meant to be (Meek, Raphael, and Stein 1977: 33–35), and several other important contributions have highlighted his place in the "skeptical Whig" tradition, in the "civic humanist" tradition, and in the prosecution of Hume's project of a "theory of justice" (Forbes 1954; Pocock 1975: 468–505; Winch 1978; Haakonssen 1981). As a result we are now able to see the contours of a typical Scottish and Smithian doctrine, the part of Smith's system of ideas most similar to a political theory in the present sense. This peculiar discipline, named natural jurisprudence, is worlds apart from nineteenth-century liberal political theories, but it also has important differences from seventeenth-century Natural Law philosophy. As a further result we are also able to appreciate how Smith's political economy—notwithstanding its recent autonomy—is still embedded in a political theory, with all the implied differences from later classical economists.

In this chapter I shall try to take advantage of this renewed image of Smith's politics as a starting point for an exploration of the connection between these doctrines and his epistemology. The connection to be explored will be rather intricate: rather than a direct link between an image of science and an image of politics, it is a devious path leading from a theory of the principles of the mind to a reconstruction of the history of natural science, and a parallel, even more twisted, path leading from the theory of the mind to a general theory of human society and of its evolution, and further on to theories of moral judgments, government, moral rules, and of the market.

In more detail, I will argue that: (1) the epistemological doctrines of Smith are led to a stalemate by the opposition between an eventually still shared essentialist ideal of knowledge and a pragmatist and instrumentalist approach to the history of science; (2) the political doctrines of Smith are still intended to serve the goal of providing a foundation to a Natural Law; (3) a weaker foundation is found in 'nature' rather than in 'reason' in order to avoid the paradoxes of rationalistic Natural Law theories; (4) as a consequence, the legitimation of several partial social orders is introduced, which may be the objects of inquiry of several specialized social sciences; (5) as a parallel consequence, we are led into a stalemate, similar to the one faced by Smith's epistemology, by the need to bring about an impossible reconciliation between the ultimate order of society and the several partial empirical orders.

Descartes and Newton

I shall begin with a brief reconstruction of the content of Smith's writings on the history of science. His masterpiece in this field, "The History of Astronomy,"[1] starts with a section illustrating the "principles" of the mind that lead to the construction of "philosophical systems." This opening section is followed by a reconstruction of the history of the astronomical systems, which followed each other, starting from ancient times and concluding with Descartes's theory of vortexes and Newton's theory of universal gravitation. The essay is unfinished and it is worth noting that it stops at the open question of the real significance of the Newtonian system (HA IV.76).

The need to formulate philosophical systems, and later on to substitute one system for another, stems from a few basic laws of the mind. The mind perceives a kind of gap every time it faces a phenomenon different from the one it was used to finding in a given sequence. Wonder, an uneasy feeling, originates in the mind as a result. The imagination tries to provide a remedy for this uneasy feeling by creating an imaginary chain to link the disconnected phenomena. The renewed perception of some kind of continuity between phenomena restores the imagination to a condition of ease (HA II.8–12).

It is important to note that the view of the principles of the mind or of human nature sketched in "The History of Astronomy" and presented in more detail in *The Theory of Moral Sentiments* (TMS I.i.1.3–8; ED 19; 88; TMS III.3.3; HA I–III) is basically identical with the "science of human nature" dealt with in Hume's *Treatise* (THN Introduction; II.i.5; II.iii.9; III.i.2). Its basic features are atomism, association of ideas, "imagination" understood as the principle that combines different ideas, custom, and sympathy. The role of sympathy, as shown later, is primary in social interaction, whereas when man is faced with nature, it is imagination that plays a prime role (Cremaschi 1984: 34–42; 87–89; Raphael and Skinner 1980: 17–21).

Smith states that theories are like "imaginary machines," or chains of ideas built by the imagination between two disjoined phenomena. The imaginary machine is supposed to link the observed phenomena while remaining out of sight behind the scenes of nature, like theatrical machinery. The best imaginary machines are chosen according to the criteria of 'simplicity' and 'familiarity' of the principles employed, of the 'coherence' produced in the domain of phenomena explained, and of the comprehensiveness of the domain the theory unifies.

The succession of systems is ruled by these four criteria: a system is accepted as a substitute for the preceding one when it is able to connect phenomena that the preceding one could not connect, or when it is able to build the chain by means of more familiar principles, or when it is able to unify to a greater extent the given domain of phenomena.

According to these criteria, the succession of the Copernican system to the Ptolemaic system is explained; the latter had grown so complicated while endeavoring to account for new phenomena that it had become useless to the imagination as a guide for understanding reality. The Copernican system was then accepted as a substitute because it explained the same phenomena in a much simpler way (HA IV.27–32).

The most interesting part of the essay is to be found in the last pages, dealing with Descartes and Newton: Descartes's theory of vortexes and Newton's theory of universal gravitation are two different attempts to complete the Copernican system, making it more comprehensive and more familiar by providing a cause for the motions of the planets. The Cartesian system of vortexes had the great merit of being able to render the rapid motions of the enormous bodies of the planets familiar to the imagination, although the idea contrasts with the habits acquired by the imagination. The very familiar idea of impulse was used to reach this result. The main difficulty in the Cartesian system derived from the fact that it accounted only for the fundamental motions of the heavenly bodies, and could not explain irregularities in their motions. Far from accommodating his system to all the minute irregularities which Kepler had ascertained in the motions of the planets, Descartes "contented himself with observing that perfect uniformity could not be expected in their motions" (HA IV.66). In this way he thought he could avoid the need to take into account the astronomers' empirical observations. This Cartesian system's inability to explain observed phenomena paved the way for the Newtonian system. Newton "first attempted to give a physical account of the motions of the Planets, which should accommodate itself to all the constant irregularities which astronomers had ever observed in their motions" (HA IV.67).

The advantage of the Newtonian system lies in the introduction of a now familiar notion, the idea of gravitation, as a hypothesis to explain the motions of the heavenly bodies. This single hypothesis accounts for all the phenomena, terrestrial and heavenly. The same hypothesis also covers observed irregularities in the heavenly motions. As a result, the Newtonian system complied more closely with the requirements of the imagination, so that Smith himself states that he has "insensibly been drawn in, to make use of language expressing the connecting principles of this one, as if they were the real chains which Nature makes use of to bind together her several operations" (HA IV.76). The imagination, by replacing one theory by another that complies better with its requirements, feels as if it had penetrated deeper into reality. Yet, in fact, every theory, the Newtonian included, is an "invention of the imagination." What we can properly say is that a theory serves the purpose, in a better or worse way, of establishing a direction amid the chaos of phenomena.

There are, however, no grounds for stating that a theory that satisfies the four criteria better is a better reproduction of the essence of reality. The manuscript of "The History of Astronomy" stops in the midst of the discussion of the Newtonian system. An editorial note warns us that, according to the notes left by Adam Smith, the part on Newton was to be considered "imperfect, and needing several additions" (HA IV.76). We are entitled, from a statement by Smith himself, to assume that he did not publish the essay precisely because he considered it imperfect, but not primarily on stylistic grounds (Corr: Letter 137).

Conceivably the source of Smith's dissatisfaction was the contrast between the need felt by the imagination to believe in the real existence of principles connecting phenomena, on the one hand, and the compulsory conclusion, reached on rational reflection, that it is impossible to know what "real chains" Nature uses to bind phenomena and that the explanatory principles have a conventional character, on the other hand (Moscovici 1956: 10; Cremaschi 1981; Hetherington 1983; Cremaschi 1984: ch. 1).

To sum up: Smith acknowledges that we are under the pull of two opposite views of science. The first is based on the idea of an internal criterion of truth (that can be used, but is at the same time "irrational," depending only on our imagination's needs); the second view is based on a "correspondence" or—rather—a "copy" theory of truth (one that cannot be given up if science is not mere fancy, myth, or artistic creation, but at the same time one that cannot be used in practice).

Grotius and Montesquieu

Adam Smith's Politics: An Overview

Smith was not able during his lifetime to fulfill the promise he had made to publish a "theory and history of law and government" or "an account of the general principles of law and government" (TMS VII.iv.37). We know however that in the last years of his life he had not "altogether abandoned the design" (TMS Advertisement 2). We cannot know exactly how relevant to this project were the papers that Smith, when he was on his death bed, ordered burned. Nonetheless we are sure he considered *The Wealth of Nations* as a partial execution of this project (TMS Advertisement 2). The discovery of the notes from the *Lectures on Jurisprudence* enables us to compare the partial execution with what can be taken as the general scheme of the wider project: *The Wealth of Nations* covers the second part of the lectures, dedicated to "justice." Our understanding of the original content of the lectures has been greatly improved by the discovery of a second set of lecture notes, less complete in coverage than the one edited by E. Cannan, but more accurate, and of another fragment of notes.[2]

The whole of Smith's work is, however, a complex, like a set of Russian dolls. As *The Wealth of Nations* is embedded in the *Lectures on Jurisprudence*, so the *Lectures* are embedded in *The Theory of Moral Sentiments*. Section 2 of the latter work covers the area that the *Lectures on Jurisprudence* explore in a much more analytical way. As the corresponding part of the *Lectures* is less analytical than the treatment of the same topics in *The Wealth of Nations*, but gives more hints about the ultimate foundation in the science of human nature of the principles put to work in the theory, so *The Theory of Moral Sentiments* goes one step further toward that central area of Smith's system of ideas—the science of human nature—to which no single work was dedicated. As I shall argue later, the theory of human nature is a point on which both lines of Smith's work, the social theory and the theory of language, art, and science, converge.

Faced with a set of works embedded in each other, in order to reconstruct the contours of Adam Smith's "politics," it may prove useful to inspect carefully the joints connecting the parts. Smith has been held for a long time to be the proponent of a "minimal state" view, one emptying the domain of politics in favor of the bordering domain of economics (see Cropsey 1963; for the opposite view see Winch 1978: 6 ff.). The traditional view is clearly based on an anachronism: the configuration in Smith of the overall social domain, with its ethical, political, and economic subdomains, is very different from the eighteenth-century view, being much nearer to a liberalized or "decentralized" version of the seventeenth-century view of the "practical science," which covered ethics, law, and politics (Cremaschi 1982).

A preliminary terminological clarification is required: Smith describes his doctrines by the terms "natural jurisprudence," "science of a legislator," "political economy," "justice," and "police." "Natural jurisprudence" is the general term that indicates Smith's political doctrines. It is a part of moral philosophy, as explicitly stated in *The Theory of Moral Sentiments*, where natural jurisprudence is said to be "of all the sciences by far the most important, but hitherto, perhaps, the least cultivated" (TMS VI.ii. Introduction 2). It is "the theory of the rules by which civil governments ought to be directed" (LJ(A) i.1), or the theory of "the general principles which ought to be the foundation of the laws of all nations" (LJ(B) 1; see also TMS VII.iv.37).

Natural jurisprudence is identical with "the science of a legislator" (TMS VI.ii. Introduction 1), that is, a figure opposed to that of the "politician": the legislator is a wise and prudent man inspired by a desire to ameliorate the conditions of his country and is directed by prudence and by well-founded principles (TMS VI.ii.2.16–18). Smith talks of the "science of a legislator, whose deliberations ought to be governed by general principles which are always the same" (WN IV.ii.39). Natural jurisprudence is divided into two parts: the first, or the theory of "justice," concerns rights of the individual. It is not a deductive legal theory but a theory of the "originall or foundation" of rights, and it performs this task by an explication, like the one given by grammar for language, of that "natural justice" dictated to us by our "natural sentiments" (TMS III.6.11; LJ(A) i.24). In this sense natural justice is included in the theory of moral sentiments, and yet it is distinguished from a "system of moralls" (LJ(A) i.15).

The second part is the doctrine of "police," which concerns the "inferior parts" of the science of a legislator. Its main object is "cheapness or plenty." It differs markedly from the first part of natural jurisprudence, being based not only on considerations of justice but also on considerations of "expediency." "Political economy" is identical with the second part of natural jurisprudence, or with "police," and it may accordingly be "considered as a branch of the science of a statesman or legislator" (WN IV.a.1).

The best·starting point for a reconstruction of the complex system of ethical-political-economic doctrines, as well as of Smith's political theory in a strict sense, is the *pars destruens* of his undertaking. His main critical targets are utilitarianism in ethics and artificialism in politics. The views he wants to criticize are primarily those of Hobbes and Locke, and secondly those of the "rationalist" Natural Law philosophers Grotius and Pufendorf and of the "moral sense" Natural Law philosopher Hutcheson. He wants to take over Hume's attempt at finding an alternative "foundation" to Natural Law, other than reason or moral sense, but he adds to Hume's solution a powerful dose of Montesquieu's genetic account of law and of the Scottish evolutionary theory of society.

Hume's attempt had been to avoid recognition of any supernatural origin of a natural law or of its origin in any explicit deliberation by human beings, while avoiding complete relativism. He had tried to reconstruct the genesis of a set of general rules of justice as a result of purely "natural" causes, i.e., individual human actions, though not as an intended result of such actions (THN III.ii.6.5–6). So justice is seen to originate as an unforeseeable result of numberless individual judgments as human beings are "powerfully addicted to general rules" (THN III.ii.9.3), and the rules of justice play the role of the traditional idea of a Natural Law: "tho' the rules of justice be artificial, they are not arbitrary. Nor is the expression improper to call them Laws of Nature" (THN III.ii.1.19).

The difficulty that Smith may have felt with Hume's approach, even if he was highly sympathetic with Hume's project, stems from the dichotomy between an abstract system of general rules and the individual judgments governed by sympathy. The lack of concrete content of the rules of justice seems to make Hume fall back from time to time into a rationalistic view of how the sympathy mechanisms work (Haakonssen 1981: 36).

In Hume's account a third category between "natural" and "artificial" seems to be required (Haakonssen: 21–26). That is why Hume's "theory of justice" is integrated by Smith with an evolutionary theory of the genesis of government and of law that follows the inspiration of Montesquieu's attempt at discovering the "spirit of laws" and that tries to provide precisely that third intermediate element. Smith's attempt is based on a much more sophisticated theory than Montesquieu's "climatic factors theory," that is, on the four-stage theory that makes the forms of government dependent upon the modes of subsistence (LJ(A) iv.4–55; LJ(B) 19–30). In contrast with Hume's approach, Smith should be able to accomplish the following: to show how, through a continuous process of adaptation, our sympathetic moral judgments continuously select, vis-à-vis changing situations, basic standards of evaluation (applying both to rules of "justice" and to other virtues) that tend to approximate an ideal standard. These standards can in a sense transcend given customs and laws (TMS VII.iv.36), and they are approximately convergent with this ideal standard because the laws of the functioning and of the evolution of human societies make virtue, and particularly justice, a precondition for the survival of society (TMS II.2.4; II.5.8; VII.iii.1.2; VII.ii.2.13).

The evolution of custom and of moral codes and, most interesting for the present discussion, the institutions of government and systems of law are dependent upon social evolution plus sympathetic judgments. Government did not originate from an original contract, nor was it created in some "state of nature," "as there is no such state existing" (LJ(B) 3; LJ(A) v.114–119; 127–129).

There has been indeed a state of society, the "age of hunters" or "the rude and early state," where society existed with "very little government of any sort" (LJ(A) iv.4). Government arose "naturally" as, in the subsequent ages of history, society grew more and more complex: its sources were the authority spontaneously accorded to older, wiser, more valiant people, the need to protect the property of the rich against the poor, and the direct influence over other people carried by wealth in pre-commercial societies (LJ(A) iv.7–12; iv.22–23).

The origin of law is more recent than the origin of government. The first forms of government, in the age of the shepherds, included only the executive power; later, in the more complex agricultural societies, a judicial power was required. Only after the institution of a judicial power did a body of laws gradually come into being (LJ(A) v.122).

The general framework that has been sketched depends on two elements: the ways in which societies function and evolve, and the ways in which sympathetic "natural sentiments" are regulated. I shall present first the background social theory presupposed by Smith. In this theory two dimensions can be distinguished: the first may be qualified as a kind of "proto-functionalism."[3] Society is often presented in functionalist terms, stressing the interdependence of the several social domains and the ability of societies to self-regulate and self-correct their internal processes. In these terms, a "contextual" explanation of the several elements of any given society is available. Such an approach comes to the fore every time Smith adopts the Stoic or Deistic attitude that has been qualified as "contemplative utilitarianism" (Campbell 1977: 528). The importance of the contemplative utilitarian attitude in Smith's system of ideas can hardly be over-estimated, though there is abundant evidence refuting Campbell's view, according to which contemplative utilitarianism is the only alternative Smith is supposed to adopt to a value-free descriptive attitude (Campbell 1971: 51). I shall argue later that the possibility of a third way between the two attitudes is essential to Smith.

According to the proto-functionalist vision, all aspects of human reality— the unintended results of individual actions, the spontaneous self-correction of our natural sentiments, the operation of the mechanisms of political and legal institutions, and a number of other human institutions such as language and exchange—interact with each other and readjust themselves in a continuous selection of appropriate behaviors (TMS I.i.3.6; I.i.4.7; V.2.10; LJ(B) 326–327; LJ(A) iv.4–55; Languages; LJ(A) vi.44–55; Haakonssen 1981: 54–61). Smith makes the assumption that the interacting elements of the social system cooperate in the long run and in a rough way leading to the prosperity of mankind: "No society could subsist a moment, in which the usual strain of men's conduct and behaviour was of a piece with the horrible practice I have just now mentioned" (TMS V.2.16; see also TMS II.3.5–6; IIII.2.6–7).

As an obvious consequence of the unintended character of this continuous process of readjustment, the extent to which conscious human action can influence what happens is limited. On the one hand, human beings can become aware of the utility of virtue: virtue contributes to the smoother functioning of the social machine by adding "beneficence" to "justice." The latter, being indispensable to the survival of society, is primarily recommended by our natural sentiments, while beneficence, being less indipensable, is suggested to us by "reason and philosophy" (TMS II.ii.6.10; VI.ii.1.1–2). On the other hand, conscious human intervention can achieve cautious reforms of artificial human institutions, such as would not hinder but rather ease the attainment of those goals that Nature would in the long run more or less unfailingly reach (TMS VI.ii.2.16–17). But the role of the "man of government" will be discussed in detail later.

The second dimension of the background social theory is evolutionary. This dimension comes to the fore in the well-known four-stage theory (Meek 1976; Skinner 1982), according to which the forms of government are determined by the "mode of subsistence" of a given society: hunting, stock raising, agriculture, commerce. The political institutions evolve through the several stages thanks to the unintended results of human action. Mankind's natural sentiments, which give origin to the standards of justice accepted in a particular society, evolve according to what it is reasonable to expect from fellow human beings in the circumstances (TMS V.2.7–9).

The primary spring of evolution is a kind of Vicoesque "heterogenesis of ends," or the principle of unintended results, according to which events originate from human action even if not from human design (Forbes 1954: 661; Forbes 1977a; Cremaschi 1982: 242–243). Not only can a "natural" functioning of the social whole be acknowledged at any given moment, but also a "natural course of things," i.e., a path of evolution that is roughly unavoidable and that is—or has been up to the present time—a way toward happiness and perfection of mankind (even though a rather transverse way to that end, as the discussion that follows will show).

What helps make this quasi-optimistic vision flexible enough to escape from apriorism is the supplementary idea of the "animal principle": nature will find its own way through the obstacles created by imperfect human institutions, and will not wait until they have been removed or perfect human institutions have been established (WN IV.ix.28; II.iii.31).

Both the functionalist dimension and the evolutionary dimension of the theory of society rely, as an ultimate basis, on the very same Humean theory of human nature on which Smith's theory of natural science was based. On the basis of the laws of the mind it is possible to account for phenomena such as the evolution of language, the desire for goods that go beyond the basic necessities also common to animals, the desire to better our condition, the distinction of ranks, the propensity to "truck and barter," the desire to be considered praiseworthy, and finally respect for every institution that is established and old (Languages 41; LJ(A) vi.13; TMS I.iii.2.1; LJ(A) vi.44–157; TMS I.iii.2; LJ(A) vi.45; TMS V.1). While imagination plays a primary role in organizing our perception of natural phenomena, and also plays an important role in social life, the more complex mechanism of sympathy (nevertheless rooted in imagination, being based on the ability to make an imaginary switch of situation) rules over social interaction. That may explain why the construction of systems in natural philosophy has been a necessity felt from the very beginning by the mind, in order to overcome apparent disorder (HA IV.8–12; WN V.i.f.25), while disorder in social life has always been felt on a small scale and has been tackled through sympathetic readjustments of moral sentiments.

Systems in moral philosophy come only at a later stage (TMS VII.ii.4.14; WN V.i.f.25; Haakonssen 1981: 79–82). A proviso should be made: as natural philosophy is ultimately dependent on the principles of the mind, but this dependence is limited by the unbridgeable gap between the principles of the mind and the real principles of nature, so the dependence of "moral philosophy" on the principles of the mind is limited by the gap between the conscious aims of human beings and the unintended results they unconsciously produce.

Mention has been made of the fact that natural jurisprudence consists of two parts: "justice" and "police." The part on justice can be viewed as directly belonging to the theory of moral sentiments; it is the part of the theory of moral sentiments that deals with a virtue more necessary than any other to the existence of society that can be treated in a much more exact way. Justice is sharply contrasted with benevolence; the former may subsist between rational egoists (TMS II.ii.3.2). At the root of justice lies resentment (TMS II.ii.1.4), which may in several instances be the principle regulating the proper use of violence (TMS II.ii.1.8–9). "Natural justice" is accordingly a standard not derived from reason but dictated by natural sentiments. Its basic character for social life is dependent on the importance of negative, as contrasted with positive, virtues. Pain and misery are felt more pungently than pleasure and happiness; sympathy with these negative feelings is accordingly much stronger (TMS I.iii; III.2.15). The role of resentment in founding the sense of justice is derived from this characteristic of sympathy (LJ(A) ii.89–90; TMS II.ii.1–9). The whole doctrine of justice is accordingly an explication and systematization of criteria dictated by our "natural sentiments." The criteria of justice are not derived from reason in any of the possible senses: neither by deduction from a cosmic *lex aeterna*, nor by contractualistic fiction, nor by utilitarian considerations.

Utilitarian considerations of a sort are admissible more for speculative than for practical purposes, and are the business of philosophers, not of men of action, or they may be appealed to in some cases for rhetorical or didactic purposes, as a partial remedy for the tearing of the natural sense of justice. Human beings may approve of a certain institution also because of its utility in view of the happiness and perfection of human life, but only post factum, once the institution has been accepted and approved by the passions and sentiments of men (LJ(A) v.119–122; Campbell 1977: 528–529; Haakonssen 1981: 73).

"Natural justice," as a consequence, is clearly for Smith a form of Natural Law, that is, a theory of "the general principles which ought to run through and be the foundation of the laws of all nations" (TMS VII.iv.37). The normative function of natural jurisprudence is beyond any doubt; its difference from seventeenth-century Natural Law lies rather in its non-rationalistic foundation. Smith rules out an original law of nature as a fixed legal code that could be deduced by reason or learned by experience. In different societies positive laws are judged against the standard provided by "natural justice" or by the "natural sentiments" of mankind. These sentiments, regulated by sympathy and by the impartial spectator, are not completely universal and metahistorical (LJ(A) i.24; ii.75; ii.162; i.36; ii.43; TMS I.i.1). This is a central feature that cannot be given up in the economy of Smith's system. But the troubles it causes to the system have been often under-estimated (as by Haakonssen 1981: 101–102). The variability of natural sentiments is necessary to avoid an aprioristic and ahistorical approach; they recognize human actions as appropriate in different ways according to the historical context, but they may be "corrupted" by fashion and by a few innate tendencies of human imagination (TMS V.ii). While the normative content of Smith's theory of justice can be ascribed, in terms of history of the climates of opinion, to the "skeptical Whig" and to the "civic humanist" traditions, it fits nonetheless significantly into the theoretical framework provided by Smith's peculiar version of Natural Law. The basic value for Smith seems to be "personal liberty":

> The great source of both the misery and disorders of human life, seems to arise from over-rating the difference between one permanent situation and another. Avarice over-rates the differences between poverty and riches. Except

the frivolous pleasures of vanity and superiority, we may find, in the most humble station, where there is only personal liberty every other which the most exalted can afford. (TMS III.3.31)

The predominance of "personal liberty" seems to be related to a Stoical underrating of the possibilities of human happiness; the real differences between the happiness that can be afforded by the different "stations" in life is greatly emphasized by the imagination. The condition of the beggar and that of the king are not greatly different (TMS IV.1.10; I.iii.2.2). The primary object of the "science of a legislator" is accordingly not so much happiness, but rather "justice" or "rights." Security is a precondition for making justice possible. If, on the one hand, the promotion of happiness cannot be the real task of a legislator, on the other, the primary aim of personal freedom must not be mistaken for the different target of "political freedom."

This last term refers to the participation of citizens in the government of the commonwealth. Smith holds "political freedom" to be highly desirable, but he stresses that personal freedom may be independent of it: "civilized monarchies," where law and order rule, can afford a high degree of personal freedom (WN V.iii.a.15–16; III.iv.4). Conversely, the two kinds of freedom may be in conflict, as the case of slavery shows; the lot of a slave is generally better under despotic governments, where the sovereign can interfere with the affairs of the slave owners, than under republican governments, where the holders of political power are the very same citizens who own slaves (Forbes 1977a; Winch 1978: ch.2).

The decisive factor in giving priority to the more limited aim of "personal liberty" over the more ambitious aim of "political liberty," and in declaring the most ambitious aim of "public happiness" almost totally delusory, is the primacy of negative virtues as foundations of rights and justice, as stated earlier. From this priority, the typically liberal distinction is between the public sphere, the proper object of political and legal regulations, and the sphere of the conscience, which must be safeguarded against interference from public authority (TMS II.iii.3.2). Some positive tasks are unavoidable for the "civil magistrate": "he may prescribe rules . . . which not only prohibit mutual injuries among fellow-citizens, but command mutual good offices to a certain degree" (TMS II.ii.1.8). But in prescribing these very rules he must be as careful as possible not to infringe upon the liberty of individuals (TMS II.ii.1.8).

Even if Smith adheres to "republicanism" on principle (Forbes 1977a; Winch 1978: ch.2), the extent to which he commits himself to the practicability of republican principles is limited by the negative sympathetic foundation of rights and justice. He contrasts the "Whig" principle of "utility" as a foundation of government with the "Tory" principle of "authority," making the prevalence of one principle dependent on historical circumstances of a given society (LJ(A) v.119–124; v. 129–132). It is impossible to base the legitimacy of governments solely on utility, i.e., on the teachings of "Reason and Philosophy" (TMS I.iii.2.3) because of the sentimentalist foundation of moral judgments, including judgments on justice. In the same line of argument is the refusal of utopias (WN V.iii.68; IV.ii.43), the refusal of attempts to achieve perfect systems of social reform by "imperial and royal reformers" (TMS VI.ii.12–18), and the refusal of seeing perfect happiness as a feasible aim of government (TMS VI.ii.2.17). "Republicanism" in principle—apart from questions about the evolution of Smith's ideas, which will be dealt with later—is some kind of ultimate standard that is however considered to be of limited use in practice.

> What institution of government could tend so much to promote the happiness of mankind as the general prevalence of wisdom and virtue? All government is but an imperfect remedy for the deficiency of these (TMS IV.ii.1).

The problems of politics are to be stated primarily in terms of constitutional machinery precisely because there are too few reasons to lay one's bet on moral progress. The scope of Smith's pessimism is a central point, requiring careful examination.

Coming to Smith's diagnosis of the historical moment, his main concern can be acknowledged to be the relation between progress of civilization and progress of liberty. His diagnosis is that the course of European history has led to a highly contingent and precarious correspondence between progress of "opulence" and progress of "liberty" both in "republican" governments (such as England) and in "civilized monarchies" (such as France) (WN III.iii.9; III.iv.4; II.i.31; III.iii.5; Forbes 1977a; Winch 1978: ch.4).

The last point that needs mention in this overview is the nature and scope of political action and discourse. The science of a legislator is wider in scope than just "justice"; it includes political economy and other parts based on the principle of "expediency," such as "security." Yet the only normative basis for the science of a legislator lies in "natural justice" (Haakonssen 1981: 96–97). As both Utopianism and a Rousseauian kind of democracy are discarded, the remainder of the science of a legislator can only be based on a prudent calculus (where "prudence" is understood in much poorer terms than in the Aristotelian tradition).

The action of the "man of government" (not of the individual citizen, who is left, after all, to his everyday business, regulated by self-interest and natural justice) may be directed mainly at smoothing the natural course of things; not even the plain and evident "system of natural liberty," dictated in political economy by the natural sense of justice and confirmed by utilitarian considerations, should be applied without some limitation (WN IV.ii.43). Apart from leaving the spontaneous market mechanisms reasonably free in their domain, the man of government can imitate the results of market mechanisms in other domains such as defense, justice, and education (WN V; Robertson 1983: 70). Last of all, the man of government should be aware of the unexpected counter-effects a highly artificial intervention may provoke, and needs to act carefully, to take into account existing conditions, rooted traditions and institutions, and even to come to terms with prejudice when he cannot overcome it, thus avoiding the loss of the second best while trying too hard to obtain the best (TMS VI.ii.2.16).

The Epicenters of Society

The peculiar theoretical framework outlined gives two main results in Smith's work. The first is a decentralization of the political order that gives origin to several partial orders: the first specialized social science, namely political economy, wins autonomy from the political discourse. The second result is a weakening of the normative strength of the order: the several partially autonomous orders all have a "weak" kind of normativity.

Let us start with the first of these results. Smith owes much of his fame to the discovery of the principle of unintended results. Ironically, his main theoretical achievement might be described as a highly unintended result: Smith started with the intention of radically reforming the "science of natural law," and ended as the founder of a "new science." Recent contributions in the history of ideas have revised the standard image of Smith as the turning point of the deflection of classical political philosophy into economic science (for this image see Cropsey 1963), and have tried to restore a balanced relationship between natural jurisprudence and political economy (Winch 1978: 6 ff.). However, as long as the main results of this restoration are not questioned, namely, that political economy for Smith is inherently a part of natural jurisprudence, and that Book V of *The Wealth of Nations* is not a mere addendum to that work, a few words may be said against the currently fashionable image of Smith as a contemporary of Machiavelli and a very remote ancestor of Ricardo.[4] Smith is acknowledged as having realized that the characteristics of modern society need to be dealt with on several levels (Dippel 1981: 99–100). I stress that it would be extremely naïve to describe this achievement in terms of a discovery of the effects of social differentiation in progress; Smith describes and makes sense of a number of aspects of complex modern society precisely because he is in a position to make a theoretical move toward a subdivision-reaggregation of the social whole, resulting in a description of a cluster of phenomena as a new unified domain: the national economy. Not arbitrarily, Smith's achievement in *The Wealth of Nations* can be compared with the ancient proponents of the system of epicenters as reconstructed in "The History of Astronomy":

> by supposing, that in the solidity of the Sphere of each of the Five Planets there was formed another little Sphere, called an Epicycle . . . in the same manner as we might suppose a little wheel inclosed within the outer circle of a great wheel. . . . Those philosophers transported themselves, in fancy, to the centres of these imaginary Circles, and took pleasure in surveying from thence, all those fantastical motions, arranged, according to that harmony and order, which it had been the end of all their researches to bestow upon them. (HA IV.10–13)

The author of "The History of Astronomy" may have finally come to terms with the apparent disorder of social life that the highly unified order of the rationalistic Natural Law was not able to reduce to order, by supposing a little wheel, that is the order of the market, enclosed within the outer circle of the great wheel of social order.

The theory presented in *The Wealth of Nations* relates to a domain whose borders are not identical with those of the domains to which it is the heir. It includes a value theory like the Lockean theory of property, a theory of equilibrium mechanisms like the Mercantilist theories of foreign trade, a theory of a natural order of production, a theory of circulation, and a theory of productive and unproductive labor like the Physiocrats' theory of the *ordre naturel des sociétés*. Most interesting, it includes a theory of gravitation like that of Newton's natural philosophy. The difference with the previous cases is that the domain of phenomena to which the theoretical mechanism applies is altogether different (Jensen 1976; Worland 1976; Lowry 1974; Cremaschi 1981).

A thesis that I have discussed extensively in earlier works is that the case of the transfer of one theoretical entity from natural to moral philosophy is not radically different in its nature from cases where the transfer is from a more limited (and partially not overlapping) domain to a newly defined domain (Cremaschi 1981; Cremaschi 1984: ch.4). Smith's theoretical revolution thus produces the new notion of "national economy," a notion that includes more than any of the definitions of the domains of ancestor-discourses (the right to property and the just price, commerce, the natural physical and moral order of societies); at the same time it includes less than any of these definitions, as it discards characteristics that turn out to be irrelevant, and severs or loosens links with other parts of the social whole (Cremaschi 1986).

A second, parallel feature of Smith's revolution is the shift in the understanding of the "laws" included in the theory. This can be described as a shift from a deductively normative concept of laws to a quasi-empirical and weakly normative concept of laws. It is this shift that gives to Smith's theory—as contrasted with the Physiocrats' discovery of a natural and essential order of societies—the character of a scientific Galilean theory. On the other hand, these are not the purely descriptive laws of the logical empiricist reading of Smith (e.g., Bitterman 1940). A central feature of the Classical paradigm, up to the time of the Marginalist revolution, will be the immediately applied and normative consequences of its pure scientific laws (Cremaschi 1986).

The most powerful enabling factor behind this twofold revolution is the "Galilean break" made by Smith: he understands moral philosophy, in the spirit of Hume's "Moral Newtonianism," as a theoretical enterprise aimed not at establishing definitions of essences, but rather at introducing non-ultimate hypotheses to "save the phenomena" (THN I Introduction; Cremaschi 1981; Cremaschi 1984: ch.3). It is the Galilean break that makes it possible to conceive of several coexisting partial orders (versus the unitary order of rationalistic Natural Law), and it is this break that allows for an understanding of these several orders as weakly normative.

It is pointless to recall how such an attitude enabled Smith's political economy to gain much more empirical content than its ancestor-discourses. It is important instead to suggest that this Galilean break was directly influenced by, or at least very similar to, the image of Newtonian natural science offered by "The History of Astronomy." The central feature of the Newtonian epistemology, i.e., the separation of the ultimate principles of reality from the intermediate principles of the theory, lies at the core of Smith's revolution in political economy. This central feature was actually a sore point, but in political economy it was also the pivotal point around which a powerful new theoretical system revolved.

Natural Justice, Prejudice, and Corruption

The Galilean break—with all its unresolved epistemological dilemmas— proved highly productive in the construction of the first specialized social science. This break was at the core of Smith's attempt at formulating a weaker system of Natural Law. In this attempt the dilemmas of the Galilean break come more urgently to the fore and can be held eventually responsible for Smith's political disenchantment, for a hopelessly pessimistic diagnosis of the development of civilization, for a discouraging appreciation of the limits of political action and—most important—for the admission of an unbreakable circular connection between "natural sentiments" and the "natural course of things" that leaves no appeal against evil in history and that leads to a reluctant but resigned surrender to prejudice, oppression, and injustice.

A few words are in order about the development of Smith's attitude. An established result of Smith's scholarship is the acknowledgment of a progressive shift of the hub of Smith's "skeptical Whiggism" from the "Whig" term to the "skeptical" term (Mizuta 1975; Forbes 1977a: 181–182). Thus, the young lecturer who incidentally still talks of "natural reason" (LJ(A) i.1; ii.29; i.24; i.54; i.26; ii.32) as a basis for valuation raises his voice much louder against "so much oppressive inequality" (ED 5) of commercial society than the old writer of the additions to the sixth edition of *The Theory of Moral Sentiments*. Along the same line, confidence in the goodness of "natural sentiments" vanished as the first edition of *The Theory of Moral Sentiments* was replaced by subsequent editions (TMS III.2.30 ff.; I.iii.3; Mizuta 1975: 127–129). It was not merely a matter of individual psychology but rather of the general climate of ideas. But the direction of Smith's evolution, even if viewed against the background of the course of development of this climate of ideas, still appears as some sort of compelled outcome of some basic aporias of his system of ideas. It is on these aporias rather than on the changing opinions that I will focus.

Highly valuable reconstructions have been made in recent literature of Smith's partially pessimistic diagnosis concerning the evolution of modern British society, of his concern with "corruption" or with decadence of "virtue," of his partly cyclical vision of the history of political institutions, of his concern—even if with partially different conclusions from Hume's—

with the risks of standing armies and even more of growing public debt (Salvucci 1966: ch.1; Pocock 1975: 504–505; Winch 1978: chs. 4 and 6). An even more important aspect that has been highlighted is his concern about the losses implied by civilization: the division of labor carries with it mental mutilation of the workers, and a loss of martial virtue and of civic spirit is consequent. The urbanization of growing masses carries with it the severing of the links that grant social control over individuals and consequently good morals. The damages of the division of labor and of urbanization carry with them that splenetic spirit that may favor "enthusiasm" (Cropsey 1957: 96 ff.; Cropsey 1963: 88–93; Reisman 1976: 63 ff.; Winch 1978: 97–99; 113–120). In terms of political doctrines, such developments render impossible any recourse to civic spirit, understood in the civic humanist tradition; the merchants are the only group able to understand the interests of society, but this group is the only one whose interests are contrary to those of the whole (Robertson 1983: 460–465).

Derived from the above diagnosis is Smith's choice of constitutional engineering, understood as a choice of the second best if contrasted with the hope of preserving civic virtue from corruption. The thesis I argue for is that the general framework of the diagnosis and the chosen strategy are determined not only by a crude description of "facts," but to a high degree by Smith's theoretical premises on unintended results, natural sentiments, self-interest, and passions.

A second question that may bring us closer to the central question concerns the limits Smith poses to political discourse. In its stricter sense (as contrasted with the overall background social theory) political discourse has a rather limited scope in comparison with the scope of the seventeenth-century Natural Law "politics" or with Rousseau's "democratic" understanding of politics. Natural jurisprudence is primarily concerned with "natural justice," a negative virtue, and when it is concerned with "police" it is limited to a strategy of the second best, exactly because the big job is done—if not in the best way, at least better than any way available to us—by functionalist readjustments of the social whole and by historical evolution. The action of the "man of government" in the complex commercial society may help solve problems of social integration on some of the several levels of this complex society (defense, justice, education) in a highly artificial way, very far from an unduly extended laissez faire attitude, but imitating solutions that are already naturally offered by the development of commercial society, such as division of labor and market mechanisms (Robertson 1984: 469–471). The "legislator," Smith's figure of ideal politician, is very different from the mythical figures of founding fathers that enchanted Rousseau: the legislator may be inspired by the principle of "utility" to better the institutions of his country, but his leading principle must be prudence, understood in very non-Aristotelian terms. The figure of the legislator is described in the sixth edition of *The Theory of Moral Sentiments* in highly Burkean terms:

> He may re-establish and improve the constitution, and from the very doubtful and ambiguous character of the leader of a party, he may assume the greatest

and noblest of all characters, that of the reformer and legislator of a great state; and, by the wisdom of his institutions, secure the internal tranquillity and happiness of his fellow citizens for many succeeding generations . . . though he should consider some of them [the established powers and privileges] as in some measure abusive, he will content himself with moderating, what he often cannot annihilate without great violence. When he cannot conquer the rooted prejudices of the people by reason and persuasion, he will not attempt to subdue them by force . . . and will remedy as well as he can, the inconveniences which may flow from the want of those regulations which the people are averse to submit to. When he cannot establish the right, he will not disdain to ameliorate the wrong. (TMS VI.ii.2.14-16)

The biggest danger in politics seems to be the "spirit of system," displayed by reformers who produce every kind of unforeseeable result while trying to achieve an abstract rational order (TMS VI.ii.2.17).

The two preceding points could not be the final proof of any kind of aporia in Smith's system of ideas. The hypothesis could be put forth at most of an "elective affinity" between such diagnoses and some latent stalemate of Smith's thinking. The third point I shall develop is what I would like to name the predicament of nature. While adding a few elements to the general picture of Smith's pessimistic attitude, it brings to the fore the latent aporias of his political thought and reveals how they are closely linked with the Galilean break.

The ultimate regulative criterion came to Smith from contemplative utilitarianism, the attitude suggested by Reason and philosophy, the one that may encourage the pursuit of virtue and wisdom in every case in which the uninstructed natural sentiments are not enough. It is important to recall that contemplative utilitarianism is not some kind of attitude for Sundays, to be contrasted with an empirical survey of actual behaviors, to which we should have recourse on weekdays (as suggested by Campbell 1971: 51–52; 219). The "natural sentiments" provide a second and more effective basis for normativity, and there is a constant interaction between the first and the second basis. The second basis holds to the extent that it is a more or less truthful approximation of the first (Cremaschi 1984: ch.2; Haakonssen 1981: 135–153). Smith's project of a natural jurisprudence is precisely the project of a renewed Natural Law free of the main shortcomings of its rationalistic versions, primarily the lack of empirical content. Within this context the notion of nature to which this natural law refers is different from the seventeenth-century notion of nature: a typical feature of the eighteenth-century notion, present in Smith, is the opposition between Reason and nature. The eighteenth-century notion of nature has long been mocked as lacking in consistency, or it has been considered too vague and too obscure to be of any interest to philosophers. What has been overlooked however is the meaningfulness this idea recovers when put into the context of the intellectual strategy of eighteenth-century philosophers such as Smith (Preti 1957: 37–43). The idea of nature seems necessary for Smith to formulate a research program—it is the bridge between two poles, the individual mind and reality-in-itself. The following discussion will try to show how this research strategy is essential both for natural science and for political theory.

Within the framework of the project of a weaker Natural Law, Smith discovers mechanisms of selection of behaviors useful to the preservation of society (Haakonssen 1981: 67–74). It is important to stress that the individual mechanisms do not fit into a general functionalist empirical theory of society, but that their discovery helps in the foundation of such a normative-empirical discourse as the part on "justice" of natural jurisprudence. A general functionalist view of society emerges only at a different level, i.e., of that "dogmatic" precomprehension of social reality offered to the contemplative utilitarian. It is this difference from twentieth-century sociology that makes the use of a term such as "proto-functionalism" appropriate. It is precisely because "natural justice" is a standard of judgment that needs to be explicated by a "grammar" of justice, i.e., by "natural jurisprudence" (TMS III.6.11), rather than the subject matter of a sociological explanation, that a number of shortcomings cannot be carelessly dealt with as mere diagnoses, made by Smith, of what is going on, since they are decisive difficulties in which his own system of ideas is caught.

The difficulties, well known to Smith scholars, are the following. First, the natural sense of justice is unavoidably blended with prejudice: the wealthier and more powerful people command our sympathy; we feel much more strongly about the smallest inconvenience to ourselves and our closest relations than about the biggest disaster that may happen to very distant people; and most of all, custom rules to such an extent over our natural sentiments that every law and institution that is old commands respect regardless of whether it is just (TMS II.ii.3–4; VI.ii.3.6; IV.2.14; VI.ii.2.11–18).

Second, human rapacity and oppressive inequality are "natural" in a sense that it is difficult to distinguish from the sense in which natural sentiments are "natural." There is a "natural wish to dominate" that belongs among the basic human passions. As a consequence, such institutions as slavery still represent, in Smith's eyes, more the norm than the exception (LJ(A) iii.130; WN III.ii.10; IV.vii.b.53–56).

Third, solutions outlive their usefulness. The most striking case was the survival of infanticide in classic societies, when the hardship was over that could have justified such a cruel practice in primitive societies (TMS V.2.14–16).

Given the last difficulty, the thesis of the generally beneficial character of the mechanisms of selection of appropriate behavior is a scant comfort and can hardly guarantee goodness of our unreflected valuations, as it still could for a confident Deist such as Smith's teacher Hutcheson. The acknowledgment of these difficulties is much more than a description of contradictions existing in reality: it constitutes a stalemate of Smith's thinking. The term "nature," in the exertion of providing a weaker and non-vacuous basis for normativity, is so twisted that a misplaced circular path arises between "natural sentiments" and "the natural course of things." The gap between the ultimate order and the Machiavellian *verità effettuale* cannot be solidly filled by our variable and corruptible "natural sentiments" (Preti 1957: 171–172).

To sum up: Smith tries to keep the main idea of Natural Law philosophy, namely the idea of a law preceding positive law, while trying to abandon the aprioristic approach of Natural Law philosophers. He departs from them, accepting the Galilean break made by Montesquieu, not to deduce the right system of law, but rather to reconstruct the genesis of the several systems of law. Within the framework provided by this approach, the possibility of a natural law is rescued via Hutcheson's and Hume's idea of moral sentiment. The "natural sentiments" of mankind should pave a midway between the ideal order of reality of the contemplative utilitarian attitude and the purely factual order of the "natural course of things." Natural sentiments, or natural justice, are the tool in a desperate attempt to stop the run from Natural Law to Historicism at some intermediate point. The attempt is doomed to failure because what is natural for Smith, in the exertion of gaining enough empirical content not to fall back into the nature of rationalistic Natural Law philosophy, ends up with appearing as prejudice and whim, as arbitrary as the positive laws it was called forth to judge.

The recognition of some kind of unbridgeable gap between an ever farther off ultimate order and the order according to which human beings actually feel and behave would have probably been the last word of Smith's unwritten work on natural jurisprudence.

> The great judge of the world, has, for the wisest reasons, thought proper to interpose, between the weak eye of human reason, and the throne of his eternal justice, a degree of obscurity and darkness. . . . If those infinite rewards and punishments, which the Allmighty has prepared for those who obey or transgress his will, were perceived as distinctly as we foresee the frivolous and temporary retaliations which we may expect from one another, the weakness of human nature . . . could no longer attend to the little affairs of this world; and it is absolutely impossible that the business of society could have been carried out. (TMS (2nd ed.) III.2.31)

Truth, Virtue, and the Unbridgeable Gap

It was a long time ago that the seventeenth century was believed to be the age of a self-confident and incurably optimistic Enlightenment. The importance of historical pessimism in seventeenth-century thought is now universally acknowledged (Günther 1984). I would like to establish a link between this pessimistic climate of opinion and the topic of the crisis of knowledge recognizable in Hume's *Treatise* and Smith's "History of Astronomy." As for Hume, the suggestion has been made that the topic of the crisis of knowledge plays a central role in the *Treatise*, a role that anticipates Husserl's *Krisis* (Davie 1977: 71). I shall suggest that Smith not only shows the same awareness of the crisis of the original promises of the "new science," but also that this awareness is connected with the feeling of the crisis of a civilization, to be acknowledged both in the history of science and in the history of civil society that has carried along "free governments." The factors felt as conflicting in the two fields are, I think, in an important sense analogous. In both domains Smith's thinking is under the spell of Cartesian presuppositions that it cannot fully overcome. How do these presuppositions generate the conflict in the two domains?

Adam Smith, in his reconstruction of the history of astronomy, concludes that we are irresistibly drawn to view the Newtonian system as the discovery of truth concerning reality. This seems to stem from an ineluctable tendency of the imagination. The needs of our imagination compel us to take for granted the possibility of theoretical progress, i.e., of a greater "truth" or of closer correspondence to reality for each successive theory. They compel us to take for granted that theory change is rational, that it does not depend on pure fashion. Strictly speaking, the criteria according to which a theory is judged better than another one provide no guarantee regarding its truth as *adaequatio*. The best theory connects the phenomena in a better way (but that implies only that it is an ingenious device, not that it reflects reality) or extends a hypothesis from a familiar domain to a new one (but that may be merely the result of an arbitrary demand of our imagination, and the choice of the hypothesis to be used can depend entirely on custom).

Smith is consequently forced to state that the only possible conclusion of a critical examination of our theories on nature is that even the Newtonian system is an imaginary machine; this imaginary machine satisfies to the utmost degree the requirements of the human mind, but that is no guarantee that the theory represents the "real chains used by Nature to connect the phenomena." The criteria of simplicity, familiarity, coherence, and comprehensiveness are not strictly criteria of truth of the theories or criteria of the rationality of theory change. These criteria are, in a sense, arbitrary, as they depend on some laws of the mind that have nothing in common with the laws of reality.

The general metaphysical presuppositions of Humean thought, shared by Smith, are the eventual reason for this aporetical status of the criteria of truth and of theoretical progress. In the critical literature on Hume it is generally accepted that Hume's main unchallenged presuppositions, which determine his skeptical-naturalistic outcome, are basically identical with the presuppositions shared by the mainstream of modern thought, and first of all, by Descartes: the presupposed separation of *res cogitans* from *res extensa*, the absolute distinction between order of ideas and order of reality, the atomistic nature of reality and of ideas, and possibly solipsism (N. K. Smith 1941: 559; Dal Pra 1967: 78–88). The historian of science Adam Smith, while leaving his "History of Astronomy" unfinished, apparently felt—two centuries before the crisis of the "standard view"—that it was impossible to account for the historical phenomenon "science" as precomprehended by our culture, so far as the Cartesian presuppositions are accepted. The separation of the order of ideas from the order of things and the atomistic nature of phenomena (which makes the individual phenomenon unintelligible) are presupppositions that make it impossible to acknowledge any kind of rationality in the history of science, or to formulate any idea of the truth of scientific theories that makes sense (Bernstein 1983: 51–108).

Let us compare now the crisis of science with the crisis of politics. All the main modern thinkers started as defenders of the rights of the individual and ended with a vindication of the rights of the collective, of the state, and of realpolitik over the individual. That may be the case for Smith as well: the biographical pattern, moving in the direction of an increasingly skeptical and decreasingly whiggish attitude, may serve as a parable for logical developments of ideas, and the inability to write the "history and theory of law and government" may be the symptom of a deeply felt trouble, like the inability to write a conclusion to the "History of Astronomy." The case of Adam Smith's natural jurisprudence may be considered an example of the failure of modern liberal political thought to fulfill the task Smith had assigned himself (Unger 1975: 83–100).

At the core of the predicament of Smith's political thought is the contradiction between the need he feels to keep a gap between the ultimate order of reality and the weaker order of "natural sentiments," and the need to postulate a convergence between the two orders that can be asserted only dogmatically. Any of the available solutions to the contradiction would make the self-imposed task impossible: it would lead back to rationalistic Natural Law if the gap were filled, or it would head toward Historicism, Legal Positivism, and "Political Science" if the mysterious convergence between the two orders were wiped out. In no case would natural jurisprudence, or a science of the principles upon which civil governments ought to be directed, still be possible. The object of modern rationalistic Natural Law, namely a universal basis for rights, could not be provided in nonvacuous terms by Rationalism. The opposite attempt, carried out by Smith in sentimentalist terms, was unable to provide that basis in universal and necessary terms.

Smith's attempt was doomed to failure because of the logical, anthropological, and ontological presuppositions he shared with Rationalism: a sharp distinction between essence and phenomena, which leaves the gap open between the ultimate order and the actual course of things; atomism, which makes the social wholes totally heterogeneous from individuals; an understanding of reason in analytic-instrumental terms, which makes practical rationality impossible in principle and leaves the natural sentiments in the condition of an empirical fact, called on to fulfill the impossible task of providing a basis for normativity.

It appears that in Smith's system of ideas the main element common to science and politics is the "crisis." In both domains the source of the antinomies seems to be the set of basic Cartesian presuppositions shared by the mainstream of modern thought. The antinomies cannot be adequately explored because of the inability of Smith and of eighteenth-century thought to focus on this common background of hidden premises.

An important part of twentieth-century thought, ranging from the Pragmatist thinkers to the later Wittgenstein, to Hermeneutics, and to the Frankfurt

School, can be interpreted as a massive critique of Cartesianism. Questions of radical redefinition of both scientific and political rationality are on the agenda (Bernstein 1983: 16–20). The exploration of one chapter of the vicissitudes of Cartesianism in science and in politics may prove useful to the present discussion.

The Crisis of Cartesian Reason

To start with, it can be suggested that there is indeed a link between Smith's political theory and his epistemology. The link can be described as a direct influence of the image of the right method—presented in "The History of Astronomy," that is, the image of Newtonian natural science, or of what seemed to be the best performance of human reason up to Smith's time—on his theorizing in the field of natural jurisprudence. The consequences of this methodological influence are twofold: first, Smith fights the "spirit of system," trying to develop a political theory free from that apriorism typical of the theories of Locke, Hobbes, Grotius, and Pufendorf. Second, Smith dismisses a unitary (descriptive and normative) order of society and brings in several different coexisting orders: his main achievement in this direction is the discovery of the (relatively) autonomous self-regulating order of the market.

A second and more interesting suggestion is based on the answer to a somewhat different question: besides the direct link between epistemology and politics, is there some kind of analogical relationship between Smith's image of science and his image of politics? Smith's account of science is forced to maintain two contradictory views of scientific truth, namely an internal psychological criterion, and an external "copy" criterion of truth. In a strikingly similar way, Smith's politics cannot give up two contradictory demands, namely the need to appeal to some kind of natural law, preceding the several positive laws and based on the natural sentiments of mankind, and the acknowledgment that the natural sentiments are not metahistorical and universal, but are dependent on social circumstances, on innate tendencies of human imagination, on deeply rooted traditions, on ignorance and prejudice. In both fields the human mind is the victim of an unavoidable, but at the same time necessary, deception. I think that what happens behind the scenes, and is responsible for this similarity, is that Smith is facing one and the same challenge in both fields, namely, he is trying to limit the consequences of the acknowledged impossibility to grasp the "order of reality" or "reason in itself," as the Rationalists still felt able to do. The substitute Smith offers is the postulate of an "order in the mind" as far as the knowledge of nature is concerned and the postulate of a reasonable (as contrasted with rational) "order of Nature" as far as social reality is concerned. These two orders are somehow of a "weaker" kind, being supposed to portray the ultimate order approximately, in a rather mysterious way. It is possible to make sense of this double move by Smith only if it is viewed as a way of dealing with the crisis of the solution that Rationalism had provided for the tasks of explaining reality and of giving a foundation to norms.

Here it must be stressed once more—against all attempts to modernize Smith through a radical translation of his theories into contemporary terms— that the idea of nature is, in this context, more essential than ever: it provides a buffer between Reason in reality and Reason in the mind. The notion of nature is appealed to in order to fulfill the dual tasks of formulating explanations and of establishing norms. This dependency on the laws of human nature or on the laws of the mind seems to confer on our theories on nature something more than a purely instrumental value, and to the valuations dictated by natural sentiments a status different from that of mere facts to be explained by a sociological theory.

I have already suggested that the eighteenth-century idea of nature, in order to make sense, needs to be appreciated in terms of the intellectual strategies it was called forth to serve. Both in politics and in natural science "nature" seems for Smith a possible bridge between two poles, the individual mind and the ultimate order of reality. Seventeenth-century Rationalism felt no need for a bridge or buffer, as there was an apparent continuity between reason in the individual mind and Reason with which reality is informed or that is the essence of reality. The idea of nature, in its typical eighteenth-century connotation, is indispensable for Smith to formulate his research program, one that might possibly find a third way for natural science between aprioristic essentialism and instrumentalism, and a third way for politics between a deductivist Natural Law philosophy and a Hobbesian or Mandevillian cynical attitude (Forbes 1977b: 43–44; Preti 1957: 37–43).

The continuation of the story, after Smith, is well known: in nineteenth-century politics the idea of nature was to be replaced by the apparently much more self-evident idea of history or—on the opposite front—an Archimedean point would be sought in a noumenal realm of values, sharply contrasted with the empirical realm of facts. In nineteenth-century natural science, a "Humean" positivism was to establish itself, resting on skeptical foundations in the theory of knowledge, but at the same time able to overlook these foundations while appealing to the undoubted success of science in the predictive control of facts. The destinies of science and of politics were to move further and further apart as the nice dual seventeenth-century framework (natural philosophy vs. moral philosophy) was replaced by an increasingly complex map of knowledge.

The crisis of reason of the eighteenth century, appearing in a striking way in Hume's *Treatise*, and developed in some of its consequences in Smith's writings, raises a number of questions that twentieth-century thought is still trying to answer. This is the crisis of unitary Cartesian Reason. Its two aspects, namely the crisis of natural science and the crisis of politics, appear as parallel exactly because they are one stage of a run that, starting from the unitary Reason of Rationalism, leads to the present proliferation of "reasons." In the culture of the twentieth century, characterized by a proliferation of different languages, bodies of knowledge, and practices, each with its own epistemological status, it would be hard to find one science to be contrasted with one politics.

The task still to be carried out, beyond the contributions of the later Wittgenstein, of Pragmatism, of Hermeneutics, and of the Frankfurt School, is both highly destructive and creative: it is the task of eliminating the last vestiges of Cartesianism that still hinder an adequate self-understanding of the markedly differentiated forms of rational practice of our culture (Bernstein 1983: 16–27). Science and politics will appear then as two out of several rational practices, and the problem of the relationship between science and politics will be solved, or rather dissolved.

Acknowledgments

This chapter has greatly benefited from comments by Don Herzog and Lorenzo Ornaghi, and from discussions with Ora Gruengard and Marcelo Dascal on several previous versions.

Notes

1. "The History of Astronomy" was never published during the author's lifetime. The essay is a part of a wider collection along with two shorter and possibly less elaborated essays on "The History of Ancient Physics" and "The History of Ancient Logics and Metaphysics," under the general heading: "The Principles which lead and direct Philosophical Enquiries."

2. See Meek, Raphael, and Stein 1977: 32–35. The two main sets of notes are published together in *Lectures on Jurisprudence*.

3. Obviously enough, I am referring to the sociological notion of functionalism. According to its founding father, Malinowski, it is "explanation of . . . facts . . . by the part they play within the integral system of culture, by the manner in which they are related to each other within the system, and by the manner in which this system is related to the physical surroundings" (quoted by Emmet 1967). The classification of Smith's background social theory as "functionalist" has been made in Campbell (1977: 528). The qualifier "proto," which I have added, is meant to convey the idea that Smith's background social theory, while very far from being a methodologically self-aware statement of such a view, is however a first step in this direction, providing an overall picture of the social system as a multi-level system of interactions.

4. Such a reactionary move has already been made by Robertson (see Robertson 1983: 482). To my taste he goes a little too far in this direction.

References

Becker, James J. F. 1961. Adam Smith's theory of social science. *Southern Economic Journal* 28(1): 13–21.

Bernstein, Richard J. 1983. *Beyond Objectivism and Relativism: Science, Hermeneutics, and Praxis*. Oxford: Blackwell.

Bitterman, Henry J. 1940. Adam Smith's empiricism and the law of nature. *Journal of Political Economy* 48(4–5): 487–520, 703–734.

Campbell, Thomas D. 1971. *Adam Smith's Science of Morals*. London: Allen and Unwin.

_____. 1977. Adam Smith and natural liberty. *Political Studies* 25(4): 523–534.

Cremaschi, Sergio. 1981. Adam Smith, Newtonianism and political economy. *Manuscrito* 5(1): 117–134.

_____. 1982. Adam Smith, l'economia politica e la filosofia morale. In Luigi Ruggiu (ed.), *Genesi dello Spazio Economico.* Napoli: Guida, pp. 147–184.

_____. 1984. *Il sistema della Ricchezza. Economia Politica e Problema del Metodo in Adam Smith.* Milano: Angeli.

_____. 1986. The idealization of economic reality in classical political economy. In Evandro Agazzi, Marco Mondadori, and Sandra Tugnoli Pattaro (eds.), *Logica e Filosofia della Scienza, Oggi. Atti del primo Congresso della SILFS,* vol.2: "Epistemologia e Logica Induttiva." Bologna: CLUEB, pp. 257–262.

Cropsey, Joseph. 1957. *Polity and Economy: An Interpretation of the Principles of Adam Smith.* The Hague: Nijhoff.

_____. 1963. Adam Smith. In Leo Strauss and Joseph Cropsey (eds.), *History of Political Philosophy.* Chicago: Rand McNally College Publishing Company, 1972 (2nd ed.).

• Dal Pra, Mario. 1967. L'astrazione nella filosofia di Hume. *Rivista Critica di Storia della Filosofia* 22(4): 435–456.

Davie, George. 1977. Edmund Husserl and 'the as yet, in its most important respect, unrecognized greatness of Hume.' In George P. Morice (ed.), *David Hume. Bicentenary Papers.* Edinburgh: Edinburgh University Press, pp. 66–67.

Dippel, Horst. 1981. *Individuum und Gesellschaft. Soziales Denken zwischen Tradition und Revolution: Smith-Condorcet-Franklin.* Göttingen: Vandenhoek und Ruprecht.

Emmet, Dorothy H. 1967. Functionalism in sociology. In Paul Edwards (ed.), *The Encyclopedia of Philosophy,* vol. 3. London: Macmillan, pp. 256–259.

Forbes, Duncan. 1954. 'Scientific' whiggism: Adam Smith and John Millar. *Cambridge Journal* 7: 643–670.

_____. 1977a. Sceptical whiggism, commerce, and liberty. In A. S. Skinner and T. Wilson (eds.), *Essays on Adam Smith.* Oxford: Clarendon Press, pp. 179–201.

_____. 1977b. Hume's science of politics. In George P. Morice (ed.), *David Hume. Bicentenary Papers.* Edinburgh: Edinburgh University Press, pp. 39–50.

Günther, H. 1984. Optimismus. In Joachim Ritter and Karlfried Gruender (eds.), *Historisches Wörterbuch der Philosophie,* vol.6. Basel-Stuttgart: Schwabe Verlag, pp. 1240–1246.

Haakonssen, Knud. 1981. *The Science of a Legislator. The Natural Jurisprudence of David Hume and Adam Smith.* Cambridge: Cambridge University Press.

Hetherington, Norris S. 1983. Isaac Newton's influence on Adam Smith's natural laws in economics. *Journal of the History of Ideas* 44(3): 497–505.

Hume, David. [THN]. 1964. A treatise of human nature. In Thomas H. Green and Thomas H. Grose (eds.), *The Philosophical Works,* vols. 1 and 2. Aalen: Scientia Verlag (reprint).

Jensen, Hans E. 1976. Sources and contours of Adam Smith's conceptualized reality in the 'Wealth of Nations.' *Review of Social Economics* 34(3): 259–274.

Lindgren, John R. 1973. *The Social Philosophy of Adam Smith.* The Hague: Nijhoff.

Lowry, S. Todd. 1974. The archaeology of the circulation concept in economic theory. *Journal of the History of Ideas* 35(3): 429–444.

Meek, Ronald L. 1976. *Social Science and the Ignoble Savage.* Cambridge: Cambridge University Press.

Meek, Ronald L., David D. Raphael, and P. G. Stein. 1977. Introduction. In Adam Smith, *Lectures on Jurisprudence.*

Megill, A. D. 1975. Theory and experience in Adam Smith. *Journal of the History of Ideas* 36(1): 79–94.

Mizuta, Hiroshi. 1975. Moral philosophy and civil society. In Andrew S. Skinner and Thomas Wilson (eds.), *Essays on Adam Smith*. Oxford: Clarendon Press, pp. 114-131.

Moscovici, Serge. 1956. À propos de quelques travaux d'Adam Smith sur l'histoire et la philosophie des sciences. *Revue d'Histoire des Sciences et de leurs Applications* 9(1): 1–22.

Pocock, John G. A. 1975. *The Machiavellian Moment. Florentine Political Thought and the Atlantic Republican Tradition*. Princeton: Princeton University Press.

Preti, Giulio. 1957. *Alle Origini dell'Etica Contemporanea. Adamo Smith*. Bari: Laterza.

Raphael, David D., and Macfie, Alan L. 1976. Introduction. In Adam Smith, *The Theory of Moral Sentiments*.

Raphael, David D., and Andrew S. Skinner. 1980. General Introduction. In A. Smith, *Essays*.

Reisman, David A. 1976. *Adam Smith's Sociological Economics*. London: Crom Helm.

Robertson, John. 1983. Scottish political economy beyond the civic tradition: government and economic development in the 'Wealth of Nations.' *History of Political Thought* 4(3): 451–482.

Salvucci, Pasquale. 1966. *La Filosofia Politica di Adam Smith*. Urbino: Argalia.

Skinner, Andrew S. 1974. Science and the role of imagination. In William B. Todd (ed.), *Hume and the Enlightenment*. Edinburgh: Edinburgh University Press, pp. 164–188. Reprinted in: A.S. Skinner, *A System of Social Science*. Oxford: Clarendon Press, 1979, pp. 14–41.

———. 1982. A Scottish contribution to Marxist sociology. In Ian Bradley and Michael Howard (eds.), *Classical and Marxian Political Economy. Essays in Honour of R. L. Meek*. London: Macmillan.

Smith, Adam. [TMS]. 1976. *The Theory of Moral Sentiments*, ed. by David D. Raphael and Alan L. Macfie. Oxford: Clarendon Press.

———. [WN]. 1976. *An Inquiry into the Nature and Causes of the Wealth of Nations*, ed. by Roy H. Campbell, Andrew S. Skinner and W. B. Todd. Oxford: Clarendon Press.

———. [Corr]. 1977. *The Correspondence of Adam Smith*, ed. by Ernest C. Mossner and Ian S. Ross. Oxford: Clarendon Press.

———. [LJ(A)]. 1977. Lectures on jurisprudence: report of 1762–1763. In Roland L. Meek, David D. Raphael and P.G. Stein (eds.), *Lectures on Jurisprudence*. Oxford: Clarendon Press.

———. [LJ(B)]. 1977. Lectures on jurisprudence: report dated 1796. In Roland L. Meek, David D. Raphael and P.G. Stein (eds.), *Lectures on Jurisprudence*. Oxford: Clarendon Press.

———. [ED]. 1977. Early draft of *The Wealth of Nations*. In Roland L. Meek, David D. Raphael, and P.G. Stein (eds.), *Lectures on Jurisprudence*. Oxford: Clarendon Press.

———. [Essays]. 1980. *Essays on Philosophical Subjects*, ed. by William P. D. Wightman, John C. Bryce and I. S. Ross. Oxford: Clarendon Press.

———. [HA]. 1980. The principles which lead and direct philosophical enquiries: illustrated by the History of Astronomy. In A. Smith, *Essays*.

———. [Languages]. 1984. Considerations concerning the first formation of languages. In John C. Bryce (ed.), *Lectures on Rhetoric and Belles Lettres*. Oxford: Clarendon Press.

Smith, Norman Kemp. 1941. *The Philosophy of David Hume*. London: Macmillan.

Thompson, Herbert F. 1965. Adam Smith's philosophy of science. *Quarterly Journal of Economics* 79(2): 212–233.

Unger, Roberto M. 1975. *Knowledge and Politics*. New York: Free Press.

Viner, Jacob. 1927. Adam Smith and Laissez Faire. *The Journal of Political Economy* 35: 198–217. Reprinted in J. Viner, *The Long View and the Short*. Glencoe, Ill.: Free Press, 1958.

Winch, Donald. 1978. *Adam Smith's Politics. An Essay in Historiographic Revision.* Cambridge: Cambridge University Press.

Worland, Stephen T. 1976. Mechanistic analogy and Smith on exchange. *Review of Social Economy* 34(3): 245–258.

5

Condorcet's Epistemology and His Politics

Richard H. Popkin

In considering the question, does a philosopher's epistemology have anything to do with his or her politics, one case study is especially interesting, that of the Marquis Marie-Jean-Antoine-Nicholas Caritat de Condorcet, 1743–1794. Condorcet was one of the foremost mathematicians, scientists, social scientists, and politicians of his day. He was the most important member of the *philosophes* to have lived into the period of the French Revolution. He played a very important role in the revolutionary governments up to 1793, when he had to go into hiding for opposing the execution of Louis XVI, and for opposing the Jacobin constitution. His most famous work, *L'Esquisse d'un tableau historique des progrès de l'esprit humain,* was written when he was in hiding. He died in March 1794 soon after he was captured during the Reign of Terror.

He began his intellectual career in the Jesuit Collège de Navarre. At the age of twenty-two he submitted a paper on integral calculus to the Académie des sciences; the paper was highly praised by Lagrange and d'Alembert. He became a *protégé* of Voltaire and Turgot. As a result of his early papers on mathematical and scientific topics he was elected to the Académie des sciences when he was twenty-six, and a few years later became the secretary of the academy and then its perpetual secretary. His constant stream of mathematical, scientific and philosophical publications led to his being elected to the Académie Française in 1782. As a disciple of Turgot's he began to apply his scientific views to social problems, and became a leading prerevolutionary advocate of social reform. He wrote against slavery, against the mistreatment of Protestants in France, and in favor of prison reform, legal reform, educational reform, and many other causes. He became head of the Société des Amis des Noirs and presented Thomas Jefferson with a plan for gradually abolishing slavery in the new United States. In 1789 Condorcet was elected to the Commune of Paris, and in 1791 he was elected to the Legislative Assembly. He served on many committees and drew up detailed plans for a new system of national education from kindergarten to graduate school (much of which was adopted after the revolution), plans for reorganizing health care, the legal system, the tax system, plus a complete liberal constitution for the French republic, which was set aside by the Jacobins.[1]

This brief account of Condorcet as mathematician, scientist, social scientist, philosopher and political actor in late eighteenth-century France shows that he was an active intellectual. As we will see, he had a well-worked out theory of knowledge, which led to his analyses of social problems and to his active participation in the movements attempting to solve these problems. Condorcet was a kind of a skeptic, and a kind of an empiricist, and apparently drew heavily on Hume's epistemological analyses as well as those of the French *philosophes*. Since Hume did not come to many of Condorcet's conclusions about social problems, and did not lead reform movements, we will explore why the two drew different conclusions about social, economic and political matters, and why they reacted so differently to some of the problems of their time. (It is not known if they ever met. Hume was in Paris when Condorcet was just becoming known, and several of Hume's French friends were Condorcet's early patrons and patronesses).[2]

Before delineating Condorcet's theory of knowledge, I should say something about some comments I made earlier about skepticism in the Enlightenment. At the First International Congress on the Enlightenment, held at Coppet, near Geneva, in 1963, I gave a paper in which I said that except for Hume there were no real skeptics during the Enlightenment.[3] The *philosophes* scorned Pyrrhonism, treated Pierre Bayle as the best of the Dark pre-Enlightenment Ages, and made positive claims about the possibility of our gaining knowledge now and in the future. My paper led my late friend, Giorgio Tonelli, to write a series of papers in which he characterized the epistemology of the leaders of the Age of Reason as one of pointing out the weakness of reason. He sought to show that the leading *philosophes* held to views that both admitted the limits and failings of reason to gain indubitable knowledge and contended that Newtonian sciences, clarified by the French mathematicians, provided a way of understanding the natural and human world. This way of understanding could be applied to human problems and yield reasonable proposals for their solution (Tonelli 1971, 1973, 1974, 1976). Tonelli's work has been supplemented by some important articles by Ezequiel de Olaso.[4] Keith Baker, in his basic study of Condorcet, provided the overall detailed background in the mathematical, scientific and social scientific developments during the Enlightenment that lay behind Condorcet's theory of knowledge (Baker 1975: 85–194). Condorcet was a skeptic of sorts, an empiricist of sorts, and a firm believer in intellectual progress.

One problem in casting Condorcet, or his mentors Turgot, Voltaire, and d'Alembert, into familiar classifications is that British and French empiricism in the eighteenth century diverge in many ways. Berkeley and Hume have been twisted and turned to make a neat progression from Locke's empirical questioning of innate ideas and substance, to Berkeley's questioning of matter, and Hume's of cause. The non-empirical sides of Berkeley and Hume have been hidden as long as possible to keep this historical schema together, so that the British empiricism of Jeremy Bentham, James Mill, John Stuart Mill, Bertrand Russell and A.J. Ayer could neatly follow. The more interesting and consistent history of eighteenth-century empiricism, however, moves from Locke to his continental followers, first Voltaire and 'sGravesande, and then to the *philosophes* from d'Alembert and the *encyclopédistes* to Condorcet. Continental empiricism is based on the French translation of Locke (by Pierre Coste) that makes the skeptical issue stand out more than is done in the original English, on the French edition of Pascal that was done by Voltaire and Condorcet, and on the legacy of Pierre Bayle. On the positive side it is based on the more mathematical formulation of Newtonian physics, developed from Leibniz's version of the calculus, and the great French mathematical tradition up to Laplace, with his complete formulation of the equations of Newtonian science. In some ways the French were more skeptical, more empirical and more mathematical than their English contemporaries.

Condorcet had said in the notes to his edition of the *Pensées* of Pascal:

> All those who have attacked the certainty of human knowledge have committed the same mistake. They have established (nor was it difficult to establish) that neither in the physical sciences nor in the moral sciences can we obtain the rigorous certainty of mathematical propositions. But in wishing to conclude from this that man has no sure rule upon which to found his opinions in these matters, they have been mistaken. For there are sure means of arriving at a very great probability in some cases and of evaluating the degree of this probability in a great number. (quoted in Baker 1975: 129)

For reasons Locke had offered in his *Essay,* Condorcet declared that a necessary science of nature was not attainable by human beings. We could observe empirically what happens, but not why it happens. Even Newton's laws do not guarantee that nature must behave in certain ways, and cannot be otherwise. So, in the study of nature and of human nature, we cannot attain the logical, demonstrative certainty that we find in mathematics. This is what Tonelli called "the weakness of reason." But does this not lead to a complete skepticism of the kind found in Pascal and Hume? For Condorcet the answer is yes and no.

In examining why we are certain about mathematics and possess only probabilities about the natural and human world, Condorcet, like Locke and Hume, saw that the problem was in the human observer, and not in the order of things. The world, for all that we know, can be completely determined, as the formulation of Laplace's system claimed. If we knew all of the laws of nature, the location and direction and velocity of motion of every particle of matter, we could predict the whole future course of the world and write its whole history.

Unfortunately, starting with what we know, we have only empirical observations and intuitively recognized relations of ideas. The laws we induce from our empirical observations are only probable, as far as we know, because we do not know if the future will resemble the past. For Condorcet the skepticism of Pascal, Bayle, and Hume made one realize the meager limits of our empirical knowledge. The development of the mathematics of probability, a branch of mathematics to which Condorcet, and his contemporaries, d'Alembert and Laplace, contributed a great deal, allowed one to formulate a mathematics of reasonable expectation, presuming nature continued to function uniformly. As a branch of pure mathematics, it revealed the relations of ideas, but not of things. As a means of estimating what might happen, it did not tell us what would happen, but what we as humans might expect would happen.

Pushing this a bit further, Condorcet, in his notes for his inaugural address to the French Academy, indicated that even the intuitively realized certainties of mathematics were open to some doubt. When one considered a proposition such as $2 + 2 = 4$, one saw it was certain. But could one be sure one's mind would continue to function so that in future times this proposition would appear certain?

The import of casting a faint doubt on mathematics, on somewhat similar reasons to those offered by Hume in his discussion in *A Treatise of Human Nature* concerning skepticism with regard to reason, was to allow Condorcet to claim that mathematical knowledge, natural science and the moral sciences (those applying to human affairs) were all to some degree empirical and only probable.[5] Or put more positively, the moral sciences can have the same kind of precision and exactitude as the natural sciences, and can attain the same kind of certainty.

The natural sciences and the moral sciences can both be stated with carefully defined terms and claims of reasoning from them. The certainty involved in this theoretical presentation—and in mathematics as well—is just probable, in that it is "founded on the constant order that I have observed, that every time I reexamine a proposition that I remember having seen rigorously demonstrated, I still find it evidently true" (Baker 1977: 44; Baker 1984: 74). Whether propositions in the natural or moral sciences are true about empirical reality depends upon what is found in experience, "fortified by the observation that the fact which was observed yesterday will be observed today if no circumstance has changed" (ibid.). The kind of certainty that we can have in the physical and moral sciences is based on the sort of order of facts we observe.

The order of facts in the physical and moral sciences can be expressed in terms of probabilities. It may be easier to ascertain these probabilities in the physical sciences, but Condorcet insisted it can also be done in the moral sciences. Therefore, even if one cannot attain the same rigorous certainty in physics and social science that one can in mathematics, it does not follow that we have no sure rule to follow in these sciences. We have sure means, as Condorcet said in his notes on Pascal's *Pensées*, of reaching a very great probability in some cases. When one applies the mathematics of probability, then one does not have to be stymied by skeptical doubts. One can proceed to develop a "true philosophy" (Baker 1975: 183; *Oeuvres*, III: 641).

Condorcet presented his "true philosophy" at his reception speech at the French Academy in 1782 and in his *Essai sur l'application de l'analyse à la probabilité des décisions rendues à la pluralité des voix* of 1785. Much to the surprise of his auditors and readers, Condorcet claimed that both moral and political sciences can be treated mathematically. All reasoning that we employ to direct our judgment as well as our conduct is based on probability. So-called rationally demonstrable propositions are based on the probability that what we have found intuitively true in the past, we will continue to find true in the future. More factors are involved in the propositions of natural and moral sciences. The first we call "mathematically certain," the second, "physically certain" and the third, that of the moral sciences, we call "probable." But these distinctions are really just different kinds of probabilities (*Essai:* x–xiv; Baker 1975: 184).

Without going any further into the details, Condorcet's epistemology led him to a skepticism of sorts. No knowledge—mathematical, physical or moral—was beyond doubt. Each kind of knowledge was probable in its own way. The powerful new tools of mathematical analysis that he helped to create and to publish allowed for a mathematics of the probabilities involved. Hence, there could be a positive, or true, philosophy stated in terms of probabilities based on the application of mathematics to the observations of experience.

What became the striking thrust of Condorcet's views from the time of his reception speech through his revolutionary career was his contention that the sciences dealing with human problems, the moral sciences, could have the same kind of certainty as the physical sciences (though not necessarily the same degree of certainty) *and* that the results of the moral sciences could be employed to solve human problems and to make people happier. Hence social science, not religion or the state, could bring people to better lives.

It might be more difficult to make observations about human affairs than about the motions of the planets, and it might be more difficult to find order in observations about humans than about physical nature. Nonetheless, Condorcet said in his notes on his reception speech that it should be possible to find the facts needed "to establish the first principles of ethics, of political, civil or criminal legislation, or of administration" (Baker 1977: 45; Baker 1984: 75). Thus, his epistemology should lead to his politics. The theory of knowledge that explained the nature of scientific knowledge should enable us to gain such knowledge in the moral sciences and to apply such knowledge in a wide range of human problems. The social sciences, whose certainty he had analyzed and justified, would not be just descriptive of how people behaved, but prescriptive as well. For Condorcet the social scientific knowledge about how people do behave would lead to knowledge about how they should behave, if certain human problems are to be solved.

Hume had denied that one could derive an "ought" from an "is," and hence denied the sort of theory Condorcet was advancing (cf. *Treatise,* III, part I, sec. i, 469–470). Condorcet was, in effect, claiming that human rights, natural rights, are known empirically. He contended that by observing people, we will find that all normal human, sensible beings capable of acquiring moral ideas will have the idea of justice and of right.[6] In a note that Condorcet added to the edition of Voltaire's works, he said that human beings might err about moral matters, just as they can err about anything else. "But"—he added—

> since every reasoning being will be led to the same ideas in morality as in geometry, it is no less true that these ideas are not arbitrary, but certain and invariable. They are in effect the necessary result of the properties of sensate beings capable of reasoning: they derive from their nature; from which it follows that it is sufficient to suppose the existence of these beings for the propositions founded on these notions to be true; just as it is sufficient to suppose the existence of a circle to establish the truth of propositions which develop its different characteristics.
>   . . . Thus the reality of moral propositions, their truth relative to the state of real beings, of man, depends entirely upon this truth of fact: that men are sensitive and intelligent beings.[7]

So, if we know man's actual state of affairs, we also know what man should do. Thus, social science would not just be descriptive, but would also prescribe how people should behave in various circumstances, in terms of what human nature is like. Making people behave in certain ways was not part of social science. It is part of a political action program, and political action is an art.

Condorcet's friend Thomas Jefferson proclaimed in 1776, "We hold these truths to be self-evident," and then listed the moral truths on which he and his co-revolutionists intended to build a new society. Jefferson's statement indicates two different contentions, (1) that the assertors of the Declaration of Independence hold as a matter of faith, or as a basic assumption, that all men are created equal, or (2) that the proposition "all men are created equal" is self-evident. Condorcet, in contrast, was holding that it is a fact that sensitive and intelligent beings will realize that all men are created equal. Hence, the natural and human rights are as obvious to sensitive and intelligent beings as the properties of circles and squares and of falling bodies. The principles of morality and politics can be defined just as certainly and precisely as those of the physical sciences. Both are based on observed facts. This would lead to basing political actions on evidence that was as good as that employed in natural science. Political action, however, was an art, an art to bring about rational social choices in actual historical conditions, based on social scientific knowledge. Men can improve their situations. They can do this rationally, scientifically, on the basis of their knowledge of the human condition.

In his final work, the *Esquisse d'un tableau historique des progrès de l'esprit humain,* written while hiding out from the Reign of Terror, Condorcet said in the Introduction that "the observation of human societies throughout the different stages of their development," enabled people to see

> the order of this change and the influence that each moment exerts upon the subsequent moment, and so ought also to show, in the modifications that the human species has undergone . . . the path that it has followed, the steps that it has made towards truth or happiness. Such observations upon what man has been and what he is today, will instruct us about the means we should employ to make certain and rapid the further progress that his nature allows him still to hope for. (*Sketch:* 4)

The wonderful optimism Condorcet retained during the last decade, and apparently the last days of his life, enabled him to see rational scientific progress going on indefinitely to improve the human world, in spite of all of the disasters occurring around him. The interrelationship of his theory of knowledge and his political reforms can be seen, perhaps, more clearly, if we look at a case history—his plans for eliminating slavery. (I offer this example, since I have devoted a separate study to it. I think approximately the same results would follow from examining Condorcet's plans for tax reform, educational reform, prison reform, constitutional reform, and so forth.[8])

From the time that he wrote his notes on Pascal's *Pensées*, published in 1776, to the *Esquisse* of 1794, Condorcet was constantly opposing slavery and advocating its abolition. (During the same period of time he was developing the theory of knowledge discussed above.) In 1781 he published *Réflexions sur l'esclavage des Nègres*. He became president and spokesman for the Société des Amis des Noirs just before the revolution, and in the early moments of the revolution issued an address on behalf of the Société, which began:

> We hold that all men are born free and with equal rights, regardless of their color, their nationality, or their condition of birth. We hold that no man can give up his freedom, that no man can seize the freedom of his fellow man, and that no society can legitimate such crime. We hold that, regardless of contrary laws, customs, and practices, the slave is always free, since the law of nature cannot be annulled. Accordingly, the restoration of a slave's freedom is not a gift or an act of charity. It is rather a compelling duty, an act of justice, which simply affirms an existing truth. (cited from *Adresse:* 328 and n. 73)

This statement exhibits Condorcet's "scientific" basis for his politics. Before analyzing it, I will step back to his larger presentations of his case in his *Réflexions sur l'esclavage des Nègres*. Condorcet based his abolitionist program on two contentions, (1) that the liberty and the rights of man are everywhere the same regardless of the color or nationality of the persons involved, and (2) that a crime is always a crime regardless of other factors. Both are supposedly derived from empirical study and have the degree of certainty that is possible in this area. Condorcet went as far as to mention that the claim that men could be deprived of their liberty is a contradiction like 2 + 2 = 5. Any attempt to accomplish this deprivation is a crime no matter what economic or social benefits may result from it.

The basic freedom of human beings, their right to be free, is obvious (maybe self-evident) to rational people. Since this is a basic property of people, they cannot legitimately be deprived of their freedom, though obviously they are being so deprived by illegitimate means. Further, people cannot legitimately give up their freedom, that is, sell themselves into slavery, though some people may foolishly do so. Therefore, no matter what the actual state of affairs is in the Americas, the slave is always free, since the law of nature cannot be abolished (Popkin 1984b: 36–38).

The actual, observable state of affairs is that the Africans are being enslaved, shipped to the Americas, sold as slaves, and kept as slaves. This is all empirical data that Condorcet and his abolitionist colleagues knew only too well. The marquis argued that regardless of the factual state of affairs, it was contrary to a law of nature, namely, that all people are free all of the time. If the observable fact is that a lot of people are enslaved a lot of the time, then what is the status of this law of nature? Presumably, given Condorcet's theory of knowledge, and its application to the moral sciences, the idea of human freedom is what reasonable sensate beings would all see belonged to the idea of man, as much as the properties of a circle belong to the idea of it. The idea of man is based on observation, but can be known clearly and precisely. Hence, slavery is a denial of a natural property of a person, a property that cannot be abrogated in the terms of the idea of human nature (Popkin 1984b: 36).

Condorcet's position is unlike Jefferson's claim that human liberty is self-evident. Condorcet's does require and rest on observation. But it does not rest on statistical observation—how many people are in fact enslaved at a given moment. It rests on the observation of the idea of human nature, carefully clarified and defined. This is like the scientific definition of a chemical element. Observation is followed by analysis to reveal the essential versus the accidental features, followed by definition. All examples of the element may be contaminated, may be mixed with other features. Nonetheless, based on observation, the element, in its pure form, can be defined, though we do not empirically encounter the pure form.

Condorcet also did not follow Jefferson, nor Condorcet's successor as the head of the Société des Amis des Noirs, the abbé Grégoire, in making human freedom rest on its cause—all men are endowed by their Creator with life, liberty and the pursuit of happiness.[9] For Condorcet rational people would realize that human freedom is an essential feature of the conception or understanding of human nature. Then, any abrogation of human freedom is a crime.

The next step for Condorcet was to claim that people have a compelling duty to restore people's freedom. In general, he contended that when people understand something about human social conduct, then they will want to do something about it. This is a law about human behavior, which obviously does not hold in all cases. The duty to act follows from reflection on the moral ideas of justice and virtue. "Our interest in being just and virtuous is founded on the pain necessarily inflicted on one sensitive being by the idea of the evil suffered by another" (quoted in Baker 1975: 216). So there can be a science of conduct for rational and sensitive beings, which will make clear what their choices are.

Thus, slavery is a denial of human rights. Rational and sensitive people will want to do something about this denial because we are pained by thinking of the bad things that are happening to other human beings. Being a reformer in politics and in social policy is the natural consequence of understanding how the human situation got to be what it is, though we realize the limitations of our understanding. But the actual reforming of the human scene is an art.

Condorcet, hence, not only tried to show the irrationality of slavery, and to rebut all of the arguments offered in its favor, he also advocated the abolition of slavery, presumably as an effect of understanding the pains being inflicted on slaves by violating their natural rights. In the *Esquisse* he noted that "the labours of recent ages have done much for the progress of the human mind, but little for the perfection of the human race; they have done much for the honour of man, something for his liberty, but so far almost nothing for his happiness" (*Sketch:* 169). In order to do something to regain the slave's liberty, and to accomplish something for his or her happiness, one had to work out a plan and apply it. This would be part of political art, applying knowledge to the actual situation in order to alter it.

Planning for the abolition of slavery involved not only achieving the goal of giving slaves their freedom, but also doing it in the context in which they exist, and in the society in which they exist, so that human happiness can result. In planning, Condorcet tried to gain as much information as he could about the situation in the Americas.[10] From Jefferson, Condorcet learned something of the realities, and the possible consequences of various schemes. He ended up proposing prior to the revolution a forty-year abolition plan, in which it was hoped that education, job training, and so forth would bring about a just and happy society for the ex-slaves and their masters. Jefferson, who shared a good deal of Condorcet's view, was at the same time too fearful of the possible violent consequences, ex-slaves killing their ex-masters, so that the enlightened United States put off the attempt to resolve the problem until the trauma of the Civil War forced some action.

Condorcet and his abolitionist friends found themselves after July 14, 1789, in a position to try to do something besides planning, with regard to slavery in the French colonies. However, now another element in the chain from the theory of knowledge to political action came into play. All of the scientific knowledge, the social scientific discoveries, the need and duty to relieve human suffering, had to be transferred from reform plans into actions. And here there is no sure science, no matter how limited, of what to do.

The field of political and social action is an art. Guided by knowledge, it can lead to human improvement and happiness. Unfortunately, neither Condorcet nor his abolitionist colleagues were the best politicians. For all of their theories and proposals, they were unable to overcome the opposition of the colonial planters (See Popkin 1984b: 42–43). So, as reformers have discovered over and over again, they have to be able to deal with the realities of making political changes as well as theorizing and planning for them. Dealing with the realities requires acting in the world of actual people. And here Condorcet was not too astute. Aside from his personality problems that antagonized some people more than necessary, he was not adept at pushing his reform projects during the factional struggles of revolutionary France. Instead of leading France to the future progress he foresaw at the end of the *Esquisse*, to "the abolition of the inequality between nations, the progress of equality within each nation, and the true perfection of mankind" (*Sketch:* 173), he became one of the victims of the final in-fighting among the revolutionaries.

Condorcet's theory of knowledge justified his claims of reasonably certain social scientific knowledge. His conviction that there were discoverable features of human nature, namely human rights, became a basis for social reform. His insistence that rational and sensitive persons want to alleviate the sufferings of others (a social scientific law) became the basis for social action (though this is an empirical observation subject to revision on the basis of the actual behavior of rational and sensitive people). The transfer of plans for social action into genuine change went beyond the theory, and required something different from scientific knowledge—political ability— which the philosopher or scientist did not necessarily have.

Condorcet drew some of his skepticism, some of his theory of probable knowledge, and some of his theory of social science from Hume. But when it came to plans of action the two diverged greatly. Before Condorcet had made his mark, Hume had already fallen out with the optimistic *philosophes*. The exchange of views between Hume and Condorcet's sponsor, Turgot, in 1764, showed that for all that the Scottish *philosophes* and the French ones had in common, they disagreed on a most basic matter—whether the human situation could really be improved.[11] Hume's analysis of human nature indicated that most people acted irrationally from fears, superstitions and ignorance. Hume's reading of history did not give him much hope that man was getting better or wiser. Condorcet proposed a complete revision of the educational system to deal with human fear, superstition and ignorance. Hume just cast skeptical doubt on plans for improvement.[12]

If one traced back the areas of disagreement, one would find that Condorcet held to a skeptical epistemology like that of Hume, in which mathematical, scientific and value judgments were open to doubt. However, for both Hume and Condorcet, a theory of belief was presented which explained why reasonable people had firm belief in certain mathematical and scientific propositions. Hume insisted that moral statements are not like mathematical or factual ones in that they are not based on rational factors, but are the result of the passions. For Condorcet, moral judgments and the propositions of the social sciences are based on the same sort of data as scientific propositions, and can be as certain. This presumes that we can know "justice" as clearly as we know "velocity," something Hume would never have countenanced.

On the other hand, Hume was one of the first social scientists in the modern sense. The second and third books of *A Treatise of Human Nature*, *The Enquiry Concerning the Principles of Morals*, and many of his essays attempt to provide reasonable analyses of human social problems based on inductions from empirical research. Unlike Condorcet, Hume contended that principles of justice depend entirely upon human traditions and inventions. One can then study empirically what principles have been adopted and what has happened when they were enforced (Norton 1982; Livingston 1984).

This kind of social science led Hume to a much more pessimistic outlook on the human scene than that offered by Condorcet. The latter saw social science as making clear what is just (e.g., that all men should be free), and leading reasonable people to try to bring about a just state of affairs; hence, the rationale for Condorcet's campaign to abolish slavery. Hume, in a rapid survey of what has been the case, declared, "I am apt to suspect that the negroes and in general all of the other species of men (for there are four or five different kinds) to be naturally inferior to the whites. There never was a civilized nation of any other complexion than white, nor even any individual eminent either in action or speculation" (Hume 1882: III, 252n.). This led Hume to be rather aloof from the abolitionist controversy. (His Scottish opponents, the students of Thomas Reid, were in the forefront of the abolitionist movement.) Hume allowed the defenders of American slavery to quote him authoritatively as justifying the denial of freedom to Africans transported to America (cf. Popkin 1977-1978, 1984a).

Condorcet, if he had accepted Hume's claim (which he knew to be empirically false), would have contended that the problem of non-white inferiority would have to be investigated, and if possible, remedied, since the equality of human beings was as certain as the fact that bodies gravitate. If people were functioning unequally, then the conditions causing this had to be discovered and altered.

In fact, the last point was one of the major reasons for Condorcet's advocacy of democracy in his proposed constitution. Each person was basically equal. Society had to be redesigned so that everyone's equal rights (as discovered in observing everyone's human nature) could be exercised, even if people did not have the same abilities to exercise their rights. His plan for a national public education system and for a national health plan would help accomplish this to the greatest degree possible.

The real advantages that should result from this progress, of which we can entertain a hope that is almost a certainty, can have no other term than that of the absolute perfection of the human race, since, as the various kinds of equality come to work in its favour by producing ampler sources of supply, more extensive education, more complete liberty, so equality will be more real and will embrace everything which is really of importance for the happiness of human beings. (*Sketch:* 184; Shapiro 1934)

Condorcet's optimism is hard to sustain in view of what has in fact happened, even in the most enlightened democratic societies. The increase in knowledge about nature and human nature has led to solving many problems, curing many ailments, but it has also led to enormous human-induced suffering. The insights we have gained in the twentieth century about human beings and their motives certainly makes one more skeptical than Condorcet was about finding certain truths about human nature. The activating factors in human behavior have turned out to be less benign than Condorcet thought. Knowledge does not necessarily lead to beneficial action. If it did, no one would still be smoking tobacco; hunger would have been eliminated; torture would not occur; and so on.

Thus, in conclusion, we can see that for Condorcet knowledge was supposed to lead to beneficial political action. In fact it does not. So, something is wrong with his theory. The weak link seems to be where Hume saw it in Turgot's theory of human progress. The best human knowledge about human beings is, for better or worse, applied to the human situation by human beings. They do not function rationally but, rather, function as the result of the complex interaction of rational and irrational factors. The skepticism that Condorcet accepted about human knowledge should have been extended as well to human ability to understand and act in human affairs. In the light of the horrors of human engineering in the twentieth century, we should be much more skeptical than Condorcet about the good that can be accomplished. But, I think, rather than fade into inaction, we should base our positive contributions to the human scene on the faith, rather than the knowledge, that man's lot can be improved, a faith reiterated in the supreme wisdom of Judaism, Christianity, Islam and Enlightenment humanism—a faith that should not be abandoned in the face of the man-made disasters of the twentieth century.

Notes

1. On Condorcet's career, see Baker (1975), Bouissounouse (1962), and Rowe (1984).

2. On whether they ever met, see Baker (1975: 139ff). See also Popkin (Forthcoming).

3. Popkin (1963). Since 1950 I have been offering my reading of Hume as a "consistent" Pyrrhonist. Many of my discussions of the character and importance of Hume's skepticism appear in the articles on Hume in Popkin (1980).

4. These have been published as a small volume (Olaso 1981). Olaso and I are preparing a volume of essays by Tonelli and ourselves on skepticism in the Enlightenment.

5. Baker (1975: 181–182). Compare with David Hume, *Treatise*, Book I, Part IV, pp. 180–183.

6. Condorcet, note to the Kehl edition of the *Oeuvres de Voltaire*, in *Oeuvres*, Tome IV, p. 540; and Baker 1984: 76.

7. Ibid. The translation is Baker's.

8. Popkin (1984b). Rosenfield (1984) also includes studies on Condorcet's views on emigration, hospitals and medical care, tax policy, education, penal legislation, and constitutional reform.

9. Popkin (1984b: 43–44). One assumes that Condorcet's skeptical caveats about knowledge apply to all his abolitionist reasoning. He kept writing his epistemological analyses throughout his life.

10. Condorcet's abolition plan is described in Popkin (1984b).

11. On the break between Hume and Turgot, see Bongie (1965: 47–52) and Popkin (Forthcoming).

12. See Hume (1953). There is a note by Hume at the beginning of the essay stating, "Of all of mankind, there are none so pernicious as political projectors if they have power, nor so ridiculous if they want it."

References

Baker, Keith M. 1975. *Condorcet, From Natural Philosophy to Social Mathematics.* Chicago: University of Chicago Press.

———. 1977. Condorcet's notes for a revised version of his reception speech to the Académie Française. *Studies on Voltaire and the Eighteenth Century* 119: 7–68.

———. 1984. Condorcet: A note on the problem of the randomness of ends. In Rosenfield (ed.), pp. 73–80.

Bongie, Laurence L. 1965. *David Hume: Prophet of the Counter-Revolution.* Oxford: Clarendon Press.

Bouissounouse, Janine. 1962. *Condorcet, Le Philosophe dans la Revolution.* Paris: Hachette.

Condorcet, M.-J.-A.-N. C. de. [*Essai*]. 1785. *Essai sur l'application de l'analyse à la probabilité des decisions rendues à la pluralité des voix.* Paris: Imprimerie Royale.

———. [*Oeuvres*]. 1847–1849. O'Connor and Arago edition. Paris: F. Didot Frères.

———. [*Réflexions*]. 1857. *Réflexions sur l'esclavage des Nègres.* In *Collection des Principaux Economistes.* Paris: 1857. [Reprinted by O. Zeller, Osnabrück. Volume 14, pp. 505–543].

———. [*Sketch*]. 1955. *Sketch for a Historical Picture of the Progress of the Human Mind,* translated by June Barraclough. London: Weidenfeld and Nicholson.

———. [*Adresse*]. 1975. Adresse de la Société des Amis de Noirs, à l'Assemblé Nationale, à toutes les villes de commerce, à toutes les manufactures, aux colonies, à toutes les sociétés des amis de la constitution de 1791. In David Brion Davies (ed.), *The Problem of Slavery in the Age of Revolution, 1770–1823.* Ithaca: Cornell University Press.

Hume, David. 1882. Of national characters. In T.H. Green and T.H. Grose (eds.), *Philosophical Works,* Vol. 3. London: Longman's, Green, pp. 244–257.

———. [*Treatise*]. 1951. *A Treatise of Human Nature.* Oxford: Oxford University Press.

———. 1953. On the idea of a perfect commonwealth. In Charles Hendel (ed.), *David Hume's Political Essays.* New York: Liberal Arts Press.

Livingston, Donald W. 1984. *Hume's Philosophy of Common Life.* Chicago: University of Chicago Press.

Norton, David F. 1982. *David Hume, Common Sense Moralist, Sceptical Metaphysician.* Princeton: Princeton University Press.

Olaso, Ezequiel de. 1981. *Escepticismo e Ilustración, La crisis pirrónica de Hume y Rousseau, Cuadernos de las Ideas,* 1. Valencia, Venezuela: Oficina Latinoamericana de Investigaciones Jurídicas y Sociales (Facultad de Derecho, Universidad de Carabobo).

Popkin, Richard H. 1963. Scepticism in the Enlightenment. *Studies on Voltaire and the Eighteenth Century* 24–27: 1321–1345.
———. 1977–1978. Hume's racism. *Philosophical Forum* 9: 211–226.
———. 1980. *The High Road to Pyrrhonism*. San Diego: Austin Hill Press.
———. 1984a. Hume's racism reconsidered. *The Journal* 1: 61–71.
———. 1984b. Condorcet, abolitionist. In Rosenfield (ed.), pp. 35–47.
———. Forthcoming. Hume and Condorcet. In David Williams (ed.), *Condorcet Studies*, vol. 2.
Rosenfield, Leonora C. (ed.). 1984. *Condorcet Studies*, vol. 1. Atlantic Highlands, NJ: Humanities Press.
Rowe, Constance. 1984. The present-day relevance of Condorcet. In Rosenfield (ed.), pp. 15–33.
Shapiro, J. Salwyn. 1934. *Condorcet and the Rise of Liberalism*. New York: Octagon Books.
Tonelli, Giorgio. 1971. The 'weakness' of reason in the age of Enlightenment. *Diderot Studies* 14: 217–244.
———. 1973. Maupertuis et la critique de la métaphysique. In *Actes de la Journée Maupertuis*. Paris: Vrin, pp. 79–90.
———. 1974. Pierre-Jacques Changeux and scepticism in the French Enlightenment. *Studia Leibnitiana* 6: 106–126.
———. 1976. The philosophy of d'Alembert. A sceptic beyond scepticism. *Kant-Studien* 67: 353–371.

6
John Stuart Mill: Fallibilism, Expertise, and the Politics-Science Analogy

Stephen Holmes

Representative government, according to J. S. Mill, is much more restless and onward-moving than government by consent. A defeated minority may agree to a decision-making procedure even while disapproving of a particular decision; but to the outcome of such a procedure, those who are outvoted, by definition, do not consent. What they *can* do is discuss and, in discussing, they can contribute vitally to a process of collective learning. Public learning is the heart of liberal democracy, or so Mill believed. His political theory was thus indissolubly linked to his theory of knowledge or, at the very least, to his theory of the growth of knowledge.

Publicity and the Growth of Knowledge

Representative government is itself a cognitive process, designed to maximize the production, accumulation, and implementation of politically relevant truths. Because he conceived of representative government in this way, Mill rejected an economic or privatistic interpretation of liberal citizenship. Voting is not a private right but a public trust. Truth does not hinge upon revealed preferences. Liberal democracy is a set of institutionally anchored procedures *both* for aggregating pregiven interests *and* for rationally transforming interests in the course of public discussion. Because of this second function, representative government cannot be adequately described in categories used for analyzing consumer satisfaction and economic exchange.

Mill is often grouped among self-realization theorists of democracy. But his profound commitment to the analogy between politics and science (to be criticized below) jars rudely with romantic interpretations of his thought. True, he considered political participation to be personally rewarding—a way to cultivate one's feelings, widen one's horizons, exercise one's higher faculties, and strengthen one's character. But his central argument was less narcissistic. Free speech is valuable because of its positive influence on the quality of collective decisions. Indeed, participation in politics has a beneficial effect on individual character only when citizens pursue a goal less personal than self-improvement. Their principal end in view should be the intelligent governance of the community.

Public debate allows truth to prevail over error. Compared with the position adopted by ostensibly "more democratic" theorists, this Miltonian thesis is quite radical.[1] Publicity is a disinfectant, a way of flushing out corruption and exposing abuses of power. But publicity also exerts a more positive influence: it is a stimulant as well as a depressant. As Mill described it, public discussion is a machine for gathering facts, correcting past errors, generating new policy suggestions, and enlisting the creative energies and decentralized intelligence of citizens in solving common problems. Not only representatives, moreover, but *all* citizens are called upon to take part in public debate: "by the utmost possible publicity and liberty of discussion . . . not merely a few individuals in succession, but the whole public, are made, to a certain extent, participants in the government" (Considerations: 436). Like an economic market, the free market of ideas mobilizes dormant resources (for example, minds working at one-half capacity), which can help make government more intelligent, better informed, and more aware of troubling side effects. Both representative institutions and freedom of the press have a crucial *mobilizing function*.[2] Autocratic governments, issuing commands and expecting their citizens silently to obey, deprive themselves of a powerful resource locked within their own citizens. Such regimes are self-impoverishing.[3]

A legally guaranteed right of opposition is an essential component of democratic government. To help make collective decisions as intelligently as possible, critics of governmental officials and policies must not only be protected but even institutionally encouraged. Uncriticizable rulers never learn of their problems until it is too late. If policies are set publicly and public criticism is rewarded, by contrast, a government can avoid self-contradictory legislation, nip crises in the bud, and promptly correct its own mistakes. Furthermore, the "collision" (On Liberty: 229) of ideas sharpens the minds of all parties, yielding suggestions no one would have conceived of in isolation and producing decisions more adequate than any proposals presented at the outset. Public opinion is a progressive force only when it is formed in a free-for-all public debate. Without institutional inducements for public criticism and opposition, in fact, political unanimity is likely to be a sign of irrational conformism.[4] For the sake of collective rationality, "a perpetual and standing Opposition to the will of the majority" must be kept up (Bentham: 108).

Beneath these political claims lies an epistemological principle that later came to be known as fallibilism. We cannot remove an idea from our minds and compare it with "reality" to determine if the two correspond. So how can we know if our beliefs are true? Mill's trenchant answer was that "[t]he beliefs which we have most warrant for, have no safeguard to rest on, but a standing invitation to the whole world to prove them unfounded" (On Liberty: 232). Indeed, intellectual honesty demands that we energetically strive to refute our own convictions. If you haven't played the devil's advocate, attempting to disprove your own opinions, you have no reason to believe what you believe.

Mill's fallibilist epistemology inspired many of his political proposals. Consider, for example, his support of a trustee as opposed to a delegate theory of representation. A delegate is a mere agent, sent to Parliament to express the opinions of his constituents and subject to immediate recall if he deviates from his mandate. A trustee, by contrast, has ampler room for maneuver: he can vote as he thinks best, disregarding occasionally and temporarily the opinions of his electors.

The delegate model is objectionable, according to Mill, because it implies that a representative has nothing important to learn from uninhibited debate with his fellow deputies. But this assumption is unrealistic: "if he devotes himself to his duty, [a representative] has greater opportunities of correcting an original false judgment, than fall to the lot of most of his constituents" (Considerations: 509). The decisive superiority of deputies over citizens lies not in higher intelligence, virtue, or education, but in the unusual nature of the legislative situation itself. Voters are parochial, seldom exposed to the clashing viewpoints of fellow citizens who live in remote parts of the country. No one is ever invited to prove them wrong or rewarded for disclosing their follies. Voters should defer to representatives, although only in the short run, because members of an elected assembly enjoy the eye-opening benefits of exposure to mutual criticism and relentless debate.

In medieval assemblies, a deputy would represent his constituents before the king or a court of nobles. In modern parliaments, citizens represent themselves to each other. A modern legislative assembly is a machine for public learning because it guarantees that the ideas of all citizens will be "tested by adverse controversy" (Considerations: 432). Deputies are encouraged not only to uncover each other's errors but also to change their own minds when they become convinced that they have been laboring under an illusion. If recanting is intelligent, it can be justified publicly, even to the voters back home. Accountability requires that deputies explain their decisions to their constituents. Because explanations of difficult issues take time, however, a system of immediate recall makes a mockery of government by discussion. Far from being antidemocratic, the trustee theory of representation simply recognizes that public learning can never be instantaneous.

Freedom and Knowledge

Mill's entire theory of personal liberty assumes that we can distinguish clearly between actions that affect the interests of others and actions that directly affect the actor alone. Interestingly enough, Mill also justified his ideal of personal liberty by advancing a striking claim about *the lack of knowledge:* "the strongest of all the arguments against the interference of the public with purely personal conduct, is that when it does interfere, the odds are that it interferes wrongly, and in the wrong place" (On Liberty: 283). We almost never have sufficient information to save someone from himself.

The Mill of *On Liberty* was less concerned with the tyranny of the magistrate than with the tyranny of social ostracism and gossip. The entire book is a defense of personal eccentricity, nonconformism, and deviance in the face of censorious peer-group pressures. But what does a handbook for heretics have to do with representative government? Mill's often-cited definition of liberty ("the only freedom which deserves the name, is that of pursuing your own good in your own way" [On Liberty: 226]) is deafeningly silent about a nation's freedom to govern itself. Thus, the political relevance of *On Liberty* is not immediately clear. It would be emphatically wrong, however, to conclude that Mill did not consider collective self-rule to be a freedom worthy of the name.

Civic shirkers unwittingly jeopardize their private independence because control of political decision making entails control of the police. Thus, even if Mill believed (which he didn't) that the only freedom worthy of the name was that of pursuing your own good in your own way, he would have advocated representative institutions: when government officials are not held accountable, they soon begin to harass private citizens, preventing the latter from pursuing their own good in their own way. The reverse is also true: when private independence is destroyed, citizen participation in collective decision making is essentially worthless. Intimidated sheep cannot criticize each other in constructive ways. Liberal democracy cannot function if citizens are routinely brutalized by the police and pseudo-consent is extorted by threats. Thus, private rights make an essential contribution to public debate: in a democratic nation, citizens must be well shielded from reprisals whenever they choose to criticize wielders of power.

On Liberty is concerned not only with personal eccentricity but also with democracy-reinforcing freedom of speech. Predictably enough, Mill stressed not the origins but the consequences of this "right." In addition to his hopes for the cultivation of character, he advanced several nonromantic arguments for near-absolute freedom of expression. For example, from the double premise that human minds are fallible and that everyone will benefit from knowing the truth, he drew the conclusion that censorship is an irrational, self-destructive policy. To censor an individual is to deprive mankind of his potential contributions to the advance of knowledge, contributions that censors will be too obtuse to discern. Because human minds are frail and mistakes are common, citizens should have the right publicly to defend *any* opinion, no matter how immoral or offensive it may happen to seem to other people. "All silencing of discussion is an assumption of infallibility" (On Liberty: 229). Such an assumption is both unwarranted by experience and damaging to the growth of knowledge.

Mill was not exactly a skeptic. For one thing, he considered censorship to be irrational because it conflicted with *indisputable facts* about human ignorance and knowledge. But while censorship is irrational, it can easily be explained. Man is a self-flattering animal. Most people minimize their own proneness to error. Human beings seldom hesitate before deciding what is right and wrong for others. They are irrationally wedded to their own parochial perspectives and expect the circumambient world pliantly to conform. Disagreement and disobedience shocks the mind. However natural, such arrogance is self-defeating in the long run.

Put simply, the epistemological principle underlying Mill's defense of free speech is that *no opinion is so certain that we can justify using force to prevent it from being criticized*. To adduce this sober claim as evidence for Mill's unhinged moral nihilism seems unwise, to say the least.[5] The theorist who shuns unfettered discussion, lacking confidence in his own views and expecting that wide open debate will demolish all universally respected truths, has a better claim to the title of skeptic than Mill. If anything, as we shall see, Mill was overconfident about the production of moral "truth" through uncensored political debate.

Skepticism, Empiricism, and Reform

Political and moral skepticism are quite distinct. Mill was a political skeptic: he did not trust unaccountable political authorities to enforce their conception of the good life on passive citizens. As every reader of *Utilitarianism* knows, doubts about the wisdom and virtue of rulers did not lead him to deny the difference between right and wrong. True, he believed that uncertainty might be politically beneficial. To undermine persecutory arrogance, he strove to make religious bigots aware that their own deepest beliefs were the fruits of chance. A religious crusader is a victim of his birthplace: "the same causes which make him a Churchman in London, would have made him a Buddhist or a Confucian in Pekin" (On Liberty: 230). No person will burn "heretics" for entertaining beliefs that that person would have held if raised in similar circumstances. Homilists who ascribe all manner of moral catastrophe to relativism and historicism should reflect upon the contribution that, according to Mill, such doctrines make to the triumph of toleration.

In many ways, Mill's reformism rested squarely on claims about knowledge:

> The practical reformer has continually to demand that changes be made in things which are supported by powerful and widely spread feelings, or to question the apparent necessity and indefeasibleness of established facts; and it is often an indispensable part of his argument to shew, how those powerful feelings had their origin, and how those facts came to seem necessary and indefeasible. (Autobiography: 269)

Opponents of reform naturally seek to demonstrate that an offending institution "cannot" be changed. In response, a reformer must not only prove that real alternatives are available. To be effective, he should also explain how the obfuscatory appearance of *false necessity* initially arose:

> There is a natural hostility between [the reformer] and a philosophy which
> discourages the explanation of feelings and moral facts by circumstances and
> association, and prefers to treat them as ultimate elements of human nature;
> a philosophy which is addicted to holding up favourite doctrines as intuitive
> truths, and deems intuition to be the voice of Nature and of God, speaking
> with an authority higher than that of our reason. (Autobiography: 269–270)

Mill's battle against innate ideas was, in part, politically motivated.[6] Fallibilism
itself was conceived as an attack on illusory certainties. Associationism,
initially introduced to undermine the dogma of original sin, turned out to
be a useful technique for shaking the self-assurance of the moral police. In
sum, the philosophy of experience was an epistemology for reformers.

While ensuring that political decisions will be based on inadequate
information, censorship also enfeebles the minds of individual citizens. If
a government allows people to think for themselves, then, in future unknown
situations, they will be more likely to act rationally without a government
official holding their hands. Rationality—the capacity to give plausible
arguments for one's beliefs and plausible justifications for one's actions—
develops with use. But the use of reason is suffocated by censorship. As a
result, opinions sheltered from criticism, far from being fortified, are impaired.
Beliefs defended not by reason but by a censor's blotter "are apt to give
way before the slightest semblance of an argument" (On Liberty: 244). A
government inadvertently confers a terrible strength on rotten arguments
by failing to allow its citizens to witness unsound ideas routinely being
trounced by sound ones.

Absolute freedom of expression should be protected, among other reasons,
because an opinion the government desires to suppress may turn out to be
true. But Mill also argued that errors themselves are worth protecting. False
beliefs serve an important intellectual function: "teachers and learners go
to sleep at their post, as soon as there is no enemy in the field" (On Liberty:
250). By assailing a correct opinion, dissenters, no matter how misled, force
those who know the truth to defend their beliefs. When we defend a belief,
we transform it from a mechanical profession into a profound conviction
capable of influencing action. The vibrancy and vitality of truth can be
sustained only in a continuous struggle with error.

To summarize: liberal democracy is the best form of government, given
a certain minimal level of education, because it protects the interests of all
citizens, develops their mental alertness and fact-mindedness, enlists their
creative capacities in solving common problems, and improves the quality
of collective decisions. All these achievements refer to knowledge. To repeat
the list, accentuating its epistemological side: representative government
protects the governed from the ignorance of the governed, promotes the
growth of knowledge among citizens, mobilizes preexistent knowledge for
public purposes, and improves legislative proposals by submitting them to
processes of mutual criticism.

The Use and Abuse of Political Ignorance

The human capacity to *withhold knowledge*, too, has important consequences for legislation and institutional design. At the time Mill wrote *On Liberty*, there was an English law excluding atheists from testifying in court because only believers were thought to have an incentive to tell the truth. According to Mill, this rule was self-convicted of absurdity: it allowed mendacious atheists to testify, depriving the courts only of testimony from atheists who told the truth.[7]

James Mill believed that the secret ballot could do for the many what ownership of land had done for a few: it could protect voters from manipulation and retaliation by the powerful. It performed this function by artificially obstructing the flow of information, i.e., by selectively replacing knowledge with ignorance. When people vote secretly, they can have a will of their own: they can vote as they think best, not as their superiors think best.

Convinced that fidgety intolerance of dissent and an ape-like urge to conform were deep-seated proclivities of human nature, the younger Mill might well have provided a ringing defense of the secret ballot.[8] To vote publicly is to expose yourself to the intolerance of others. The desire to "fit in" might impoverish political life in a society where all participation was publicly exposed. But Mill attacked the secret ballot. What were his reasons?

His principal argument was psychological. Institutions, such as the mode of voting, make an indirect impression on the citizen's mind, leading him to conceive citizenship in a particular way. The secret ballot teaches voters to regard their votes as private possessions. In other words, the secret ballot educates citizens to ignore the common interest and act for selfish motives even in public life.

Renowned for his hostility to paternalism, Mill nevertheless argued that citizens must be subjected, against their will, to the moral education provided by public voting. They need to learn that the suffrage is a public trust and not a private right; and they must be psychologically coaxed, in the act of voting, to focus on the broad public advantage rather than on their own puny selves. Public voting will not lead to slavish conformism, he optimistically promised. It will merely compel citizens to concoct plausible rationales for unpopular causes: "To be under the eyes of others—to have to defend oneself to others—is never more important than to those who act in opposition to the opinion of others, for it obliges them to have sure ground of their own" (Considerations: 493). In other words, Mill supported public voting because of its effect on public knowledge. The glare of publicity, it turns out, is an irresistible spur to moral behavior: "Even the bare fact of having to give an account of their conduct, is a powerful inducement to adhere to conduct of which at least some decent account can be given" (Considerations: 493). This last statement should tantalize students of Mill's life. Bitterly wounded in his private existence by public pressure to conform to conventional standards of decency, Mill nevertheless proposed using a threat of shame to induce thoughtful participation in public affairs.

To limit government is not to deprive it of all positive social functions. At the very least, the government has an affirmative duty to disrupt those monopolies which form "spontaneously" in the social world. Many illiberal social patterns depend upon asymmetries of information. Knowledge is power; and if a seller can prevent a buyer from knowing the price of a product at a competitor's shop, he can earn an extortionate profit that no genuinely "free" market would tolerate. To correct this sort of problem, according to Mill, the government must become an aggressive purveyor of information (e.g., Coleridge: 156). The *Principles of Political Economy* contains an enthusiastic endorsement of "the course so seldom resorted to by governments, and of which such important use might be made, that of giving advice and promulgating information" (*Principles:* 443). For all his antistatism, Mill insisted that the government should achieve "the greatest possible centralization of information, and diffusion of it from the centre" (On Liberty: 309). The state must provide essential social preconditions for individual autonomy; and the most important of these is universally accessible knowledge.

Elitism and Expertise

A liberal-democratic regime will mobilize the critical and creative talents, the imagination, knowledge, and intelligence of its citizens for the solution of common problems. Such admirable traits are not distributed evenly throughout the population, however. A landed aristocracy has little to offer the community; but a scientifically educated elite can make a contribution to political life out of all proportion to its small numbers. Here we encounter what unfriendly critics have derided as Mill's elitism, including his avowed wish that most people be guided "by the counsels and influence of a more highly gifted and instructed One or Few" or by "the acquired knowledge and practiced intelligence of a specially trained and experienced Few" (On Liberty: 269; Considerations: 434).

Bentham's principle of utility was essentially antiauthoritarian: it decentralized the authority to define happiness, dispersing it into the hands of individuals.[9] Mill found the egalitarian and republican implications of Bentham's theory quite congenial. Nevertheless, he notoriously departed from Benthamite premises when he claimed that "some *kinds* of pleasure are more desirable and more valuable than others" (Utilitarianism: 211). When exercising our higher faculties, we experience a "higher" form of pleasure. To rank one pleasure above another, obviously enough, is to make a cognitive claim: rankings can be true or false. Just as Aristotle (that "judicious utilitarian" [On Liberty: 235]) had said: human beings are so constituted by nature that they necessarily attain the greatest utility when engaged in superior forms of activity. This is an empirical claim about universal traits of human psychology. The correct ranking of pleasures cannot be established by counting noses. When comparing two activities, the majority should defer to "the judgment of those who are qualified by knowledge of both" (Utilitarianism: 213).

Here we find the moral, and morally questionable, foundations of Mill's (somewhat inconsistent) praise for intellectual authority in political affairs. Consider, as a supplementary example, his commentary on the claim that local government is a "school"[10] of political capacity:

> But a school supposes teachers as well as scholars: the utility of the instruction greatly depends on its bringing inferior minds into contact with superior, a contact which in the ordinary course of life is altogether exceptional, and the want of which contributes more than anything else to keep the generality of mankind on one level of contented ignorance. (Considerations: 539)

Intelligent politics requires not merely robust and wide open debate but also a "deference to mental superiority" on the part of most citizens (Considerations: 508). Such passages reveal the surprisingly narrow limits of Mill's antipaternalism.

In his chapter on the suffrage, Mill argues bizarrely that people with university degrees should be granted three or four votes while uncertified individuals should be allotted only one. Why Mill believed that an academic education would create useful citizens remains unclear.[11] Having never attended school, he probably overlooked the oppressive dimension of institutional education, viewing academic training unrealistically as nothing but a means of liberation from conventions and prejudices. The extra votes awarded to those who had received higher university degrees, in any case, were primarily symbolic (Considerations: 476). Plural voting must not allow the "educated class" to impose its minority views on an uneducated majority. That would be exactly the sort of class legislation Mill consistently opposed.

Indeed, a generous interpreter might argue that Mill advocated plural voting for the same reason he supported public voting. Both institutions were designed to make an impression on the minds of average citizens; both teach that knowledge is preferable to ignorance. "It is not useful but hurtful that the constitution of the country should declare ignorance to be entitled to as much political power as knowledge" (Considerations: 478). To induce future citizens to become knowledgeable participants in public controversies, a prize for knowledgeableness, i.e., symbolic prestige for thoughtful and informed citizens, must be built into the constitutional system itself.

"No progress at all can be made towards obtaining a skilled democracy," according to Mill, "unless the democracy are willing that the work which requires skill should be done by those who possess it" (Considerations: 440). And he didn't hesitate to employ Platonic metaphors to underscore the need for democratic deference to a knowledgeable class: "The people ought to be the masters, but they are masters who must employ servants more skilful than themselves: like a ministry when they employ a military commander, or the military commander when he employs an army surgeon" (Tocqueville: 72). In passages such as these, the instructed minority consists of technical experts, not glowing moral exemplars. The educated few have skills that make them better qualified for certain specialized tasks than untrained individuals. The extent to which ordinary citizens should defer to technical specialists on broad questions of public policy, however, remains obscure.

Doubts About Expertise

Mill stressed the cumulative and slighted the self-destructive side of scientific progress. He emphasized the present generation's contribution to truth, not the near certainty that today's beliefs will be ridiculed in the future. Despite his fallibilism, in other words, Mill hesitated to acknowledge that science had made knowledge permanently unstable: "As Mankind improve, the number of doctrines which are no longer disputed or doubted will be constantly on the increase: and the well-being of mankind may almost be measured by the number and gravity of the truths which have reached the point of being uncontested" (On Liberty: 250). As a young man, under the influence of the Saint-Simonians and Comte, he declared that the present was "an age of transition" (Spirit: 3) and that, if the instructed few managed to provide a coherent set of beliefs, intellectual authority would be reestablished in the future. Doubt is seasonal; criticism is a waking interlude between dogmatic slumbers. Even in his mature writings, Mill sometimes suggested that freedom of discussion is only a provisional virtue, appropriate solely for the disoriented present (On Liberty: 252).

Most people, in any case, will *never* be able to grasp truth with their own unaided intelligence. Fortunately, except during ages of cultural confusion, the majority of mankind will (and should) defer to intellectual superiors. That, according to the early Mill, is nothing more than what the division of labor demands.[12] Among those who think scientifically, a moral and political consensus does not yet exist; but it will eventually emerge. This is fortunate because social cohesion ultimately hinges upon the integrating power of a coherent set of beliefs. When a new and well-rounded belief system finally takes shape, the unschooled will acquiesce in an intellectual elite's authoritative opinions with becomingly submissive minds.

Mill's exaggerated confidence in intellectual superiority may have been reinforced by his experience as an administrator in the East India Company. Making decisions about a country so different from England required "professional knowledge" and, indeed, "specially Indian knowledge and experience" (Considerations: 574, 575). It could not be left to an ignorant populace and their elected representatives. Indeed, despite his enthusiasm for parliamentary debate, Mill expressed a general contempt for the competence of legislative assemblies: "a numerous assembly is as little fitted for the direct business of legislation as for that of administration" (Considerations: 428). A long time observer of Parliament, he wrote that "[t]here is hardly any kind of intellectual work which so much needs to be done not only by experience and exercised minds, but by minds trained to the task through long and laborious study, as the business of making laws"

(Considerations: 428). Unfortunately, British lawmakers were not qualified to do this job.

Mill's fondness for expertise and intellectual superiority, in other words, led him to retreat from what at first seemed an unreserved commitment to government by public discussion: *"doing* [including lawmaking], as a result of discussion, is the task not of a miscellaneous body, but of individuals specially trained to do it" (Considerations: 433). Laws must meet certain minimal standards of rationality, such as consistency with themselves and other laws. Elected legislators, lacking intellectual discipline, will inevitably write bills one at a time and in response to a variety of pressures and problems. Their mindless incrementalism will breed a host of practical confusions. Mill's proposal for a solution was the establishment of a standing panel of experts. If a special commission prepared bills, then "legislation would assume its proper place as a work of skilled labor and special study and experience" (Considerations: 432).

To be sure, Mill's fantasies about an authoritative clerisy were less extreme than these passages, cited out of context, might suggest. For one thing, he insisted that elected generalists should control appointed specialists. Lacking narrow expertise, legislators may nevertheless possess breadth of mind, an ability to see the connectedness of things, which no technical education could provide. Experts, in any case, should be on tap, not on top. Parliament approves and rejects bills; and it can charge the Commission of Legislation with preparing bills on designated topics. The panel of experts would "merely" be the intelligence enabling legislators to carry out their will in a coherent and effective manner (Considerations: 430).

Mill's miscellaneous views on the political value of intellectual superiority may not be completely consistent. His skepticism about expertise, at any rate, is expressed most eloquently in his discussions of pedantocracy. He wrote admiringly of Rome and Venice: their policies were intelligent because public business was consigned to "governors by profession" (Considerations: 438). They were not aristocracies so much as bureaucracies. But specialists are quite unspecial in one respect: like everyone else, they have a bias toward their own particular interests. Technical knowledge, unlike Platonic wisdom, makes no one virtuous. Even if an expert understood the interests of nonexperts better than they could understand these interests themselves, there would be no reason to suppose he would respect them.

Moreover, useful knowledge becomes obsolete with time. Truths do not simply accumulate like stones heaped upon a pile; some are destroyed by the advance of knowledge. Thus, bureaucrats and specialists can be crippled by what they "know." Hard-won insights tend to become objects of veneration and irrational loyalty—as we are reminded by all those generals anachronistically fighting the last war.[13] Necessary innovations, in fact, are usually introduced against the drag of bureaucratic inertia. As a result, final control of the government must never rest with professionals. Only a "popular element" (Considerations: 439), happily free from the debilitating effect of obsolete expertise, can cure bureaucracy of its fixation on stale truths.

Another antielitist strand in Mill's argument appears in his principle of the "pinching shoe."[14] The people most likely to initiate needed reforms are those most adversely affected by bad laws. That is a crucial argument for universal suffrage. Knowledge is not distributed evenly throughout society; but neither is it monopolized by a university-trained elite. Indeed, the ignorance of technical experts is encyclopedic. Firsthand knowledge of what problems need to be solved is concentrated among those who suffer directly from such problems. Victims are grass roots experts, so to speak. Mill's belief in the all-importance of knowledge, in other words, had a significant democratic side. Without universal suffrage, the knowledge of disenfranchised citizens will be unavailable to policy makers. As a result, the working class must be represented in Parliament.

The Authority of Science

An intriguing but misleading analogy lurks in the background of Mill's theory of representative government: the analogy between political and scientific discussions.[15] Voters must not express their preferences but rather choose the right answer. Like scientists, they must abstract from all personal, sectional, or group interests and devote themselves solely to increasing the GNT, the gross national truth.[16] This argument usefully highlights a fundamental difference between politics and markets. It also shows that Mill did *not* view politics principally as an arena for individual self-realization. But despite its virtues, the notion that political discussions produce political "truth" goes too far. It leaves no room for ordinary horse-trading among private interests; and no room is not enough. Not enough even on Mill's own account.[17]

In *On Liberty*, Mill fails to distinguish clearly between freedom of scientific thought and freedom of moral choice. We must tolerate public disagreement because it promotes intellectual progress. To argue in this manner about political and moral questions does not seem completely plausible, however. Notoriously, questions such as "how should I live?" or "what should I do?" have no single correct answer. Certainly, allowing people to do whatever they want will not lead them to an inevitable convergence on *the* true answer to practical questions. But Mill clearly suggested that freedom would generate consensus in morals as well as in science. This may have been due to his conviction that the "worth" of different modes of life is a cognitive question to which a univocal answer is inscribed in human nature (cf. On Liberty: 261). Scientific metaphors, at any rate, pervade his moral writings. For example, he wrote quite casually of successful and unsuccessful life experiments. Experience shows which modes of conduct and existence are superior to others. If we want to be rational, we must profit from "the ascertained results of human experience" (On Liberty: 262).

At times, it is true, Mill emphasized the "experimental" character of politics in order to dishearten arrogant fanatics pretending to have all the answers in advance. Referring to communist revolutionaries aiming "to substitute the new rule for the old at a single stroke," he wrote the following:

> It must be acknowledged that those who would play this [revolutionary] game on the strength of their own private opinion, unconfirmed as yet by any *experimental* verification—who would forcibly deprive all who have now a comfortable physical existence of their only present means of preserving it, and would brave the frightful bloodshed and misery that would ensue if the attempt was resisted—must have a serene confidence in their own wisdom on the one hand and a recklessness of other people's suffering on the other, which Robespierre and St. Just, hitherto the typical instances of those united attributes, scarcely came up to. (Chapters: 336)

Science suggests a questioning attitude, opposed to the dogmatism and arrogance of revolutionaries. But it also suggests a sure-footed progress toward incontestable truth. This second suggestion underlay the most dubious aspects of Mill's political theory.

Character and Choice

What is the relation between human character and human choice? At times, Mill wrote that character is the *result* of choice: individuals sculpt their own lives, hurling themselves voluntarily into personality-shaping circumstances and thus actively forming their own characters. A person's way of laying out his own existence is best because it is his *own* way. In other passages, however, Mill treats character as a preexistent natural standard which, far from being choosable, itself guides (or should guide) all choice. Individuals must select a life to "suit" their characters, just as shoppers pick shoes which fit their feet (On Liberty: 226). The "worth" of a life is a cognitive question not only because of what human nature in general demands. Each individual has a unique pregiven nature, which a style of life can either violate or match. Mill did not simply delight in diversity. He justified tolerance for moral nonconformity in much the same way as he justified tolerance for scientific disagreement. Both lead to "the truth." By tolerating an abundance of life experiments, society helps individuals discover the peculiar lives which their idiosyncratic natures demand.

We can choose shoes to fit our feet; but we cannot very easily choose our own foot-size. Despite his obsession with liberty, Mill sometimes seems so devoted to the pregiven uniqueness of each individual's character that he denies any significant character-shaping role to choice. This (inconsistent) denial of alternatives is expressed most clearly in his queer metaphor of the man-tree: "Human nature is not a machine to be built after a model, and set to do exactly the work prescribed for it, but a tree, which requires to grow and develop itself on all sides, according to the tendency of the inward forces which make it a living thing" (On Liberty: 263). Trees make no choices; they do not have to. Incumbent on an oak is merely the strain of unfolding a promise inchoate in the acorn. That, to say the least, is a curious way to conceive the moral life of human beings.

Conformists are miserable creatures: "by dint of not following their own nature, they have no nature to follow" (On Liberty: 265). But what does it mean: to follow one's own nature? In a brilliant essay (Nature), Mill demolished the fallacious belief that "nature" can serve as a moral standard. In his ethical writings, however, he sometimes ignored such warnings. Preferences should be judged not only by their natural worth but also by their correspondence with individual character. He insisted that "our desires and impulses should be our own" (On Liberty: 263). But what does personal "ownership" contribute to inherent value? And what does it mean to call a desire "our own" anyway? Mill's entire discussion, in fact, hinges upon a latent distinction between autonomous and heteronomous desires. He never even tries to make such a controversial distinction clear and intelligible, however.

Mill lapsed into the same fallacy which plagues all philosophers who rely on "athletic arguments" when advancing moral claims. An individual has many capacities which are unique to himself or to his species (e.g., the capacity to be absurd). But his "possession" of these capacities is obviously not a moral reason for exercising them. A Darwinist perspective helps illuminate the hidden teleological premises behind Mill's wholesale assertion that human beings should realize their inborn potentials and exercise their authentic capacities. Many people have the ability to flash hot with aggression because, at some earlier stage of evolution, such a capacity was useful for the survival of the species. Changed circumstances, however, have made this "inborn capacity" obsolete and even into an albatross needlessly hampering and shortening human life. In other words, to assume that people have a moral obligation to realize their natural potentials is to assume that these potentials were purposely granted by God or nature and were not the result of selective adaptation to ephemeral circumstances.

Consent and Assent

Indifferent to individual preferences, "truth" is also independent of majority will. To the extent that Mill believed political problems susceptible to correct solutions ("correct" in the scientific sense of dictating the acquiescence of all rational minds), he also denied that popular consent could ever legitimate a political choice. This undemocratic conclusion results inevitably from a reliance on the science-politics analogy. A commitment to "truth" in politics makes "consent" redundant—which may explain why Mill so often displays an unwarranted confidence in intellectual superiors. His scientism also surfaces in his disembodied and overintellectualized conception of public debate. His political discussions have been so thoroughly sanitized of love and hatred, of partial interests and partial loyalties, that they do not even resemble university seminars. The politics-science analogy suggests that if members of a community discuss moral and practical questions long enough, they will eventually reach agreement about what to do. But this assumption is unrealistic if fundamental conflicts between rival values cannot be resolved by rational argument.

To preserve the core of Mill's argument, we must distinguish between *consent* and *assent*. Assent is agreement to empirical or mathematical truths. We assent to the proposition that "it is snowing in Chicago," and our assent is essentially redundant: it will still be snowing whether we say so or not. In fact, it makes little sense to categorize acquiescence in empirical truths as either voluntary or involuntary. The truth that "Paris is in France" depends in no way on our accepting it; nor does accepting it in any way diminish our freedom.

Neither personal nor political choices are of this sort. For such choices, knowledge is necessary, but not decisive. Collective decisions to break a military alliance or build a nuclear reactor are risky ventures. The question of what to do in such circumstances does not have a true or false answer. For this reason, political choice demands consent, not assent. Indeed, political decisions require consent precisely because they may prove to have been foolhardy. If things turn out badly, a community will have only itself to blame for a decision based on popular consent.

The distinction between consent and assent suggests that freedom of political debate must be justified in a different manner than freedom of scientific discussion. Debate on important public issues is not desirable because it produces "true answers," but for other reasons. For one thing, wide-open discussion and tolerance for criticism helps encourage government flexibility, awareness of alternatives, self-correction, and the ability to rethink and respond again. Political debate may not guarantee the triumph of truth; but it remains a useful method for challenging false certainties and promoting the trial of new ideas.

The politics-science analogy is telling to the extent that public discussion helps uncover relevant facts. But political debate also keeps public consciousness focused on rival, perhaps irreconcilable, values; and it simultaneously fosters private and sectional bargaining. Discussion is a perfect medium for the simultaneous pursuit of factual knowledge, moral agreement, and pragmatic compromise among clashing values and conflicting interests. Mill was right to note that public debate can set in motion a process of preference transformation. But this process takes time; and time is scarce. Decisions often have to be made in haste and, as a result, the labor of reshaping individual and group interests will sometimes be cut short. Thus, the transformation of preferences will always have to be supplemented by the aggregation of preferences (Elster 1983: 38). Within all public discussions, as Mill would probably have recognized, both processes go on.

Private Fallacies and Public Insights

"I acknowledge that the tendency of all opinions to become sectarian is not cured by the freest discussion, but is often heightened and exacerbated thereby" (On Liberty: 257). This is a stunning admission by the nineteenth century's premier advocate of free debate. Discussion can undermine both individual and collective rationality. Open debate may lead to a hardening of battle fronts, far beyond what would result from a silent assessment of conflicting interests. Because of the plentiful opportunities it offers for cornering, insulting, embarrassing, losing face, and tripping over one's own feet, public discussion can cause disputants irrationally to dig in their heels. Controversies also have a certain dynamic of their own. Controversialists may come to appreciate the sweet benefits of facing bitter opponents. After all, enemies help clarify life. Once a friend-enemy pattern has been established, moreover, an individual's willingness to acknowledge the valid insights offered by his antagonist markedly shrinks, "the truth which ought to have been seen, but was not, being rejected all the more violently because proclaimed by persons regarded as opponents" (On Liberty: 257).

A voter should vote not for his private interests but for the public advantage, "exactly as he would be bound to do if he were the sole voter, and the election depended upon him alone" (Considerations: 490). There is no suggestion here of an invisible hand, producing public benefits from private vices: each citizen must be completely public minded and must act with the common good in mind. At other times, however, Mill makes greater concessions to the metaphor of a free market of ideas. He argues, for example, that one-sided and even bigoted debaters are naturally led, through a process of near mindless "collision," to produce something resembling the whole truth. Invisible to the debaters, such a fortunate outcome can nevertheless be appreciated by lucky bystanders. This particular *Harmonielehre* requires no directing intelligence, but only the watchfulness of an observing intelligence. Debate can be justified because it induces debate observers to see both sides of an issue; but it cannot be justified from the standpoint of the controversialists themselves.

The broad-minded attempt to see the whole picture is only valuable when all parties make the same effort. Unfortunately, this seldom occurs because "in the human mind, one-sidedness has always been the rule and many-sidedness the exception" (On Liberty: 252). When popular truths are one-sided, as they often are, they can be effectively opposed only by equally one-sided fanatics. Evenhanded debaters will be completely ineffectual. If one individual is fanatically biased and another strikes a reasonable balance, the outcome of a compromise between the two is likely to be skewed toward the selfish commitments of the former. In other words, what is rational for the individual (to see both sides) may not necessarily be rational for society.

After an obligatory nod to intellectual superiority, Mill acknowledges the importance of an invisible hand for the successful functioning of the free market of ideas: "Truth, in the great practical concerns of life, is so much a question of the reconciling and combining of opposites, that very few have minds sufficiently capacious and impartial to make the adjustment with an approach to correctness, and it has to be made by the rough process of a struggle between combatants fighting under hostile banners" (On Liberty: 254). Useless or even harmful to the debaters, public controversy is beneficial to society as a whole. It broadens the horizons of third parties able to appreciate the composite truth that emerges from the clash of two one-sided views.[18] Private errors produce public truths.

At one point in *On Liberty*, Mill recklessly wrote that "no belief which is contrary to truth can be really useful" (On Liberty: 234). This assertion is spectacularly contradicted by his claim that one person's error can fortify another person's truth. Even those who are hopelessly wrong can prevent teachers and learners from sleeping at their posts. This instrumental attitude toward the false beliefs of the deluded is expressed most clearly in the *Autobiography*. Looking back, Mill wrote:

> I . . . earnestly hoped that Owenite, St. Simonian, and all other anti-property doctrines might spread widely among the poorer classes; not that I thought those doctrines true, or desired that they should be acted on, but in order that the higher classes might be made to see that they had more to fear from the poor when uneducated, than when educated. (Autobiography: 179)

Deluded individuals are stepping-stones to a higher consciousness that they can never themselves hope to attain. This conclusion should have been— but apparently was not—disturbing to a liberal such as Mill. Marxists are usually the ones accused of conspiring to make omelets by breaking eggs, willingly sacrificing the happiness of the present generation, which has but one chance to be happy, to the bliss of later generations. Without being so callous toward other people's suffering, Mill came close to making a parallel argument. The virtue of some individuals, e.g., their evenhandedness, must be sacrificed to promote the advancement of the species. Mill doesn't quite say that one man's disability is justified by its contribution to another man's ability, but he says something similar. Do "the permanent interests of man as a progressive being" (On Liberty: 224) really *justify* the mistakes of individuals, however? Did Mill's enthusiasm for scientific progress require him to embrace an updated form of theodicy? Did his belief in an alliance between liberal politics and scientific inquiry lead him—as other beliefs had led Marx—to espouse a doormat theory of the present generation? Arguments can be given on both sides. What Mill's writings reveal unambiguously, in any case, is a tension between his epistemology and his ethics, between his commitment to science and his commitment to individualism. From its very inception, modern science pursued the growth of knowledge ruthlessly, with no particular regard for individuals.

Notes

1. Rousseau, for example, denied that disagreement can be politically creative just as adamantly as any exponent of absolute monarchy.

2. Cf.: "the general prosperity attains a greater height, and is more widely diffused, in proportion to the amount and variety of the personal energies enlisted in promoting it" (Considerations: 404).

3. Conversely, public discussion is a practical strength, not merely a moral norm. This thesis is advanced by Samuel Beer (1979), to whom I am much indebted.

4. For this reason, "unity of opinion, unless resulting from the fullest and freest comparison of opposite opinions, is not desirable" (On Liberty: 260).

5. That is nevertheless the gist of Gertrude Himmelfarb's (1974) imaginative diagnosis.

6. "The notion that truths external to the mind may be known by intuition or consciousness, independently of observation and experience, is, I am persuaded, in these times, the great intellectual support of false doctrines and bad institutions" (Autobiography: 233).

7. If atheists told the truth, of course, as the rule assumes they would, then the rule itself was senseless (On Liberty: 239–240).

8. See the forthcoming history of the secret ballot by Andreas Teuber.

9. The state must promote the greatest happiness of the greatest number, and happiness should be defined by unsupervised individuals in a variety of eccentric ways. Political officials cannot prescribe obligatory goals or overrule diverse ideas of happiness on the grounds that wise statesmen must be their brothers' keepers. From a *political* point of view—and the restriction is crucial—pushpin is as good as poetry. If political authorities could legitimately define happiness, resistance to governmental authority would be extremely difficult to justify. On all these points, see Shirley Letwin (1965: 127–188).

10. Only someone who never went to school could consider this high praise.

11. Other sorts of education may well serve civic purposes: e.g., Rousseau believed that individuals should be taught habits of identification with their fellow citizens. But academic education does not seem well suited for any such task.

12. "Those persons whom the circumstances of society, and their own position in it, permit to dedicate themselves to the investigation and study of physical, moral, and social truths, as their peculiar calling, can alone be expected to make the evidence of such truths a subject of profound meditation, and to make themselves thorough masters of the philosophical grounds of those opinions of which it is desirable that all should be firmly *persuaded*, but which they alone can entirely and philosophically *know*. The remainder of mankind must, and except in periods of transition like the present, always do, take the far greater part of their opinions on all extensive subjects upon the authority of those who have studied them" (Spirit: 12–13).

13. "The disease which afflicts bureaucratic governments, and which they usually die of, is routine. They perish by the immutability of their maxims; and, still more, by the universal law that whatever becomes a routine loses its vital principle, and having no longer a mind acting within it, goes on revolving mechanically though the work it is intended to do remains undone" (Considerations: 439).

14. Clearly expounded in Dennis Thompson (1976: 20ff.).

15. Mill also employed an equally interesting and unsatisfying analogy between citizens voting and jury members delivering a verdict.

16. A phrase of Samuel Beer's.

17. For example, Mill explicitly praises representative government as the regime best able to protect the *interests* of the poor.

18. Mill never explained why the adversary system would necessarily bring *all* sides of every issue to the consideration of observant bystanders. Adversaries might despise each other and yet conspiratorially decide to repress relevant facts and viewpoints because, despite their differences, they have some interests in common. Mill simply assumed that this would seldom be the case.

References

Beer, Samuel. 1979. The strengths of liberal democracy. In William Livingston (ed.), *A Prospect for Liberal Democracy.* Austin: University of Texas Press, pp. 215–229.

Elster, Jon. 1983. *Sour Grapes: Studies in the Subversion of Rationality.* Cambridge: Cambridge University Press.

Himmelfarb, Gertrude. 1974. *On Liberty and Liberalism: the Case of John Stuart Mill.* New York: Knopf.

Letwin, Shirley. 1965. *The Pursuit of Certainty.* Cambridge: Cambridge University Press.

Mill, John Stuart. (1831). [Spirit]. The spirit of the age. In Gertrude Himmelfarb (ed.), *Essays in Politics and Culture.* New York: Doubleday, 1963.

———. (1835). [Tocqueville]. Tocqueville on democracy in America, Vol. I. In *Politics.*

———. (1838). [Bentham]. Bentham. In *Ethics.*

———. (1840). [Coleridge]. Coleridge. In *Ethics.*

———. (1848). [*Principles*]. *Principles of Political Economy,* vol. 2. New York: Colonial Press, 1899.

———. (1859). [On Liberty]. On liberty. In *Politics.*

———. (1861). [Considerations]. Considerations on representative government. In *Politics.*

———. (1861). [Utilitarianism]. Utilitarianism. In *Ethics.*

———. (1873, published posthumously). [Autobiography]. Autobiography. In *Autobiography and Literary Essays,* ed. by J.M. Robson. Toronto: Toronto University Press, 1981.

———. (1874). [Nature]. Nature. In *Ethics.*

———. (1879, published posthumously). [Chapters]. Chapters on socialism. In *On Politics and Society,* ed. by Geraint Williams. Glasgow: Collins, 1976.

———. [*Ethics*]. 1969. *Essays on Ethics, Religion and Society,* ed. by J.M. Robson. Toronto: University of Toronto Press.

———. [*Politics*]. 1977. *Essays on Politics and Society,* ed. by J.M. Robson. Toronto: University of Toronto Press.

Thompson, Dennis. 1976. *John Stuart Mill and Representative Government.* Princeton: Princeton University Press.

7

The Logic of Political Life: Hegel's Conception of Political Philosophy

Myriam Bienenstock

The reader who expects to find a normative political theory in the *Principles of the Philosophy of Right* (1820),[1] Hegel's main work on political philosophy, cannot but be disappointed. In this book, Hegel consistently refrains from formulating judgments about the way in which society, or the state, ought to be organized. In the Preface, he declares that the *Philosophy of Right*,

> inasmuch as it contains the science of the state, must be nothing other than the endeavour *to conceive and depict the state as something inherently rational.* As a work of philosophy, it must be poles apart from the temptation to construct a *state as it ought to be.* The instruction which it may contain cannot consist in teaching the state what it ought to be; it can only show how the state, the ethical universe, is to be known. (PhR, par. 26; par. 11)

Frustrated in his most basic expectations, the reader may well be tempted to hypothesize that the position Hegel vindicates in his book is none other than the position commonly known as "legal" or "ethical positivism." As Karl Popper puts it in *The Open Society and Its Enemies,* Hegel would have wanted to demonstrate that whatever *is* the case also is what *ought* to be—that "might is right."[2]

This, however, would imply that Hegel's main purpose in the *Philosophy of Right* was to provide us with a normative political theory—a paradoxical and untenable one, perhaps, but still an essentially normative one. It makes much more sense to postulate, I think, that in this work Hegel had a very different aim in mind. In this chapter, I will argue that in the *Philosophy of Right* Hegel engages in a kind of conceptual clarification: he endeavors not so much to justify the normative judgments which we enact in our political behavior as to elucidate the meaning of the concepts upon which we rely in these judgments. My contention will be, indeed, that according to Hegel the justification of normative judgments is contingent upon a preliminary clarification of the meaning of the concepts we use in them. Hegel believed, I think, that it is precisely such a clarification which will ultimately enable us to justify the final ends of our political behavior. In the *Philosophy of Right*, he focused upon that clarificatory task.[3]

Arguing that the justification of normative judgments is contingent upon a preliminary clarification of the meaning of the concepts we use in them does not necessarily entail a vindication of "legal positivism." Whether or not this argument entails such a vindication obviously depends upon the way in which the task of "conceptual clarification" itself is defined. But how does Hegel understand this task? What is, for him, a "concept" (*Begriff*)? As is well known, his own definition of this term is idiosyncratic: it draws its meaning from his conception of a "philosophical science" (*philosophische Wissenschaft*). In the *Philosophy of Right*, Hegel himself puts strong emphasis upon this point: in the introduction to this book, he explains that the "science of right" is a part of the system of "philosophical science" as a whole, and that as such it draws its "concepts" from this system (PhR, par. 2). He also refers his readers to the *Science of Logic*. This latter book alone contains, he says, a presentation and defense of the approach proper to philosophical science: the dialectics (PhR, par. 31).

From this it follows that for us to understand what Hegel wants to do in his political philosophy, we must turn to his major systematic works, and attempt to elucidate the meaning of his conception of a "philosophical science." I cannot pretend to achieve this task in a fully satisfactory way in the present chapter, but I would like at least to indicate what seems to me the correct direction of research. To this end, I will take as a lead a definition of philosophy Hegel puts forward in the Introduction to his *magnum opus*, the *Encyclopaedia of the Philosophical Sciences*. In this Introduction, he writes that

> philosophy may be said to do nothing but transforming representations into thoughts—and further transforming the mere thought into the concept, of course [dass die Philosophie nichts anders tue, als die Vorstellungen in Gedanken zu verwandeln,—aber freilich fernerhin den blossen Gedanken in den Begriff]. (Enz., par. 20 A.)

I will attempt to show that Hegel's political philosophy itself partakes of this overall purpose: one may rightly say that in this part of his philosophical system Hegel focuses upon the "representations" (*Vorstellungen*) that we adopt as the purposes of our actions, and also upon the "representations" we make for ourselves of the social and political institutions in which we live, and that he endeavors to transform them into "thoughts" (*Gedanken*). He tries to show that a "concept" or, rather, an "Idea" is implied by them: the idea of freedom.

It is still a quite common practice, among Hegel scholars, to try to clarify the meaning of Hegel's idiosyncratic philosophical approach—the "dialectics"—by confronting it with "positivism." In the first part of this chapter, I will try to clarify the issues at stake in this confrontation, and also to determine whether or not it is right to ascribe to Hegel a vindication of the ominous "might is right" thesis. My contention will be that the attempt to characterize Hegel's dialectics by opposing it to positivism rests upon an unsatisfactory account of the meaning of Hegel's philosophical enterprise as a whole. In the second part of this chapter, I will focus upon this latter enterprise or, more exactly, upon what I take to be one of its central features: the transformation of "representations" (*Vorstellungen*) into "thoughts" (*Gedanken*); and I will try to shed some light upon the meaning of this transformation. Finally, I will attempt to show that Hegel's political philosophy itself shares the overall purpose of his system.

Positivism and Dialectics

The term positivism is used today in so many different senses that the discussion of Hegel's attitude toward this conception of knowledge may well seem hopelessly confused. Still, it is worth noticing that in his work Hegel himself made much use of the notions of "positivity" and "positive sciences." There undoubtedly is a common ancestry to both his use of these terms and our contemporary recourse to the notion of positivism. To identify what is at stake in the repeated attacks launched by contemporary Hegel scholars against what they call positivism, I will first try to clarify the meaning of Hegel's own terminological practice.

To this end, I will focus upon his early, 1802/1803 article on "The Different Scientific Forms of Treatment of Natural Right" (JS 434–530). In the Introduction to this article, Hegel writes that Natural Right has long been acknowledged as a "philosophical science," but that modern scientists no longer understand the true meaning of this expression: the properly philosophical part of science, he says, is now relegated to metaphysics; and science is believed to be wholly independent of this branch of study. Scientists are thus induced to adopt as their basic principle of research the reliance upon empirical experience. For them, science turns out to be no more than a collection of empirical reports (JS 434; 55). This evolution, Hegel argues, characterizes both the natural sciences and the sciences of right: a "positive" science of right, just like a "positive" science of nature, is one which "holds itself to be outside philosophy and, inasmuch as it itself gives up philosophy, believes it possible to escape its [philosophy's] criticism" (JS 440; 59).

Everything happens, then, as if Hegel ascribed to the notion of positive science a meaning quite akin to that which twentieth-century positivists have given to it: he characterizes it by its opposition to philosophy and, more particularly, to metaphysics. But far from wanting, like our contemporary positivists, to vindicate, as against metaphysics, a purely empirical conception of science, he makes empiricism as a positive science the very target of his criticism: he argues that by severing their links with philosophy, the empirical sciences make nonsense of their own claim to scientific objectivity (ibid.).

Some Hegel scholars have not hesitated to infer from this argument that in his work as a whole Hegel sets his mind upon denying the validity of any and every form of empirical science.[4] This inference is, I think, inaccurate. It is true that, in the first part of the article on Natural Right, Hegel criticizes what he calls the empirical sciences of right, and that one can infer from this criticism a criticism of the empirical sciences in general. But it is worth noting that neither in this article nor in his other works does Hegel disavow the intention of empirical scientists to rely upon experience. Rather, he explicitly vindicates this intention. His contention is that philosophy itself must be directed toward experience. As a matter of fact, he even gives primacy to the orientation toward experience over any a priori philosophizing: even if it is inconsistent, he insists, the reliance upon empirical experience is much more adequate as a philosophical or, for that matter, a scientific method than the attempt to construct political theories in an a priori way (JS 449f.; 67f.).

But, he says, most often, empirical scientists are unfaithful to their own ideal of knowledge: they do not adequately account for experience. For, he explains, empirical scientists themselves, if they want their work to be scientific, cannot limit themselves to the mere recording of sense-impressions, or to the enumeration of a multiplicity of empirical qualities. They must also attempt to introduce a unity, or at least some relationships, among these qualities: they must use concepts. Intuition, he insists, however pure it may well be, needs to be expressed in concepts (JS 450; 68).

But how are these concepts formed? Empirical scientists themselves contend that they take these concepts from experience: they would resort to a purely empirical procedure of abstraction, one enabling them to single out or "abstract" from experience its general features. Indeed, Hegel says, had this been their actual way of proceeding, they would have had every right to be praised. But, he argues, the principle of selection to which they resort is most often not an empirical one: far from drawing the distinction between the general and the particular, the necessary and the contingent, from their observation of experience, empirical scientists instead rely upon ready-made abstractions. They borrow their concepts from the then prevalent theories, and also from common language: it is typical of them to resort to mere commonsensical distinctions, ideas or notions usually taken for granted in the culture of their time (JS 450–453; 68–70).

This misleading conceptualizing practice is not due to mere oversight. Rather, it is grounded in an inadequate definition of science: empirical scientists, Hegel contends, lack any criterion enabling them to distinguish, in their experience, between the universal and the particular, the necessary and the contingent (e.g., JS 445; 64); and because they lack such a criterion, they cannot ground their own claim to objectivity.

Here, Hegel criticizes pure empiricism as a theory of knowledge. It is worth noting, though, that this criticism does not induce him to vindicate a non-empirical, purely a priori form of knowledge. In the article on Natural Right, he contends that it is just as impossible to build a science upon concepts alone as it is to build it upon pure intuitions: the attempt to formulate a priori, "absolute" principles, and to deduce from these principles the blueprint of a political state as it ought to be organized, he says, is as self-defeating as would be the limitation to empirical political theorizing. "Formal" Natural Right scientists, he writes, claim to exclude whatever is empirical from their apriority and scientificity. But they, too, rely upon experience. For in the first place, if they want to give a positive content to their theory, they must relate their formal concepts to the empirically given. At every stage of their demonstration, they must resort to experience; and from this it follows that they are even more dependent upon empirical necessity than the empirical scientists (JS 443; 62).

Furthermore, the principles of formal Natural Right scientists are themselves not really a priori: they are formed by a process of abstraction from empirical experience, one strikingly similar to the abstracting practice used by empirical scientists, and as little grounded as this latter practice. To obtain their concepts or principles, formal Natural Right scientists, too, rely upon experience: most often, they merely take apart one determination of experience, and they raise it to universality. But this means that they, too, just like the empirical scientist, must distinguish between the universal and the particular, the accidental and the necessary. In this matter, however, they are in no better position than he is. For they have no criterion which would enable them to make this distinction in a nonarbitrary way. Their principles, too, are no more than determinations of experience, arbitrarily elevated to universality and necessity.

Just as Hegel had criticized the empirical sciences of right for introducing unaccounted-for abstractions or concepts in their allegedly purely empirical description of experience, he now castigates formal Natural Right scientists for an uncritical reliance upon experience in their allegedly purely a priori demonstrations. He puts together the empirical and the formal treatments of Natural Right; and he argues that both forms of science are inadequate. Both, he says, consist in nothing other than in an impure mixture of empirical and formal representations: "When the empirical seems to enter into a fight with the theoretical, the former as well as the latter are usually proved to be an intuition already vitiated and sublated by reflection, and an inverted reason" (JS 452; 69).

Here, he takes as an example the notion of a state of nature, which Natural Right theoreticians adopt as a principle. This notion, he says, is neither an empirical nor a purely a priori one. Indeed, he writes quite often, Natural Right scientists are not even clear about the status they want to ascribe to it: is it a state which has once really existed, or a fiction—or, perhaps, a mere possibility (JS 444f.; 63)? Furthermore, he says, even when it is explicitly posited as a purely theoretical principle, the notion of the state of nature is a priori only in name. For, he asks, how does the scientist obtain it, if not by "abstracting" from his own experience, i.e., from the historical situation in which he lives? The political scientist excludes all that seems to him merely particular, or merely historical—i.e., here, merely given—and he retains only those features of man's character which seem to him more important, or more "essential," than the others: the drive to survival, for example.

But he has no criterion which may allow him to justify his distinction. No wonder, then, that he makes distinctions according to what he wants to demonstrate. If, for example, what he ultimately wants to do is to demonstrate the necessity of the state, he will be tempted to assign to man's "nature," or to the "state of nature," precisely those qualities which can "explain" the state: either indirectly, as in those theories in which the "good" men would strive to reach is defined as the direct opposite of the chaos proper to the state of nature, or directly, when man is endowed with a so-called sociability instinct. "The directing principle for that a priori [of the state of nature] is the a posteriori" (JS 445ff.; 63f.).

What Hegel dismisses here is, once again, "abstract" political theorizing: his criticism of both the empirical and the formal modes of treatment of Natural Right is a criticism of their abstraction. To fully clarify the meaning of this criticism, however, one must pay attention to the idiosyncratic way in which he resorts to the notion of 'abstraction' in his work: it must be kept in mind that what underlies his opposition of the 'abstract' to the 'concrete' is not the opposition of the universal to the particular or, for that matter, of that which only exists in thought to that which would be real or actual but, rather, the opposition of the part to the whole. In Hegel's thought, let it be unequivocally asserted here, abstracting fundamentally means separating, taking a part from a whole, a totality; and only the totality, the whole, is said to be 'concrete.' But this means that what Hegel calls abstract is not just the universal, that which is taken apart or singled out from experience by means of an empirical generalization. The particular, too—that which is allegedly given to our empirical observation—can be said to be abstract (e.g., JS 520; 125): for Hegel, the very fact that we call given features of reality "particular" shows that we have abstracted them, i.e., separated them, or taken them apart from the whole, the concrete, to which they actually belong.

In Hegel, it is precisely the abstract character of modern political theories which accounts for their positivity: as Hegel explains in the fourth part of the article on Natural Right, the difference between positive and non-positive sciences concerns not the *content* but the *form* of these sciences. Positivity, he explicitly states, results from the fact that something which is merely "unilateral" is "isolated, posited for itself and expressed as something real" (JS 516; 122). From this it can be inferred that for Hegel, formal Natural Right itself is just as positive a science as empirical theories of right. Indeed, Hegel writes, formalism

> tears up intuition with its identity of universal and particular, opposes the abstracted universal and the abstracted particular to each other, and takes for positive whatever can be excluded from this void but subsumed under the

abstracted particular—without being aware that by this opposition the universal becomes as positive as the particular. (JS 520f.; 125)

We commonly assume that Natural Right and positivism—or, for that matter, legal positivism—are the names of rival theories. In Hegel's time, indeed, it was already common practice to oppose the 'positive' or the 'historical' or, for that matter, the given to the 'natural,' or 'rational.' But the passage of the article on Natural Right I have just quoted shows that it is precisely this opposition which Hegel criticizes as 'positive': he objects to the very opposition of the positive to the natural, and of positivism to Natural Right. He argues that merely opposing something is no way of justifying it, or of grounding it in reason: the principles which are obtained by merely opposing the positive, he contends, can themselves only be positive.[5]

In the article on Natural Right, he thus writes that principles such as freedom and equality are "abstractions without essence and negations formulated positively" (JS 451; 68): what he criticizes in this passage, let it be unequivocally stated already at this point, is not the idea of freedom as such but, rather, the abstract conception of freedom vindicated by Natural Right revolutionary thinkers; and he criticizes this conception precisely because, he says, it is obtained by merely negating or opposing the given; according to him, this latter procedure makes the idea of freedom philosophically or, for that matter, scientifically ungrounded. Furthermore, he insists, it also makes this idea politically inapplicable: "abstract" political theorizing "can have no application and contradicts the necessary practice" (JS 452; 69).

What Hegel castigates in the famous 1820 Preface to the *Philosophy of Right* is similarly "the idea that freedom of thought, and of mind generally, evinces itself only in divergence from, indeed in hostility to, what is publicly recognized"; or the opinion that "thinking knows itself to be free only when it diverges from what is universally recognized and valid and when it has discovered for itself some particular character" (PhR, par. 15; par. 4); here again, he does not dismiss the idea of freedom itself. As we shall see in the third part of this paper, he makes this idea the very basis of his philosophy of right. But he argues, just as he had done in the article on Natural Right, that in recent times the aspiration to freedom has been perverted into a principled opposition to any and every given social order, because and inasmuch as this order is given. It is this latter perversion which he condemns.

I have already pointed out that in the article on Natural Right Hegel gives preference to empirical modes of treatment of right over formal ones: he rates the orientation to experience much higher in scientific value than any a priori philosophizing. Political philosophy, he writes, must be applicable to reality; and to be applicable to reality, it must concern itself with individual systems of existing constitutions and legislations, which belong to a determinate people and a determinate time (JS 451; 69 and 510; 117). Still, this privilege which Hegel grants to the orientation toward experience does not turn him into a "positive" scientist. As a matter of fact, the fourth part of the article on Natural Right is wholly devoted to an attempt to distinguish a properly philosophical account of right from the account put forward by the "positive sciences of right." In this part Hegel argues that it is just as mistaken to consider the social and political institutions which already organize our life as in principle unjustifiable as it is to vindicate them *en bloc*, for the very reason that they are already given. Both practices, he says, are conducive to "positivity."

To sustain this argument, he focuses on the notion of "experience" (*Erfahrung*), upon which positive scientists rely in their work; and he points to its ambiguity. The fundamental shortcoming of the positive sciences of right, he says, is that they give us no means of distinguishing, in experience, between what is morally justified and the merely subjective, the contingent:

> In the first place, the positive sciences include in the actual reality [*Wirklichkeit*] to which they claim to relate not just the historical, but also the concepts, principles, relationships and, in general, much of what belongs in itself to Reason and is to express an inner truth and necessity. However, it must be acknowledged that it is in and for itself inadmissible to call upon actual reality and experience on this matter [on what belongs to Reason] and to hold it [what belongs to Reason], against philosophy, as something positive. For it is impossible that anything which is philosophically proved to be nonreal truly comes out in experience. . . . Only philosophy can determine whether something is a subjective point of view or an objective representation, an opinion or a truth. (JS 511; 117f.)

Here, Hegel relies upon a definition of experience and, indeed, of actuality (*Wirklichkeit*) very different from the one commonly accepted by empirical scientists: for him, noticeably enough, only philosophy can determine what is to count as experience and, indeed, as actual (*wirklich*).[6] According to him, indeed, principles, too—whether scientific or moral—can be called actual (*wirklich*). But what can this mean? In what sense, indeed, can a moral principle be called objective or objectively true? And how can the determination of the objectivity of a moral principle be gained from a consideration of experience? How can it be called actual?

At the end of the article on Natural Right, Hegel also strongly insists that philosophy must "teach us to honour necessity" (JS 522; 126).[7] This has induced some of his interpreters to read into his writings a vindication of "Historicism," i.e., of the contention that whatever makes social or political institutions historically necessary also makes them right, i.e., morally justified. In the article on Natural Right, Hegel explicitly denies the validity of this thesis: he distinguishes between what he calls a philosophical account of right and a merely historical one. He contends that "necessity" is not to be confused with historical necessity: according to him, the necessary character of an institution, its "objectivity," does not arise from its being historically given (e.g., JS 526; 129f.).[8] He would undoubtedly have denied, then, that his endeavor to turn political philosophy into a science is nothing other than an attempt to vindicate the thesis that might is right, that what *is* historically the case also is what *ought to be*.

But is this denial justified? And if it is, what can ground the objectivity of our juridical and political representations? How are the principles according to which we direct our actions to be defined, if not as "abstract" ones? What, indeed, may be "concrete" moral or ethical principles of action? To answer these questions, we must try to determine what it is which Hegel calls a philosophical science. We must endeavor to clarify the relationship of this science to metaphysics. This is the task in which I will engage now.

The Transformation of Representations into Thoughts

The very reliance of the "positive" sciences of right upon the "common form of representation" (*die gemeine Vorstellungsart*), Hegel writes in the article on Natural Right, calls for a philosophical justification (JS 510; 118): the crucial yet ambiguous role played by the notion of representation in his analysis of the process of knowledge is already emphasized in his Jena period. This emphasis is a constant of his work as a whole: as I have pointed out in the Introduction, one of his fundamental theses is that philosophy consists in a transformation of representations into thoughts. I will now try to clarify the meaning of this thesis.

Here again, I begin with an examination of Hegel's Jena writings. This examination shows that Hegel's own elaboration of the notion of *Vorstellung* builds upon Kant's use of the term: when, in the article on Natural Right, Hegel argues that the widespread reliance of scientists upon the "common form of representation" calls for a philosophical justification, what he has in mind is undoubtedly Kant's attempt to distinguish, among representations in general, between mere "sensations" (*Empfindungen*) and "objective perceptions" or "knowledge" (*Erkenntnis*). Kant, we should remember, considered both "intuitions" (*Anschauungen*) and "concepts" (*Begriffe*)—concepts of the understanding as well as concepts of reason—as representations (*Vorstellungen*) (Kant 1971: B376ff.). He contended that objective knowledge requires intuitions as well as concepts. However, he argued that the distinction between objective knowledge and mere opinion does not depend on representations themselves but, rather, on the form of our judgments. Instead of asking, as had been done before, whether representations—or, for that matter, "ideas" in general—are impressed upon our mind by sensory means or are innate, he examined the form of the connection established by the judgment between intuitions and concepts. He analyzed the different ways in which intuitions and concepts are related in our judgments; and he argued that an objectively valid relationship, a judgment, holds only where those representations are not simply taken together in our mind but related to one another according to certain rules—the categories—and this, on the basis of a necessary unity: the original synthetic unity of apperception.

In "Faith and Knowledge," an article which was written at approximately the same time as the article on Natural Right (1802/1803), Hegel explicitly endorses this account: he praises Kant's assertion, according to which intuitions without concepts are blind and concepts without intuitions are empty. Kant, he also writes, rightfully acknowledged that synthetic a priori judgments are only possible under the presupposition of some transcendental power of unification, of synthesis: the capacity of the original synthetic unity of apperception. But, he argues, Kant was ultimately unfaithful to his own discovery. This is the point at which he puts forward what will come to be known as the most fundamental assumption of his philosophical system as a whole: the "idealistic" thesis of identity between thought and being (e.g., JS 302; 67).[9] Kant's fundamental mistake, he says, is to have failed to acknowledge the validity of this thesis. Kant's philosophy "remains entirely within the opposition" (*schlechthin in dem Gegensatze verweilt*): Kant took for granted a fundamental opposition of spirit to the world, soul to body, self to nature. To account for the "objectivity" of our representations, however, we ought to "sublate" (*aufheben*) the opposition (*Gegensatz*), and to acknowledge the identity of "subjectivity" with "objectivity." Furthermore, we ought to consider this identity, not just as a postulate, but as the starting point of philosophy and its sole content (JS 302–307; 67–72). What is the meaning of these sentences? How, indeed, should Hegel's "absolute idealism" be interpreted?

Interpreters often see in it nothing other than an extreme form of subjective idealism: Hegel, they say, would have argued that since it is preposterous to say anything at all about an object that can have no relation to our consciousness, since it is impossible to speak of a reality apart from a subject, consciousness itself must be proclaimed the ultimate and unconditioned reality: hence the identification of reality with thought. My contention is, however, that this interpretation is erroneous. Furthermore, it distorts the meaning of Hegel's philosophy as a whole. As a matter of fact, Hegel himself disowned it: he did not just dismiss subjective idealism as a theory of knowledge. As we shall see below, he also criticized any and every philosophy focusing upon "consciousness" as the knowing subject and bearer of representations. It is this latter criticism which makes it impossible, I think, to consider his own system as yet another version—albeit extreme— of subjective idealism.

Hegel's criticism of Kant in the *Encyclopaedia of Philosophical Sciences* (1830) hinges precisely upon the assumption that consciousness (*Bewusstsein*) is the bearer of representations and thus of knowledge: Reinhold, Hegel writes, accurately grasped the meaning of Kant's philosophy when he characterized it as "a theory of *consciousness* (*eine Theorie des Bewusstseins*), named the *power of representation*" (*Vorstellungsvermoögen*: Enz., par. 415 Z.). This mention of Karl Reinhold is illuminating: one may rightly say, it seems to me, that Hegel's criticism of Kant is not so much a criticism of Kant's philosophy itself as a criticism of the conception ascribed to Kant by Reinhold. I will now attempt to spell out the meaning of this criticism. This will enable me to determine what Hegel has in mind when he castigates what may be called the point of view of consciousness.

Reinhold, who was one of Kant's most popular interpreters in Hegel's time, had argued that philosophers should adopt as the basis and fundamental point of departure of their enterprise a universal principle or, rather, a "fact"—one which is not itself demonstrable but rather immediately evident: the "fact of consciousness" (*die Tatsache des Bewusstseins*). The mere reflection over the "fact of consciousness," Reinhold wrote, shows that all our rational activity rests upon one central function, viz., "representing." Furthermore, it shows that every one of our representations is made of two different, heterogeneous elements: the material stuff, which results from the stimulation of our senses by the "object," by things in the outer world, and the form, stemming from the knowing "subject," from thought. Still, the very fact that our representations have a twofold origin means that we cannot know the world as it is in itself, or the subject in itself, but only what exists between the two: the world of phenomena.[10]

Reinhold's doctrine, which purported to be a systematic reconstruction of Kant's theory of knowledge, actually turns this theory into nothing other than a psychology: according to Reinhold, one may say, Kant's theory of knowledge ultimately consists of a purely descriptive analysis of the contents of consciousness. It makes sense to argue, indeed, that Reinhold's reconstruction of Kant comes very close to Locke's purely "historical," i.e., merely descriptive account of knowledge. Reinhold's own account, to be sure, reaches beyond mere description: in his reconstruction, Reinhold allows himself to refer to a subject and an object of knowledge. He contends that the "matter" (*Stoff*) of our representations is *given*, whereas their "form" is *produced* by us. But he insists, just like Kant, that we cannot know or even think the thing-in-itself—the very factor which allegedly provides us with the matter of our representations. His own original contention is that we cannot make ourselves a representation of the thing-in-itself. Yet the presupposition of a thing-in-itself plays an essential role in his reconstruction: it alone enables him to refer to an "object" of knowledge which would be "given" to us, and to oppose to this given object the spontaneity of the "subject," i.e., of thought. From this it may be inferred that Reinhold, his own assertions notwithstanding, provides us with yet another dogmatic and metaphysical account of the process of knowledge.

Hegel believes Reinhold's account to be faithful to the spirit of Kant's philosophy—but he holds this account against Kant himself: in "Faith and Knowledge," Hegel takes the assumption of the thing-in-itself to be an essential presupposition of Kant's thought; and he contends that this assumption induced Kant inadvertently to replace the attempt to account for the objectivity of knowledge with a causal explanation of the way in which impressions affect the mind (JS 310f.; 76f.). He also draws attention to the alleged similarity between Kant's and Locke's accounts of knowledge, and he criticizes both: it should be obvious, he says, that a causal or genetical explanation cannot account for the "objectivity" of our knowledge.

At the root of Kant's mistaken ascription of intuitions to the causal effect of the thing-in-itself upon our mind, Hegel argues, is the contention that the subject of representations is "consciousness"—or that categories belong to consciousness, i.e., to a subjective ego.[11] Kant's fundamental mistake,

Hegel explains, was his failure to distinguish in a clear enough way between that which accounts for the representations, i.e., the capacity of the original synthetic unity of apperception, and "the representing [ability]," that empty I, which allegedly accompanies all our representations: Kant related the synthetic unity of apperception to a consciousness, which he ultimately defined in a psychologistic way, by means of the different psychological faculties embodied in it. He fell thereby into a merely "psychological idealism," one which cannot account for the objectivity of our knowledge (JS 308f.; 75).

It is worth noting, too, that in "Faith and Knowledge" Hegel does not hesitate to define consciousness by the opposition of concepts to intuitions, and to assimilate it to the act of seeing (JS 305; 70). His criticism of all the philosophies in which the bearer of representations is consciousness may well be considered as, basically, a criticism of all the conceptions according to which knowing consists in nothing else than seeing. At Jena, Hegel repeatedly criticizes "reflective" forms of thought: forms of thought which are modeled upon visual metaphors and rest upon the process by means of which a subject "reflects," in the literal sense of this metaphorical term, i.e., brings back to himself, the image of an object. This criticism, let it be emphasized at this point, should not be taken to mean that according to Hegel the acquisition of knowledge involves no reliance at all upon perception. Hegel instead argues that the act of seeing proper cannot be the ground, the foundation of our representations: had we only been endowed with "consciousness," i.e., with the faculty of seeing, he says, we would never have been able to form representations of our subject matter, and therefore to know. Although Kant himself acknowledged this point, he would have believed consciousness to be the sole bearer and ultimate foundation of representations; and this would mean that he remained caught in a reflective conception of knowledge. His own assertions notwithstanding, Kant would thus have been ultimately unable to account for our very representative capacity.

By denying the common association of representations to consciousness, Hegel thus wants to shift our attention from whatever "appears" to our consciousness—i.e., from knowing as seeing—to the logical or, rather, the categorial form in which we couch our assertions about reality. In his Introduction to the *Science of Logic* (1812), he points out that this book consists of a critical presentation of the categories or "forms of thought" (*Denkformen*), which "in general run through our mind instinctively and unconsciously" (WdL I, 18; 39) and which are "displayed and stored in human language" (WdL I, 9; 31): this is but another way of describing his endeavor to transform representations into thoughts. This endeavor may well be considered, fundamentally, as an attempt to clarify the conceptual, or categorial, presuppositions of our judgments.

In the passage of the *Science of Logic* I have just quoted, Hegel also draws attention to language. In the *Encyclopaedia* itself, he deems language one of the primary forms of "representational thinking" (e.g., Enz., par.

459). One privileged way of accounting for the meaning of his attempt to transform representations into thoughts would thus be to examine his conception of language. In this examination, too, one ought first to pay attention to his criticism of the point of view of consciousness: Hegel contends that it is just as erroneous to ascribe language to consciousness as it is to consider consciousness as the bearer of representations in general. One cannot account for language, he says, as long as one assumes as a point of departure a fundamental opposition of the self to the world, one on the basis of which man would consciously ascribe names to given objects in the world.

In the *Encyclopaedia*, he ascribes language to "spirit" (*Geist*): he argues that language is an essentially "spiritual" activity. This argument matches his more general thesis: that *Anschauen* and *Vorstellen*, intuitive and representational thought, ought to be related to spirit (*Geist*), not to consciousness (*Bewusstsein*: Enz., pars. 445–468). The notion of *Geist*, one should remember, is the fundamental notion of his system: his is an idealism of the "spirit," not of consciousness. But what is the difference between ascribing representations or, for that matter, language to spirit, and ascribing them to consciousness?

On these questions, the examination of the Jena writings is again illuminating:[12] at Jena, in 1802/1803, Hegel writes that language does not and cannot exist as the language of an individual, but only as the language of a collectivity, a people.[13] But the ascription of language to the "spirit" of the people in which it develops is a typical Romantic thesis: it quite naturally calls to the mind Herder's (1772; in Herder 1960) considerations on language in his famous *Treatise upon the Origin of Language* (cp. Berlin 1976). Indeed, one striking feature of Hegel's philosophy of language at Jena is its indebtedness to the terminology of Romanticism—the terminology proper to all those Romantic trends of thought which developed precisely during the years of Hegel's stay at Jena (1800–1807), at and around the town of Jena itself (see Bienenstock 1979). It is thus tempting to argue that in his criticism of "reflective" philosophies, Hegel chimes in with his Romantic contemporaries and, beyond them, with Herder, one of their main sources of inspiration: just like Herder, Hegel would have denied that language is merely an instrument which man—as an individual—would invent in order to communicate his ideas to other men. He would have contended that man's thought, far from preceding language, is rather shaped by it: by using language, a man would take in nothing less than the whole vision of the world of the community, the people, to which he belongs. The world as it appears to us, Hegel would thus have believed, always has a meaning for us, even before we consciously relate to it. To put this in Romantic terms, one may well say that according to him this world always already "speaks" to us. "Nature" itself, indeed, would appear to us as always already informed by a language, i.e., by categories, and therefore by thought: this would account for the meaning of Hegel's fundamental thesis of identity between thought and reality, subject and object.[14]

It cannot be denied that Hegel's "absolute idealism" builds upon motives traditionally identified as Romantic ones. But it seems to me that the feature which connects Hegel's philosophy to Romanticism is the emphasis not so much upon the collective and historical dimension of language as upon its mythical origins: one of the most characteristic features of myth, one may say, is the lack of distinction in it between word and thing, between the real and the ideal, meaning and being. Where we see a mere symbol or representation, myth assumes a real identity: the image would not represent the thing, it would be the thing itself. The word, or the sign, would not merely refer to or designate something. It would be the object itself: it would include within itself the object, together with the powers this object is believed to have. Everything happens as if Hegel, just like many Romantics of his time, had endorsed this mythical account of language. For he contends that if the world always already appears to us as informed by a language, as meaningful, this is because the thing is originally identical with the word, *Sache* with *Sage* or *Kategorie*.[15]

He assumes that categories are not just determinations of thought but also inform the world—the social and historical world as well as nature itself: just like Kant, he argues that consciousness must abandon the idea of an objectivity independent of its knowledge and recognize that everything is "permeated" by categories. As against Kant, however, he contends that categories are not just formal determinations of statements or of thinking, but rather grasp the order of reality itself. Here, he rehabilitates what he takes to be the position of classical metaphysical thought. In the *Encyclopaedia*, he thus writes that "this science [metaphysics] considered thought-determinations as the *fundamental determinations of things;* by this presupposition, that whatever *is* is also known *in itself,* inasmuch as it is *thought,* it stands higher than the later critical philosophizing" (Enz., par. 28). Here, he states his fundamental thesis of identity between thought and being. One may well read into this thesis, I think, a vindication of the contention that language and, beyond it, knowledge itself are grounded in myth.

Commentators often take this thesis to mean that according to Hegel we possess not just empirical intuitions of phenomena, but also metaphysical intuitions: by vindicating, as against Kant, the existence of intellectual intuitions, Hegel would have wanted to assert that we can gain an absolute knowledge of the world as such, not just a knowledge of phenomena, of the world as it appears to us. Such an interpretation is, it seems to me, inadequate, and also very misleading: it may well induce us to turn Hegel's philosophy into a philosophy in which knowing ultimately means nothing other than "seeing" or intuiting an object; whereas, as I have attempted to show above, Hegel sets his mind upon criticizing this very conception of knowledge.

It is worth noting, indeed, that although Hegel praises classical metaphysics for its acceptance of the thesis of identity, he also sharply criticizes this traditional branch of learning; and he criticizes it precisely because of its reliance upon what he calls "immediate intuition" (*unmittelbare Anschauung*).

Thus, to quote just one example here, in the Preface to the 1807 *Phenomenology of Spirit*, his Jena masterpiece, Hegel inveighs against all those conceptions according to which, as he puts it: "the True exists only in what, or better *as* what, is sometimes called intuition, sometimes knowledge of the Absolute."[16] The conceptions he has in mind then are Jacobi's "immediacy philosophy," but also, first and foremost, Schelling's mythical *Naturphilosophie*. What he criticizes in these conceptions is the attempt to ground knowledge upon pure metaphysical intuitions.

Acknowledging that Hegel drew much of his inspiration from the mythical conception of language and thought proper to certain of his Romantic or pre-Romantic contemporaries does not mean, then, that he merely endorsed their *Weltanschauung*. My contention is, as a matter of fact, that far from endorsing this *Weltanschauung*, Hegel instead took issue with it: he made it the main target of his criticism. His own account of language is not, I think, a mythical one but, rather, an attempt to break with the Romantic conception of language, to move from *mythos* to *logos*: he sets his mind upon exposing the fundamental errors of a mythological conception of language; and he endeavors to show that what is presupposed by our ability to speak is Reason itself, as *logos*.

It is in Aristotle's philosophy of mind that Hegel hoped to find means of refuting the then popular mythical conceptions of language and of thought. I cannot engage in this chapter in a detailed examination of the reading Hegel makes of Aristotle's *De Anima*. But I would like to emphasize that Hegel's own conception of "representational thinking" undoubtedly draws mainly upon Aristotle's philosophy: in a way strikingly similar to Aristotle, he defines "spirit" as "the essence of consciousness" (*das Wesen des Bewusstseins*).[17] Here, he contends that our soul is ontologically in harmony with the world, and that it is precisely because it is in such a harmony with the world that we can gain knowledge. To understand how knowledge is possible, he says, we must assume some fundamental community of nature, an identity of sorts, between the self and the world, matter and spirit, body and mind. It is this "identity" which explains how knowing or representing is possible.

It is also this identity which accounts for the fact that although the representations we make ourselves of the world are proper to a certain people and a certain time, although they are framed in a determinate language, they can be established as objectively valid. It is, I think, Hegel's appeal to Aristotle's philosophy which induced him to believe that he could escape the harmful subjectivist implications of the immediacy philosophies typical of that Romanticism which was so popular in his time. But how, then, can one determine, according to him, the "objective" validity of a representation?

According to him, it is dialectics which fulfils this role. Although Hegel considers "representational" thinking (*vorstellendes Denken*) as a necessary stage in the acquisition of knowledge, he also criticizes it; and it is precisely as against representational forms of knowledge that, in the Preface to the

Phenomenology of Spirit, for example, he sets his own dialectical or, for that matter, "speculative" thinking. I would not hesitate to say that "dialectics," in Hegel, draws its meaning not so much from an opposition to positivism as from an opposition to metaphysical forms of thought which rely upon immediate intuition and representation.[18] Here again, however, one must keep in mind Hegel's main thesis: that representations are anchored in "spirit," not in "consciousness." This thesis can be taken to mean, I think, that representations, but also intuitions, are always already informed—albeit in an immediate way—by logic, or by categories. According to Hegel, it is not consciousness which has logic, but logic which imbues consciousness.[19] In the *Encyclopaedia,* Hegel writes that whether we are aware of it or not, logical categories are what we always already have at our disposal (Enz., par. 24 Z.): the "logical," he says, is natural to us; it impregnates all our behavior. For him, then, dialectics is the approach that enables us to extract the logical or categorial form from those material intuitions or representations in which it is embedded. This is the means through which we can engage in the ascent from "representations" to "thoughts" (*Denkformen*) or categories, and from "thoughts" to the "Concept" (*Begriff*): to the "Form," which accounts for the unity, the coherence, of both our thought and the world itself. One may well say, indeed, that dialectics is essentially an endeavor to define this Form.

The Foundations of Theory and Practice

I will now attempt to show that Hegel's attempt to transform representations into thoughts can be made to account for the meaning of his practical philosophy as well as for that of his theoretical philosophy: just as, in his theoretical philosophy, Hegel contends that the representations scientists make themselves of nature stand in need of a philosophical justification, so in his practical philosophy, too, he argues that the representations we make ourselves of the purposes of our moral and political activity can and must be accounted for philosophically. The reason why modern political theorists do not see the need for any such justification, he says, is that they relate these representations to man's consciousness. Instead of this, however, they should relate them to the spirit, i.e., to the total way of life of the people who develop them: they should explicate the inner logic of this life: the Idea or Form of this life.

Already in the Introduction to the *Principles of the Philosophy of Right,* Hegel draws attention to the essentially representational character of the human will. He also infers from this character far-reaching implications: that the human will, in contradistinction to any merely instinctive, animal behavior, is directed by the representation of a purpose shows, he says, that the sharp distinction contemporary philosophers want to establish between theory and practice is misguided.

> The theoretical is essentially contained in the practical. This goes against the representation that the two are separate, for one cannot have a will without

intelligence. On the contrary, the will contains in itself the theoretical: the will determines itself and this determination is in the first place internal, because I represent to myself what I want, this is an object for me [was ich will, stelle ich mich vor, ist Gegenstand für mich]. An animal acts on instinct, is driven by an inner impulse and so it too is practical, but it has no will since it does not represent to itself what it desires [weil es sich das nicht vorstellt, was es begehrt]. (PhR, par. 4 Z.)

What Hegel has in mind in this polemical passage is the clear-cut distinction that Kant had established between theoretical and practical philosophy. Kant himself, we should remember, had not denied that our voluntary actions are directed by representations. But he had distinguished between, essentially, two kinds of actions: technical actions, and properly practical ones. Strictly speaking, he had said, the technical application of theoretical laws ought to be considered as merely a corollary of theoretical philosophy: technical propositions, which concern the production of objects, rest upon theoretical representations. To formulate them, we need to first represent to ourselves the object which we want to produce; and also the theoretical laws, the causal relationships, by means of which we think it possible to produce this object. We must assume the validity of causal relationships: relationships between a cause—in this case, the will itself, which may be considered as a natural cause—and an effect, the object to be produced. We then put these relationships to use: we apply them to particular cases.

But, Kant had said, practical philosophy in its proper sense does not deal with the technical application of theoretical knowledge. Rather, it deals with acts grounded in freedom, actions in which the essence and purpose of the will is freedom; and these are actions directed not by "concepts of nature"—essentially, the category of causality—but by the "concept of freedom." However, no theory can account for freedom. For scientific knowledge requires both concepts and empirical intuitions. Yet although we do have a concept of freedom, this is a concept of reason, not one of the understanding; and we can have no intuition corresponding to it. Having an intuition of freedom would mean having an intuition of the thing-in-itself—a metaphysical intuition, an intuition of the supersensible, and there are no such intuitions: "the natural concept represents its objects in intuition, not as things in themselves, but as mere phenomena; the concept of freedom, on the other hand, represents in its object a thing in itself, but not in intuition" (Kant 1951: Introd. I and II). According to Kant, then, the reason why we can gain no knowledge of freedom is that we lack any intuition or representation of the object of freedom. It is also because we lack such an intuition that the distinction between theory and practice (as studied by practical philosophy) is necessary.

In the *Philosophy of Right*, Hegel explicitly vindicates Kant's conception of freedom. In the Introduction to this book he writes, just like Kant, that "a will is truly a will only when what it wills, its content, is identical with itself, when, that is to say, freedom wills freedom" (PhR, par. 21 Z.). He unambiguously posits as the basis of his practical philosophy as a whole and also, more particularly, of his political philosophy, the concept of the free will; and he contends that right in general, and also the state, are grounded upon this concept (PhR, par. 4). The state, according to him, is not the outcome of natural necessity or, for that matter, of an instrumental calculus men would make in order to determine the best means of preserving their own individual rights, or of furthering their welfare. To put this in Kantian terms, one may well say that according to him the state does not result from a hypothetical imperative but, rather, from a categorical imperative as fundamental and essential to our nature as the moral imperative, which tells us how to behave in our relationships with other individual human beings.

In contrast to Kant, however, Hegel contends that a theoretical knowledge of freedom is possible. It is tempting to argue here that the reason why he thinks such a knowledge possible is that, unlike Kant, Hegel is convinced that we have, not just empirical intuitions, but also intuitions of suprasensible objects, metaphysical intuitions: it would be because Hegel asserted the existence of metaphysical intuitions, not just of empirical ones, that he thought it possible to gain "objective truth" in moral and political matters. But this answer is very misleading, I think, about the meaning of Hegel's political philosophy as a whole: as I have attempted to show in the second part of this chapter, Hegel, far from making his political philosophy contingent upon the existence and validity of metaphysical intuitions, makes these intuitions the main target of his criticism. This also applies to his practical philosophy: just as, in his theoretical philosophy, he castigates the reliance upon immediate intuition as a form of knowledge, so in his practical philosophy, too, he denies that the truth about the state can be grounded upon any immediate intuitions.

Noticeably enough, indeed, he accuses Kant himself of having contributed to the justification and propagation of the political Romanticism which spread in his time: that "the true itself cannot be known," he writes, has induced many to conclude "that what is true is what every individual lets rise in his heart, out of his emotion and enthusiasm, about ethical matters, especially about the state, the government, and the constitution" (PhR, par. 18; par. 5). Modern political philosophy thus ends up merely vindicating the immediacy of feelings and intuitions. But, Hegel insists, the attempt to ground moral and ethical principles on "the authority of inner feeling and of the heart" (PhR, par. 14; par. 3)—i.e., I take it, on immediate ethical intuitions—is politically disastrous.

Hegel's political philosophy itself is prompted by the intention to cope with the contention that in matters of religious, ethical, or moral feelings, no rational discussion is possible. It purports to provide an answer to those who claim that a political organization, a state, draws its strength and justification from *immediate* feelings. One may well say, indeed, that the main target of Hegel's political criticism was the *Gefühlsrevolution*, which spread throughout Germany during his lifetime: just like many of his contemporaries, Hegel acknowledges the weight of religious and moral feelings. He also recognizes their political meaning. As a matter of fact, he considers such feelings as the very basis, the ground of the state. But he maintains that the identification or *definition* of these feelings is the very purpose of political philosophy; and he repeats, over and over again, that immediate feelings or aspirations cannot be vindicated as such, as immediate. If considered in their immediacy, he says, such aspirations include the best, but also the worst; and there is no assurance that what is vindicated in them is indeed moral. In fact, it is quite clear that most often this is not the case.

But how can freedom itself be defined? In the Introduction to the *Philosophy of Right*, Hegel refers his readers to the methods whereby classical theories of right hoped to define their basic concepts, and he criticizes them:

> The procedure was to presuppose the *representation (Vorstellung)* of the will and to attempt to derive from it a precise definition; then the so-called *proof* of the will's freedom was extracted, in the manner of the old empirical psychology, from the consideration that the different feelings and phenomena of the ordinary consciousness, such as remorse, guilt and the like, can only be *explained* in the light of a *free* will. But it is more convenient of course to arrive at the same point by taking the short cut of supposing that freedom is *given* as a *fact* of consciousness (*Tatsache des Bewusstseins*) and that we must *believe* in it. (PhR, par. 4, A.)

According to Hegel in this passage, classical theories of right are no better than modern conceptions: they, too, are unable to provide us with an adequate definition of freedom. For in them, just as in Kantian and neo-Kantian accounts of practical philosophy, consciousness is assumed to be the bearer and foundation of our representations. But relating representations to consciousness induces us to remain at the level of representational thinking, and prevents us from raising from representations to thoughts, and from thoughts to the Concept.

At this point Hegel refers the reader to his *Encyclopaedia*. It is in this book, he says, that he exposed the premises of his argument:

> that *spirit* to start with is *intelligence*, that the determinations through which it passes in its development, from *feeling (Gefühl)*, through *representing (Vorstellen)*, to *thinking (Denken)*, are the road along which it produces itself as *will*, and that will, as practical spirit in general, is the truth closest to intelligence. (PhR, par. 4, Z.)

This, then, is the link which relates Hegel's practical philosophy to his system as a whole: the transformation of representations into thoughts, and of thoughts into the Concept, he argues, is a process just as fundamental to practical as to theoretical knowledge.

Accounting for the objectivity of practical or, for that matter, political knowledge requires that we correctly understand the nature of this process. To this end, we must refrain from relating representations to consciousness. In the Introduction to the *Philosophy of Right*, Hegel explicitly states that in this book he will not consider separately the "conscious" form of the will. This form, he writes, is one in which "the *formal* will of self-consciousness . . . *finds* an external world *facing* it." The "relation of consciousness," as he defines it, is grounded in the opposition of a self-certain I to an independent object, one which would be external to the I. But taking such an opposition for granted, Hegel explains, prevents us from determining which "determinations of the will" (*Willensbestimmungen*) are merely subjective, and which ones are truly rational (PhR, par. 8).

In the Introduction to the 1820 *Philosophy of Right*, he also points to the ambivalence of the commonsensical opposition of subjective to objective. It is only for representational thinking and for the understanding, he says, that the logical categories of subjectivity and objectivity have a "hard and fast meaning"(PhR, par. 26 and Z.): here, he undoubtedly draws upon his fundamental thesis of identity between thought and being. I have mentioned in the second part of this chapter one quite common, very popular way of interpreting this latter thesis: Hegel would have wanted to argue that objectivity itself—indeed, the actual world—should be considered as the product of our consciousness. This interpretation, first put forward as an attempt to account for Hegel's "absolute idealistic" conception of knowledge as such, is most popular with those commentators who focus upon Hegel's social and political philosophy. It makes much sense to argue, many of them say, that Hegel's absolute idealism draws its meaning from an attempt to envisage the social and political world in which men live as the product, or the expression, of their actions. Whether or not this thesis makes sense in the natural sciences, they note, is highly problematic. But, they insist, it should be acknowledged that it is quite cogent in the human and social sciences (see Taylor 1975).

Thus their interpretation turns Hegelianism as a whole into a philosophy of human subjectivity: these commentators posit as the fundamental starting point of their reconstruction the notion of subjectivity; and they endeavor to determine how this subjectivity expresses or objectifies itself in actuality. To be sure, they may well want to define this subjectivity in various ways. They may want, for example, to emphasize the social or political nature of man: by ascribing political and social representations to spirit rather than to consciousness, Hegel would then have wanted to say that the subject of history is not man as an individual but rather a human collectivity, a people. Furthermore, Hegel would have argued that man himself—as an individual— is most often not aware of the collective purposes of the people to which he belongs. However, Hegel's main intention would precisely have been to show how or in what ways man can become aware of these purposes: has he not defined history as a whole as "progress in the consciousness of freedom"?

Much of the contemporary discussion over the meaning of Hegel's political philosophy thus focuses upon the definition of man—this true subject of history—that Hegel would have endorsed.[20] Whatever the definition of human subjectivity adopted in this discussion, it is taken for granted that

Hegel developed nothing other than what I have called earlier in this chapter a philosophy of consciousness. As I have already attempted to show, however, Hegel's absolute idealism is not and should not be considered as merely an extreme form of subjective idealism. Hegel's thesis of the identity of theory and practice itself does not rest upon the contention that man's mind—or a people's mind, or God's mind itself, defined in analogy with the human mind—is creative or productive of actuality. Hegel himself, let it be repeated here, explicitly criticized all possible variants of subjective idealism: he claimed that these variants tend to replace the attempt to ground the objectivity of knowledge with an inquiry into its origins; but that no genetical description of the process of knowledge can account for its validity.

Ends vs. Purposes

In the *Philosophy of Right* Hegel nowhere examines the origin of the representations we adopt as the purposes of our actions. He does not attempt to relate these actions or, for that matter, the institutions which we would create through such actions, to purposes or intentions we would have set ourselves, whether collectively or as individuals. Rather, he relates them to what he calls their end (*Zweck*) or final end (*Endzweck*). But he explicitly distinguishes between the categories of *Zweck* and *Endzweck* on the one hand and the notions of "purpose" (*Vorsatz*) and "intention" (*Absicht*: PhR, pars. 115–128) on the other hand. This distinction is crucial to the understanding of his political philosophy. As a matter of fact, it is precisely because many commentators overlook it—they inadvertently reduce the notion of *Zweck* to yet another kind of "purpose"—that they are led to turn Hegel's political philosophy into only a philosophy of human subjectivity. I will now try to clarify its meaning.

In Hegel's thought, both purposes (*Vorsätze*) and intentions (*Absichte*) are representations (*Vorstellungen*). Hegel makes this unambiguously clear in the passages of the *Philosophy of Right* in which he deals with "purposive" and "intentional" actions. In an action directed by a purpose, he says, "the will has before itself an existing situation upon which it acts. But in order to be able to do this, it must have a representation [*Vorstellung*] of this situation." Indeed, he continues: "the responsibility [for the action] is truly mine only inasmuch as I had knowledge of the situation confronting me" (PhR, par. 117, Z.). Furthermore, he insists: "that I acknowledge only that which was my representation [*Vorstellung*] marks the transition to the intention [*Absicht*]. That is to say, one can impute to me only what I knew of the circumstances" (PhR, par. 118, Z.).

In his analysis of an "intentional action" (*absichtliche Handlung*), Hegel also plays upon the etymological roots of the German term *Absicht*, which means *absehen* or abstracting: he contends that to define our intentions, we resort to a process of "abstraction." This is worth noting: according to him, when we act intentionally we engage in a process quite similar to the one which we use in our theoretical scientific work. We single out from the situation as a whole what we take to be its "universal" character; and it is this character which we adopt as the purpose of our action. But as I have tried to show in the first part of this chapter, Hegel dismisses abstract political theorizing: he deems "abstract" both the allegedly purely empirical and the allegedly a priori forms of political theorizing. His discussion of the structure of purposive and intentional actions sheds additional light, I think, upon the meaning of that criticism. It is true, Hegel now acknowledges, that, juridically speaking, we can only be held responsible for those universal representations which we acknowledge as our intentions. But, he says, the discussion of the notion of responsibility is only one part of political philosophy. In fact, it is not its proper, ultimate aim. For political philosophy proper does not deal with matters of juridical responsibility. It does not purport either to call for this or that action. The role of the philosopher is not so much to call for action as to focus upon the principles which are supposed to direct this action, and to analyze them; to try to determine what, in matters of morality, is objectively true; or what it is, to be free; and to determine which of our actions are actually free—or which are "objectively" moral—we must relate them not to our purposes or intentions but, rather, to the final end (*Endzweck*) we pursue in them.

Yet it ought to be acknowledged that whereas both purposes (*Vorsätze*) and intentions (*Absichte*) are representations (*Vorstellungen*), the notion of *Endzweck* is not a representation. Purposiveness (*Zweckmässigkeit*) is not definable in terms of human desires; and teleological explanations, explanations by means of the notions of *Zweck* or *Endzweck*, are not explanations in terms of such subjective, human purposes and desires as vary from person to person. For Hegel, relating men's actions to their final end does not consist in relating them to human desires or intentions, whether these desires be conscious or unconscious ones. The notion of *Zweck* rather is a category or, more exactly, a Concept (*Begriff*)—in the full Hegelian sense of the term. It performs a categorial role: it introduces unity in a manifold. To put this in yet other terms, one may well say, I think, that it is that which accounts for the connection of representations which we establish in our judgments: by arguing that men's practical judgments are directed by an "end," Hegel wants to say that they themselves—but also men's actions and, beyond these actions, men's way of life as a whole are structured by an underlying unity, a rationality of their own. Whether we are aware of it or not, he argues, our actions and, indeed, our way of life as a whole are articulated by a conceptual structure; and the task of the political philosopher consists in bringing out this conceptual structure.

In Hegel as in Kant, then, what is "practical" is not the relationship of human purposes or intentions to men's actions themselves or to the way in which these actions manifest themselves in social and political institutions but, rather, the relationship of categories to reality. In Hegel's system itself, let it be unequivocally stated here, the subjective is not the mental or the intentional but, rather, the Concept; and the objective is not just that which is external to us, or that which reaches us from the outside by means of sense perception. Rather, this is "that which is *in and for itself*," or *"the absolute being of the Concept"* (WdL II, 358; 709f. See also Enz., par. 41 and Z.): Hegel defines "objectivity" as the realization—albeit incomplete—of the conceptual structure of the world in which we live.

One should note, too, that the representations Hegel examines in the *Philosophy of Right* are not just those representations which we set ourselves as purposes or intentions, but also the representations we can make ourselves of already existing, actual institutions. In the Introduction to the *Philosophy of Right*, indeed, Hegel makes it explicit that in this book he will examine the "content" of the will as such, and that this means considering the inner, as yet unrealized purposes of our actions, but also purposes already realized, i.e., already present in the institutions within which we live (PhR, par. 9). The *Philosophy of Right* consists mostly of an examination of the representations we make ourselves of already existing institutions: the institution of private property or private right in general, for example.

This should arouse no surprise: one may rightly wonder how indeed it is possible to extract the logical form, the conceptual unity of actions which have not yet been realized, and which are present in us only under the form of immediate intuitions. In the Preface of the *Philosophy of Right*, Hegel strongly insists upon the fact that it is actually only after an action has been performed that philosophers can endeavor to extract its logical form. Philosophy, he says, always comes too late.

No wonder, then, that according to Hegel political philosophy can hardly formulate a normative doctrine about the way in which we ought to act in our political life. It must rather endeavor to transform the realm of representations. But this is far from being practically insignificant. Wasn't Hegel right, indeed, when he wrote: "I am getting convinced more and more every day that theoretical work brings about more in the world than practical work; once the realm of representation is revolutionized, actuality does not hold [ist erst das Reich der Vorstellung revolutioniert, so hält die Wirklichkeit nicht aus]"?[21]

Acknowledgment

Comments by Ora Gruengard on earlier drafts were very helpful.

Notes

1. For the abbreviations of Hegel's works, see the references. I shall follow the usual practice of citing only the paragraph numbers of the *Encyclopaedia (Enz)* and the *Principles of the Philosophy of Right (PhR)*. All translations are mine. But I have been greatly helped by the following translations (to which the second page number in parentheses refers): *Natural Law. The Scientific Ways of Treating Natural Law, Its Place in Moral Philosophy, and Its Relation to the Positive Sciences of Law*, tr. by T.M. Knox, University of Pennsylvania Press, Philadelphia 1975; *The Difference Between Fichte's and Schelling's System of Philosophy*, tr. by H. S. Harris and W. Cerf, State

University of New York Press, Albany 1977; *Faith and Knowledge,* tr. by W. Cerf and H. S. Harris, State University of New York Press, Albany 1977; *Hegel's Science of Logic,* tr. by A. V. Miller, Humanities Press, New York 1976; *Hegel's Philosophy of Right,* tr. by T.M. Knox, Oxford University Press, Oxford 1967.

2. Popper (1963: 41f., 392–395). See also the similar and more recent criticism of Ernst Tugendhat (1979: 351).

3. Compare Fulda (1982).

4. See here, first and foremost, Marcuse (1960: 27).

5. It is quite typical of Hegel to play upon the opposition, common in language, of the "positive" to the "negative." Hegel assumes that vindicating the given consists of "positing" it, i.e., in affirming it. He then contends that principles which are formed by the mere negation of this affirmation or position are just as dependent upon the given and therefore just as "positive" as principles directly extracted from experience: they are just as ungrounded. From this it can be inferred that by "opposition," he means here contradiction.

6. When, in the *Philosophy of Right,* Hegel entreats his readers to acknowledge that "what is rational is actual and what is actual is rational" (PhR, par. 24; par. 10), he presupposes, just as in the article on Natural Right, that only philosophy can determine what counts as actual.

7. These sentences echo the lapidary declarations of the somewhat earlier manuscript on the German constitution, according to which men should acknowledge that what *is* also is what *ought to be* (*Frühe Schriften,* Suhrkamp Verlag, 1971, p. 463; *Hegel's Political Writings,* tr. by T.M. Knox, Oxford, 1964, p. 145; and also the famous epigram of the *Philosophy of Right*—quoted in the Introduction to this chapter—which ascribes to philosophy the role of comprehending what is, and no more).

8. See also, in the *Philosophy of Right,* the following passage: "Spurning that difference [the difference between the historical and the philosophical study of law] induces one to displace the point of view and to slip over from the question of the true justification to a justification by an appeal to circumstances, to deductions from presupposed conditions which are in themselves inappropriate to play this role [the role of a true justification], and so forth. To generalize, by this means the relative is put in place of the absolute and the external appearance in place of the nature of the thing. When those who try to justify things on historical grounds confound the origin in external circumstances with the origin in the concept, they unconsciously achieve the very opposite of what they intend. Once the origin of an institution in determinate circumstances turns out to be fully adapted [to the circumstances] and necessary, the demands of the historical standpoint are fulfilled. But if this is supposed to pass for a general justification of the thing itself, it turns out to be the opposite, because, since those circumstances are no longer present, the institution, so far from being justified, has rather lost [by their disappearance] its meaning and its right" (PhR, par. 3, A.).

9. See also, for a vindication of this thesis, Hegel's article on "The Difference Between Fichte's and Schelling's System of Philosophy" (1801; JS 9–138).

10. On Reinhold see, e.g., Cassirer (1923: 35–58).

11. Kant's "chief thought," Hegel writes in the *Science of Logic,* "is to vindicate the *categories* for self-consciousness as the *subjective ego.* By virtue of this determination the point of view remains confined within consciousness and its opposition; and besides the empirical element of feeling and intuition it has something left over which is not posited and determined by thinking self-consciousness, a *thing-in-itself,* something alien and external to thought—although it is easy to perceive that such an abstraction as the *thing-in-itself* is itself only a product of thought, and of merely abstractive thought at that" (WdL I, 45; 62).

12. As the recent scholarship on Hegel has shown, it is precisely during the years of his stay at Jena that Hegel moved from a philosophy of consciousness to a philosophy of spirit, and elaborated his notion of *Geist*. The study of Hegel's philosophical development at Jena may therefore be expected to shed light upon the questions Hegel had in mind in this move. See here my review (Bienenstock 1985).

13. See, e.g., *Jenaer Systementwürfe*, I (*Gesammelte Werke* 6, ed. by K. Düsing and H. Kimmerle, Felix Meiner Verlag, Hamburg 1975, 318f.); tr. by H.S. Harris and T.M. Knox in *Hegel's System of Ethical Life and First Philosophy of Spirit*, State University of New York Press, Albany 1979, 244f.

14. For this interpretation, see, especially, Taylor (1975).

15. *Jenaer Realphilosophie*. Vorlesungsmanuskripte zur Philosophie der Natur und des Geistes von 1805–1806, ed. by J. Hoffmeister, Felix Meiner Verlag, Hamburg 1969, p. 183. On Hegel's attitude toward mythical conceptions of language see, in particular, Gadamer (1976).

16. *Phänomenologie des Geistes*, Suhrkamp Verlag, Frankfurt a/M, 1970, 15. *Phenomenology of Spirit*, tr. by A.V. Miller, Oxford University Press, Oxford, 1977, 4.

17. Compare Aristotle's definition of the soul as the "substance corresponding to the principle (*logos*) of a thing" (*De Anima*, 412b11–12). Hegel's definition of "spirit" as "the essence of consciousness" appears for the first time in his 1803/1804 *Jenaer Systementwürfe*, I, 273ff. But Aristotle's philosophy of mind is also vindicated throughout the Philosophy of Spirit of the *Encyclopaedia*.

18. Compare here the interpretation of Hegel's *Science of Logic* which the leading Hegel scholar Michael Theunissen puts forward in his recent and already famous *Sein und Schein* (1980): in this book, Theunissen argues—rightly so, I think—that the purpose of Hegel was to release classical metaphysics from the essentially "representational" form of thought proper to it. Theunissen, however, assimilates Hegel's criticism of *Vorstellen* to a criticism of "positivism." This, I think, is quite confusing: such an assimilation only too easily induces us to think that Hegel wants to dismiss any and every form of empirical knowledge. Yet as I have attempted to show in the first part of this chapter, this would be a misinterpretation of Hegel's thought. Hegel's contention rather is that it is the very attempt of empirical sciences to do without philosophy—i.e., to be "positive"—which makes them liable to metaphysical speculations. See, on this point, the passage of the *Encyclopaedia* in which Hegel criticizes empiricism: "The basic illusion in scientific empiricism is always this, that it uses the metaphysical categories of matter, force, also of one, many, universal, also infinite etc.; further, that it follows, in its reasoning, the thread of such categories and thereby presupposes and applies the forms of this reasoning; and does not know, in all this, that it itself contains and practices metaphysics and uses those categories and their associations in a completely uncritical and unconscious way" (Enz., par. 38). Hegel, let it be emphasized here once again, does not reject the ideal of knowledge put forward by the empirical sciences. His contention is that the empirical scientists' failure to acknowledge their use of rational concepts or categories induces them to inadvertently endorse metaphysical presuppositions—and thereby to be unfaithful to their own ideal of knowledge. It is with the unacknowledged metaphysical presuppositions of knowledge that he quarrels.

19. Just like Aristotle, Hegel explains that knowledge does not begin with the relation of a fully conscious subject to an object but, rather, with preconscious stages, i.e., with sensation (*Empfindung*) and empirical imagination. In these stages, he says, the opposition of "subject" to "object," of self to world, proper to "consciousness," is not yet present. At this stage of the process of knowledge, that which is intuited is in "spirit," as yet indistinct from it: no "consciousness" is present. *Jenaer Real-*

philosophie, 179f.; also *Jenaer Systementwürfe,* I, 282ff. Compare Aristotle in *De Anima* III 2: for Aristotle as for Hegel later on, sensation itself manifests an identity between "subject" and "object," not a separation between the two. It is only a later reflection which infers from the fact that "I" have a sensation that there is a "thing," an "object" there in the world.

20. The young Marx's interpretation of Hegel (Marx 1975) may itself be considered as one variation on this theme: in contrast to Hegel, Marx would have ascribed primacy to man's ability to work rather than to his "cultural" aspirations. But his own philosophy, just like Hegel's, would be nothing other than basically a philosophy of human subjectivity.

21. *Briefe von und an Hegel,* I, ed. J. Hoffmeister, Hamburg 1952–60, p. 253.

References

Berlin, Isaiah. 1976. *Vico and Herder.* London: The Hogarth Press.

Bienenstock, Myriam. 1979. Hegel at Jena: nationalism or historical thought? *Archiv für Geschichte der Philosophie* 61: 175–195.

_____. 1985. On Hegel's Jena writings: recent trends of research. *Bulletin of the Hegel Society of Great Britain* 11: 7-15.

Cassirer, Ernst. 1923. *Das Erkenntnisproblem in der Philosophie und Wissenschaft der neueren Zeit.* Berlin: B. Cassirer.

Fulda, H. F. 1982. Zum Theorietypus der Hegelschen Rechtsphilosophie. In D. Henrich and R.P. Horstmann (eds.), *Hegels Philosophie des Rechts.* Stuttgart: Klett-Cotta.

Gadamer, Hans-Georg. 1976. *Hegel's Dialectic. Five Hermeneutical Studies.* New Haven and London: Yale University Press.

Hegel, G. W. F. [Enz]. 1970. *Enzyklopädie der philosophischen Wissenschaften* (1830), 3 volumes. Frankfurt am Main: Suhrkamp.

_____. [JS]. 1970. *Jenaer Schriften 1801-1807.* Frankfurt am Main: Suhrkamp.

_____. [PhR]. 1970. *Grundlinien der Philosophie des Rechts.* Frankfurt am Main: Suhrkamp.

_____. [WdL]. 1963. *Wissenschaft der Logik.* Hamburg: Felix Meiner.

Herder, Johann Gottfried. 1960. *Sprachphilosophische Schriften.* Hamburg: Felix Meiner.

Kant, Immanuel. 1951. *Critique of Judgment* (1799). New York: Hafner Press.

_____. 1971. *Kritik der reinen Vernunft,* 2nd ed. (1787). Leipzig: Verlag Philipp Reclam.

Marcuse, Herbert. 1960. *Reason and Revolution.* Boston: Beacon Press.

Marx, Karl. 1975. *Early Writings.* London: Penguin Books.

Popper, Karl. 1963. *The Open Society and its Enemies,* volume 2. New York: Harper and Row.

Taylor, Charles. 1975. *Hegel.* Cambridge: Cambridge University Press.

Theunissen, Michael. 1980. *Sein und Schein.* Frankfurt am Main: Suhrkamp.

Tugendhat, Ernst. 1979. *Selbstbewusstsein und Selbstbestimmung.* Frankfurt am Main: Suhrkamp.

8

Absolute Fruit and Abstract Labor: Remarks on Marx's Use of the Concept of Inversion

Robert Paul Wolff

> The wealth of those societies in which the capitalist mode of production pre-
> vails presents itself [*erscheint als*] as "an immense accumulation of commodi-
> ties," its unit being a single commodity. Our investigation must therefore begin
> with the analysis of a commodity.
>
> —*Karl Marx*

A coat is an article of clothing capable of protecting its wearer from the
weather. But it is not, in virtue of that or any of its other natural properties,
a commodity. If a coat *were* a commodity in virtue of its capacity to protect
its wearer from the weather, then it would remain a commodity no matter
where or when it existed, for as a natural object it always possesses that
natural capacity. But coats are commodities only in societies with systems
of production for market exchange. A coat removed from its setting in a
system of market exchange retains its physical properties but loses its
commodity character. And, be it noted, among the natural physical properties
of a coat is the property of having been produced by certain specific concrete
human labors, including the labor of tending and shearing the sheep, carding,
spinning, and weaving the wool into cloth, sewing the cloth into a coat,
and so forth. These, like texture, shape, and size, are natural physical
properties (and relations) and it is *not* in virtue of any of these, or of all
of them taken together, that an object is a commodity.

A commodity, strictly speaking, is not an object of sense perception at
all. Ten yards of linen, *qua* cloth, can be seen, felt, cut, sewn, folded,
packaged, and transported from a factory to a retail outlet. But ten yards
of linen, *qua* commodity, cannot be seen, felt, or physically manipulated.
For a commodity is a queer thing, a thing full of metaphysical subtleties
and theological niceties. Only the doubting Thomases of this world sniff

the sacramental wine as the chalice is passed to them, expecting somehow that through the miracle of transubstantiation the sweet odor of wine will give way to the stench of blood.

But if commodities are not physical objects, what then are they? Or to put the same question somewhat differently, *in virtue of what* are the linen, the coat, the corn, and the iron commodities?

> If then we leave out of consideration the use-value of commodities, they have only one common property left, that of being products of labour. But even the product of labour itself has undergone a change in our hands. If we make abstraction from its use-value, we make abstraction at the same time from the material elements and shapes that make the product a use-value; we see in it no longer a table, a house, yarn, or any other useful thing. Its existence as a material thing is put out of sight. Neither can it any longer be regarded as the product of the labour of the joiner, the mason, the spinner, or of any other definite kind of productive labour. Along with the useful qualities of the products themselves, we put out of sight both the useful character of the various kinds of labour embodied in them, and the concrete forms of that labour; there is nothing left but what is common to them all; all are reduced to one and the same sort of labour, human labour in the abstract.
>
> Let us now consider the residue of each of these products. It consists of the same unsubstantial reality in each, a mere congelation of homogeneous human labour, of labour-power expended without regard to the mode of its expenditure. All that these things now tell us is, that human labour-power has been expended in their production, that human labour is embodied in them. As crystals of this social substance, common to them all, they are values—commodity values. . . . The labour, however, that forms the substance of value, is homogeneous labour, expenditure of one uniform labour-power. The total labour-power of society, which is embodied in the sum total of the values of all commodities produced by that society, counts here as one homogeneous mass of human labour-power, composed though it be of innumerable individual units. (Marx 1967: 38–39)

The exchange value of a commodity—or, more precisely, the exchange value in virtue of which a commodity *is* a commodity, the exchange value that constitutes the commodity-ness of a commodity—is a *crystal of abstract homogeneous social labor.* The quantum of exchange value congealed or crystallized in each commodity can neither be seen nor felt nor smelt nor tasted. This homogeneous, infinitely divisible, non-sensory stuff, this *value,* is contained in the products of labor as a consequence of their being produced by workers hired by capitalists in a system of market exchange regulated by competition. In the production process, portions of this stuff congealed in previously produced commodities are transmitted or passed on to newly produced commodities. As the spindle turns, it smoothly, invisibly, magically passes on infinitesimal bits of its value to the thread that collects around it. When the spindle breaks and must be discarded, it is emptied of its crystals of value, exhausted, spent—unless of course, it has yet some resale value as a used spindle, in which case it will be found to have held back a little cache of its secret value to bring, as a dowry, to its new owner.

The passionate aim and single-minded purpose of the hard-headed businessmen from Manchester and Liverpool, London and Sheffield, is to accumulate as much of this transcendent ectoplasmic stuff as possible, as fast as possible. They want it not for its attractive and gratifying sensory qualities—for it has no sensory qualities at all—but for its magical ability to increase in quantity. They want it, that is to say, so that they may get more of it, which they want in order to get still more. When they grow old and rich, these metaphysical entrepreneurs may decline into sensation, and cash in their crystals of value for inferior things of the flesh, for houses and clothes and rare paintings. But so long as they are young and vigorous, they shun all such temptations and pursue the holy grail of self-expanding value.

What can Marx possibly have in mind by advancing so manifestly absurd an account of the commodity? That he considers this theory of "crystals of abstract homogeneous socially necessary labour" to be absurd is manifest by the language in which he chooses to expound it. The chapter on commodities, in which this extraordinary doctrine is introduced, is strewn with religious metaphors. Marx sets himself to trace the "genesis" of the money form of exchange value. As coats and linen change and exchange, as if in a ghostly minuet, the linen, he says, "acquires a value-form different from its physical form," an echo of the miracle of transubstantiation. (Indeed, all exchange is a kind of inverted transubstantiation, for in the miracle of the Mass, the sensory accidents of the bread and wine remain unaltered, while their essence or substance is changed into that of the body and blood of Christ, whereas in commodity exchange, while the sensory accidents of one commodity are exchanged for the sensory accidents of another, their substance—value—remains unaltered.) "The fact that [the linen] is value," Marx says, "is made manifest by its equality with the coat, just as the sheep's nature of a Christian is shown in his resemblance to the Lamb of God" (Marx 1967: 47, 52).

Lest there be a reader so insensitive to even the broadest mockery as to imagine that this account of the inner essence of commodities is meant literally as a straightforward description of what makes anything a commodity, Marx breaks the ironic tone of his discourse momentarily to tell us that such talk is deranged, crack-brained, crazy—*verrückt:*

> When I state that coats or boots stand in relation to linen, because it is the universal incarnation of abstract human labour, the craziness [*die Verrücktheit*] of the statement is self-evident. Nevertheless, when the producers of coats and boots compare those articles with linen, or, what is the same thing, with gold or silver, as the universal equivalent, they express the relation between their own private labour and the collective labour of society in the same deranged form [genau in dieser verrückten Form]. (Marx 1967: 76)

The key to Marx's meaning here is his use of the notion of *inversion*, which he takes from Hegel. The notions of inversion (*Verkehrung*) and of the inverted world (*die verkehrte Welt*) are introduced by Hegel in his discussion of understanding (in the Kantian sense of the cognitive faculty that orders the given materials of experience in law-like structures) and the relationship between appearance and that which appears. Hegel's account of these notions, like so much of his philosophy, is exceedingly obscure, but the central theme is a rejection of Kant's claim that the perceived world, the world of scientific investigation and daily experience, is merely an appearance of a real world of things as they are in themselves, lying behind the presented appearances. In effect, what happens is something like this: we begin *in medias res* with a multiplicity of events and objects in relation to one another, and by a process of abstraction and cognitive organization we posit a system of laws as the order, or form, or structure of the experienced world. This "world" of laws is "supersensible" in the sense that it is posited by the mind's own cognitive powers, not apprehended in sense-experience. It is a world characterized by universality rather than by particularity, for the events and objects with which we begin are individual, local, particularized as occurring or existing at a specific time and in a specific place, whereas the laws of the "supersensible" world are universal, general, applicable to all times and all places. Furthermore, the supersensible world is characterized by necessity rather than by contingency, for the laws of nature are conceived as laws of necessary connection, causal laws, whereas the concatenation of events in the world of sense-experience is experienced merely as given, as happening without necessity.

Now, however, by an inversion (*Verkehrung*) this supersensible world of laws is construed as the *real* world of which the realm of particular events and objects is only an instantiation, an unfolding, an embodiment. What was ectype is now construed as archetype. As Hegel says:

> By means of this principle, the first supersensible world, the changeless kingdom of laws, the immediate ectype and copy of the world of perception, has turned round into its opposite. The law was in general, like its differences, self-identical; now, however, it is established that each side is, on the contrary, the opposite of itself. The self-identical repels itself from itself, and the self-discordant sets up to be selfsame. In truth, with a characteristic of this kind, distinction is only inner distinction, or immanent distinction, since the like is unlike itself, and the unlike like itself.
>
> This second supersensible world is in this way the inverted world, and, moreover, since one aspect is already present in the first supersensible world, the inverted form of the first. (Hegel 1910: 151–152)

It is extremely instructive to follow Marx in his deployment of the notion of inversion from its earliest appearances to the quite subtle form that it takes in the opening chapters of *Capital*. Let us begin with the "Contribution to the Critique of Hegel's Philosophy of Right," where Marx repeatedly turns the notion of inversion against Hegel, with devastating results.

Marx sounds the theme of his critique early in the essay. After quoting a passage from Hegel's *Philosophie des Rechts*, he observes: "It is important that Hegel everywhere makes the idea the subject and turns the proper, the actual subject, such as 'political conviction,' into a predicate. It is always on the side of the predicate, however, that development takes place" (Marx/ Engels 1975: 11). He elaborates this theme two paragraphs later, referring to the "inversion" (*Umkehrung*) of subject and predicate. The key to the critique is Marx's argument that Hegel persistently treats what is abstract, dependent, derivative as though it were concrete, independent, creative. "The existence of predicates is the subject, so that the subject is the existence of subjectivity, etc. . . . Subsequently the actual subject appears as a result, whereas one must start from the actual subject and look at its objectification" (Marx/Engels 1975: 23). As applied to the analysis of the state, this critique becomes a rejection of the idealist notion that the state takes precedence, ontologically and also politically, over its subjects:

> So in this case sovereignty, the essential feature of the state, is treated to begin with as an independent entity, is objectified. Then, of course, this objective entity has to become a subject again. This subject then appears, however, as a self-incarnation of sovereignty; whereas sovereignty is nothing but the objectified mind of the subjects of the state. (Marx/Engels 1975: 24)

As Marx says somewhat later in a slightly different context, "The correct method is stood on its head. The simplest thing becomes the most complicated, and the most complicated the simplest. What ought to be the starting point becomes a mystical outcome, and what ought to be the rational outcome becomes a mystical starting point" (Marx/Engels 1975: 40).

Finally, near the end of the essay, in a passage that displays him at his wittiest and most penetrating, Marx plays with inversion to mock Hegel's discussion of the rights of the first-born:

> Concerning the entailment of estates in primogeniture two elements need stressing: (1) That which is enduring is the *ancestral estate*, the *landed property*. It is the lasting element in the relationship, the *substance*. The master of the entailed estate, the owner, is really a mere *accident*. The different generations represent *anthropomorphised* landed property. *Landed property*, as it were, continually *inherits* the first-born of the House as the attribute fettered to it. Every first-born in the series of landed proprietors is the *inheritance*, the *property* of the *inalienable estate*, the *predestined substance of its will* and its *activity*. The subject is the thing and the predicate the human being. The will becomes the property of the property. (Marx/Engels 1975: 106)

This critique of Hegel was written in the spring and summer of 1843. The next year, Marx and Engels cooperated on an enormously bloated, bizarre, uproarious attack on the Bauer brothers, Bruno and Edgar, and their associates, the Young Hegelians. In an attack on F.Z. Zychlinski's discussion of Eugène Sue's popular novel, *Les Mystères de Paris*, Marx develops a brilliant burlesque of the logic of Idealist metaphysics. Partly because Marx's method in this passage bears so important a relation to the treatment of abstract labor in Chapter 1 of *Capital*, but partly also because the passage is such fun, I shall quote from it extensively.

The mystery of the Critical presentation of the *Mystères de Paris* is the mystery of *speculative*, of *Hegelian construction*. . . . A few words will suffice to characterise speculative construction *in general*. . . .

If from real apples, pears, strawberries and almonds I form the general idea "*Fruit*," if I go further and *imagine* that my abstract idea "*Fruit*," derived from real fruit, is an entity existing outside me, is indeed the *true* essence of the pear, the apple, etc., then—in the *language of speculative* philosophy—I am declaring that "*Fruit*" is the "*Substance*" of the pear, the apple, the almond, etc. I am saying, therefore, that to be a pear is not essential to the pear, that to be an apple is not essential to the apple; that what is essential to these things is not their real existence, perceptible to the senses, but the essence that I have abstracted from them and then foisted on them, the essence of my idea—"*Fruit*". I therefore declare apples, pears, almonds, etc., to be mere forms of existence, *modi*, of "*Fruit*." . . . Having reduced the different real fruits to the *one* "fruit" of abstraction—"*the* Fruit," speculation must, in order to attain some semblance of real content, try somehow to find its way back from "*the* Fruit," from the *Substance* to the *diverse*, ordinary real fruits, the pear, the apple, the almond, etc. . . . If apples, pears, almonds and strawberries are really nothing but "*the* Substance," "*the* Fruit," the question arises: Why does "*the* Fruit" manifest itself to me sometimes as an apple, sometimes as a pear, sometimes as an almond? Why this *semblance of diversity* which so obviously contradicts my speculative conception of *Unity*, "*the* Substance," "*the* Fruit"?

This, answers the speculative philosopher, is because "*the* Fruit" is not dead, undifferentiated, motionless, but a living, self-differentiating, moving essence. . . . The different profane fruits are different manifestations of the life of the "*one* Fruit"; they are crystallisations of "*the* Fruit" itself. . . . We see that if the Christian religion knows only *one* Incarnation of God, speculative philosophy has as many incarnations as there are things, just as it has here in every fruit an incarnation of the Substance, of the Absolute Fruit. (Marx/Engels 1975: 57–59)

This disquisition on the Absolute Fruit may seem little more than youthful buffoonery on Marx's part, but it takes on a richer significance when it is compared with his treatment of abstract labor in the first chapter of *Capital*. Let us recall that Marx accorded to his account of abstract labor pride of place as the most important single idea in his great work: "the best things in my book" (he says in the 24 August 1867 letter to Engels) "are: 1. (on this depends *all* understanding of the facts) the *double nature of labour*, according as it is expressed in use-value or exchange value—which even in the *first* chapter is prominently displayed" (Marx/Engels *Werke*, 31: 326). A close look at the text shows that Marx, with all seriousness, develops the concept of abstract homogeneous socially necessary labor in a manner parallel to the satirical exposition of the concept of the Absolute Fruit. When we have grasped the inner significance of this odd convergence, we shall be a good deal closer to a satisfactory understanding of Marx's conception of the crazy structure of social reality.

The development of the concept of abstract labor begins in the opening section of Chapter 1. We start with concrete particular physical objects whose natural properties make them capable of satisfying various human wants, and whose existence results from particular concrete acts of human laboring—specific acts of weaving, sewing, spinning, and so forth. We "make abstraction from" or "put out of sight" both "the useful character of the various forms of labour" embodied in those physical objects, and also "the concrete forms of that labour." What is left when we have completed this process of abstraction is merely "what is common to them all," namely "human labour in the abstract" (Marx 1967: 38).

Thus far, we are describing a familiar process of intellectual or conceptual abstraction, of the sort that is required to bring many particular concrete instances under one general heading. In Marx's deliberately untendentious phrase, we "leave out of consideration" the individuating characteristics that distinguish one commodity from another and one productive act from another, just as we leave out of consideration the individuating characteristics of the apple, the pear, and the almond when we form the general concept of a fruit. We "no longer" regard the coat as the product of the activity of a tailor, the table, of the activity of the carpenter, but it is clear that tailoring and joining are the real activities and "labouring as such" the abstraction, just as it is clear that apples, pears, and almonds are real existences, and fruit-as-such a conceptual abstraction.

Now, however, a series of quite complex conceptual and theoretical shifts take place. According to Marx, when commodities exchange, "their exchange-value manifests itself as something totally independent of their use-value" (Marx 1967: 38), from which he draws the conclusion that "the common substance that manifests itself in the exchange-value of commodities, when-ever they are exchanged, is their value." And a useful article *has* value, according to Marx, "only because human labour in the abstract has been embodied or materialised in it" (Marx 1967: 38). After setting aside the superficial error of supposing that a commodity less efficiently, and hence more laboriously, produced will thereby acquire greater value—a natural enough error, so long as we confusedly think of abstract labor as some peculiar sort of human activity engaged in by abstract laborers in an abstract factory—Marx sums up his analysis: "We see then that that which determines the magnitude of the value of any article is the amount of labour socially necessary, or the labour-time socially necessary for its production" (Marx 1967: 39). Echoing the language of *The Holy Family*, Marx says, "In general, the greater the productiveness of labour, the less is the labour-time required for the production of an article, the less is the amount of labour crystallised [sic] in that article, and the less is its value" (Marx 1967: 40).

The natural interpretation of these remarks about abstract homogeneous socially necessary labor time, the interpretation suggested by modern philo-sophical analyses of theoretical models and theoretical terms in those models, is to construe them as shorthand ways of asserting a relationship between several different variables in a formal model of a competitive commodity-producing capitalist economy. Thus, the statement that the exchange value of a commodity is determined by the quantity of abstract homogeneous socially necessary labor crystallized within it—a statement that appears wildly metaphysical on its face—is interpreted as asserting a functional relationship in a formal linear reproduction model between the equilibrium price of the commodity and the labor value of the commodity, where "labour value" is defined to mean "quantity of labour directly and indirectly required for production under the assumptions of fixed technical coefficients and perfect competition." But as Marx continues his exposition in the first chapter of *Capital*, he seems to take an entirely different tack.

We have been citing passages from the first section of the chapter. In the second section, a subtle shift takes place. Marx is elaborating on "the two-fold character of the labour embodied in commodities," and he observes that the coat and linen in the simple example he has been pursuing are, insofar as they are values, "things of like substance, objective expressions of essentially identical labour." But tailoring and weaving, taking them as actual concrete human activities, are "different kinds of labour" (Marx 1967: 43). So if exchange is to be based on the equating of quanta of abstract labor whose concrete instantiations are quite diverse, some sort of process of *real* abstraction must take place (ibid.).

There is a linguistic oddity in Marx's discussion, which if we subject it to a strenuous construal, is revelatory of a very profound and important conceptual shift. Marx says not that the coat and linen *have* value but that they *are* values. Now, this is a peculiar diction. We might at first be inclined to treat "the coat and the linen are values" simply as elliptical for "the coat and the linen are objects which have value." But that would be a mistake. To say that the coat and the linen, *qua* commodities, *are* values is to say that the coat and the linen, *qua* commodities, are not natural objects at all. Indeed, it signals the possibility that commodities, strictly so-called, are not substantives, save in a quite superficial grammatical sense, and that, in the language of modern logic, "commodity" and its cognates are syn-categorimatic terms which can be defined only by explicating the contexts in which they characteristically appear. If this is in fact the case, then the question "what is a commodity?" would be grammatically misleading, and the "correct" answer, namely, "a commodity is a crystallization of abstract homogeneous socially necessary labour" would be thoroughly metaphysically misleading.

Marx begins the conceptual reversal of particular and universal by suggesting that "tailoring and weaving . . . are each a productive expenditure of human brains, nerves, and muscles, and in this sense are human labour" (Marx 1967: 44). Thus far he sounds quite matter of factly materialistic, although the use of the word "productive" should serve as a warning, for what counts as *productive* in a competitive capitalist economy is a function of equilibrium prices and profit rates, not of human nerves and muscles. Now, however, he asserts that the tailoring and weaving "are but two different modes of expending human labour-power" (ibid.). This, I suggest, is an echo of the satirical remark, written twenty years earlier, that "apples, pears, almonds, etc. [are] mere forms of existence, *modi*, of 'Fruit.'" The remark is deliberately absurd when made of apples and almonds. It can hardly be meant to be taken as unambiguously serious when made of tailoring and weaving.

By the time Marx is deep into his exposition of value, the inversion is far advanced. After a complex passage in which Marx, mocking the classical economists, speaks of the "mystical character of gold and silver" (a clear sign that things are not what they seem), he writes:

> The body of the commodity that serves as the equivalent, figures as the materialisation of human labour in the abstract, and is at the same time the product of some specifically useful concrete labour. This concrete labour becomes, therefore, the medium for expressing abstract human labour. If on the one hand the coat ranks as nothing but the embodiment of abstract human labour, so, on the other hand, the tailoring which is actually embodied in it, counts as nothing but the form under which that abstract labour is realised. In the expression of value of the linen, the utility of the tailoring consists, not in making clothes, but in making an object, which we at once recognise to be Value, and therefore to be a congelation of labour, but of labour indistinguishable from that realised in the value of the linen. In order to act as such a mirror of value, the labour of tailoring must reflect nothing but its own abstract quality of being human labour generally. (Marx 1967: 58)

Tailoring and weaving are human activities. Abstract homogeneous socially necessary labor is an abstraction derived *from* tailoring and weaving by "leaving out of consideration" the myriad particular ways in which they differ from one another. Abstract labor has no existence outside our minds, any more than The Fruit has an existence outside our activity of abstracting from the particularities of apples, pears, and almonds. But now an inversion has begun to take place. Hedging slightly, Marx says, "If on the one hand the coat ranks as nothing but the embodiment of abstract human labour . . .," thereby leaving open the possibility that it is merely *we* who so construe it. But the assertion is made flatly a few pages further on. "The manifold concrete useful kinds of labour, embodied in these different commodities, rank now as so many different forms of the realisation, or manifestation [*Verwirklungs—oder Erscheinungsformen*] of undifferentiated human labour" (Marx 1967: 64). What is this but a direct echo of the crack-brained notion, attributed in *The Holy Family* to "the speculative philosopher," that "the different ordinary fruits are different manifestations of the life [*verschiedene Lebensausserungen*] of the 'one Fruit'"?

Finally, in the section devoted to the "The Fetishism of Commodities and the Secret Thereof," Marx tells us flat out that this way of speaking and thinking is crazy.

> When I state that coats or boots stand in a relation to linen, because it is the universal incarnation of abstract human labour, the craziness [*die Verrücktheit*] of the statement is evident. Nevertheless, when the producers of coats and boots compare those articles with linen, or *What is the same thing* with gold and silver, as the universal equivalent, they express the relation between their

own private labour and the collective labour of society in the same crazy form. (Marx 1967: 76, my emphasis)

To speak of tailoring and weaving as manifestations of, embodiments of, forms of the realization of abstract human labor is as crazy, as manifestly inverted, as to speak of man as having been made in God's image, or of apples and pears as different manifestations of the Absolute Fruit. And yet, having alerted us to this absurdity, having burlesqued it in his youth and anathemized it in his maturity, Marx persists in speaking this way throughout *Capital.* Why?

Marx tells us the answer in the paragraph immediately succeeding the assertion that the producers of coats and boots "express the relation between their own private labour and the collective labour of society in the same crazy form." "The categories of bourgeois economy," he says, "consist of such like forms. They are socially valid, hence objective forms of thought for the relations of production belonging to this historically determined mode of production, i.e., commodity production."[1] *They are socially valid, hence* objective. . . . In this phrase is encapsulated Marx's revolutionary theory of the objectively crazy (or contradictory) nature of capitalist social reality, and the radically new epistemological and literary standpoint following therefrom. At this point we must attempt a direct statement and analysis of the fundamental elements of that theory.

What does it mean to say that crazy forms of thought are socially valid, and hence are the objective forms of thought for commodity production? Without taking too prolonged a detour into the philosophy and methodology of science, we can, I think, clarify this puzzling but very important notion sufficiently to grasp Marx's meaning.

The study of nature presents relatively simple problems of concept formation. If we suppose that nature has an objective, essential structure which it is the aim of science to grasp, then the concepts employed by science will be objective insofar as they identify and articulate the actual structures of natural things. A cosmology based on the distinction between terrestrial and celestial matter, or on the notion of natural place, will prove relatively unsuccessful in explaining the existence and nature of comets or the motions of bodies in space. The scope and power of explanation and prediction achieved by the unification of the laws of terrestrial and celestial motion, or by the notion of inertia, is taken to constitute a demonstration of the objective validity of these concepts relative to that of their predecessors.

In the study of human affairs, matters become considerably more complex. The problem, as has often been pointed out, is that the participants in a social interaction themselves possess concepts of their own activities and relationships, as well as of the natural world in which they live. These concepts, in quite complex ways, guide, distort, shape, and condition their interactions. The problem arises in a familiar and much explored way in the work of cultural anthropologists, who must determine precisely what use to make of the concepts which play a central role in the thought and action of the subjects of their investigations. In particular, when religious or magical beliefs, which the anthropologists know to be false, constitute a significant portion of the salient belief system of a people, how—in what voice, with what caveats, with what degree of identification of speaker with subject—shall the investigator express those beliefs in the course of characterizing or analyzing the subject culture?

Some social concepts have a self-confirming objectivity, in the familiar sense that they acquire their legitimacy as *descriptions* of social reality from their adoption, acceptance, and employment by the participants in the social situation to which they purport to apply. For example, the various terms associated with property relations have this character. The statement, "She owns the house at Number 23 Elm Street," which is in its paradigmatic usage ascriptive rather than descriptive or prescriptive, acquires its objective validity from its place in a system of beliefs, actions, expectations, and decisions which, taken all together, constitute part of the institution of property in the society in question. The truth of the statement as a description rests on the acceptance by the relevant members of the society of the ascription made by the statement in its primary function. To say of a person that she owns a house is not, in the first instance, to *discover* something about her, nor is it to make a claim about what *ought* to be the case. Rather, it is to attribute to her a certain status—that of property-owner—in a social structure of property rights defined at least partially by some institutional arrangements for deciding property relations, resolving conflicting claims, and so forth. It makes no sense to say of a person who lives in a society lacking the institution of property that he *really* owns a cow, regardless of whether the society knows it or not. We might, to be sure, offer the opinion that *if* the society were to develop the institution of property, it would probably adopt a set of property practices in the context of which this man *would* "own" the cow. But in the strict sense, property terms are descriptively objective *because*, to invoke Marx's phrase, they are "socially valid," which is to say because the participants in the society employ them, shape their actions and expectations by them, and thereby embody them in their practices.

There is, however, nothing inherently crazy about the beliefs expressed by statements of property rights and relations, nor are the concepts in which they are expressed crack-brained (at least not so far as anything we have said thus far is concerned—later on, of course, we may find Marx calling into question the rationality of certain rights and relations of property). Property concepts, like kinship concepts, for example, are rational concepts which quite straightforwardly acquire their objective reference from their social validity.

The situation is utterly different with regard to the concepts and associated practices of political authority. The central concept of politics is the concept of *de jure* legitimate authority. A state is a person or group of persons who successfully claim *de jure* legitimate authority within a territory or over a people. This claim is a normative claim—a claim to the right to issue commands, and the correlative claim to have the right to be obeyed. A person or group of persons who make such a claim and succeed in getting it accepted by the preponderance of those against whom the claim is made are said to "be a state," or more strictly to be a *de facto* legitimate state. By the nature of the case, no group claims merely to have *de facto* legitimacy, for such a factual claim would, in effect, undermine its claim to *de jure* legitimacy. So kings, prophets, presidents and parliaments, workers' councils, synods, and popes issue claims of *de jure* authority and by and large succeed in winning acceptance for their claims. Those who acquiesce in claims of legitimate authority—the subjects—acknowledge themselves to have a moral (or religious) obligation to obey the commands of their legitimate rulers. They do not merely recognize themselves to be in a position of subordination to superior power. To be sure (as Max Weber and others have pointed out), the perversity of the human spirit is such that men and women frequently develop a belief in the legitimacy of the authority of those who have power over them *merely because of that power*. But conceptually, and operationally, there is all the difference in the world between a conquered people who submit to superior force and a subject people who accept the authority of their rulers.

Now, the traditions of hereditary monarchy, the personal qualities of charismatic leadership, and the constitutional procedures of representative democracy do not confer *de jure* legitimate authority on kings, prophets, or elected legislatures. In fact, nothing can confer *de jure* legitimate authority on any person or group of persons who put themselves forward as the state. Hence, all authority claims are illegitimate, and all beliefs in the authority of states are irrational. Nevertheless, the concept of legitimate authority acquires objectivity by virtue of its social validity, despite the fact that it is, as philosophical analysis reveals, an incoherent concept. In other words, a correct description and analysis of the political institutions and behavior of a society cannot be developed without the invocation of the notion of legitimate authority.

Marx held—and I would concur—that claims of legitimate authority are supported by a network of conceptual inversions and mystifications whose purpose it is to represent the state as having a being independent of the subjects whose beliefs, expectations, habits, and agreements constitute it, so that eventually, in the higher reaches of the Idealist rationalizations for the authority of the state, individual real human beings are crazily portrayed as mere instantiations or fulfillments of the being of the state. The demystification of the state proceeds in the first instance by a series of revolutionary political upheavals which destroy the aura of majesty of monarchy or parliament. It is the decapitation of a king, rather than the dissection of the concept of monarchy, which accomplishes the demystification most thoroughly.

Nevertheless, when philosophers make their contribution to the debunking of statehood, a problem arises concerning the language in which that debunking must be carried out. Insofar as both the author and the audience are in the grip of the mystifications of political authority, so that the process of debunking is at one and the same time a self-criticism by the author and an attack on the beliefs of the audience, an ironic voice may be required in order to express the continuing mystifying appeal of the discredited claims of legitimacy. Historically, the appeal of legitimacy has worked so powerfully on even the most skeptical souls that attacks on the authority of one's own state have characteristically been couched either in the language of appeal to a higher, divine authority (hence the attractiveness in the civil disobedience movement of religious appeals to conscience) or in a language of appeal to the more legitimate authority of some alternative claimant to legitimacy: History, The Proletariat, The Movement, A People, or even, most absurdly, yet another existing nation-state.

The objective absurdity of claims of *de jure* legitimate authority makes the institution of the state potentially unstable, for its existence and successful functioning depend essentially on the perseverance of false beliefs and confused thinking among the participants—both rulers and subjects. The clearer men and women become about the real nature of the state—the clearer they become therefore about the illegitimacy of all authority claims— the less able are the persons who comprise the state to get their commands obeyed (in the strict sense of "obeyed," which is "complied with because they are legitimate commands"). Force must replace *de facto* legitimacy, with counter-productive results. If we could show (as I rather think we cannot) that ongoing changes internal to *de facto* legitimate states must have the effect of raising the level of self-conscious understanding of the true nature of political authority, then we could conclude that the state is an actually, as well as potentially, unstable institution, and a dialectical argument, like that offered by Marx with regard to the self-destructive tendencies of capitalism, could be advanced in support of the thesis that the modern state is moving inexorably toward anarchism.

Some of the beliefs concerning the legitimate authority of the state are simply false, as, for example, are all beliefs that a state possesses *de jure* legitimate authority. Such beliefs are meaningful, however, and the concepts in which they are framed are not absurd, for they are moral beliefs concerning our obligations, and the concept of moral obligation is philosophically coherent.

Some of the concepts invoked by the discourse on political legitimacy are absurd, however, including most centrally the notion of the state as an entity existing independently of, and ontologically prior to, its subjects. This conception, as we have seen, is the focus of Marx's acute critique of Hegel's philosophy of the state. The concept of the state *is* indeed a crack-brained or absurd concept which acquires objective meaning from its social validity as the mystified illusion on which the *de facto* authority of the state rests.

An analogous line of argument can be developed with regard to the religious beliefs and institutions of a society. The concepts and doctrines of the various religious faiths are, at least as elaborated by the higher religions, simply absurd. No coherent meaning can be given to the notion of an infinite, timeless being which creates the universe *ex nihilo* and then periodically interacts with it to accomplish revelations, incarnations, and salvations. But religious beliefs, like political beliefs, cannot be dismissed as mere errors, confusions, or expressions of ignorance. The illusions of religion clearly express deep-rooted fantasies, needs, projections, and inversions whose grip on us persists even in the face of the most devastating critiques. Kant spoke of Reason's need to unify the materials of knowledge in ways which led inevitably and ineluctably to dialectical illusion.

Nevertheless, as a consequence of the secularization of bourgeois society, it has become possible, at long last, to treat religion unambivalently as mere superstition, and to speak of it therefore in the neutral voice of scientific detachment. The triumph of the secular, despite the endless evangelic revivals by which the primitive returns to mock us, marks perhaps the greatest single intellectual victory of the Enlightenment. To be sure, the mystified notion of *geistliche Natur* reappears as the modern heresy of environmentalism, but a celebration of the snail darter and the blue whale is a far cry from the magisterial pronouncements *ex cathedra* of God's Vicar.

The same cannot be said, alas, for the mysteries of the state, which persist in less obvious but equally absurd form as the universal belief in the moral legitimacy of the democratic state. Sovereignty counts among its champions legions of philosophers and political theorists, while divinity these days can muster few defenders whose commitment extends beyond irrational faith.

When we come to the concepts of the market, the categories of bourgeois political economy, we find Marx claiming for them the same anomalous status, the same philosophical absurdity but social validity, and hence objectivity, which characterizes the concepts associated with the state and the church. In the case of the central concepts of bourgeois political economy, however—commodity, value, money, and capital—we can extract from Marx's discussion a much fuller and more precise account of the ways in which the operations of the market confer social validity on them. As we shall see, the canons of bourgeois efficiency and profitability demand that capitalists and workers alike embrace the illusions of the market and regulate their thinking by the crack-brained premises of value theory.

Consider, for example, the concept of the commodity with which Marx begins *Capital*. As natural being, a commodity is a material object with a variety of physical, chemical, and other properties which make it more or less useful in the satisfaction of human needs. But a commodity is not, *qua* commodity, a natural object. A commodity is a quantum of value. Its natural properties are accidental and irrelevant to its true inner essence, which is the crystal of abstract homogeneous socially necessary labor that lies concealed within it.

This is an absurd notion, as should by now be obvious. But Marx insists that it is nevertheless a *socially valid* notion, and hence an objective form of thought for those participating in and theorizing about the particular social relations of production and exchange characteristic of capitalism. Let us see exactly what this means.

Economic efficiency demands that both entrepreneurs and merchants abstract entirely from the natural properties of the commodities they produce and sell, attending only to their exchange value. The prudent capitalist cannot allow his economic decisions to be influenced by his normal human responses to the accidents of his wares. The tailor in love with his worsteds is not better than a whiskey priest drunk on sacramental wine. A sensuous affection for fine cloth, lingering from a pre-capitalist craft pride, may incline him to a more costly suiting than the market demand justifies. Soon he will find himself driven to the wall by rational tailors whose fingers are numb to feel the good wool, but whose metaphysical consciousness can discern the exact quantum of value in each yard of goods.

The senses are too coarse to apprehend the miracle of self-expanding value. No mechanic, however keen his eye, can perceive in the bustle of an automatic assembly line the measure of its profitability. Only the accountants, those eremites of capitalism, for whom all sensory qualities fall away to reveal the transcendent crystals of value, can discern whether a firm is earning an appropriate rate of return on the value of its invested capital. Romantic entrepreneurs, enticed by the stench and heat and fire of the blast furnaces, will soon yield place to the Pythagoreans of the market, for whom only numbers are real.

Competition standardizes commodities, substitutes abstract calculation for concrete technical judgment, stifles passions and affections which are inappropriately aroused by the natural properties of goods, and breeds up by ruthless selection a new capitalist man for whom only exchange value is real. The same historical process of development produces a mass of workers who, in the homogeneity of their culture, their mobility, and their lack of particularized skills, approximate ever closer to the inverted ideal of abstract labor. As the rational becomes real, the real becomes ever more irrational. These absurd forms of thought—the commodity as quantum of crystallized value, the worker as petty commodity producer of abstract labor—acquire social validity and hence objectivity, which is to say that successful day-to-day interaction with the world of work and consumption, of production and circulation, requires workers and capitalists to apprehend their environment, interpret their experience, and guide their actions by means of them.

But if socially valid, which is to say effective in operation and confirmed in experience, then how absurd? The answer is twofold, on the side of the worker and on the side of the capitalist. Subjectively, the worker as purveyor of abstract, averagely efficient labor is torn between her natural human needs and the needs of capital. Her mind and body require a graceful, rational, integrated development if she is to achieve a healthy fulfillment of her nature. But the exigencies of profitability demand the services of a neutral, adaptable labor power unencumbered by such obstructive predispositions as natural body rhythms, craft traditions, or a preference for participation in the planning, direction, and evaluation of the activity of production.

The concept of abstract labor is *socially valid* because the more fully the worker construes his actual work situation in its terms, the more successful he is, as measured by the criteria implicit in the concept itself—criteria endlessly reconfirmed by employers, fellow workers, ministers, teachers, and even by the members of his own family. The more completely he remakes himself in the image of abstract labor, the more likely he is to get and hold a job, win the praise of those around him, and weather the periodic economic storms. This repeated social confirmation confers objective validity on the concept, so that finally it comes to seem that resistance to the regime of the machine is mulish stubbornness, rejection of the authority of the bosses is sinful rebelliousness, and dissatisfaction with a subsistence wage is self-indulgence. The absurdity, the crack-brainedness of the concept of the commodity is thus, on the subjective side, made manifest in the increasing misery of the increasingly productive, increasingly twisted and thwarted, ever more alienated workers.

On the objective side, on the side of capital, the immediate and irrefutable evidences of the absurdity of the categories of bourgeois political economy are the periodic crises that threaten to bring to a disastrous halt the processes of reproduction and accumulation. Economic crises, Marx argues, are the direct consequences of the attempt by capitalists to conform their economic decisions to the tenets of rationality enshrined in the socially valid, and hence objective, categories of bourgeois political economy. It is the social relations of production and circulation, not the technology of capitalism, that produces crises. The self-destructiveness of capitalism results naturally from the capitalists' reduction of all economic decisions to profitability, to the quantitative measurement of self-expanding value. The concepts of value, of money, and of capital achieve social validity through their short-term success. Capitalists unable or unwilling to live by the ascetic rule of profit maximization are driven to the wall in the competition of the market. The craziness of these concepts is manifested in the crises which periodically destroy even the most economically rational of entrepreneurs.

Thus we see that there is an inner theoretical connection between Marx's economic doctrines of exploitation and crisis, his psychological theory of alienation, and his metaphysical thesis of the objective irrationality of capitalist social formations. It follows in turn from these conclusions that a different, more conceptually and stylistically complex mode of discourse is required to express that irrationality in our social theory. I shall argue, in a future work, that the ironic voice of Capital is Marx's solution to this epistemological and literary problem.

Marx's philosophical, as opposed to his economic, doctrines have often been construed in ways that make them relatively impervious to discon-firmation. It is therefore perhaps worth concluding with the observation that if this reading of Marx is correct, then the soundness of his philosophical conception of the objective irrationality of capitalism depends essentially both on his claim that capitalism produces a progressive alienation of the working class and on the thesis that capitalism is fatally prone to ever more serious economic crises. If the evidence leads us to give up these hypotheses, then we lose the critical perspective from which we can issue a negative evaluation of capitalism. But, of course, this is the price of non-vacuous theory.

Notes

1. Marx 1967. I have altered the translation to bring out the precise logical stucture of Marx's assertion. The original reads: "Es sind gesellschaftlich gültig, also objektive Gedankenformen für die Produktionsverhaltnisse dieser historisch bestimmten gesellschaftlichen Produktionsweise, der Warenproduktion."

References

Hegel, G.W.F. 1910. *The Phenomenology of Mind*, trans. by J. B. Baillie. London: Swan Sonnenschein and Co.

Marx, Karl. 1967. *Capital*, Vol. I, trans. by S. Moore and E. Aveling, ed. by F. Engels. New York: International Publishers.

Marx, Karl, and Friedrich Engels. 1958–1966. *Werke*, 39 Bände mit Erganzungsbände. Berlin: Dietz Verlag.

_____. 1975. *Collected Works*. New York: International Publishers.

9
Marxism and Individualism

Jon Elster

Individualism is both an epistemological and a political attitude. In this chapter I discuss how these two aspects of individualism are related to each other within the Marxist tradition. For a very long time, the conventional wisdom was that Marxism is inherently opposed to political individualism and, therefore, to epistemological or methodological individualism (MI). I shall contest the premise, the inference and the conclusion of this argument.

I shall not proceed, however, in exactly that order. In the first section I explain what, for the purposes of this study, I shall understand by "Marxism." Clearly, it is not possible to refute someone who insists that the methodological holism not infrequently found in Marx is essential to what it is to be a Marxist. I believe, however, that a more fruitful definition is to define Marxism in terms of its more viable elements—by what is living rather than by what is dead. The second section is a brief statement and defense of the doctrine of MI in the social sciences. Although I cannot help thinking that the doctrine is trivially true, I know that others think differently, and so an argument is needed. In the third section I discuss the relation between Marxism and MI. Did Marx's work rest on a denial of this principle? How much of it can be restated within a strictly individualist framework? In the final section I state the doctrine of political individualism in two distinct versions. I then address two questions: What is the relation between political individualism and MI? Is political individualism compatible with Marxism?[1]

Marxism: What Is Living and What Is Dead?

The corpus of Marxist thought, from Marx to the present, may be divided into three parts. First, there is a general theory of historical change, usually referred to as historical materialism. Second, there is a theory of capitalism as an economic, social, political and ideological system. Third, there is a normative theory of communism, which can be succinctly described as a society which has overcome alienation and exploitation. I shall provide thumbnail sketches and brief evaluations of each of these, with a view to laying the groundwork for later sections.

Historical materialism proposes a theory of the relation between productive forces and relations of production, together with a theory of the relation between the economic base and the legal, political and ideological superstructure. The structure of the former theory has now been clarified, definitively in my opinion, by G. A. Cohen (1978).[2] Relations of production rise and fall according to their capacity to promote the growth of the productive forces. A given set of relations obtains as long as and because they are optimal for this development, and ceases to obtain when and because another set of relations supersedes them in this respect. The reason why a given set of relations ceases to be optimal is to be found in the very development of the productive forces which these relations have promoted. A set of relations which are optimal at one level of development of the productive forces may be inferior when a higher level is achieved. Each mode of production lays the foundations for its own ultimate abolition.

This is a functional explanation of the relations of production in terms of their impact on the productive forces. It allows us to state both that the forces "determine" the relations (since the relations are explained by the forces) and that the relations "determine" the force (since the development of the forces is shaped by the relations), without turning the theory into a trivial statement of reciprocal influence. Cohen argues that there is an analogous functional connection between the economic base and the superstructure: legal, political and ideological phenomena can be explained by their stabilizing impact on economic relations. I agree that many Marxist accounts of superstructural phenomena correspond to this description, but I don't think all do. When Marx argues, for example, that mercantilist theories embody a cognitive fallacy directly related to the class position of capitalists, I take this to be a paradigmatic case of reduction of superstructure to base, and yet it is difficult to see how these false theories could stabilize the relations of production (see also Elster 1985: 31–34, 487ff., 494ff.).

Be this as it may, historical materialism as just stated proves difficult to apply to specific cases. Marx's account of the transition from feudalism to capitalism has at best a vague resemblance to the general theory, whereas his remarks on earlier transitions directly contradict it. Nor, finally, is it plausible that the transition from capitalism to communism should occur "when and because" communism emerges as a superior form of development for the productive forces. It is very difficult to escape the conclusion that Marx was under the sway of a teleological conception of history. The theory of the development of the productive forces is a secular theodicy. Attempts to apply the theory of base and superstructure have also been flawed by a tendency to rely on arbitrary functional explanations or on implicit conspiratorial assumptions. Often, from the observation that a phenomenon appears to serve some interest of the capitalist class it is concluded that this also provides an explanation of the phenomenon, without any attempt to support it by a mediating mechanism or a lawlike regularity.

In his writings on capitalism, Marx ranged remarkably widely, from pure theory to detailed historical narrative. At one extreme, there are the economic analyses of *Capital*, Volumes 2 and 3. With one exception,[3] these are all invalid. The labor theory of value, intended to provide a deep explanation for the economic phenomena as they appear at the level of market prices, fails utterly. For one thing, the concept of labor value turns out to be ill-defined on all except the most simplistic assumptions; for another, even when well defined it has no explanatory role to play. The theory of the falling rate of profit—which is the other cornerstone of Marx's economic theory—is in no better shape. Whereas the other classical economists had argued that the rate of profit would fall because of insufficient technical progress, Marx argued that innovation was the very vehicle of that fall— a view which turns out to be contrary not only to intuition but to truth as well.

Capital, Volume 1, is not a work of economic analysis in the strict sense defined in Schumpeter's *History of Economic Analysis*, but of economic history and economic sociology. Here, Marx is at his unsurpassable best in the chapters which study the interplay of property relations, power, technology and rational decision-making at the factory level. Less focused, but also masterful, are the analyses of capitalism as a *system* of firms—of competition, of the transition from manufacture to machinofacture, of accumulation, growth and technical change. In my opinion, Marx's greatness as an economic theorist comes across in his mastery of details, made possible by his vast erudition and analytical skills, although he is of course known mainly for his grand theories.

Another great achievement was Marx's analysis of class structure and politics in Germany, England, and France in the mid-nineteenth century. Here he captures the interplay between class consciousness, class struggle and class coalitions in a way that remains exemplary in many respects. The analyses of "divide and conquer" and "two-front wars" in the class struggle are especially striking. His analysis of politics as the continuation of class struggle by other means is less convincing. In particular, his a priori assumption that all state policies could be explained in terms of their usefulness for the capitalist class led him to use Ptolemaic devices to save the phenomena. When around 1850 it became clear that the bourgeoisie in the three countries was not assuming its historical role by directly taking political power, Marx tried to explain this as ultimately being in the bourgeoisie's own interest. Again, this represents a functional explanation unsupported by specific evidence or general regularities.

Marx also attempted to explain the ideological elements of the capitalist superstructure, or at least some of them. The three volumes of *Theories of Surplus Value* are, among other things, an attempt to write the history of economic thought from James Steuart to John Stuart Mill as reflecting the development of economic relations during the same period. As usual, his views range from teleological and functional to more acceptable causal explanations. (An instance of the latter is his analysis of mercantilism, briefly mentioned above.) These writings exemplify how Marx's functionalism can play on several different registers. If a given theory cannot be explained as supporting and stabilizing the existing property relations, he can argue instead that it prepares the ground for the relations which will replace them. The physiocrats, for instance, believed that they glorified feudal landed property when they labeled industry as "sterile," whereas in reality, Marx says, they paved the way for the bourgeoisie by arguing that industry, being sterile, should be exempt from taxation. Not content with observing the irony of the situation, he had to turn it into the Ruse of Reason.

Let me turn, finally, to the normative components of Marxism. These can, I believe, be summarized in two propositions. First, the good life for man is one which is organized around active self-realization rather than around passive consumption.[4] The deepest form of alienation, for Marx, is man's alienation from his creative powers, whether this takes the subjective form of an unfulfilled desire for self-realization or the objective form of the absence of this desire. Marx differentiates himself to his right from Adam Smith, who believed that work was doomed to remain a "curse," and to his left from Fourier, who believed it could be made into mere amusement or play. For Marx, if work can be deeply satisfying it is because and not in spite of the fact that it is strenuous and demanding. There are some Utopian elements in Marx's view, notably the view that in a communist society each and every individual will develop and deploy each and every of his potential abilities. Yet shorn of this exaggeration, and suitably supplemented by other considerations—*Arbeit und Liebe*, not just *Arbeit*—the ideal of self-realization through work remains an immensely valuable guide to industrial and political reform.

Second, in the communist society scarce resources will be distributed "according to need." Exactly what Marx intended by this principle remains unclear. On one reading it could mean that there will be abundance in an absolute sense, so that when all have taken what they want from the common stock there will be something left over of each good. Although Marx occasionally expresses himself in ways compatible with this view, the principle of charity in textual interpretation should make us look for more plausible readings. Given the context in which the principle is stated, the most natural way to understand it is as a claim for equal satisfaction of needs, which in turn, given my earlier argument, might be thought to consist of equality of self-realization. Or in the light of problems raised by this conception (see Elster 1986 and Dworkin 1981a), one might try to understand it as a principle of equal opportunity for self-realization (Dworkin 1981b). This notion, however, also turns out to be problematic (Roemer 1985). To sort out these difficulties, a full-blown theory of justice would be needed, a task that cannot be attempted here.

One may, however, understand what's unjust about capitalism without having a full theory about communist justice. Capitalism is unjust because it rests on exploitation. Because some individuals lack access to means of production, they are forced to sell their labor power to capital owners in return for a wage that allows them to buy consumption goods embodying less labor than that which they have performed. Although, for various reasons, exploitation in this sense is not a fundamental moral concept (see Elster 1985: Ch. 4.3), it can in a large number of historical cases serve as a guide to moral assessment. I believe, for instance, that in contemporary capitalist societies workers and employees are unjustly and unnecessarily exploited by owners and top managers. Again, this idea can be a powerful guide to industrial and political reform.

I believe that these two normative ideas—the critiques of alienation and exploitation—are the *sine qua non* of Marxism, if that notion is to retain some usefulness. The positive and explanatory concepts of Marxism will, if valid, just become part of mainstream social science. If invalid, they should simply be discarded. In neither case do they constitute reasons for talking about Marxism as a distinct intellectual tradition. The normative components, on the other hand, will not be similarly absorbed or refuted in the foreseeable future.

Methodological Individualism

The term "methodological individualism" was coined by Joseph Schumpeter (1908: 88ff.). Later it was associated especially with other Austrian philosophers and economists (Popper, Hayek) and their students. Debates over MI were frequent and heated in the 1950s, but seem to be less so today, probably because most social scientists and social philosophers have come to accept the view as the truism it is. Still, resistance lingers in some quarters, among Marxists of more or less fundamentalist persuasions[5] and among sociologists and social anthropologists who see *social norms* as irreducibly supra-individual entities that guide and constrain individual behavior.[6]

An absurd and untenable version of MI is the view that social science could in principle eliminate all references to social wholes, collectivities, systems, and the like. The objection to this view is well known and simple. When social aggregates are the object of individual beliefs and desires, one cannot always substitute, *salva veritate*, coextensional individual referents. In the statement, "The US fears the USSR," the first reference to an aggregate entity can be decomposed into statements about the fears of individual Americans; indeed, the statement has no meaning unless so decomposed. The second reference, however, resists disaggregation. What the individual American fears may well be "the USSR" as a threatening, collective entity with goals of its own,[7] not any particular collection of Soviet citizens with heterogeneous goals which are somehow aggregated into national decisions which are in turn implemented by individual citizens. For the two reasons implied by the preceding phrase—the problem of aggregating individual preferences into a coherent social preference and the problem of having the social decision carried out without being distorted by the self-interest of the executors—the social scientist should never assume that aggregates are unitary actors.[8] Yet if people entertain and act upon this unfounded assumption, it will have to be part of the explanation of their behavior.

What I have just stated is the minimal concession any methodological individualist must give to holism: because and to the extent that people as a matter of fact have and act upon beliefs and desires which include references to social aggregates, the latter must be part of the explanation of their behavior. It might appear as if this minimal concession is all that is demanded by Maurice Mandelbaum in his critique of MI: "in attempting to analyze societal facts by means of appealing to the thoughts which guide an individual's conduct, some of the thoughts will themselves have societal referents, and societal concepts will therefore not have been expunged from our analysis" (Mandelbaum 1959: 480). It is clear, however, that Mandelbaum would not be satisfied with the minimal concession. I suggested above that if people entertain notions about aggregates with beliefs and goals of their own, they are irrational. If they really understood what it means to believe something, to desire something, or to act, their beliefs and desires would not contain references to supra-individual beliefs, desires, and actions. Mandelbaum, however, argues that beliefs with "societal referents" are not eliminable from social life. They are involved, by conceptual necessity, in innumerable acts of everyday life, such as cashing a check. These, in his opinion, necessarily involve beliefs about social organizations such as "the banking system," together with beliefs about social roles such as "the bank teller." Each of these concepts, in turn, presupposes and refers to further beliefs about societal facts, such as the monetary nature of the economy, the legal system, and so forth. To get rid of these beliefs by redescribing them as beliefs about individuals would involve us in an infinite regress, since the conditions under which an individual assumes a social role can only be stated with reference to societal facts.

For the version of MI to be defended here, it would not matter were I to extend the concession to include Mandelbaum's claim. Once one has granted that supra-individual entities do occur irreducibly within intensional contexts, it does not matter much whether one sees them as occurring contingently or necessarily. I am not sure, however, that the claim must be conceded. It seems to me that Mandelbaum does not distinguish sufficiently between two concepts of individuals. On the one hand, there are what in logical theory are called individual constants, referred to by proper names or definite descriptions. Clearly, it is absurd to believe that beliefs about social facts could ever be restated, without loss of content, as beliefs about individual constants. I may have beliefs about the bank teller without having any beliefs about him as an individual. On the other hand, there are individual variables, bound by the existential or the universal quantifier. Statements about social roles, and indeed about the whole network of roles and institutions, could be restated in terms of such individual variables and their relations to one another. Even for very simple cases, it would be tedious to carry out this restatement, but I do not see why it should lead to an infinite regress. There might be complex interdependencies among roles, but that is another matter.[9]

I shall not pursue this argument, since my main interest is elsewhere. I want to argue that once we have taken account of the need to refer to social entities *qua* objects of desires, beliefs, and other attitudes, all further references to such entities can in principle be dispensed with in social science explanations. This is not to say that reference to the properties, desires, beliefs, and behavior of individuals is sufficient. Thus to explain the income of farmers in any given year, it is not sufficient to know the production decisions of farmers, the preferences of consumers, the subsidies from government and the like: we must also know something about the weather. Let me, however, take the relevance of environmental conditions for granted; also, allow me to forget about supra-individual entities within intensional contexts. MI then is the claim that all social phenomena—events, trends, behavioral patterns, institutions—can in principle[10] be explained in ways that refer to nothing but individuals—their properties, goals, beliefs, and actions. In addition, MI claims that explanations in terms of individuals are superior to explanations which refer to aggregates. In a word: reduction is both feasible (in principle) and desirable. The denial of MI is methodological holism. Given the conjunctive character of MI, holism is disjunctive. The holist may argue that some social phenomena (perhaps all social phenomena) resist explanation along strictly individualist lines and that aggregates enter irreducibly into the explanation, or he may argue that individualist explanations, when feasible, need not be superior to holist ones.

Thus stated, I find MI trivially true. It is difficult to argue for it because it is difficult to understand how anyone could disagree with it. Let me, nevertheless, adduce three arguments for the desirability of scientific reductionism in general and for methodological individualism in particular. Afterward, I shall briefly address an influential recent objection related to the question of feasibility.

First, reductionism is desirable for what one might call aesthetic reasons. Even if we have perfect confidence that a macro-phenomenon (e.g., the rate of unemployment at t_2) can be explained by another macro-phenomenon (e.g., the rate of inflation at t_1), it does not really satisfy our curiosity. To be fully satisfied, we want to know exactly *how* it comes about that inflation generates unemployment: we want to have a look at the mechanism inside the black box. We might want to know whether the causal chain operated through the actions of employers or of wage earners; what if any was the role of speculative behavior; and many other things. Sometimes we might have to be satisfied with a halfway-house explanation, in terms of the behavior of trade unions and employers' associations rather than of individual workers and employers, but this would still be an improvement on the stark statement we began with. MI is an ideal whose value is that of pointing in a certain direction. Any step in that direction is an approximation to the ideal, even though there may be many more steps to take.

Next, reductionism also improves our confidence in an alleged explanation, i.e., our belief that it does not rest on a spurious, non-explanatory connection. When we go from macro to micro, we typically also go from longer to shorter time intervals.[11] The effect is broken down in first-order effects (the immediate reactions of the individuals), second-order effects (reactions to the effects of those reactions), and so forth. By reducing the time span between *explanans* and *explanandum*, the risk of spurious explanation is also reduced. The latter risk arises in two main ways: by the confusion of explanation and correlation and by the confusion of explanation and necessitation. The first occurs when there is a third variable that generates both the apparent cause and the apparent effect; the second when the effect is brought about by some other cause that preempts the operation of the apparent cause. Both risks are reduced when we approach the ideal of a continuous chain of causes and effects, i.e., when we reduce the time lag between *explanans* and *explanandum*. This in turn is closely connected with going from the aggregate to the less aggregate level.

Third, reduction to lower levels is necessary to understand the stability and change of aggregates. This is most obvious with respect to change, whether endogenously or exogenously induced. By definition, endogenous change must be explained in terms of the internal structure of the aggregate under consideration. Families break up because the members are unable to get along with each other; organizations split because of power struggle or divergent individual priorities. To explain the impact of exogenous shocks, we must also know something about the medium of propagation, i.e., the internal structure of the aggregate. Technical diffusion, for instance, may be rapid or slow, depending on the incentives and beliefs of the group in question. It is slightly less obvious that the explanation of stability also requires reduction to lower levels. There is no "principle of inertia" for institutions or behavioral patterns. If they persist over time, it must be because the individuals concerned react to the steady stream of external and internal perturbations in ways that tend to nullify rather than amplify them. Nor, however, is there a general presumption for social homeostasis. It must be shown, for each particular case, that the forms of interaction are such as to maintain rather than destabilize the aggregate pattern.

Using examples from Marxist (and non-Marxist) social theory, Richard Miller adduces two arguments against MI. First, certain social phenomena must be explained "as due to objective interests, not to psychological dispositions." Thus,

a typical major capitalist identifies the bourgeois and the national interest because such belief serves a variety of his desires and goals. For one thing, he has a goal of promoting this belief in others. And it is easier and less tense to encourage a belief in others if you share it. Also, he possesses overwhelming evidence that policies of lay-off, speed-up, pollution and war which he investigates or encourages hurt most people. If he were to accept this conclusion, he would feel much the worse for it. So, to achieve the peace of mind he desires, he must encounter the evidence strongly prejudiced toward the belief that the interests of big business actually coincide with the interests of most people, despite apparent evidence to the contrary. Of course, these desires and goals are not *his* reasons for making the crucial identification. He would emphatically, honestly, and serenely reject this explanation of his belief. (Miller 1978: 398)

This argument confuses the distinction between psychological dispositions and objective interests with the distinction between conscious and non-conscious interests. Clearly, the capitalists described by Miller are engaged in a piece of dissonance-reduction. Unbeknownst to themselves, their desire for "peace of mind" leads them to look at the evidence in a biased way. If this desire is not a psychological disposition, I don't know what is.[12]

Miller's second argument is that MI tends to confuse explanation of phenomena with description of their causes. I believe that his argument can, without distortion, be brought out by the following example. Consider a myopic and reckless pedestrian who is killed by a car when he steps out in the street. Miller would say that a "description of the cause" of that event, i.e., the true causal story leading up to his death, does not provide an explanation of it since it does not help us see why it was "bound to happen." MI, being wed to description of causes, is thereby shown to be inadequate for explanatory purposes. This argument seems unconvincing. The explanation of why an accident was bound to happen relies on psychological dispositions of the *individual*, viz. his myopia and recklessness. We can change the example and say that "a world war would have broken out around 1914, even in the absence of the chain of events involving the assassination of Archduke Ferdinand . . . given the political and economic relations among major capitalist powers at the time" (Miller 1978: 405). But why should we believe this in the absence of a plausible story about what individuals would have done?

Marxism and Methodological Individualism

In the history of the social sciences, Marx was in several ways a transitional figure. While his social theories had deep roots in speculative philosophy, he also embraced the emerging positive mode of social analysis. As a consequence, holist and teleological elements coexist in his writings with impeccably individualist explanations which use what has become the standard causal-cum-intentional language of the social sciences. The *Grundrisse* are especially striking in this respect. Here we find, almost next to each other, obscure Hegelian deductions and brilliant analyses of the un-intended consequences produced by uncoordinated rational action. One may cite, for instance, his striking anticipation of Keynes's theory of self-reinforcing demand crises. Like the theory of the falling rate of profit, this proto-Keynesian analysis suggests that the capitalists find themselves in a Prisoner's Dilemma, in which individually rational behavior yields collectively disastrous outcomes. The theory of the falling rate of profit is invalid, but not because it violates MI.

Many of Marx's analyses of the capitalist entrepreneur and his workers rest on sound microfoundations. The entrepreneur is shown to choose between alternative techniques of production in terms of their impact on short-term profit and on the class consciousness of the workers, which in turn is an important determinant of long-term profit. Workers are shown to have some freedom of choice both as workers and as consumers. Transaction cost reasoning and strategic arguments are deployed; elements of bargaining theory are presented; and so on. Yet the labor theory of value prevented Marx from working out all the implications of the rational-choice approach. He believed that the ultimate determinants of market prices are not individual choices by workers and capitalists, but labor values, which are logically prior to these choices. Similarly, he believed that the notion of "capital" is logically prior to the many individual capitals, and that competition among the latter is just the working out of what is already implicit in that notion. In the whole of Marx's corpus, I know of no more explicit denial of MI than the following:

> The predominance of capital is the presupposition of free competition, just as the despotism of the Roman Caesars was the presupposition of the free Roman 'private law'. As long as capital is weak, it still relies on the crutches of past modes of production, or on those which will pass with its rise. As soon as it feels strong, it throws away the crutches, and moves in accordance with its own laws. As soon as it begins to sense itself and become conscious of itself as a barrier to development, it seeks refuge in forms which, by restricting free competition, seem to make the rule of capital more perfect, but are at the same time the heralds of its dissolution and of the mode of production resting on it. Competition merely *expresses* as real, posits as an external necessity, that which lies within the nature of capital; competition is nothing more than the way in which the many capitals force the inherent determinants of capital upon one another and upon themselves. (Marx 1973: 651)

"Capital" as a collective entity with (explanatory) interests and goals of its own has a central role in Marx's thinking and in that of many later Marxist writers. Here are some examples: (1) Marx suggests that the explanation of upward social mobility under capitalism is that it "reinforces the supremacy of capital itself, expands its base and enables it to recruit ever new forces for itself out of the substratum of society" (Marx 1967b: 600). (2) Several writers have suggested that the explanation of the preponderancy of labor-saving innovations is due to the benefits they bring to "capital" by lowering the demand for labor and thereby the wage rate (Marx 1967a: 638; see also Offe and Wiesenthal 1980). The argument neglects the free-rider problem that no individual capitalist firm would have a motivation to engage in the collectively rational behavior. (3) Marx suggests that the British Factory Acts were passed because of the need of "capital" for a curb on the relentless profit-maximizing behavior of individual capitalist firms (for references and discussion see Elster 1985: 186ff.).

Another collective actor endowed with explanatory goals and interests is Humanity. In Marx's conception of history, all events are ultimately to be explained in terms of their contribution to communism as the end— goal and final stage—of Humanity. This view underlies his tripartite scheme of historical development. In the first stage, society is characterized by a primitive, undifferentiated unity, which in a second stage is rent asunder by alienation and class struggle. The "meaning" (Marx 1844: 241) and "inherent purpose" (Marx 1973: 832) of this second stage is to bring about the third and final stage, in which the unity is reestablished, but without loss of differentiation and individuality. The quasi-mystical character of Marx's thought is well brought out in the following passage:

> [Although] at first the development of the capacities of the *human species* takes place at the cost of the majority of human individuals and even classes, in the end it breaks through this contradiction and coincides with the development of the individual; the higher development of the individual is thus only achieved by a historical process during which individuals are sacrificed, for the interests of the species, as in the animal and plant kingdoms, always assert themselves at the cost of the interest of individuals, because these interests of the species coincide only with the *interests of certain individuals*, and it is this coincidence which constitutes the strength of these privileged individuals. (Marx 1972: 118)

These speculative conceptions have direct implications in various domains. I do not think there can be any doubt that they form the matrix from which Marx derived his theory of the productive forces. Marx does not even try to provide microfoundations for the view that the relations of production change when and because they cease to be optimal for the development of the productive forces. Nor have later Marxists been more successful in this respect.[13] By contrast, Marx's theory can be deduced immediately from the assumption that historical development is guided by the interests of Humanity, since then any form of economic organization will be discarded when it is no longer on the shortest path to communism.

Marx's political theory and practice also demonstrate the importance of these speculative conceptions. He asserts that when the workers "opposed the bourgeoisie, as they did in France in 1793 and 1794, they fought only for the attainment of the aims of the bourgeoisie, even if not *in the manner* of the bourgeoisie. *All French terrorism* was nothing but a *plebeian way* of dealing with the *enemies of the bourgeoisie*" (*Neue Rheinische Zeitung* 15 December 1848). The temporary victory of the proletariat was "only an element in the the service of the *bourgeois revolution* itself" (*Deutsche Brüsseler Zeitung* 11 November 1847). Marx might well have used a phrase that he employs elsewhere: the workers were the "unconscious tool of history" (*New York Daily Tribune* 25 June 1853), a pawn placed by the Ruse of Reason. One might object that these are rhetorical phrases, not to be taken seriously and literally. Against this view, however, we may cite the fact that Marx's own practice in the German revolution of 1848–1849 shows him to have been under the sway of teleological views. Initially he acted as if he believed the German bourgeoisie to be mere puppets of their historical destiny, doomed to accept an alliance with the workers so that the latter could more easily move on to take power for themselves. He was frustrated when they turned out to be moved by their self-interest rather than by their historical role (for details see Elster 1985: Ch. 7.2).

So far I have discussed cases in which Marx's adherence to methodological holism led him seriously, indeed irreparably, astray. In other cases the lack of microfoundations is reparable. In particular, Marx's theory of class struggle and class consciousness can be reconstituted so as to respect MI. In *The Eighteenth Brumaire of Louis Bonaparte* and elsewhere, Marx cites structural conditions that must obtain for the transformation of a class in itself (without class consciousness) to a class for itself (with class consciousness). These include notably spatial proximity among the members, good means of communication, low rates of turnover and cultural homogeneity. If we define class consciousness as the ability to overcome the free-rider problem in collective action, we must ask how it is promoted by the structural conditions just cited. Between these structural macro-causes and the macro-effect (successful collective action), we must insert mediating mechanisms to show why, under these conditions, individuals would be motivated to initiate or join collective action. Although Marx did not attempt to do this, the enterprise does not look unfeasible. Rational-choice theories of collective action suggest, for instance, that voluntary cooperation by self-interested individuals is more likely to occur in small, stable groups (Axelrod 1984; Taylor 1987).

More generally, I believe that the research program for today's Marxists is inseparable from MI. Marxism traditionally has been strong on insights and intuitions, but weak on arguments and mechanisms. Thus I unreservedly subscribe to the following summary by Pranab Bardhan:

> Overall, in development economics, as in much of social science in general, the most valuable contribution of the Marxist approach is the sense of history with which it is imbued, its focus on the tension between property relations and productive potential in a given social formation, and on the importance of collective action and power in enhancing or thwarting processes of institutional change to resolve that tension, its insistence on bringing to the forefront of public policy debates an analysis of the nature of the state and the constellation of power groupings in civil society, and, of course, its abiding commitment to certain normative ideas on questions of exploitation and injustice. Its processes of reasoning, however, leave much to be desired, with its frequent substitution of convenient teleology for explanatory mechanisms and of a kind of murky institutionalism for rigorous rationale of contractual arrangements, and its failure to base aggregative results firmly on consistent actions of economic agents at the micro-level, ignoring as a consequence incentive compatibility problems, issues of contract enforcement and repetitive transactions, strategic interactions of agents (even with commonality of class interests), the free rider problem in class formation and action, and disequilibrium dynamics of adjustment paths. (Bardhan 1986: 76)

Political Individualism

Schumpeter defines political individualism (PI) as the view "that freedom contributes more than anything else to the development of man and to the general good *(Gesamtwohle)*" (Schumpeter 1908: 90). Later developments have produced a bifurcation in PI. On the one hand there are those who praise freedom—more specifically free market competition unrestrained by state intervention—mainly as a means to the efficient production of economic welfare. On the other hand there are those who praise freedom as a value in itself, i.e., who deny—on non-instrumental grounds—governments any right to interfere with voluntary economic transactions. On the former view, PI is a value-neutral theory about ends-means relations. On the latter it is explicitly about values, more precisely about rights. Roughly speaking, one may think of these two versions as represented by Milton Friedman and Robert Nozick respectively. Many actual positions do not fit neatly into this dichotomy. The strain within John Stuart Mill's philosophy between liberty as a means to social welfare and liberty as an end in itself is well known. Similarly, it is not obvious that F. A. Hayek or James Buchanan fit well into the deontological, rights-based tradition to which they are often assigned. This does not show, of course, that their views are ambiguous or ambivalent. It might show only that the dichotomy is pretty simplistic. Yet I believe it can be useful, since there are some views which fit unambiguously into the one or the other category.

On Schumpeter's view, PI and MI are independent of each other, in the sense that all combinations of acceptance and rejection of the two are possible and coherent (Schumpeter 1908: 91). I agree with this view. The value-neutral version of PI expresses a substantive view about social causality, whereas MI, being a methodological prescription, is not committed to any substantive propositions. True, PI in this version is compatible with MI since it is stated in individualistic language, but so is the denial of PI, e.g., the view that free competition can lead to Pareto-suboptimal outcomes. I discuss below whether the denial of MI is compatible with instrumental PI. The non-instrumental, value-oriented version of PI is similarly independent of MI. Although both are normative views, they address very different issues. The methodological norms of scientific inquiry bear no relation to the norms of rights assignment. All of these statements are, I believe, trivial and quite generally accepted.

There is, however, an undeniable sociological connection between MI and PI. In the two-by-two table of possible combinations of views, not all cells are equally well populated; in fact, one seems to be empty. The list of those who strongly advocate both MI and PI includes, prominently, Hayek (at least the early Hayek), Popper, and their followers, as well as others, too numerous to mention. The list of those who oppose both views comprises not only the followers of Hegel (including Marx), but also the followers of Comte (including Durkheim). There are also many adherents of MI who oppose PI. In most Western countries most social scientists are liberals or social democrats of a sort, meaning that they oppose PI in its more extreme versions. They also routinely follow the prescriptions of MI. By contrast, I cannot think of a single unambiguous instance of a defender of PI who rejects MI.[14] Although it is easy to find examples of right-wing organicism which definitely denies MI, it is invariably of the Tory rather than the Whig variety of right-wing politics. Hegel and others in this category defend state intervention and view unrestricted free competition with deep suspicion.

It is instructive to try to construct the views of a defender of PI who denies MI. As an opponent of MI, he must believe that aggregates have independent explanatory power. As a defender of PI, he must believe that freedom of the individual is to be valued, either on instrumental or on intrinsic grounds. Instrumental PI would commit him to the view that the achievement of the general good, when it occurs, can be explained in terms of freely acting individuals and not, for instance, as the realization of the *Weltgeist.* This is not inconsistent with methodological holism, at least in the version of that doctrine which simply insists that *some* phenomena are irreducible to individual actions. Yet there might be a strain in holding this combination of views. It might appear easier to combine a denial of MI with the non-instrumental version of PI. One might hold, that is, that the normative assessment of societies depends on the extent to which they promote and protect the (negative) freedom of the individual, and yet believe that in the explanation of societies supra-individual entities enter in an irreducible way. Yet the fact seems to be that no one unambiguously holds this combination of views.

The relation of Marxism to PI might seem straightforward. Traditionally, Marxists have invariably been hostile to the market system on several grounds. First, they have insisted on the anarchy of the market as a regulative system. To overcome market failures, such as the insufficient provision of public goods and periodically recurring economic crises, central planning is required. Second, they have argued that a market economy inevitably tends to turn into a capitalist economy, with the concomitant injustices of exploitation. Third, they have argued that the arm's length character of market transactions prevents the emergence of genuine community. In capitalism, more specifically, labor power itself is turned into a commodity, with dehumanizing effects. The work is treated as a means to profits, not as part of the self-realization of the individual. Markets, in other words, generate inefficiency, exploitation and alienation.

Yet these arguments appear less persuasive when we look more closely at the alternative to the market. The experience from Soviet-type economies massively indicates that central planning is no paradigm of efficiency, not even with respect to static resource allocation (as Schumpeter [1961: 193ff.] thought) and certainly not in any dynamic sense. There are also strong theoretical grounds for believing that this problem will not be easily overcome. As noted above, central planning is vulnerable to difficulties of preference aggregation, information collection, and policy implementation. Although some forms of exploitation or, more generally, economic injustice are absent from these economies, others are highly prominent (Roemer 1982: Ch. 8). Also, it is hard to see that the vast bureaucracies of central planning are less alienating and dehumanizing than impersonal markets. Finally, the economic freedom allowed by the market system may be regarded as a good thing in itself, even if one does not believe that it dominates all other values.

Given their values—a society without exploitation and alienation—Marxists might consider *market socialism* as an alternative to capitalism.[15] In a market socialist economy, the workers of any enterprise would have full ownership and control of their firm. There would be competitive markets for all products, but no labor market. To limit market failures, there would have to be a state sector and some macro-economic regulation. (In this respect there would be no difference between market socialism and modern capitalist economies.) As in any market economy, unjustified income inequalities might emerge. There would be no exploitation within firms, but there could well be exploitation between firms.[16] To limit these inequalities, income transfers might be required. For efficiency reasons, however, inequalities should not be eliminated. There would be less alienation, since workers would be free to organize the production process in ways that give more scope to self-realization and participation. There might or might not be a loss of economic freedom, depending on whether the freedom to create a capitalist firm was retained or eliminated. On all except the most optimistic assumptions, it would probably have to be eliminated. Nevertheless, market socialism would have much more scope for economic freedom than a centrally planned economy.

I shall not here discuss whether the balance of argument favors market socialism over capitalism. I tend to think that it does, but the argument remains to be worked out. More importantly, only experience can show if market socialism in practice has the properties suggested by theory. For the present purpose, my point is simply that there is no reason why contemporary Marxists should retain the traditional, aprioristic aversion to the market system. When combined with workers' self-management and tempered by macro-economic regulation, competitive markets need not have all the bad effects traditionally ascribed to them.

It is important to keep in mind that Marx, if not all later Marxists, subscribed to what one might call ethical individualism (EI). This is the metaethical view that ethical theories should be stated exclusively in terms of concepts defined at the level of the individual, whether these be concepts of individual welfare, individual rights, or individual autonomy. EI excludes from consideration ethical theories which invoke supra-individual or non-individual concepts as rock-bottom moral notions. An example of supra-individual theories is the view that public policy ought to aim at equality between the sexes or equality among nations, even if this should occur at the expense of greater inequality among individuals. Examples of non-individual theories are the views that policy ought to aim at the protection of nature or the growth of scientific knowledge, regardless of how these affect the welfare and rights of individual human beings. In the passage from *Theories of Surplus Value* cited above, Marx makes it clear that communism, in his view, is defined by the self-realization of men, not of Man.[17] Class societies have seen great achievements in arts and science, at the expense of the personal development of most individuals. Although great advances of mankind, these achievements could not justify the suffering of the vast majority—except by laying the foundations for a society in which each and every individual would attain what in the past was reserved for a tiny minority.

When Marx wrote, "Above all we must avoid postulating 'society' again as an abstraction *vis-à-vis* the individual" (Marx 1844: 299), we should read it as a statement of EI. He was not committed to the view that some particular mode of economic organization is intrinsically desirable, regardless of how it affects individuals. Hence if we can show that the mode he favored, that of central planning, affects individuals in a way he would have thought undesirable, we are acting in his spirit if we look for alternative solutions.

Notes

1. For several of the ideas in this paper I draw extensively on Elster (1985).
2. Important further clarificatory work was done by P. van Parijs (1984).
3. The reproduction schemes of *Capital*, Vol. 2, while flawed in various respects, do represent genuine contributions to economic analysis. They are also, however, much less distinctively "Marxist" in their political implications.
4. I have tried to spell out the Marxian ideal of self-realization in Elster (1986).
5. See for instance the contributions of S. Meikle and C. Slaughter to the symposium on *Making Sense of Marx* in *Inquiry* 29 (1986). Although somewhat less critical, the contributions by A. Wood and M. Taylor also take issue with my espousal of MI.
6. A philosophical statement of this position is Taylor (1971). See also Bourdieu (1977).
7. Note, however, that the objects of the fears of different Americans may differ widely. There is no such thing as *the* American view of the Soviet Union. Nor is there, *pace* Taylor (1971), any such thing as *the* American way, which different individuals perceive differently, in the sense in which there is such a thing as Mount Everest, which is perceived differently by differently situated individuals.
8. In addition there is the problem, much emphasized by Hayek and his followers, that the decentralized and fragmented information available to members of a group usually cannot be collected and centralized in useful form. I discuss these problems in Elster (1987).
9. I am not very confident in the argument of this paragraph, because the level of generality is such that it is difficult to get a good handle on the problem. Let me mention an analogous question which arises in recent discussions of personal identity. One can deny the objective reality of personal identity without denying its subjective reality, i.e., its reality *qua* object of thought. "Persons must be mentioned in describing the *content* of countless thoughts, desires, and other experiences. But . . . such descriptions do not claim that these experiences are *had* by persons" (Parfit 1984: 226). The question then becomes whether, if the reductionist view of the self is accepted, one could *in principle* eliminate all references to persons (beginning with oneself) from one's thoughts.
10. I do not assume that "can in principle" implies "will sooner or later." Some phenomena might be so complex and unstable that computational demands and inevitable measurement errors will forever keep them outside the grasp of individualistic explanation. Yet one can still entertain the thought experiment of a sufficiently powerful computer and sufficiently fine instruments and ask whether, within the confines of that experiment, there is any reason to think that individualistic explanation is impossible.
11. This is an empirical statement, not a conceptual truth. For a hypothetical counterexample, consider an explanation of low rates of investment at time t_2 in

terms of low consumer incomes at time $t_2 - 30$. When spelled out, the story behind the explanation could be analogous to the one mentioned in the text: a succession of reactions, of reactions to reactions, etc. It could also be, however, that people growing up in poverty became permanently disposed to a certain form of saving behavior.

12. On this point see also Elster (1983: 24–25). I note in passing that the mechanism suggested by Miller in the second and third quoted sentences is highly implausible. There is no evidence that the unconscious mind is capable of sophisticated strategic reasoning of this kind.

13. This is a weak point in Cohen's defense and exposition of Marx's theory. The brief suggestion on pp. 292–293 of *Karl Marx's Theory of History* (Cohen 1978) to the effect that the class most able to develop the productive forces will attract allies from the other classes has no empirical or logical plausibility. (It looks, in fact, very much like the argument from *Theories of Surplus Value* just cited.) For further argument on this point, see Elster (1981).

14. There are two possible exceptions to this statement. Robert Nozick (1974: 22) seems to suggest that "filter-explanations" are incompatible with MI. Since he does not define his conception of MI, it is hard to evaluate this claim. I cannot think of any version of MI which would (1) render Nozick's claim true and (2) bear some resemblance to what has traditionally been understood by MI. Also, the later writings of Hayek might seem to be an exception. His strong reliance on cultural group selection, and the concomitant neglect of the free-rider problem, might seem to violate MI, as argued by Gray (1986: 52ff.) and Vanberg (1986). In the absence of explicit arguments against MI in Hayek's writings, I nevertheless hesitate to conclude that he falls in the (otherwise) empty cell. For an elaboration of Hayek's theory which is perfectly consistent with MI, see R. Sugden (1986).

15. The following brief remarks are amplified in the Introduction to Elster and Moene (eds.) (Forthcoming).

16. For an account of such horizontal exploitation, see Roemer (1982: Ch. 1).

17. For this distinction, see Cohen (1974).

References

Axelrod, R. 1984. *The Evolution of Cooperation*. New York: Basic Books.

Bardhan, Pranab. 1986. Marxist ideas in development economics. In J. Roemer (ed.), *Analytical Marxism*. Cambridge: Cambridge University Press, pp. 64–77.

Bourdieu, Pierre. 1977. *Outline of a Theory of Practice*. Cambridge: Cambridge University Press.

Cohen, G.A. 1974. Karl Marx's dialectic of labour. *Philosophy and Public Affairs* 3: 236–261.

————. 1978. *Karl Marx's Theory of History: A Defence*. Oxford: Oxford University Press.

Dworkin, Ronald. 1981a. What is equality? Part 1: equality of welfare. *Philosophy and Public Affairs* 10: 185–246.

————. 1981b. What is equality? Part 2: equality of resources. *Philosophy and Public Affairs* 10: 283–345.

Elster, Jon. 1981. Un marxisme anglais. *Annales: Economies, Sociétés, Civilisations* 36: 745–757.

————. 1983. *Sour Grapes*. Cambridge: Cambridge University Press.

————. 1985. *Making Sense of Marx*. Cambridge: Cambridge University Press.

_____. 1986. Self-realization in work and politics. *Social Philosophy and Policy* 3: 97–126.

_____. 1987. The possibility of a rational politics. *Archives Européennes de Sociologie* 28: 67–103.

Elster, Jon, and K.O. Moene (eds.). Forthcoming. *Alternatives to Capitalism.*

Gray, J. 1986. *Hayek on Liberty*, second ed. Oxford: Blackwell.

Mandelbaum, Maurice. 1959. Societal facts. In P. Gardiner (ed.), *Theories of History*. New York: The Free Press, pp. 476–487.

Marx, Karl. 1844. *Economic and Philosophical Manuscripts*. In K. Marx and F. Engels, *Collected Works*, Vol. 3. London: Laurence and Wishart.

_____. 1967a. *Capital*, Vol. 1. New York: International Publishers.

_____. 1967b. *Capital*, Vol. 3. New York: International Publishers.

_____. 1972. *Theories of Surplus Value*, Vol. 2. London: Laurence and Wishart.

_____. 1973. *Grundrisse*. Harmondsworth: Penguin Books.

Miller, R. 1978. Methodological individualism and social explanation. *Philosophy of Science* 45: 387–414.

Nozick, Robert. 1974. *Anarchy, State and Utopia*. New York: Basic Books.

Offe, C., and H. Wiesenthal. 1980. Two logics of collective action. *Political Power and Social Theory* 1: 67–115.

Parfit, Derek. 1984. *Reasons and Persons*. Oxford: Oxford University Press.

Parijs, P. van. 1984. Marxism's central puzzle. In T. Ball and J. Farr (eds.), *After Marx*. Cambridge: Cambridge University Press, pp. 88–104.

Roemer, John E. 1982. *A General Theory of Exploitation and Class*. Cambridge, Mass.: Harvard University Press.

_____. 1985. Equality of talent. *Economics and Philosophy* 1: 151-188.

Schumpeter, Joseph. 1908. *Das Wesen und der Hauptinhalt der theoretischen Nationalökonomie*. Leipzig: Duncker & Humblot.

_____. 1961. *Capitalism, Socialism and Democracy*. London: Allen and Unwin.

Sugden, R. 1986. *The Economics of Rights, Cooperation, and Welfare*. Oxford: Blackwell.

Taylor, Charles. 1971. Interpretation and the sciences of man. *Review of Metaphysics* 25: 3–51.

Taylor, M. 1987. *The Possibility of Cooperation*. Cambridge: Cambridge University Press.

Vanberg, V. 1986. Spontaneous market order and social rules: A critical examination of F.A. Hayek's theory of cultural evolution. *Economics and Philosophy* 2: 75–100.

10

Otto Neurath: From Authoritarian Liberalism to Empiricism

Gideon Freudenthal

I. Introduction

In this chapter I shall attempt to substantiate the thesis that the empiricist philosophy developed and advocated by Otto Neurath was dependent on his political views.[1] Since both my thesis and its manner of justification are liable to be misunderstood, I shall first explain some of my presuppositions and outline the course of the argument.

By "dependency" of one theory on another or on a set of propositions or beliefs not systematically elaborated (e.g., of epistemology on sociology or on socio-political views), I do not mean that the dependent theory is logically entailed by the other theory, but rather that it presupposes the truth of propositions which it cannot itself justify and which are in fact taken over from another domain, on which it is, therefore, dependent. It is immaterial in this connection whether these propositions are explicitly justified in the other domain or whether they are merely a generally accepted view in that domain. A theory may hence be dependent on another in the sense of importing from it some of its propositions without, however, being directly entailed by it.

My thesis is that the empiricism of Otto Neurath was dependent in various ways on his socio-political views. Neurath's political views involved (as do everyone's views) some descriptive, factual propositions about the nature of Man and society that were not the result of sociological analysis but actually preceded such an analysis. Epistemology can depend on these views in two ways. On the one hand, epistemology can directly depend on propositions about the nature of Man and society, because the attribution of epistemological properties to the agent of cognition must be compatible with the attribution of properties to the agent of socio-political activity, if the propositions are to form a comprehensive and consistent theory. Of course, the agents of cognition do not have to be identical with the agents of socio-political activity, and propositions about the former do not necessarily entail propositions about the latter, nor vice versa; but since these agents all belong to humanity, the propositions about different agents may, if unchecked, turn out to be inconsistent. If consistency is attempted, propositions in one domain will put constraints on propositions in the other and the latter is, therefore, dependent on the first. On the other hand, epistemology can depend on socio-political views in an indirect way, inasmuch as an epistemology may be developed as a reflection on science or on a specific scientific discipline believed to be representative of human knowledge. This science may in turn depend on prescientific views about Man and society. Such a dependence is much more likely to hold in the social than in the natural sciences.

It may, of course, also be the case that the direct and the indirect dependencies of epistemology on socio-political views are not clearly distinguishable. This will happen if the prescientific views to some extent determine the subject matter of the scientific discipline and if the scientific theory developed in the discipline confirms and reinforces these views. If this is the case, it will hardly be possible to disentangle the direct dependency of the epistemology on the prescientific socio-political views from its indirect dependency on these views, mediated by the dependency of the scientific theory on them.

The claim that a scientific theory is dependent on socio-political views or on any other "external" factor needs to be justified. This justification, in turn, requires first that the theory be shown to be deficient according to its own standards. For if the theory is adequate (according to these criteria), then no discussion about further determinations by "external factors" is called for. Of course, a theory may in fact be (over-)determined by external factors, but this cannot be *shown* if the theory can be reconstructed by referring only to its "internal" determinations. To *demonstrate* that a theory is dependent on so-called external factors thus requires first that it be shown that the internal reconstruction fails, i.e., that the theory falls short of the standards accepted at the time. Similarly, the choice of one particular theory from among available alternatives can be explained on the basis of external factors, but here, too, it is first necessary to show that there are not sufficient internal factors to explain the choice, i.e., that according to the relevant criteria the different theories are equally adequate.

Since Otto Neurath understood his sociology to be Marxist and was recognized by contemporaries as a Marxist scientist and philosopher, it is Marxism that must be used as the standard when one argues that his socio-political views and his sociology are deficient according to the standards he himself adopted. Showing that Neurath develops a "Marxist" theory which, according to Marxist criteria, is deficient and that he does not offer an acceptable alternative to those Marxist theorems he does not endorse, is sufficient to justify the search for external factors that may explain this deficiency. This argument is of course independent of any endorsement or rejection of the Marxist theory on my part or the reader's.

I shall argue that Neurath's deficient theory is dependent on his socio-political views, in particular that his abstraction from the productive activity of humans, which is considered in Marxism to be the very basis of social theory, is dependent on his liberal socio-political views. In his social theory Neurath concentrated on questions of distribution of social wealth without paying attention either to production or to the dependency claimed by Marxism of the forms of politics and distribution on the forms of production and property.

The dependency of Neurath's empiricism on his socio-political views is, according to my interpretation, both direct and mediated by his sociology. The direct influence consists in the fact that conceiving the acquisition of knowledge in a materialist fashion while abstracting from production and therefore also from the change of its forms in the course of human history leads, as will be shown below, to abstracting both from the active nature of cognition and from the role of the historically developed and accumulated means of cognition. These abstractions are presuppositions needed for maintaining empiricism within so-called Marxism. In contrast, Marx's version of materialism views the acquisition of knowledge as a form of production and therefore both as an active process and as dependent on and developing with the means of cognition, conceived as analogous to the means of production.

The indirect dependency of Neurath's epistemology on his socio-political views as mediated by his sociology is also rooted in his abstraction from the practical activity of humans. Since, as I will argue below, Neurath's political views did not require a theory of change in human societies (change was, on the contrary, conceived as imposed on society by the ruling powers), this sociology could be conceived as a "social behavioristics." Social behavioristics has, in Neurath's view, above all the merit that it can be formulated in "physicalist language," i.e., in terms of propositions about spatio-temporal relations between observable objects. Since no other sociological theory current in Neurath's time conformed to this ideal, I shall claim that the endorsement of physicalism was dependent on the endorsement of social behavioristics. If I succeed in showing that social behavioristics is deficient (according to the standards Neurath accepted) and that its endorsement can be explained on the basis of Neurath's political views, I will have substantiated my claim that his epistemology was indirectly dependent on his political views.

Moreover, the materialist sociology of Neurath, which did not consider Man as a producer, conceived of human beings as in principle not different from animals. Therefore, the acquisition of knowledge, too, had to be explained on the basis of faculties which are common to Man and other animals, and Neurath's epistemology indeed endeavored to show that the acquisition of knowledge can be explained on the basis of such faculties.

Finally, Neurath believed that social behavioristics (but none of the alternative sociological theories) could be reduced to biology and then to chemistry and physics. Since Neurath and other members of the Vienna Circle believed that physics can be reformulated in a "physicalist" language, it followed that sociology, too, could eventually be formulated in this manner.

Hence there are three forms in which Neurath's epistemology is dependent on his sociology. The direct dependency consists in the adoption of sociological propositions about human beings which put constraints on epistemology. The indirect forms of dependency are, first, that the sociological theory developed allowed for an empiricist epistemological interpretation; and second, that the further reduction of sociology to physics allowed the presupposed empiricist interpretation of physics to be applied to it. Leaving aside the question whether or not physics itself can really be formulated in a physicalist language, it is my claim that, had Neurath conceived of Man primarily as a producer in Marx's sense, he would not have believed that behavioristics is an adequate sociological theory nor, therefore, that sociology is reducible to physics and that it can be formulated in a physicalist language. In my interpretation, all forms of dependency of Neurath's epistemology on his socio-political views are thus rooted in his abstraction from the practice of humans and from its influence on cognition and on the forms of societal life.

Since I shall argue that Neurath's empiricist epistemology is dependent on the concept of the human being developed in his sociology and on the fact that social behavioristics seems to conform to an empiricist epistemological interpretation, I shall concentrate on the argument for the dependency of Neurath's sociology on his political views, trusting that the dependency of his basic empiricist position on this sociology will clearly appear in the course of the discussion of his sociology. Since I do not argue that specific formulations of his empiricism are dependent on his sociology and political views (I rather believe the opposite), I will not discuss the differences of opinion within the Vienna Circle nor the development of Neurath's own epistemological views.

I will now outline Neurath's political views and try to explain how his abstraction from production and human practice in general was dependent on his political views.

I.1

As I will explain at length below, Neurath's political views, although they were in accord with the prevailing interpretation of Marxism in central Europe at the time, can be characterized as "authoritarian liberalism." By "liberalism" I understand a social theory according to which capitalist society is composed of independent and equal individual proprietors. These proprietors are free insofar as they are personally independent of one another, and they are equal vis-à-vis the law. The state is conceived in liberalism as a socially neutral institution installed by these individuals to regulate their common affairs. By "authoritarian liberalism" I understand a basically liberal social theory which, in addition, holds that the state can and should install rules of distribution to achieve particular social aims in the interest of society as a whole.

Liberalism is hence the view that the constitutive social relations in capitalist society are best represented as contractual relations which in fact do presuppose personal independence and legal equality of the partners. When class relations are scrutinized in this framework, they are interpreted as consisting in unequal distribution. In *authoritarian* liberalism there is an additional theory about the compatibility of different forms of social and political institutions (all within the framework of liberalism) so as to guide the planning implemented or advocated.

The basic tenets of authoritarian liberalism are thus that a particular political structure and the particular rules of distribution determining the relations between distinct groups of the population (classes) and their standards of living are compatible with different forms of production and property. Accordingly Neurath's economic and sociological theory can separate forms of distribution from forms of production and deal with the latter without considering their social and political conditions and consequences.

From this and on the basis of materialism (the adoption of which can perhaps be explained but remains contingent on authoritarian liberalism) it follows for Neurath that production in its various historical forms is conceived as dependent on the natural, i.e., biological, characteristics of Man. Along with all other human activities it is part of "human behavior" and is explained within the framework of social behavioristics, which is based on biology. The development and change of forms of production is to be explained by a kind of biological theory of "evolution." Hence Neurath attempts to explain animal and human knowledge on the basis of their similar biological constitution. This, in turn, requires the reconstruction of human knowledge as dependent only on sense perception and extrapolation— and this is the core of Neurath's empiricism. The combination of this form of empiricism with Neurath's version of materialism is what he called physicalism. Neurath's physicalism is thus dependent, via empiricism, on his authoritarian liberalism and materialism, as mediated by his sociology and the concept of Man inherent in it.

If my interpretation is correct, then it is the concept of Man which connects the political, sociological and epistemological views. This is the case since a socio-political theory (whether scientific or pre-scientific) implies or builds on a concept of Man as does epistemology too. If social theory and epistemology are to be consistent with one another they mutually put constraints on one another through the concept of Man involved in both. This mediation through the concept of Man is, I believe, generally valid for cases where socio-political views influence epistemology.

I.2

My argument will be based exclusively on the work of Otto Neurath, and hence my conclusions do not apply directly to other members of the Vienna Circle, but I will suggest that they may apply *mutatis mutandis* not only to other members of the Vienna Circle but to "Neo-Positivism" in general. The justification for this suggestion is that I shall argue my case by addressing considerations of consistency, i.e., the compatibility between socio-political views on the one hand and epistemological claims on the other. An argument from consistency as opposed to one based on biographical evidence has the advantage of addressing necessary conceptual dependencies and not accidental biographical circumstances. Thus the argument concerns a theory and not a person and may apply generally.

Focusing on Otto Neurath has some advantages for my present purpose. As has been increasingly recognized in recent years, Neurath was not only a very bold and original philosopher: he also worked in the social sciences and engaged in politics. Hence his work is especially suited for the study of possible connections between political position, science, and epistemology.

I.3

Since my argument concerns consistency, i.e., interdependencies between elements of a theory, it cannot *exclude* the possibility that the socio-political views are dependent on the epistemological ones rather than the other way around. Here, I can only indicate the reasons for not accepting this possibility. The first reason is that epistemology consists in reflection on knowledge and, therefore, presupposes first-order knowledge. Of course, it may well be the case that an epistemology is formulated on the basis of knowledge in one particular scientific discipline and that a choice between different theories in another discipline is then made on the basis of considerations of consistency between these scientific theories and the epistemology already endorsed. In this case epistemology would be both reflection on first-order knowledge (in one discipline) and the criterion of choice between different theories (in another discipline).

There is, I believe, no way to exclude this possibility in principle, and it should be considered in every particular investigation. In general, however, I find it much more plausible that epistemology is what it claims to be, namely, reflection on knowledge, than to believe that the extravagant demand of some philosophers that science should follow epistemological prescriptions is actually realized.

Furthermore, should I succeed in establishing that Neurath's epistemology is dependent on his socio-political views not only by mediation of his sociology but also directly (i.e., by showing that his epistemology is consistent with his sociology and socio-political views but not with other alternative social theories at hand), then reversing the order of dependency would entail not only Neurath's sociology but also his political views being dependent on his epistemology. Although also this possibility cannot be ruled out in principle, I find it even less likely that political views depend on epistemology than the already implausible suggestion that science follows epistemology. These considerations are, of course, dependent on a set of assumptions known well at least since Hobbes, that socio-political views involve interests and that interests may affect reasoning, while epistemology is far more remote from such interests. These assumptions cannot be discussed and justified in the present context, but I believe that there are good arguments in their favor.

The dependency of social science on political positions—which is a necessary link in my argument for an indirect dependency of epistemology on political views (mediated by social science)—is further based on the claim that every political view necessarily includes views about the nature of society, since a political opinion cannot be expressed without supposing some descriptive statement about society. Such views may determine to some extent further scientific social research and theories. Prescientific social views thus mediate the influence of political positions on theories in social science. Based on my considerations concerning the implausibility of a dependency of scientific theories—and even more so of political views— on epistemology, I will argue for a dependency of Neurath's theories in the social sciences and in epistemology on political positions and prescientific social views, and for the dependency of epistemology on theories in the social sciences, wherever I can show that constraints imposed by consistency between the domains may explain a deficiency of the scientific or episte-mological theory. It is only on the basis of the considerations above that I believe that the demonstration of consistency may be read as an argument for dependency.

II. Neurath on Socio-Economic Position and Epistemology

II.1

Some members of the Vienna Circle discussed possible interdependencies between the "scientific conception of the world" and social, political and ideological processes during the period between the two world wars in Europe. Some such interdependencies are explicitly stated in the "manifesto" of the Vienna Circle (cf. Vienna Circle 1929). Since my interpretation of these interdependencies will be very different from Neurath's interpretation, I shall first present and discuss the latter.

According to Neurath, the development of the "modern process of production, which is becoming ever more rigorously mechanized . . . leaves ever less room for metaphysical ideas." Moreover, the contest between metaphysics and science "seems to be based on the fierce social and economical struggles of the present":

> One group of combatants, holding fast to traditional social forms, cultivates traditional attitudes of metaphysics and theology whose content has long since been superseded; while the other group, especially in central Europe, faces modern times, rejects these views and takes its stand on the ground of empirical science. (Neurath 1973: 317)

And the masses "along with their socialist attitudes tend to lean towards a down-to-earth empiricist view" (1973: 356). It is true that an "increase of metaphysical and theologizing leanings" can be observed, but there are many adherents of the scientific conception of the world who "in view of the present sociological situation, look forward with hope to the course of events to come" (1973: 317). Hence, the struggle is between progressive and reactionary orientations in social, political, and philosophical respects and the outcome of this struggle is dependent on social development.

Neurath believed that Marx and Engels correctly held themselves to be "resolute materialists" since they were "quite at home with its basic empirical outlook" although they were "extremely critical of the materialism of their day" (1973: 349). "Marx and Engels are 'materialists' insofar as they speak only of what one can observe by means of the senses" (1973: 349). Marxism is opposed to metaphysics which "builds on transcendent entities" (1981: 289) and "of all attempts at creating a strictly scientific unmetaphysical physicalist sociology, Marxism is the most complete" (1973: 349). The new physicalism is at present the most consistent form of materialism, just as Marxism was in the nineteenth century. "To profess materialism today means to stand up against bourgeois intellectualism and to bring out a new mode of thought, a new popular philosophy which will be quite anti-theological and at best will link up with certain exact thinkers among modern logicians and philosophers" (1973: 287). Since the Vienna Circle resumes the work of these "exact thinkers" the conclusion is drawn in its program that empiricism (and, therefore, materialism) have taken a "strong shape" in the philosophy of the Vienna Circle (1973: 317).

On Neurath's own interpretation, there is thus an essential connection between approving technical and social progress and empiricism, which is identified with materialism, of which Marxism is "the most complete" form. The scientific conception of the world is the heir of Marxism in philosophy— it is the "philosophy of the socialist proletariat" (1973: 289)—just as Marxism was the heir to the materialism of the Enlightenment.

II.2

In addition to the socio-historical interpretation of the role and function of the philosophy of the Vienna Circle, Neurath attempted to explain why logic and mathematics, which were traditionally associated with rationalism, could be at the core of the empiricism of the Vienna Circle. He also attempted a socio-historical explanation of the fact that the intellectual and institutional conditions for the emergence of the new empiricism were present particularly in Austria.

Neurath applied here a procedure of classification which he had developed earlier. He specified in a table (see Table 1) those "elements" of the philosophy of the Vienna Circle which were part of a previous philosophy (1981: 694). One easily sees that, of all philosophies considered, the philosophy of Leibniz contains the greatest number of elements which are considered characteristic of the philosophy of the Vienna Circle, and that after Leibniz these elements are in decrease. The question raised above can now be put in a more concrete form, namely, what were the socio-historical reasons why Kantianism and its successors (German Idealism from Fichte to Hegel) did not develop in Austria, and why the one element absent from Leibniz's philosophy— "Anti-metaphysics"—developed just there?

Table 1
Vienna Circle: Philosophical Elements from Earlier Philosophy

	Anti-metaphysics	Empiricism	Logic	Mathematics
Pythagoreans	−	−	−	+
Epicureans	+	−	−	−
Scholasticism	−	−	+	−
Leibniz	−	+	+	+
Kant	−	+	−	+
Fichte	−	−	−	−
Scientism	+	+	+	+

Neurath summarized his answer under the title "Austria Dispenses with the Kantian Intermezzo" (1981: 676). He explains that until the first half of the nineteenth century anti-Kantianism in Austria was a result of the "anti-revolutionary engagement of government and church" (1981: 691), who rejected the philosophy of Kant and of speculative Idealism "as products of the French Revolution" (1981: 677); later anti-Kantianism resulted from the anti-German attitude of Austrian liberalism: there were many intellectuals outside the university who "were in distance to the national way of thought and who adhered in the first place to ideas of liberalism, later to those of socialism, utilitarianism, pragmatism and empiricism in various composi-tions" (1981: 691). The strength of Habsburg Catholic conservatism was hence the reason for the dominance at first of scholasticism in Austrian universities, which cultivated logic and mathematics; the strengthening of the bourgeoisie was the reason for the rise of empiricism and anti-metaphysics. The achievements of scholasticism could merge with empiricism because Catholic conservatism spared Austria the "Kantian Intermezzo."

Neurath's interpretation of the connection between socialism, Marxism and empiricism, as well as his emphasis on the existence of traditions of empiricism and logic in Austrian universities, may at first seem convincing. But on second thought it leaves too many questions open. Neurath himself mentions the "increase of metaphysical and theologizing leanings" at that time. Furthermore, it is well known that not all workers were socialists, not all socialists Marxists (the Catholic labor movement!), not all Marxists materialists (Max Adler!), and not all materialists empiricists in Neurath's sense (Lenin!). On the other hand, not all empiricists were opposed to metaphysics (empirio-criticists!), nor were they all materialists or Marxists (Schlick!). In short, Neurath's characterization of the connection between empiricist epistemology and socialist and Marxist views turns out to be quite questionable and so is, therefore, his explanation of the basis of these connections.

Nevertheless, at least Neurath's claim to being a Marxist himself and the fact that he was so considered by many contemporaries have to be taken seriously; and since I claim that he was an authoritarian liberal, the question arises, why a liberal at that time could pass for a Marxist. To answer this question and to elucidate further the concept of "liberalism" I shall now turn to the most influential liberal interpretation of Marxism in Western Europe at the beginning of this century and concentrate on some crucial issues. I will then show that Neurath's theoretical views are in full agreement with this liberal interpretation, and then add some direct evidence showing that Neurath supported the political course of action justified by this interpretation. The purpose is to establish that the prevailing interpretation of Marxism at the turn of the century in central Europe conformed in fact to a kind of liberalism, that Neurath shared this interpretation, and thus that, even though he did not share Marx's views he could *bona fide* believe he was a Marxist and was considered to be one.

III. Bernstein's and Neurath's Liberal Marxism

III.1

The most important central European discussion on Marxist theory at the turn of the century began in 1896 with the publication of a series of articles by Eduard Bernstein ("Probleme des Sozialismus," in *Die Neue Zeit*). These articles were followed in 1899 by a book of the same content, *Die Voraussetzungen des Sozialismus und die Aufgaben der Sozial-Demokratie* (The Prerequisites of socialism and the tasks of the Social Democratic party), whose English translation bears the title: "Evolutionary Socialism."

Bernstein, a prominent leader of the Social Democratic party (SPD), formulated his position on the basis of the observation that the politics of the party was incompatible with its theory. He proposed to reform the theory in order to establish "a unity of theory and reality, of slogan and action." The party had to find the courage "to make up its mind to appear as what it is in reality today: a democratic, socialistic party of reform" and not a party of revolution (Bernstein 1961: 197, cf. 198f, 145).

Bernstein justified his solution to the incompatibility between theory and practice by changing the theory (not by changing the practice) by means of a critique of the Marxist theory. According to Bernstein, Marxist theory claims that the development of capitalism brings about a centralization and a concentration of the means of production in the hands of few capitalists, while the middle class is expropriated. Hence, a polarization takes place in society. On the one hand a small class of capitalists is formed and on the other hand the proletariat, which constitutes the majority of the population, becomes continuously more impoverished. As a result of the contradiction between social production and private appropriation, ever more severe economic crises would occur which would lead to a social crisis and to the "collapse" of capitalism. The proletariat would then take over the power and implement socialism. Understood this way, Marxism conceives the collapse of capitalism, the taking over of power by the proletariat, and thus the transition from capitalism to socialism, as an inevitable outcome governed by a law of nature.

According to Bernstein, this theory had been refuted in all its essentials. The theory of concentration and centralization of capital is wrong in two respects: the emergence of cartels and trusts, which occurred after Marx's death, enabled capitalism to control its development and to avoid the outbreak of economic crises (1961: 79–91, 92–93). On the other hand, property of the means of production was not concentrated in the hands of a few capitalists; on the contrary: the concentration of enterprises took place only in a few branches whereas in general the number of small and middle-scale plants was not reduced (1961: 59–71); moreover, the existence of joint-stock companies had the effect that "wealth" (*Vermögen*) was distributed among ever more "proprietors" (*Besitzende*), even if enterprises were concentrated (1961: 48). Hence no social polarization into two classes had taken place and no "collapse" of the system was to be expected (1961: 72). In short: the foundation of the Marxist theory of the transition to socialism was refuted.

In the light of this analysis Bernstein concluded that the idea of a socialist revolution should be given up as impracticable, and that the policy of the Social Democratic party should be planned on the basis of the existing parliamentary political system. Bernstein believed that this conclusion did not mean abandoning socialism since socialism can and will be achieved on the basis of thoroughly implementing the principles of parliamentary democracy. In practice the Social Democratic party was already demanding universal suffrage (1961: 145/6), and "democracy is in principle the suppression of class government, though it is not yet the actual suppression of classes" (1961: 143–144). Universal suffrage would thus enable the introduction of socialism by the state, i.e., by further development of the "liberal organizations of modern society" (1961: 163). The facts spoke for the success of this policy. The enormous increase in the number of votes for the SPD from 102,000 in 1871 to 1,787,000 in 1893, the achievements of the party in the *Reichstag*, and the improvement of the social conditions spoke for themselves: "We see in politics that the privileges of the bourgeoisie give way step by step to democratic institutions" (ibid.).

Moreover, the policy could be justified in the name of "living Marxism," since Engels himself pointed to the possibility of taking over power by means of elections to parliament (cf. Engels's introduction of 1895 to Marx's "Class Struggles in France"; Marx/Engels *Werke* 22: 509–527).

The kernel of Bernstein's view is thus that capitalism consists in economic and social inequality and that this will be changed by the state if political equality (universal suffrage) is attained and thus the interests of the working class are better represented in parliament.

This view is based on a rejection or on a misunderstanding of Marx's theory of the value of commodities, to which I will now turn. Marx's theory of the value of commodities has been controversial since the end of the nineteenth century. Here only two aspects of the theory which are important for Neurath's views are of interest. These are the socio-political aspect of the theory and the "empirical" arguments of some of its critics.[2]

III.2

Bernstein's presupposition was that the implementation of democratic principles (political equality and freedom of the citizens) subverts class rule. Marx's theory of value was developed in opposition to this view and attempted to explain how the opposition of classes in capitalism is reproduced precisely within the framework of democracy. It can be summarized as follows.

The value of a commodity is determined by the amount of social labor (measured by time) necessary for its production. Under the presupposition that all proprietors of commodities are equal and free, and that commodities are sold at a price corresponding to their values, no surplus value can be appropriated by buying and selling commodities, where surplus value is defined as an excess of the value appropriated over the value expended. Hence it seems that the origin of capital and its reproduction on an ever larger scale cannot be explained on the basis of this theory of value. Marx suggested a solution of the problem in the following way: there is one commodity whose *consumption* can produce more value than is necessary for its production. This commodity is labor power.

The value of labor power is determined by the value of the means of subsistence necessary for its (the worker's) reproduction, say six hours labor. But this labor power can be exerted for more than just six hours and can thus produce commodities of more value, say of eight hours. Hence, if labor power and its products are exchanged according to their values, then the purchaser of the labor power (who thereby owns its products too) can appropriate a surplus value produced by this surplus labor, and his invested money becomes capital. Capital is hence a social relation of free and equal owners of commodities, some of whom own means of production, the others, only labor power. The sociological import of this theory is to explain how class relations are reproduced in bourgeois capitalist society on the basis of the equality and freedom of all participants, whereas in precapitalist societies class rule is based on inequality maintained by means of force.

This theory of Marx need not be discussed further here. It should be noted, however, that Bernstein and Neurath (see below) do not mention it at all. This abstraction from the social determinations of the concepts used suggests that the concepts are all conceived as merely designating quantities of objects: "property," "wealth," and "capital" seem synonymous, if it is not taken into consideration that money will function as capital in industry only in a society in which the immediate producers do not own the means of production. This misunderstanding of central concepts leads to Bernstein's judgment on Marx's concept of capital (for Marx a social relation, for Bernstein a sum of money). According to Bernstein, Marx has "personified [capital] as a mystical entity" (1921: 91). And since Bernstein believed that the abolishment of privileges and the realization of equality and freedom (which according to Marx are prerequisites for the development of capitalism) would abolish capitalist class rule, he attributes the reproduction of class relationships to the state.

Even more important than these differences, in our context, are their implicit presuppositions and consequences for the construction of social theory. According to Marx, the core of social theory is the concept of Man as a producer; this is not only the definition of Man ("a tool-making animal"), but is also the basis of Marx's labor theory of value and of the explanation of the role of value in regulating the social division of labor in commodity-producing societies. Moreover, it is by conceiving material production as dependent primarily on the means of production that Marx conceived the property of these means of production as decisive for class formation. Finally, it is on commodity production in capitalist societies that the distribution by exchange on the market depends, and this, in turn, presupposes that all owners of commodities (including the owners of labor power) are considered as free and equal proprietors. Liberalism is, therefore, considered as the political system adequate to this form of distribution.

The situation is very different in Bernstein. For Bernstein, it is the state which determines the class structure of society and the state itself is conceived as neutral vis-à-vis the functions it performs. Social change is thus not conceived as determined by economic development but only as political change. Hence there is in Bernstein a division between the economic and the social sphere. Moreover, since society is conceptualized in the tradition of liberalism as composed—or as tending to be composed—of equal and independent proprietors, the experienced existence of classes is itself conceptualized in this tradition as consisting in differences of income and in privileges rather than in a necessary struggle rooted in the process of production between proprietors of means of production and proletarians. Since he attributed class privileges to political measures imposed by the state on society, Bernstein concluded that if the state is taken into the service of the working class as the outcome of elections, then class privileges can be abolished and society transformed. It follows that, for Bernstein, there is no connection between production and social structure and there is no need to refer to production and to the concept of Man as a producer in the analysis of social structure and change. This irrelevance of the productive activity of Man to Bernstein's social theory shows up in his economic theory as well, since he rejected the labor theory of value which Marx had adopted and developed. Moreover, this rejection of the labor theory of value is justified *inter alia* with the help of epistemological arguments which shed light on an important aspect of empiricism, namely the rejection of "theoretical" concepts which do not directly refer to empirical entities. Bernstein did not realize that the quasi-empirical entities evoked are not "given" by nature but dependent on previous human conceptualization of their economic activity in a specific mode of production, nor that to evoke the "empirical" reference of economic concepts may turn out to be to demand that a theory must conform to the prevailing conceptualization.

Above all, however, it is of paramount importance that neither in Bernstein's social and political theory nor in his economic theory, to which I will now turn, was there any allusion to man as a producer. This fundamental Marxist concept plays no role whatsoever in Bernstein's theories.

III.3

In Bernstein's view, Marx's theory of value should explain only the prices of commodities. But since, according to Marx, the price of a commodity does not have to coincide with its value, Bernstein rejects the theory as "metaphysical" (1921: 262). As is well known, it is still controversial whether Marx's explanation of the "transformation" of values into "prices of production" (in the third volume of *Capital*) is satisfactory. But here only the argument with which Bernstein rejects Marx's theory is of interest: it is the demand that each and every concept of a theory should refer to an empirical entity.

Consider the following case. Marx introduced the concept of value as produced only by labor to explain that "salary" is not the "price of labor" (corresponding to its value) but the price of "labor power." A part of the value produced by putting labor power to work is equivalent to its own value, and the "surplus value" (the difference between the value produced and the value of the labor power) is shared by different capitalists as their "profit" ("rent" of land is not considered here). Thus Marx intended to overcome an obvious inconsistency in previous theories between the assumption that all commodities are exchanged according to their values and the existence of profit. Bernstein considered "value" and "surplus value" as referring immediately to the salary of any employee (whether engaged in production or not) and to the profit of capitalists respectively.[3] The resulting inconsistencies between Marxian and "bourgeois" economic theories are, according to Bernstein, the proof that Marx's concepts do not refer to empirical entities. Bernstein's view is a consistent elaboration of his adoption of a theory so widely accepted that its categories seem to be undisputable reflections of objective reality. Instead of discussing the incompatibility of Marxist economic theory with empiricist economic theory, he identifies prevailing *conceptualizations* with what is empirically the case and finds Marxism inconsistent with purported empirical facts.

On the basis of such an attempt, Bernstein concludes that the concept of "value" is a "purely abstract entity" just as the theory of marginal utility is grounded in "abstractions" (1961: 34). Bernstein therefore rejects both theories. In general, he identifies theories and inferences within them with rejected Hegelian dialectics: they are the fundamental evil of Marx's system and they are responsible for Marx's and Engels's mistakes in economics and politics (1921: 53–55, 57–58, 59, 61, 71, 145).

But if only those concepts should be used which refer to "empirical entities" of actual economic practice, then "actual" capitalist production would be identified with social production in general. In this case, empiricism implies that capitalist production is implicitly declared as the only form of social production. This had already been seen by Marx (Letter to Kugelmann, July 11, 1868, in Marx/Engels *Werke* 32: 552–554). And conversely: if the capitalist form of production is identified with social production in general, then one is inclined to overlook the sociological aspect of Marx's theory of value and it must seem to be "metaphysical." From the Marxian point of view, this "empiricism" implies the acceptance of current conceptualizations of social reality as a faithful representation of that reality.

The appeal of Bernstein's position to liberals was based not only on his theoretical revisions but also on his political course. Bernstein's recommendations that the Social Democratic party should give up the ideal of seizing power, and that it should cooperate with bourgeois parties, explain the fact that, as he stated, his book was "enthusiastically welcome in the bourgeois newspapers and showered with praises" (1921: 260). The leader of the "National Liberals," Ferdinand Naumann, was of the opinion that "Bernstein is our forward post in the camp of the Social Democracy" (1921: 260). And indeed, Bernstein supported even the German colonialist policy proposed by Naumann (1961: 176–179).

III.4

Bernstein's positions were controversial in the SPD. On June 16, 1903, the SPD had an important success in the elections (the party received 31.7 percent of the votes) and at the next convention in Dresden (September 13–20, 1903) the revisionist position was condemned: "The convention condemns most emphatically the revisionist attempt to change our current successful tactics, based on class struggle and crowned with victory, in such a way as to adopt a policy of accommodation to the existing order instead of seizing power by overcoming our adversaries."[4] The party demanded of the faction in parliament that it "combat even more energetically than was possible until now militarism and gunboat policy, colonial and world-power politics."

Otto Neurath, then a twenty-one-year-old student, read the protocol of the convention "with interest," since he had the "opportunity to get acquainted with revisionist circles" in Berlin, but with "mixed feelings."[5] In the two decisive issues, namely the alternative between class struggle and accommodation to the existing order, and in the question of colonial policy, Neurath shared the view of the revisionists and even seemed to go a step further in this direction: after the election of 1907 he was interested in the possibility of a "pact" between the National Liberals and the Social Democrats and inquired whether among the liberals elected there were many "followers of Naumann" (*Naumannleute*).[6] Neurath explained the relatively poor showing of the SPD in these elections (the SPD had almost as many votes as in 1903 but the number of its seats in parliament was reduced from 81 to 38) as the result of its anti-colonial policy and believed that the revisionist's position was "more reasonable."[7]

III.5

In his textbook on political economy (*Lehrbuch der Volkswirtschaftslehre*, 1909), his first full-scale publication in the social sciences, Neurath stated explicitly his position on some of the main issues mentioned above. As to the theory of value, his position is unequivocally that of the theory of marginal utility. As did Böhm-Bawerk, he too ascribed "value" to all "goods" and not only, as did Marx, to products of human labor, and maintained its magnitude to be dependent on subjective needs; even the classical example of the "value" of water for the thirsty in the desert was adopted (1909: par. 1).[8]

Neurath went even beyond the rejection of the labor theory of value; he later rejected all theory of value. He believed value theory to serve only for the calculation of prices, and that a theory of prices could be developed independently of any theory of value (1981: 38). Giving up all theory of value should have only the effect that language will have one term less than before (1981: 27, 40). Instead of calculating values and prices one can investigate all systems of "goods displacement" (*Güterverschiebung*) while abstracting from the question "which human needs condition these displacements" (1981: 35). Having abstracted from value, the issue of wealth was conceptualized as "pleasure and displeasure" (*Lust und Unlust*) and the question investigated became: what respective constellations of pleasure and displeasure result from different "systems of displacements"? (1981: 41). With this, "the problem of the maximum pleasure" was posed (1981: 47–55; 1973: 113–122), and Neurath attempted to develop an adequate calculus.

But the creation of a system which guarantees an overall pleasure maximum encounters unsurmountable problems unless the decision is entrusted to a single person. The choice can be made either "with the help of an inadequate metaphysical theory or in some other way. Tossing coins would be much more honest" (1973: 122). However justified, such a procedure can be imagined only if the existence of an authority is presupposed which—with help of the "auxiliary motive"—would make decisions and be able to implement them. If the decision is made within society itself, then it will be determined by struggle alone (1981: 55; 1973: 122). Moreover, the possibility of planning social relations rests on the presupposition "that the economic is not something given, which is alien to us, but a machinery which we can also operate" (1981: 31).

But who is "we"? If the members of society are entrusted with this function, then, as Neurath said, struggle would determine the outcome. The end, to realize a maximum of pleasure for the greatest number of individuals, presupposes the existence of an authority which acts in the interest of society "as a whole." This is, according to Neurath, the state. It is therefore the "statesman" who should implement the calculus of happiness (1981: 52).

III.6

Like Bernstein, Neurath also believed that the creation of joint-stock hold companies "enables the individual easily to become co-entrepreneur"(1909: 53).[9] Nobody will, of course, question property of the means of production in a society of entrepreneurs: whether this property is advantageous for the "whole" depends on whether the enterpreneur is able or not.[10]

In a society of private proprietors there is, moreover, no opposition in principle between class interests. Employer and employee (*Arbeitgeber und Arbeitnehmer*) should cooperate in the common interest and the state "takes interest in the welfare of the whole" since it represents the whole. It is only when "certain groups with vested interests [*Interessengruppen*] have the power in their hands, that damaging regulations of government may occur" (1909: par. 51–54, 182).

Liberalism must have seemed self-evident to Neurath, since he considers alternative conceptions only as political programs and not as alternative economic and social theories. Mistaking liberal conceptualizations for the immediate expression of social and economic facts, Neurath could only conceive of alternatives as differing political programs based on the same theoretical analysis. Marxism is therefore discussed under the heading "economic parties of the present," i.e., as political contenders but not as an alternative theory in social science. In contradistinction to the "utopians," "who invented new economic structures as technicians invented new machines," the "new version of Socialism," founded by Marx, claims that "the accumulation of great wealth" on the one hand, and the "general misery" on the other, tend to increase, "until at last the old economic structure will collapse of *itself*" [sic] (1909: par. 208).

Neurath rejected at that time this view as all other "religious materialist conceptions of history" which conceived all events as necessary and in the last analysis as of "divine origin" (1909: par. 431). Neurath's own conception tended toward those of the "utopians"; in later years he illustrated social change frequently with the metaphor of the invention and construction of new machines. It is important to note that a theory of social change and social struggle is indeed superfluous if one believes that a desirable social structure can be implemented by decree and if the state is supposed to act in the interest of the "welfare of the whole."

III.7

Neurath's ideas were reinforced but somehow changed before and during World War I.[11] Between 1911 and 1913 Neurath traveled several times to the Balkans (sponsored by the Carnegie Endowment for International Peace). His experiences during the Balkan wars were the empirical basis of his "economy of war," on which he lectured to "headquarters officers." He published his lecture in May 1914.[12]

In Neurath's view the economy of war is an alternative model to the "economy of money." In war times economy is *planned* according to the general interest. Measures in kind (related to satisfaction of needs), are much more important to such planning than measures in money. Moreover, restrictions on production do not occur here: while in the private "economy of money" the curbing of production may serve to maximize profits, it is the aim of the economy of war to supply products, and the capacities of production are hence exploited fully without considerations of profit.[13]

These developments are relevant for peace economy as well. For in "serious times" the "public interest" restrains money economy as the product of "un-organized, individualistic classes and epochs" (1919: 102) and organizes the "whole of social life" more rationally (1919: 107), while on the other hand the operation of armament forces social reforms. It seems plausible to expect, then, that a world war would transform the money economy into "state controlled economy-in-kind in a large scale" (1919: 103).[14]

The political *naïveté* these hopes show is even more manifest in Neurath's confidence in April 1919—i.e., a few weeks before the suppression of the Bavarian Republic—that socialism was about to be implemented with his help in Bavaria (1919: Preface). But this *naïveté* was consistent with Neurath's liberal views, that is, with his belief in the neutrality of the state and his disregard for class structure and class interest. Even in April 1920, after the suppression of the republic and after Neurath's own imprisonment and release, he still maintained explicitly that a planned economy is independent of property relations, i.e., that there is no inconsistency between a socialist planned economy and private property of the means of production, and that a planned economy can be implemented by an independent political authority. As for colonialism his only reservations involved humanistic considerations regarding the natives (1920: 27).

IV. Empirical Sociology

IV.1

Before turning to Neurath's sociology it seems appropriate to consider what must be shown in order to maintain that it was dependent on his "authoritarian liberalism." As outlined in the introduction, I want to argue that his sociology was dependent on his authoritarian liberalism but not that it was entailed by it. This means that his sociology depends on assumptions which result from his authoritarian liberalism, while on the basis of the same authoritarian liberalism different sociological theories could be conceived. A further clue to what we are looking for is provided by the fact that Neurath declares his sociology to be Marxist. Hence, the adoption of a particular Marxist thesis does not merit much attention, while the omission or significant modification of a basic Marxist thesis calls for an inquiry into its reasons.

The most famous characterization of Marxism (open, of course, to very different interpretations) is the opening passage of the "Preface to the Introduction to Political Economy":

> In the social production of their life, men enter into definite relations that are indispensable and independent of their will, relations of production which correspond to a definite stage of development of their material productive forces. The sum total of these relations of production constitutes the economic structure of society, the real basis, on which rises a legal and political superstructure, and to which correspond definite forms of social consciousness. The mode of production of material life conditions the social, political and intellectual life process in general.

The paramount importance which Marx attributes to material production shows up in practically all of his systematic writings on social theory. Thus, for instance, the first volume of *Capital* deals with the "production process of capital"; Marx's economic theory builds on the concept of "value," the value of a commodity being conceived as determined by the social labor necessary for its production; the formation of classes is analyzed as rooted in necessary relations arising with a specific mode of production, and so on.

I have shown that Neurath did not refer to the process of production in his writings prior to *Empirical Sociology* but concentrated exclusively on phenomena in the sphere of distribution: in his characterization of all members of society as proprietors, in his definition of classes according to income (i.e., distribution), in his misunderstanding (and later in his reasons for the rejection) of the Marxist concept of "value," and in his concentration on "prices." Now, all these positions are incompatible with Marxism but very well compatible with authoritarian liberalism. In fact, the abstraction from production and the conceptualization of the structure of society according to phenomena in the sphere of distribution (where, in fact, all members of society are equal as proprietors) is typical of, and perhaps even essential to, liberalism.

However, while liberalism itself may be taken to be an adequate theory of social reality and to require no external factors for the explanation of its genesis, the liberalism of Neurath's sociology cannot be understood in this way. Even before the publication of his *Empirical Sociology* and in this text itself, Neurath calls himself a Marxist and praises Marxism as the best existing scientific theory of society. Moreover, he promises to give an up-to-date presentation of Marxist sociology. Thus, if it should turn out that Neurath's sociology does not use social production and changes in production as an explanatory basis for social phenomena, and *a fortiori* if it does not analyze production at all, then I believe that this fact requires an explanation, since it is simply impossible to conceive of any sociology which appeals in some way to Marxism and which simply "overlooks" production. There may be many reasons for the neglect of production in a theory claiming to be Marxist; however, I have already shown (1) that Neurath shared the view of "authoritarian liberalism" which indeed neglected production, (2) that in its Bernsteinian version it consisted in a revision of Marx's theory in this central point, and (3) that it was nevertheless not only considered to be Marxist but even to be the most modern and competent presentation of Marxism. I will now suggest that the liberal-authoritarian Bernsteinian views of Neurath's provide a sufficient explanation both for the fact that he developed a theory which neglected production and for the fact that that theory could pass for Marxism.

IV.2

Neurath's empirical sociology explicitly attacks the division between natural sciences and "mental sciences" (*Geisteswissenschaften*). Sociology is a *Real-wissenschaft* and its propositions are about "lawful regularities of empirical states of affairs" (1981: 424); hence they can in the end be reduced to "observation statements" on the behavior of men (1981: 425) as one can "photograph" it (1973: 361). Sociology is "social behavioristics" (1981: 468): "dream constructions of a dying theology" as "will" and "aims" are thereby excluded from the start. "The man who is moved by the earth (gravitational field), by a blow or by a shout, is a physical structure moved in a physical process. Physicalism deals with nothing else!" (1973: 362; 1981: 470). Sociology deals with stimulus-related biological groups, and in some respects only with one such group (mankind) (1973: 364). The societies studied are complexes built up of single individuals (1973: 386) just as a mountain is built up of rocks. The determination of a more specific subject of study than the "human cover of the earth" necessitates the classification of the habits of men (1973: 367) in "groups of customs" (1973: 370f), which enables the delineation of single social structures, e.g., peoples (1973: 359). In the "empirical sociology" which should unify history and political economy (1973: 345–353), the "theory of social customs has a dominant position" (1973: 373).

Having rejected the view that social change can be explained by genetic changes (1973: 372)—a view which he endorsed in his early years—Neurath explains the emergence of a "group of customs" with the help of behaviorism. Behaviorism describes what reactions follow on what stimuli; by "extra-polation," which can already be seen in animals, reactions become "customs"; thus sociology and ethology become one and the same discipline: "Should we really want to place the theory of human societies in one discipline, the theory of animal societies in another? Should the 'breeding,' 'slavery,' 'war' of ants be treated in natural science, and the 'breeding,' 'slavery,' 'war' of men in the mental sciences [*Geisteswissenschaften*]?" (1983: 69; 543–544; cf. 410). The much more developed capability of man to extrapolate must be explained by "the unique transformation of the central nervous system . . . which enables such behavior" (1981: I, 485). And this is the basis of the superiority of humans over animals.

This conception gives rise to the following difficulty: if the genetic material of humans did not change considerably in the course of known history, and if customs are handed down to the next generation by "tradition," then it is unclear why these "customs" should ever change considerably. Neurath does not give any clear answer to this question. But one finds in his sketches of human history from the prehistoric times to the twentieth century two models of explanation. According to one of them, some of the customs built by extrapolation from reactions are chosen by a super-social authority and fixed into coherent "groups of customs." This conception is in full accord with Neurath's general authoritarian liberal outlook discussed above. The historical succession of such social structures is constituted therefore by the struggle between such super-social authorities. "Seen in the perspective of mankind: the pre-magician is defeated by the magician, the magician by the theologian, and the theologian by the scientist" (1973: 378). This model has two flaws: the first is that if "customs" can be imposed by a super-social authority, then they are not conceived any more as extrapolations from reactions. The second flaw is that the change in the "methods of extrapolation" of the rulers and constructors of society themselves is not explained. This is the basis for Neurath's second and dominant model:

> If we consider sociologically the change of customs then we must also derive sociologically the change of customs of the teachers, in such a way that we do not deal with interferences which show "beside" the given processes, but with the change of entire systems of customs, within which there are the customs of the "teachers," the magicians, the priests, the hygienists, the politicians, the novelists, etc. (1981: 481)

But if the rules of extrapolation themselves are considered as "customs," and if there are numerous different rules of extrapolation, then there is no explanation for the production of specific customs, and one must assume that many different possible reactions and customs emerge and that these are later selected. Historical development can be thus interpreted according to a "theory of evolution" according to which the fittest prevail: "In the competition of the peoples, the better weapons, better means of production and better habits with far-reaching extrapolations lead to victory" (1973: 379f.). It only remains to be explained why a custom crystallizes in the first place. But if sociology can be reduced to behavioristics, behavioristics to the properties of the central nervous system, and these to chemistry and physics, it follows that sociology can be finally reduced to chemistry and physics: "Should we penetrate to the innermost limits of the knowable laws, however, we might in the end have to deal with nothing but atoms and other particles" (1973: 363, cf. 405). This is the classical position of traditional reductionist materialism.

It is important to note not only that production was neither analyzed in Neurath's sociology nor used to explain other social phenomena, but also that this sociology obviously fails to give an adequate description of human activity at all, whether productive, social, or political. Two extreme examples will suffice as illustrations. Even when dealing with the increasing human dominance over nature, Neurath does not pay any attention to the production process or to the means employed in it: "In the past when a man and a swamp came together, man disappeared; but now the swamp disappears" (1973: 395). Note that neither in this description, nor to my knowledge anywhere else in Neurath's writings, is the production process discussed. And therefore it is always "man" on the one side, the natural object on the other which are considered. Never is notice taken of the fact that if the "swamp" is to disappear, "man" must possess and apply appropriate means developed in the historical course of the production process when he "comes together" with the swamp. The same shortcomings are evident in Neurath's treatment of social and political processes. The processes disappear and stationary photos of constellations remain. Consider the extreme example of a revolution which disappears in Neurath's description:

Successive changes in customs can lead to sudden social changes. There are unstable sociological situations which make sudden changes possible. In general, orders of life are most persistent; even when certain kinds of behavior have greatly altered, the colossus still stands, even though on clay feet. The French Revolution was thoroughly prepared. Members of the middle class had long been doing the real work in science, art, and administration, the peasants unsettled, the monarchy powerless. But nobody realized this clearly. When the Assembly was called, it became clear that the old balance of representation no longer existed, and the façade crumbled [by itself?]. The redistribution of land followed abruptly [by itself?]. The old habits had to be linked with a new environment. Most of the old customs survived in the new way of living, but they changed their social functions. (1973: 372–373; 480)

It is evident that these views on the quasi-automatic change of the socio-political structure conform to the views which Neurath had attributed to Marx many years earlier; in 1909 Neurath had thought Marx claimed that as a result of economic development "the old economic structure (i.e., capitalism) will collapse of itself" (1909: par. 208; cf. III.6 above).

Now, since I have argued that "authoritarian liberalism" differs from Marx's views exactly in those issues in which Marx refers to production in his explanations, I suggest that Bernstein's and Neurath's interpretation and revision of Marxism depended on their prior adherence to authoritarian liberalism. To conceptualize social structure in the framework of liberalism at that time actually meant to abstract from the production process and from the claim that social structures emerge in this process. Turning to Marxism after such abstractions meant professing socialist intentions based on a liberal social and political theory and professing a materialist position very different from that of Marx since it is not based on the notion of production. The question still open is how these views are related to Neurath's epistemological views proper. In what follows I will first explain briefly the difference between Marxist and reductionist materialism and cite the core propositions of Neurath's epistemology in order to suggest that these and his reductionist materialist approach to science are dependent on his socio-political views and on his sociology, insofar as both abstract from productive labor in particular and from human practice in general.

V. Neurath's Materialism and Empiricism

V.1

It is in the adoption of reductionist materialism and empiricism that the differences between Neurath's and Marx's conceptions reach philosophical grounds. As is well known, Marx considered himself to be a materialist, and I have quoted above Neurath's expressed agreement with Marx's materialism and empiricism (II.1). However, I have claimed that Marx's materialism is altogether different from Neurath's and that Neurath's statement that "Marx and Engels speak only of what one can observe by means of the senses" (1973: 349) is straightforwardly false. In fact, the empirical science to which Marx was committed has nothing to do with empiricism in Neurath's sense, and the kind of materialism endorsed by Neurath was severely criticized by Marx. Since these differences are little known or even obliterated by the prevalent usage of the terms in much of contemporary philosophy, I shall briefly sketch the difference between these conceptions.

Marx outlined his philosophical position in 1845 in his *Theses on Feuerbach*. He there criticized empiricism and indicated what he meant by materialism:

> The chief defect of all previous materialism (that of Feuerbach included) is that things, reality, sensuousness are conceived only in the form of the *object*, *or of contemplation*, but not as *sensuous human activity, practice*, not subjectively. Hence, in contradistinction to materialism, the *active* side was set forth abstractly by idealism—which, of course, does not know real, sensuous activity as such. (First Thesis on Feuerbach [1845]; Karl Marx, Friedrich Engels: *Collected Works*, vol. 5, London, Lawrence & Wishart, 1976, p. 3)

This criticism has two aspects. The first touches directly on the empiricist assumption that knowledge has to be based on sense perceptions; the second touches on the conception of materialism as referring to the objects of human cognitive activity instead of to human activity itself. These two characteristics of empiricism and materialism are rooted, according to Marx, in adopting sense perception as a starting point and in assuming the inherent separation between the perceiving ("subject") and the perceived ("object"). Moreover, when empiricism is conceived in a materialist fashion, the subject too is conceived as an object (of perception) and the active nature of cognition is then either neglected or explained by deviating from the materialist framework.

Marx suggests a different point of departure, which is both material and active and in which subject and object of activity are not separated. This is the material practice itself of humans, and Marx maintains that it is only in this practice that truth claims can be warranted. Of course, human practice as the core of Marx's theory is not only significant for epistemology, but much more so for Marx's theory of the structure of society and its change.

Both Marx's materialism and its connection to his commitment to empirical science (not to empiricism) are conspicuous in the characterization of his presuppositions. These presuppositions, the real prerequisites of human existence, "from which one can abstract only in imagination," are "the real individuals, their actions and their material living conditions, both the given and those produced by their own action. These prerequisites are thus ascertainable in a purely empirical manner" (Marx/Engels *Werke* 3: 20). Marx is a materialist insofar as he does not invoke in any of his explanations non-material entities; but this does not commit him to the view that all experience (whether in the domains of the social or the natural sciences) can be reduced to a language which addresses only spatio-temporal relations of observable objects or to the material entities of physics and to the laws pertaining to their interactions. For him, neither science nor materialism depends on such a reduction.

On the contrary: according to Marx, perceptions are not brute sense data; they are endowed with meaning, dependent on actual practice and on social structure as well as on previous practice and social structure embodied in explicit or implicit knowledge given by tradition. Similarly, the notion of reasoning according to unchanging formal rules does not make much sense in this framework. Actual inferences are dependent on the meaning of the concepts in a theory and change along with these meanings. Just as there is for Marx no actual "production in general" but only a historically specific and changing production, so too there is no unchanging experience which would be independent of social productive practice and of Man's historical changes in this practice. In short: a "historical sociology"—as one could call Marx's social theory—is compatible only with a "historical epistemology."

Thus, I claim that empiricism is incompatible with Marx's social theory but indeed compatible with liberal socio-political views when these do not include considerations of social production, its historical change, and its possible influence on socio-political structures or on experience. Furthermore, if it is more plausible to assume that epistemology is dependent on socio-political views than the other way around, it seems plausible to conjecture that Neurath's disregard within a Marxist framework for historically changing human experience depended on his disregard for practice in general and for production in particular, and that this disregard for practice was, in turn, dependent on the authoritarian liberal views that also guided his interpretation of Marxism.

V.2

Up to this point, Neurath's empiricism and reductionist materialism have been discussed in the context of his sociology, and I have argued that Neurath's empiricism is dependent on his socio-political views and on the sociology which is also dependent on these views. I will now turn to his specific epistemological theses and consider whether they require a further explanation or whether they are consistent with the empiricist positions already discussed and can be considered as a further elaboration of them.

There are three philosophical theses to be considered here: (1) that protocol statements should be the basis of science; (2) that physicalism provides the basis of unified science; (3) the coherence theory of truth.

1. The empiricist claim that knowledge could be based on a firm fundament of sense-perceptions, or rather on elementary statements about immediate sensory experience, met with the obvious criticism that sense-experience is private and cannot be made the basis of inter-subjective science. To meet this criticism and to integrate statements about sense-experience into the realm of statements about objective, publicly accessible physical objects, Neurath suggested that science be based on protocol-statements which actually are about physical objects (the perceiving human being). For example: "Otto's protocol at 3:17 o'clock: [Otto's speech-thinking at 3:16 o'clock was:

(at 3:15 o'clock there was a table in the room perceived by Otto)]" (1983: 93). Thus all propositions could be formulated in physicalist language about spatio-temporal relations of physical objects and yet the empiricist basis of science retained.

2. The common physicalist language of all sciences allows one to conceive of all scientific disciplines as together forming the physicalist and empiricist "unified science": "The various scientific disciplines together make up the 'unified science'" (1983: 53–54). "In a sense unified science is physics in its broadest aspect, a tissue of laws expressing space-time linkages—let us call it: *physicalism*" (1983: 49).

3. However, the protocol-statements which were substituted for statements about immediate sense-perceptions did not share the latter's privilege of being infallible. Protocol-statements, like all physical statements, could be wrong and corrigible. Hence their foundational status was only relative. Moreover, since "experience" or "reality" were only accessible as protocol-statements, the comparison between statements and experience was conceived as a comparison between different statements. The truth of a statement no longer meant that it was adequate to the facts but only that it was consistent with protocol-statements. Thus, a coherence theory of truth was adopted:

> We call a content statement 'false' if we cannot establish conformity between it and the whole structure of science; we can also reject a protocol-statement unless we prefer to alter the structure of science and thus to make it into a "true statement." The verification of certain content statements consists in examining whether they conform to certain protocol-statements; therefore we reject the expression that a statement is compared with 'reality,' and the more so, since for us 'reality' is replaced by several totalities of statements that are consistent in themselves but not with each other. (1983: 102)

Now, according to the principles outlined in the introduction, one should look for "external factors" to explain a theory only if it could be shown that it is deficient according to its own criteria. This applies also to epistemology. Hence, I would have to look for further explanations for Neurath's epistemology only if it was deficient on the basis already accepted. I shall argue below that this is not the case and that Neurath's epistemology is consistent with the positions already endorsed and that the basic tenets of authoritarian liberalism and its consequences suffice to explain the essentials of his epistemology. Of course, I do not argue that another variant of Neurath's empiricism would be inconsistent with authoritarian liberalism nor, therefore, that his epistemology follows necessarily from his socio-political views. This is also not necessary in order to justify the claim that the former is dependent on the latter.

As mentioned above, Neurath's introduction of protocol-statements into epistemology served (among other things) to avoid the so-called danger of solipsism inherent in the empiricist grounding of knowledge in sense-perceptions. However, it is important to note the specific way in which the obvious problems were circumvented. Neurath did not cast doubt on the empiricist assumption nor did he look for an alternative to it, but rather he tried to reconcile it with the thesis of physicalism, by letting the foundational statements too be formulated in physicalist language about spatio-temporal relations of observable physical entities. He thus endorsed and explicitly advocated the position which in Marx's view was the main flaw of "previous materialism," i.e., conceiving "reality . . . only in the form of the *object* . . . but not as . . . *practice.*" The partisanship for this position within the framework of Marxism presupposes, as I have argued, a liberal interpretation of Marxism, including the abstraction from human practice.

It is easy to see that Neurath's additional theses as quoted above are consistent with this approach. Having substituted protocol-statements for perceptions and sense-data, it was possible to maintain that the physicalist language applies also to elementary statements using perception terms. It was thus possible to maintain also the thesis of "unified science" in the framework of physicalism. Finally, the introduction of protocol-statements allowed him to replace the comparison of statements with facts by the comparison of statements with statements and thus to adopt the coherence theory of truth.

Thus, I believe that no additional explanation of Neurath's specific epistemological positions is necessary; they are consistent with, and even reinforce his positions discussed earlier, and they can be explained as dependent on his adoption of the liberal interpretation of Marxism current at his time.

However, if we consider Neurath's specific reductionist program, then there is even a stronger dependency of Neurath's epistemology on his sociology. Physicalism (as the theory that maintains that all scientific propositions are about spatio-temporal relations of observable objects) may be independent of a reduction of all sciences to physics, but a reduction of all sciences to physics and chemistry surely implies the applicability of physicalist language if this is understood as the language actually used in physics and chemistry. The same applies to the thesis concerning unified science: it may be possible to endorse an interpretation of the thesis without commitment to a reductionist program, but endorsing a reductionist program entails the thesis of unified science. I have shown that Neurath believed that all sciences—sociology in particular—can be reduced to physics and chemistry, and I have argued that this reduction depended on the abstraction from human activity (in particular from production) and that this abstraction within the framework of Marxism was in its turn dependent on Neurath's authoritarian liberalism. Hence, I believe that no further explanation for his physicalism (in the above specified sense) and for the thesis of the unity of science is necessary.

It is important to note that my argument does not depend on the biographical and hence accidental fact that Neurath maintained both the reductionist and the physicalist theses, but on a necessary dependence of physicalism, as endorsed in the Vienna Circle, on reductionism. This is so because both the physical and the social sciences were already established scientific disciplines in the first third of the twentieth century, and it was obvious that none of the very different schools in the social sciences met the requirement of using physicalist language only. Hence the argument for physicalism depended also on showing that theories of the social sciences can be reformulated in a physicalist language without loss of cognitive content. The only attempt at such a reconstruction was Neurath's empirical sociology. This sociology depended either on a reduction of sociology to social behavioristics or even to physics and chemistry. Hence the thesis of physicalism of unified science in the Vienna Circle was either based on Neurath's reductionist sociology or not justified at all. It is hence irrelevant for my argument whether both reductionist sociology and physicalism of unified science were formulated by the same person or not.

In addition to the inherent weaknesses of reductionism, physicalism in Neurath's sense, i.e., the restriction of scientific propositions to those that can be based on protocol-statements, shows another difficulty as well. Even the thesis that the concepts of physics can be based on protocol-statements, that is, on sense-perceptions, itself lacked satisfactory justification. In fact, the difficulty of reducing even the concepts of the natural sciences to sense-perceptions had been amply demonstrated since the 1930s by the failure to reduce dispositional terms (e.g., "solubility") to protocol-statements. Hence even the successful reduction of other sciences to physics would not yet substantiate the physicalist thesis.

To be sure, Neurath may have believed that protocol-statements might serve as the basis of the language of physics and that existing difficulties would be overcome; he may well have been of the opinion that the only real difficulty is to express in physicalist language some particular sciences (sociology, psychology): Neurath already suggests this interpretation in his review of Carnap's *Der logische Aufbau der Welt* (1928). Whatever the case may be (Neurath mentions the problem of dispositional terms in passing but himself never discusses it; cf. 1981: 754f.), it is immaterial here, since this belief itself had to be justified. That Neurath did not hesitate to introduce this thesis although it lacked justification can be explained by reference to the fact that this thesis was also a conclusion of an altogether different argument: Neurath was compelled by the concept of Man inherent to his social theory to base science on sense perceptions and so-called extrapolations, because he had to explain the acquisition of knowledge on the basis of properties which were common to human beings and animals alike.

The bearing of Neurath's various suggestions concerning physicalist language are well elucidated by the philosophical importance he attributed to the picture language he had developed (ISOTYPE). Neurath believed that this language—an ingenious method for graphical representation—can, like Egyptian hieroglyphs in his interpretation of them, represent facts in a "neutral" way, generate new concepts (by combination of symbols) and exclude *a limine* so-called senseless sentences and thus metaphysics (cf. 1973: 234; 1983: 218). In these respects it is an ideal "physicalist" language.

Whatever the enlightened intentions of the demand to base scientific language on protocol-statements or, in general, of the "materialist" approach may have been (criticism of metaphysics), the only point of interest here is that it was pursued by reduction of the social sciences to biology (and of biology to physics and chemistry), thus necessitating an interpretation of human activities on the basis of individual biological properties only. The conception of knowledge as based on sense-perceptions of non-social individuals and as expressed in language only is the basis of the coherence theory of truth too. If all knowledge can be traced back to protocol-statements, and if all experience is to be expressed in protocol-statements, then both the consistency of a theoretical system and its conformity to experience can be expressed in terms of consistency among statements.

VI. Conclusion

On my interpretation, it is the concept of the human being as reduced to its biological characteristics which was conditional for Neurath's empiricism and the explanation of human acquisition of knowledge on the basis of sense-perceptions and extrapolations. I believe that the key role attributed by me to the concept of Man in Neurath's formation of a unified conception of the world applies to similar attempts too. The reason is obvious: an explicit or implicit concept of Man is an essential element in every social theory. Epistemology, on the other hand, deals with knowledge produced by Man. Hence the explicit or implicit concepts of man applied in both disciplines have to be consistent if a unified conception of the world is to be attempted. However, my claim that the constraints resulting from the attempt to achieve consistency are to be understood as a dependency of epistemology on determinations of the concept of Man as formed in scientific or prescientific social theory, rather than the other way around, is itself dependent on an assumption which could not be elaborated in this context. This assumption is that socio-political views involve interests which may affect reasoning while no such interests are directly involved in epistemology. On the basis of this assumption, I believe that Neurath's epistemology is dependent on the shortcomings of his social theory—whether systematically elaborated in his sociology or tacitly presupposed in other contexts.

While I believe that a strong case can be made for the dependency of Neurath's social theory on his political views and of his epistemology on the concept of Man inherent to his social theory, it seems to me quite difficult to distinguish between a dependency of Neurath's empiricism and physicalism on his socio-political views as distinguished from his sociology proper. I suggested in the introduction that separating the two would perhaps be impossible if the sociological theory endorsed confirms and reinforces already existing prescientific views. I believe that this was indeed the case in Neurath. It may even be argued that it is impossible to endorse an epistemology and to then develop a sociology which employs concepts which do not conform to the epistemological views adopted, and that if my argument concerning the dependency of Neurath's epistemology on his early liberal interpretation of Marxism is accepted, the consistency with his later sociology is gratuitous. However, it seems to me important to distinguish between the different layers of social theory as a theory implicit in socio-political views and as an elaborated sociological theory. The reason is that the adoption of empiricism in principle does not yet guarantee that the scientific theory to be developed will not employ concepts which prove to be irreducible to sense-perception. Once we conceive a theory not as a set of existing propositions in a Platonic realm but as elaborated by human beings in time, then we should realize that not all implications of known propositions are actually known, too. Thus, elaborating a sociological theory and showing that it is in fact consistent with a presupposed concept of Man does indeed enrich and confirm the theory. Thus, I believe that we could explain Neurath's epistemology on the basis of his early and unsystematic liberal interpretation of Marxism, but that nevertheless the demonstration that Neurath's elaborated sociology and his epistemology are consistent adds much to the argument. And indeed, Neurath's sociology not only fulfills the requirements of his epistemology, but Neurath also points explicitly to this fact in his major treatise (cf. the quotations in IV.2 above).

However, since the adoption of this sociology itself was interpreted as dependent on authoritarian liberalism, I do not claim that Neurath's epistemology was dependent on two distinct sets of presuppositions (socio-political views and sociological theory), but rather that it is important to distinguish between different layers of such presuppositions. It is important to remember that Neurath's sociology was developed within an authoritarian liberal interpretation of Marxism and that a commitment to materialism in some sense of the term was a matter of course. However, whether or not the philosophy of empiricism was compatible with Marxist sociology could only be ascertained by articulating each and attempting a synthesis. Neurath made the attempt, and as we have seen, the two turn out to be incompatible. Psychologically speaking, Neurath could expect them to be compatible because their proponents were in fact political allies in Austria at the time and because the Marxism he endorsed lacked precisely those elements which were incompatible with his empiricism (and with his political views). Whether Neurath's epistemology was indeed biographically dependent on his sociology, and thus not only directly on his socio-political views but also indirectly via his sociology, is of no importance here; the justification of his claim that all science can be reduced to sense-perceptions depended on showing (in Neurath's case, in sociology) that this can actually be done.

I have argued that empiricism presupposes an abstraction from human practice and that Marxism's emphasis on human practice, especially on production, renders it incompatible with empiricism. But I did not argue that liberalism, which is dependent on abstraction from the sphere of production, is not compatible with a historical epistemology. However, it should be expected that the development of a historical epistemology based on the notion of human practice within the framework of liberalism will not include a consideration of productive labor, which in Marxism is the fundamental form of human practice. A good illustration of this expectation is the historical epistemology of Ernst Cassirer, in my view the most elaborate historical epistemology developed between the two world wars. Cassirer not only developed an as yet unsurpassed historical epistemology but was also aware of the fact that the concept of man was the touchstone for testing the consistency of his views on natural and social sciences, on culture and history. For this reason, he summarized his philosophical work in an *Essay on Man*. And indeed Cassirer does not consider production at all, and even forgets it when he enumerates all kinds of "work" characteristic of man: "Man's outstanding characteristic, his distinguishing mark, is not his meta-physical or physical nature—but his work. It is this work, it is the system of human activities, which defines and determines the circle of 'humanity.' Language, myth, religion, art, science, history are the constituents of the various sectors of this circle" (Cassirer 1944: 68).

Within the framework of liberalism the abstraction from human productive practice was, therefore, the basis of both an idealist, non-reductionist historical epistemology and of a materialist reductionist empiricism. Thus I believe that Marx was correct in his brief sketch of the two possibilities open to an epistemology which does not conceive of human acquisition of knowledge as material practice (cf. V.1 above): either a contemplative materialism which conceives of reality only as an object of perception or idealism which emphasizes "activity" but conceives of this activity as non-material. If this suggestion does indeed capture the main trends of epistemology since Descartes and if my claim concerning the dependency of Neurath's epistemology on liberalism is correct and can be generalized to both post-Cartesian epistemological alternatives, then the persistence of the underlying presuppositions of these epistemologies could be interpreted as dependent on the preservation of basic liberal views on the nature of society and the human individual.

For the period under discussion, the crucial question is, therefore, why no materialist, non-reductionist historical epistemology was developed in a non-liberal framework as an alternative to reductionist materialism and historical transcendentalism. Since non-liberal materialism was present at that time in the form of Marxism, the question is just a corollary to the question why the liberal interpretation of Marxism prevailed in central Europe at the beginning of the twentieth century. The answer to this question would presumably involve rewriting considerable parts of the history of the socialist movement in the nineteenth century.

Acknowledgments

I am especially grateful to Marcelo Dascal for his many helpful suggestions which helped me to clarify my arguments, and to Peter McLaughlin for thorough discussions of my theses. I am also indebted to two anonymous referees whose comments drew my attention to many possible misunderstandings of a previous version of this chapter.

Notes

1. None of the numerous studies on the socio-political aspects of the history of the Vienna Circle address systematically the dependencies between socio-economical and epistemological views. I have found the following studies most useful: Dvorak (1981), Fleck (1979), Nemeth (1981), Stadler (1982a), Stadler (1982b), Mohn (1977).

2. Eugen von Böhm-Bawerk had criticized Marx's theory of value and surplus value as early as 1884. In 1894 the third volume of *Capital* appeared, in which Marx developed a "transformation theory" to explain why, in capitalism, commodities are not bought and sold at prices proportional to their values but at prices corresponding to the "price of production" and "average rate of profit" without violating the law of value. In 1896 Böhm-Bawerk published an extensive critique of Marx's theory (see Sweezy 1975). I will not discuss here the still ongoing controversy on Marx's theory of value. Only one aspect of this discussion is relevant in the present context and was formulated already in Rudolf Hilferding's answer to Böhm-Bawerk's criticism. Hilferding points out that in Marx's theory "the law of value becomes a law of motion for a definite type of social organization based upon the production of commodities, for in the last resort all change in social structure can be referred to changes in the relationships of production, that is to say to changes in the evolution of productive power and in the organization of labor. We are thereby led, in the most striking contrast to the outlook of the psychological school, to regard political economy as a part of sociology, and sociology itself as a historical science. Böhm-Bawerk has never become aware of this contrast of outlooks" (Sweezy 1975: 186). The subjective stance, says Hilferding, "is unhistorical and unsocial. Its categories are natural and eternal categories" (Sweezy 1975: 133).

3. In Bernstein's view, the employees in commerce produce "surplus value" for the merchant, but no "social surplus value" (1961: 36–37). Since, according to Marx, surplus value is produced in production only, Bernstein accuses Marx of a "certain arbitrary dealing in the valuing of functions" (1961: 38). Bernstein's interest in the "valuing of functions" is presumably related to his disappointed expectation that the theory of value would provide a standard of "justice" for the relations between capitalists and workers: "The theory of value gives a norm for the justice or injustice of the partition of the product of labor just as little as does the atomic theory for the beauty or ugliness of a piece of sculpture" (1961: 39). For the use of "wealth," "possession," and "capital" as synonymous cf. Bernstein (1921: 48, 93, 271).

4. "Protokoll über die Verhandlungen des Parteitages der SPD." Abgehalten zu Dresden vom 13. bis 20. September 1903. Berlin, 1903: 418f.

5. Letter of Otto Neurath to Ferdinand Tönnies, November 19, 1903. Neurath reports that his "understanding of politics" developed only since 1903 or 1904 and "quite slowly"; Tönnies's introduction into politics "meant much" to him. Cf. Neurath to Tönnies, February 26, 1906. Tönnies, Oskar Simony and Gregor Itelson are the three scholars who—in addition to Neurath's father—had the greatest influence on him. Cf. Neurath to Tönnies, June 25, 1906; cf. Curriculum Vitae in Neurath's Ph.D. dissertation: *Zur Anschauung der Antike über Handel, Gewerbe und Landwirtschaft,* Berlin 1906. Neurath's letters to Tönnies date from 1903 to 1922 (with one additional postcard from January 29, 1929) and are kept in the Schleswig-Holsteinische Landesbibliothek. Marie Neurath permitted me to read her copies of the letters and was extremely kind and helpful in answering my questions.

6. Cf. Neurath's letter to Tönnies, February 7, 1907. In 1896 Ferdinand Naumann (1860–1919) founded the "Nationalliberaler Verein," the aim of which was to win over workers organized in the SPD for "national responsibility." The SPD should

become a "productive, state-supportive socialist party—national socialism on the basis of freedom." ("Was will die Sozialdemokratie?" *Die Hilfe*, May 4, 1899). Naumann presented his expansionist ideas in the book *Mitteleuropa* (1915).

7. "It is not at all clear to me what ideal of foreign policy the SPD concretely envisions. If one adds all [their] single declarations, Germany should presumably act very much like Switzerland. . . . A grave flaw of the SPD is among others the absence of a Utopia" (Neurath to Tönnies, February/March 1907). In general, Neurath is quite catholic in his search for political allies. "With the socialists one sees readily that the organization of life is one whole, in which ethics, custom, law and politics are but accidental delineations. . . . Among the modern Austrian Christian-Socialists it is Vogelsang who elaborated most a sort of an ideal of a comprehensive life organization" (Neurath to Tönnies, no date). Neurath mentions in this letter his work on the *Lesebuch der Volkswritschaftslehre* (1909); hence the letter was presumably written in 1909. The fact that the ideologue of the Christian-Socialist movement, Karl Freiherr von Vogelsang (1818–1890) advocated a Christian-corporative organization of society rather than socialism is insignificant to Neurath since the rejection of "money economy" and the ideal of a "comprehensive life organization" are his only criteria.

8. The labor theory of value is mentioned in its pre-Marxist version only in reference to "hunter-peoples" on a "low cultural level" (1909: 27). This position is of special importance because Neurath knows the discussion about Marxian theory of value; he studied with L. V. Bortkiewicz and mentions his paper "Wertrechnung und Preisrechnung im Marxschen System" (1918: 28, note 14). Neurath not only abstains from a criticism of Marxian economic theory but he does not even mention Marx in his review of *German Political Economy of the Nineteenth Century* (1909: par. 207). In the *Lesebuch der Volkswirtschaftslehre*, which Neurath edited together with his wife, he indicates his responsibility for the selection of texts out of all three volumes of *Capital* (cf. Neurath and Shapiro 1909: vii). In his editorial note, Neurath writes that Marx's "views on political economy" had "great influence on thinkers of all orientations just as did his doctrine of the dependence of all historical phenomena on economic facts."

As in other writings, here, too, there is a general, not very precise critique of Marx. Marx is said to have had the ability "to integrate many complicated relations into one picture" but "not always with sufficient clarity" (Neurath and Shapiro 1909: 198). This general critique is often repeated but never explicated. Neurath's interest in the "Vienna School" dates back to his studies in Berlin. Neurath criticizes, in his "Zur Theorie der Sozialwissenschaften" (1910), the psychological foundation of the theory of marginal utility but not its validity for capitalist economy (cf. 1981: 32). At the same time he believes that the theory of prices is independent of the theory of value (1981: 38). Neurath is not so much interested in the laws of capitalist economy as in a general theory of "displacement of goods," in which "all possible cases" are systematically investigated (1981: 37), and which would be valid for an "economy without labor" too (1981: 28).

On April 23, 1904, Neurath informs Tönnies that he will "presumably work on the 'concept of value' of the Vienna School"; with Professor Wagner he works on "value and price" (Letter to Tönnies, May 29, 1904). After his Ph.D. he intends to deal "exclusively for some time with mathematical political economy (Cournot, Walras, Jevons, etc.) and with the theoreticians of value (especially with the Austrian School)." Besides economics he is fascinated by mathematical logic (December 30, 1904). Many years later, Neurath recalls that the Austrian School seemed to him at that time "— and rightly so—as disguised Manchesterian" (unpublished letter of Neurath to Josef

Frank, July 8, 1939). Neurath also reports his inclination toward Empiricism and enumerates the philosophers, who "very much attracted" him: Mill, Guyau, Bentham, Fouillée, Tarde, Wundt.

9. In agreement with this conception, Neurath repeats without criticism the "theory of factors of production" (land, labor, capital) (1909: par. 23) and the theory of the three "kinds of income" (pars. 158ff.), which was ridiculed by Marx as "the trinitary formula" (*Capital*, Vol. 3, Chapter 48).

10. "Private property is advantageous for society as a whole when it incites one individual to be of use to another in his own interest, e.g., to cultivate much corn." It can be disadvantageous for the whole when the proprietor e.g., "artificially creates a famine by destroying corn in order to raise prices in his own interest." "It is one of the most difficult questions, how to reduce the disadvantages of private property without abolishing its advantages." One suggestion is to change the laws of inheritance "in their private extension," "because it often grants totally incapable people great power" (1909: par. 5).

11. Conceiving the state as the authority which represents the interests of the whole prevents Neurath from asking questions about interests involved in World War I. "It is horrible, how many people have to live under unceasing pressure [i.e., under fear for relatives at the front] and still humanity [sic] forgets it all and begins a few decades later a World War again. It is terrible" (Letter to Tönnies, August 6, 1917). This remark is especially astonishing since a few days earlier (August 2, 1917) the first revolt of the German navy's sailors had taken place, not to mention the developments in Russia. Neurath expresses similar views in 1919, cf. preface to "Von der Kriegswirtschaft zur Naturalwirtschaft" in Neurath (1919).

12. *Einführung in die Kriegswirtschaftslehre*, Wien 1914. Reprinted in Neurath (1919: 42–133). Citations are according to this edition. Cf. Neurath's letters to Tönnies of January 23 and April 24, 1914. Neurath emphasizes that the theory of war economy is "a science like ballistics, which is also independent of whether one advocates the use of cannons or opposes it (cf. 1919: 42, 43, 132).

13. "If the money system does not function properly then the installation of a comprehensive economy in kind would be most plausible. After all, it is in war the supreme principle of the politicians to look after the public well-being and for the objective of the war; the traditional order is for him nothing but a means to this end" (1919: 99). Neurath expresses these views also in his letters to Tönnies: "The administration of the army has no sympathy for restrictions on production in the profit interests of capitalists. The administration is interested in a planned and regular increasing production. . . . It does not even shy back from state socialist interventions" (Letter to Tönnies, January 23, 1914). Neurath believes that the strains imposed on the people by armament are so great that only a "socially most healthy body" of the people will be capable of enduring them; the military had, therefore, an interest in social reforms (Letter to Tönnies, April 26, 1914).

14. "The generals and politicians of recent years have endeavored to do everything in the service of military success disdaining the traditional order of society. . . . It is so incomprehensible if ever more people ask whether the objectives of peace could not be pursued in a similar way . . . whether the great generals and politicians of the struggle for human happiness could not install new orders of life disregarding traditional forms and rearranging industry" (1919: 230).

References

Bernstein, Eduard. 1921. *Die Voraussetzungen des Sozialismus und die Aufgaben der Sozialdemokratie*. Stuttgart/Berlin: Dietz/Vorwarts.

————. 1961. *Evolutionary Socialism. A Criticism and Affirmation*, translated by Edith C. Harvey. New York: Schocken.

Cassirer, Ernst. 1944. *An Essay on Man.* New Haven: Yale University Press.

Dvorak, Johann. 1981. *Edgar Zilsel und die Einheit der Erkenntnis.* Wien: Löcker.

Fleck, K. 1979. *Eine biographische und systematische Untersuchung.* Ph.D. Dissertation an der geisteswissenschaftlichen Fakultät der Universität Graz, September 1979.

Marx, Karl, and Friedrich Engels. 1956ff. *Werke.* Berlin: Dietz.

Mohn, E. 1977. *Der Logische Positivismus—Theorien und politische Praxis seiner Vertreter.* Frankfurt am Main: Campus.

Nemeth, E. 1981. *Otto Neurath und der Wiener Kreis.* Frankfurt/New York: Campus.

Neurath, Otto. 1909. *Lehrbuch der Volkswirtschaftslehre.* Wien: Holder.

————. 1919. *Durch die Kriegswirtshcaft zur Naturalwirtschaft.* München: Callwey.

————. 1921. *Jüdische Planwirtschaft in Palästina.* Berlin: Welt-Verlag.

————. 1928. Review of *Der Logische Aufbau der Welt* and of *Scheinprobleme der Philosophie*, by R. Carnap. *Der Kampf* 21: 624–626.

————. 1973. *Empiricism and Sociology*, ed. by M. Neurath and R. S. Cohen. Dordrecht: Reidel.

————. 1981. *Gesammelte Philosophische und methodologische Schriften*, 2 vols., ed. by V. Haller and H. Rutte. Wien: Hölder-Pichler-Tempsky.

————. 1983. *Philosophical Papers. 1913–1946*, ed. by R. S. Cohen and M. Neurath. Dordrecht: Reidel.

Neurath, Otto (ed.). 1906. F. Marlow (L.H. Wolfram). *Faust.* Neu herausgegeben und mit einer biographischen Einleitung versehen von Otto Neurath. Berlin: Ernst Frensdorff.

Neurath, Otto, and Anna Schapiro (eds.) 1909. *Lesebuch der Volkswirtschaftrslehre*, 2 vols. Leipzig: W. Klinkhardt.

Stadler, F. 1982a. *Vom Positivismus zur 'wissenschaftlichen Weltauffassung'.* Wien: Locker.

————. 1982b. *Arbeiterbildung in der Zwischenkriegszeit.* Wien: Locker.

Sweezy, Paul (ed.). 1975. *Karl Marx and the Close of his System* (Eugen von Böhm-Bawerk) and *Böhm-Bawerk's Criticism of Marx* (Rudolf Hilferding). London: Merlin Press.

Vienna Circle. 1929. *The Scientific Conception of the World: the Vienna Circle* (preface signed by Hans Hahn, Otto Neurath and Rudolf Carnap). In Neurath 1973, pp. 299–318.

11

Politics and Feyerabend's Anarchist

Alastair Hannay

Defending Anarchism

One man's thief is another man's parson. Some see in the anarchist a perverse devotee of chaos; others, a naïve optimist about natural human capacity. Either he shocks because he wants to topple the traditional pillars of social organization, or else he invites worldly scorn for supposing that buried under those pillars there lies a stifled human talent that can do the job of organization as well or better. Any defense of anarchism must hover uneasily between these extremes; to defend the anarchist against those whom he shocks one must give arguments which, if too much is made of them, will turn shock into scorn.

One way of preventing too much being made of them is to allow that anarchism works but only in certain circumstances; to accept, for example, that the general anarchistic drift, the anarchist's conception of alternative, "centrifugal" sources of social cohesion, can be a healthy countercurrent to a tendency to concentrate too much power in central institutions, but not because it is always healthier not to have central institutions than to have them. However, as a defense of anarchism this obviously doesn't carry the argument far enough. To allow that the centrifugal drift might go too far, that in certain circumstances it might be positively unhealthy, is to deny even the minimal anarchistic presumption that the onus of justification is on those who allege that there can indeed be circumstances in which no case for anarchism can be made.

If that can be called containing anarchism in social time, another, no better defense, would be to contain it in social space: to defend anarchism only within a well-defined social sub-context. In Lutoslawski's compositions there are strictly delimited intervals where the players are allowed to make what sounds they like with their instruments, and they have to make some. Similarly in social life at large, there are activities and interests in which individuals are freer than in others to do more or less what they like; but enveloping these activities and interests is a dense web of regulated behavior and legitimized expectation. Kindergartens allow their attendees a measure of freedom not tolerated outside, not extended, for instance, to drivers on public roads. And religious life in most Western societies is left to the individual, but only because, and insofar as, matters "spiritual" are out of public harm's way. Anarchism thus contained can surely be defended for all sorts of external reasons, and also for internal ones, but again, anarchism's merits, whatever they may be, will count only so long as the contained freedom supports, or at least does not interfere with, interests and goals defined in an overriding context, and these need not at all be anarchistic.

In *Against Method* Paul Feyerabend argues that development in science is not due to adherence to "fixed and universal rules" (1975b: 295). Historically, he claims, what is generally acclaimed as growth in science has not been the result of applying a "unique set of standards" (1975b: 216); in fact we owe such "episodes" in the history of science as the Copernican revolution, the acceptance of the kinetic theory, and the rise of quantum theory to *violations* of "rules and standards which both philosophers and scientists [have] regarded as essential parts of rationality" (1978b: 13). Feyerabend adds that indeed any attempt to enforce rules of rationality will be "detrimental to science" since it "neglects the complex physical and historical conditions which influence scientific change" (1975b: 295). As for a general rule for scientific advance which takes adequate account of these conditions, and of all that can actually aid scientists in their work (1975b: 15), the best one can propose is: Anything goes (1975b: 28, cf. 215).

As its subtitle, "Outline of an Anarchistic Theory of Knowledge," clearly indicates, *Against Method* addresses science. The knowledge in question is knowledge of nature, not political knowledge, so one might think that the author's case for the theory was based exclusively on its scientific appeal, and that the anarchism it advocates was a contained one in the second of the above two senses (though within science itself a watered-down anarchism contained in the first sense could also be prescribed from time to time as an antidote to a tendency for science to become hidebound and inhibited by internal mandarinism). Yet both in this work and in others Feyerabend appeals often to a wider audience, namely mankind (e.g., 1978b: 215). There are references to humanity, human dignity, and the like. Furthermore, *Science in a Free Society* comes as a sequel to *Against Method:* it "resume[s] the argument" of the latter by extending that argument to "society as a whole" (1978b: 7); in other words we begin with the critique of scientific practice and then apply its lesson to practice in society in general.

Is Feyerabend claiming that because science serves mankind, whatever is good for science is good for mankind? That truism would hardly call for the large-scale defense provided in *Science in a Free Society*. Moreover, the truism conceals an important *non sequitur:* whatever science is (resistance to the tyranny of nature, conversion of mystery into commonplace, or however else we choose to define it), there is no guarantee that every measure adding to science's total output of humanly beneficial knowledge gives a net overall human gain, let alone involves no increment of human loss. So the claim that epistemological anarchism benefits mankind calls for some wider justification.

At times Feyerabend sounds as if he assumed the wider justification were already given, while it is the application to science that needs special argument. In the passage referred to above he says he is convinced that "Mankind, and *even* Science, will profit from everyone's doing his own thing" (emphasis added). Not science and *therefore* mankind, but mankind and perhaps *even* science! And in arguing later in the same work that the idea that science should be run according to fixed and universal rules is "pernicious" because any attempt to enforce the rules is "bound to increase our professional qualifications at the expense of our humanity," Feyerabend says that "*[i]n addition*, the idea is detrimental to science" (1975b: 295; emphasis altered). All this sounds as though what Feyerabend had in mind was not first and foremost epistemological anarchism at all, at least as an anarchism confined to scientific practice, but some more general policy of "doing one's own thing" which in this instance, he is saying, can also, and in spite of intuitions that tell us that science is after all a collection of scientific *disciplines*, be extended to science. Perhaps, then, it is only in this general sense, and not in its application to the theory of knowledge, that Feyerabend is claiming anarchism to be to the advantage of mankind? But no. At the very beginning of *Against Method*, which outlines a theory of knowledge, he admits that anarchism is "perhaps not the most attractive *political* philosophy"; what it is, is "excellent medicine" for "epistemology" and "philosophy of science" (1975b: 17; original emphasis). Thus it seems that it is indeed the health it brings to the latter that Feyerabend wants us to see as the source of the advantages of anarchism for "society as a whole."

To find the nature of the intended link we must ask what are the precise involvements of epistemological anarchism in the wider, political sphere? This chapter looks at a number of ways in which Feyerabend actually specifies that involvement, as well as at one which is not made explicit but which I believe can be shown to be the only one on which his widest claims for the political relevance of epistemological anarchism can be based. This latter way can be illustrated by a parallel Feyerabend himself draws with the separation in Western societies of church and state (1975b: 299). That separation is based on the idea of freedom of individual worship, a freedom in which the state is (ideally) involved solely as its guarantor. In this political arrangement (which of course also leaves the state free to pursue an unencumbered *Realpolitik*) religion is reduced to the status of private ideology; the lords spiritual and their minions in the field—priests and parsons—can no longer exert a spiritual dictatorship. To recycle my opening sentence, the parson has been convicted of theft, not by embezzling church funds or living too well at public expense, but because in the exercise of his duties he deprives the citizen of the right of free exercise of judgment in matters of conscience. So too in our day with *die Gelehrtenrepublik*, the lords scientific and their minions, in matters of knowledge. Feyerabend's argument is that such judgments are the proper preserve, not of a scientific elite, but of ordinary citizens. However, to see what this amounts to we must distinguish between the preserve's being "properly" theirs because this makes for better science, and its being "properly" theirs because this forms an improved basis for society as a whole. In what follows it will be noted that I am less concerned with questioning Feyerabend's claim that anarchism in science makes for better science than with looking for ways in which this claim can be relevant for the purposes of *political* improvement.

Some Lexical Law and Order

The term "anarchist" (from the Greek *an archos*, or "no government," though with inflections also in the direction of "no beginning" and "based on no principle") is thought to have originated as a pejorative for those opposed to order as such (Woodcock 1967: 111). But the devotee of chaos is a poor anarchist, and although room must be made for the inveterate destroyer, at any rate in the field of entertainment—the punk anarchist (probably very far from poor)—in modern times anarchism is associated with the belief in a society's ability to regenerate itself by the release of centrifugal capacities in place of control from the center. Feyerabend's anarchist, although his lines are often those of the entertaining destroyer or "flippant Dadaist," and in spite of his wish not to be remembered as a *"serious* anarchist" (1975b: 21 fn 12, emphasis added; and 33 fn 4), is clearly formed in this mold. But in tracing the epistemological anarchist's ancestry Feyerabend mentions other anarchisms. Take the "political" anarchist, who "believes in science and in the natural reason of man." Far from being bent on destruction, this anarchist believes he holds the key to social harmony. "Remove all boundaries, and natural reason will find the right way. Remove educational methods, and man will educate himself. Remove political institutions, and he will form associations that express his natural tendencies and may thus become part of a harmonious (un-'alienated') life" (1975c: 176; cf. 1975b: 188). Now it is true that the epistemological anarchist, in Feyerabend's portrait, does not believe in science, the established order in that area being precisely what he opposes. But he still believes in something very like the natural reason of man, namely the "natural shrewdness of the human race" (1978b: 98), and it seems clear that sentiments like these are ones Feyerabend intends the epistemological anarchist to be able to echo.

However, since the anarchist has as much to gun against as to gun for, there is some danger of confusion if we do not know from which of these he derives his qualifying title, a confusion not altogether absent in Feyerabend's own account. "Political" anarchists "oppose political institutions" in the name of science, but "religious" anarchists oppose the physical world as such (as a "lower realm of being") in order to be guided *by* religion (though not by religious institutions) (1975c: 176; cf. 1975b: 187). This would make the political anarchist a *scientific* anarchist, as the former rule would make the religious anarchist a *secular* or *sublunary* anarchist, or some such.

What then are we to make of the "epistemological" anarchist? Well, he is against institutionalized science, but since he propounds a theory of knowledge, an anarchistic theory, he must be counted as being both for and against. And that suggests a third labeling rule which would qualify an anarchism by the domain within which the anarchist recommends achieving centrifugally what an existing order insists on achieving centrally. Using the same rule we might call, say, a "philosophical" anarchist not someone opposed to philosophy (the first rule), nor opposed to everything but philosophy (the second rule), but someone concerned with shifting power from the domain's center (e.g., the philosophy departments) to some more centrifugal location (e.g., the philosopher in the street).

"Philosophy" once meant, in its widest sense, the pursuit of wisdom, a discipline covering all spheres of life, directing, among other things, the course of political and social debate; and what is traditionally called "philosophical anarchism," the view that a person obeying his natural inner light needs no authority in any sphere (cf. Brinton 1967: 523), reflects this. Nowadays, however, few philosophical storms overflow the rims of common-room teacups. Nevertheless, if we allow ourselves to adopt the old, wide sense of "philosophical" we can form a fourth labeling rule: the terms "political," "religious," "epistemological" can be used to specify that sphere of life in which the "philosophical" anarchist sees the promise of a centrifugal basis for the good life. Thus a religious anarchist, according to this rule, is one who sees the hope of the good life quite generally in religious terms, and who therefore seeks to promote the anarchistic drift by strengthening individuality in the religious domain. The Parliamentarians' opposition to the divine right of kings was politically motivated but still within the domain of religion. It was philosophical because it was backed by principles about the nature of the good life. It was also a centrifugal move, though because of the residual elitism of the Puritans, not yet anarchistic. It became anarchistic when Gerrard Winstanley and the Diggers (often referred to as "religious" anarchists) opposed the victorious Puritans of the New Model Army for using their power to appropriate land (as just reward) instead of treating it as mankind's common treasury. One might regard these religious anarchists as anarchists in the philosophical sense, because they saw the promise of a centrifugal basis for the good life in religious individualism. My purpose in drawing attention to this usage is to anticipate the suggestion that epistemological anarchism might also take the form of a species of philosophical anarchism in the good old wide sense of "philosophical."

Subsystem Anarchy

Anarchism in *Against Method* is defended as being good for epistemology and philosophy of science. As indicated, what Feyerabend is attacking here is the belief, fostered in these disciplines, both that there is a universally valid scientific procedure or set of procedures, and that whatever successes science has enjoyed can be attributed to the use of these. Removing the prestige these theoretical disciplines have bestowed on science by their propagating such falsehoods will bring about a general release of cognitive energy. And if one assumes that the point of arguing that something is good "medicine" for epistemology and philosophy of science is that it helps these to promote the activities they have been established to guide, one will conclude that Feyerabend believes that the releasing of cognitive energy in projects hitherto classified as non- or unscientific will serve *cognitive* goals. Feyerabend has specified the goals of science as the understanding of nature and the mastery of the physical environment (1975c: 173). Let us assume that these are also the goals of the epistemological anarchist. If so, he earns his title by virtue of the third of our four labeling rules: he is called "epistemological" because it is within epistemology that he seeks to undermine oppressive forms of authority, and it is in terms of what is now sought regarding our understanding of nature and mastery of the environment through central control that he thinks more can be achieved centrifugally, by freeing natural capacity.

Now suppose an anarchist believes, as Feyerabend's "political" anarchist does, that science can achieve the ends of *political* institutions better than these institutions themselves can. It will be natural for him to describe these ends as speaking to the good life; and insofar as politics is perhaps for him not just the art but the science of that life, the ends can still be said to be political. The way in which science improves on political institutions will therefore be specified in terms of its superior contribution to such cardinal political goods as justice and freedom. But then what about knowledge and truth? Will it be because of the assumed ability of scientific institutions to grasp truth that he defends these, or because they facilitate the establishment of the good life? Now Feyerabend calls the political anarchist's acceptance of science "naïve and childlike" (1975c: 177 and 1975b: 188), and of course we can say that it is part of the political anarchist's *naïveté* that he believes the pursuit of truth has the good life as its automatic by-product. But then what if, like Feyerabend's epistemological anarchist, he overcomes his *naïveté* about science and discovers that scientific institutions are politically oppressive? Will he not then be faced with a choice of goals—scientific or political? He may want to oppose scientific institutions because they inhibit a politically preferable "centrifugal" capacity. But there would be no automatically provided political reason for opposing them if it is only the search for knowledge and truth or some correspondingly epistemologically preferable capacity that they inhibit. While if he should indeed find it necessary to oppose centralized epistemological institutions for political reasons, his opposition would in principle be quite independent of his having the conviction he presumably does have that anarchism in epistemological matters was good for science. He might in fact believe the best science was centrifugal science but think that such science was politically oppressive, just as anyone who, on the contrary, believed politically oppressive epistemological institutions to be necessary for effective science might waive that consideration in the interests of political freedom.

So we have the possibility of opposing or defending scientific institutions for reasons that are not epistemological, and of having good epistemological reasons for opposing or defending scientific institutions, reasons which are outweighed by political considerations. In effect what we have is the ability to ask, if someone advocating anarchism asserts that people should be allowed to do and have the science they want to do and have, whether that is (1) because it will make science better; or (2) because they will be freer, happier people, gain dignity, humanity, and the like; or (a variant of the former alternative) even whether it is (3) because science itself will gain from their greater freedom, happiness, humanity, etc. What we do not have is the possibility of opposing or defending scientific institutions for good epistemological reasons that imply (or are themselves) correspondingly good political reasons. We are not yet allowed to expect people to be said to have the science they want because that is in itself a political justification.

On the assumption, then, that political anarchism and epistemological anarchism define separate goals, though allowing that one domain might be called upon in pursuance of the goals of the other, let us note that once anarchism is qualified as other than political, its goals will normally be regarded as subordinate to those of political life. Science is a subsystem. That means that whatever the merits of epistemological anarchism in its own field, the exploitation of those merits is conditional upon their serving, or at least upon their not defeating, certain extra-scientific goals. However, we should note too that these extra-scientific goals need by no means be liberal ones. There is indeed no reason why epistemological anarchism should not serve, or at least be tolerated because it did not defeat, the ends of a totalitarian state; just as little reason as there is for supposing that it would not be rejected in an "open" society because it tolerated procedures which in the political domain not even an open society can put up with. Take the analogy of religion which Feyerabend often refers to in support of the separation of science and state. The political center may remain tolerant of religion, as in East Germany, only so long as the "church within socialism" confines its practices to hallowed ground and its goals to such otherworldly ends as the salvation of souls. Its tolerance ceases once churchgoers and the clergy begin ignoring the boundaries and secularize these goals by relating them to physical death and disease, avoidance of war, and the placement of nuclear-armed rockets (see Dimbleby 1982). Similarly, in a totalitarian state, science together with the host of discarded "non-scientific" traditions might be given free rein for all sorts of political reasons, from "divide and rule," through containment of otherwise politically dangerous creative energy, to obtaining the widest possible catchment area for the production of politically needed technology. An analogy can be drawn. Anarchy in the kindergarten could fulfill almost any shade of political goal: freeing expenditure on child minders for whatever other purpose, encouraging self-reliance, creativity, or the anarchic virtues in general in the young, but also selecting efficient bullies, confining disruptive creativity, diverting it into harmless play, or inculcating through experience of the horrors of chaos a healthy respect for control from above. So too can anarchy in the epistemological sphere, in theory, be tolerated or actively promoted for almost any kind or shade of political end.

Civilian Involvement in Science

The epistemological anarchist, as now circumscribed, is concerned as anarchist only with the freeing of natural "knowing" capacities. What are these and where are they to be found? In *Against Method* Feyerabend refers us to scientists, but not as users of some special scientific procedure. We are referred to the scientist's moods, whims, passing fancies and preoccupations, though also to his or her wider interests such as "social peace," on the one hand, or the desire to arouse colleagues and contemporaries from their dogmatic slumbers on the other. All these are to determine a scientist's attitude to a scientific theory (see 1975b: 191–195), the scientist's snap judgments and personal assessments being more potent sources of scientific advancement than conformity to universal standards, laws, or ideas (1975b: 189). The epistemological anarchist will accordingly lend his elbow to whatever upsets a conviction in "laws of reason," "standards of rationality," or "immutable laws of nature" (1975b: 190–191).[1] The reason is that the anarchist's "non-method . . . has a greater chance of succeeding than any well-defined set of standards, rules, prescriptions," a claim backed by such observations as that "argument, judiciously used, could have prevented the rise of modern science . . . while deception is necessary for advancing it" (1975b: 195). In *Science in a Free Society*, however, the centrifugal shift is extended past the scientist to the layman. This, anarchistically, is a very significant move, driving the constructive element, as it does, to the centrifugal limit, namely the normal intelligence of the ordinary citizen. But how does one justify, in terms of the growth of understanding and control, such a "surrender" of professional judgment to the masses?

Feyerabend's first answer distinguishes scientific research from what scientists claim about its application. Laymen are not to *do* science, they are to "supervise" it, to pass judgment on what scientists say is to be achieved by it, e.g., in medicine, psychological testing, prison reform, safety of nuclear reactors. In such matters "it would not only be foolish but downright irresponsible to accept the judgment of scientists and physicians without further examination" (1978b: 96). The examination is to be made by "duly elected committees of laymen" willing to put the experts through the kind of cross-examination that can expose "the uncertainty, indefiniteness, the monumental ignorance behind the most dazzling display of omniscience." In this way "science is not beyond the reach of the natural shrewdness of the human race." Feyerabend suggests that shrewdness "be applied to all social matters which are now in the hands of the experts" (1978b: 98).

Feyerabend's initial illustrations of the need for lay supervision of science are cases in which scientists (1) lend their prestige to the rejection, say, of astrology or phrenology, but in significant ignorance of what it is they are rejecting, or (2) assure politicians and the public of the correctness of their own findings (e.g., about the expected "low" levels of radiation released from nuclear power plants), but with insufficient grounds. In both of these cases it is the prestige of a politically influential group, a whole scientific tradition or some group of scientists, that takes the upper hand over science. Scientists fail, for reasons of personal interest, to do their science properly. In such cases lay supervisors provide what might be regarded as an appropriately objective, that is, impartial, corrective. As a kind of watchdog service to protect the people's investment, they help prevent the kind of situation described recently by a (scientifically trained) critic of the International Commission on Radiological Protection who accused the commission of being a "self-perpetuating organisation of scientists with a vested interest in the use of radioactive material, not a society based on general professional excellence" (see Caldecott 1983). But the lay supervisors would not be restoring scientific integrity here by adding more science; they would be watching over the scientists' professional competence, holding them to the straight and narrow. In order to answer to the anarchic idea of a centrifugal natural capacity (the scientific shrewdness of natural man) replacing central authority, or an elite, *in the context of science,* the members of the supervisory committees, in exercising their natural shrewdness, would have to be considered as actually complementing the work of the professionals. So far, however, Feyerabend's lay supervisors look more like political than like scientific functionaries.

More recently, however, Feyerabend has enlarged on the role of his lay councils in a way which more strongly suggests their participation in science itself. He argues as follows: first, since the really fundamental disputes between traditions concern core matters of which the scientists themselves, if only they are honest, must confess they have no scientific knowledge, decisions by laymen on these issues are at least as good as those of the scientists; but second, the latter decisions are in fact better because they are not burdened by considerations of professional prestige (the ignorance can therefore be faced) (1980a: 15–17; and 1980b, Einleitung); third, in a democratic society which permits its members to live as they think fit, including the right to pursue what they take to be true (1978b: 86), and which protects the various corresponding traditions from forcing one another out of business through being able to call on some form of political aid, democratic councils will be able to settle such fundamental disputes more adequately by virtue of the richer basis of comparison available to them. The political arrangement here is called "democratic relativism," but, because it is clearly in the service of knowledge, it also deserves the title "epistemological." It is designed not only to protect liberal rights, but also to be "a most useful research instrument for any tradition that accepts it" (1980a: 17). Siding with John Stuart Mill, Feyerabend commends "proliferation," not just as "an expression of [the] liberal . . . faith that [a] plurality of life styles and modes of thought will be an advantage to all," but because it is also "an essential part of any rational inquiry concerning the nature of things" (1980a: 7; emphasis removed).

In this latter respect, then, democratic relativism functions as a centrifugal alternative to rationalism. In place of rationalism's distinction (corresponding to explicit and universally applicable rules of selection, which of course Feyerabend denies have been used to put modern science where it is, except in the sense that the "myth" of their having done so has concealed the real reasons for its being there) between the proper and the improper use of reason, democratic relativism gives us the distinction between effective and ineffective choices of theories and traditions. What we have now is the epistemologically justified democratic choice of theory, justified both because the specialties of the specialists do not extend to those fundamental features of their disciplines on which crucial choices of scientific theory depend, and because keeping choices out of the hands of narrow specialists prevents the impoverishment of the background of traditions against which the choices are made. In this way we can see that scientific considerations can be used to justify a certain, and in this case democratic, political arrangement—not only democratic, but also anarchistic in the sense that important decisions are no longer controlled by a central institution.

Quite clearly, however, the democratization of science itself is not at all the same as the democratization of society (anarchistically) through science. From a political point of view, in which science appears as an instrument of society, the failure of science to be measured by an objective standard need have no practical consequences whatever. Science will be judged, in a humanitarian society, by its measurable practical results, by its human utility, and not by its conformity or lack of conformity with universal laws of reason. The same applies even if, instead of science as we have it today, we assume the epistemological anarchist has succeeded and the instrument society has at its disposal is a plurality of heterogeneous epistemological traditions. What liberated science calls knowledge is for the politician no more than what he finds useful to further what he advertises as humanitarian ends.

In that case, the anarchistic claims of *Against Method* and the democratic relativism of its sequel are entirely gratuitous. Whether true or false the epistemological niceties of the former will be beside the political point, while political support for the methodology of democratic relativism will be as dependent politically on non-epistemological concerns as any other would-be scientific procedure. Of course if science can be held responsible for political oppression, in the sense perhaps that the cult of science and its domination by a particular scientific tradition force our lives into an unhealthy mold, so that people in general would lead better lives if the results of science were withheld or replaced by something less "scientific" or even something wholly "unscientific" (e.g., their own wits), then the niceties of *Against Method* will not be altogether without interest to the politician. Preaching epistemological anarchism will help to undermine any one tradition's monopoly of science, as well as the cult of science in general. If a significant hindrance to removing oppressive science is a naïve respect for science—on the part of the oppressed, but perhaps also on the part of the oppressor—due to the belief that scientists owe their success to actually following universal laws of reason and that scientific knowledge is a political necessity, then an anarchistic attack on reason and science will be in order, politically, that is. It will also be in order when the oppression is due to politicians interested in exploiting science to further their interests. But then, politically, the attack would be in order even if it were epistemologically mistaken. That is, in circumstances like these it would be politically correct to spread the word of *Against Method* to all corners of society even if those responsible were convinced that it was epistemological nonsense. Likewise, even in the relativistic society envisaged by *Science in a Free Society*, where ideally people get the science they want, it will always be possible to distinguish methodological reasons from political reasons for their wanting the science they have. And it will always be possible, therefore, to envisage a political circumstance that will call for a revisal of the epistemologically advantageous proliferation of scientific modes of thought, that is, of the very relativism of that society, assuming it to be based only on general epistemological considerations.

These remarks show the insufficiency of an appeal to the fact that science is a "social issue" for establishing a link between good science and good politics. It is one thing to say that there are aspects of science which should be the concern of society because they affect the lives of ordinary citizens—that is a political issue. It is another to say that scientific issues are to be decided by society or its representatives. If any issues *in* science are social, that is not because the scientific subsystem makes itself felt in other subsystems or their embracing system; it must be, at least partly, because science itself goes better if treated as a *social* enterprise.

The link might be established, however, by a redefinition of science. A "socialization" of science could be argued on the analogy of Quine's "naturalization" of epistemology. Just as one drops questions of the "validation of the grounds of empirical science" in epistemology in favor of questions of "how science is in fact developed and learned" (Quine 1969: 75 and 78), so one could drop questions of the validation of the choice of scientific theories in favor of questions of which theories or practices benefit society most or embarrass it least. Once a traditional problem set by a discipline proves insoluble, so the argument goes, the thing to do is settle for any soluble problems that can still be viewed within its scope, these then being regarded as the true heirs to those left unsolved (see Quine 1969: 83). In the case of scientific theories, control of the environment seems a good candidate. It has always been at least one ultimate justification for science. So if it is true (as *Against Method* claims) that no particular method can account for the choices actually made between alternative scientific theories and traditions, and testing the extent of control over the physical environment afforded by a scientific theory requires no special techniques or learning, then, provided the central issue is now agreed to be control over the physical environment, the value of theories and traditions can be left to popular judgment. To revert to our earlier analogy, it is one thing to defend kindergarten anarchy on the strength of its influence in promoting the harmonious association of adults (perhaps by fostering in future adults a nascent and socially valuable talent to create harmony out of discord or even just by getting children off present adults' backs for a while), or to oppose it for alleged destructive social consequences—in both cases what goes on in kindergartens is properly regarded as a social issue, but not yet a scientific one. It is another to maintain that the expertise needed to decide how best to run kindergartens in terms of what goes on within their walls is to be found among those who have never ventured inside them. The justification of the enlistment of the layman as *kindergärtner* would require a denial that there is indeed a relevant expertise in this area and a corresponding redefinition of the area of competence that makes an adept of any naturally shrewd human being.

However, one consequence of such a redefinition of science would be that science, or any epistemological tradition for that matter, could no longer be said to have as a principal aim the *understanding* of nature. The sole criterion for evaluating a scientific theory or tradition would be the degree to which it gave one control over the environment, something which requires no theoretical insights to test and which would sanction open acceptance of incompatible theories. It may be that Feyerabend would be willing to accept as an implication of the relativism that denies to any one tradition the right to speak for *the* truth a rejection of the idea that the goal of truth should regulate epistemological or scientific inquiry at all. However, the position he seems most consistently to hold is not that the notions of truth and knowledge should be abandoned. Rather, he argues for the view that the idea of there being just *one* truth of any matter is itself one tradition among others (see, e.g., 1984). Its standing as knowledge (and truth) should be evaluated democratically in competition with traditions that do not make that claim. Not only is it more consistent with his relativism to relativize a particular notion of truth rather than abandon truth altogether; without truth as a goal one could hardly refer to relativism as an instrument of research. So this reductive way of making science into a social issue seems not to furnish the link Feyerabend apparently assumes between epistemological anarchism's being good for epistemology and its being good for society as a whole.

Knowledge and Dignity

So far I have examined the political implications of Feyerabend's anarchism on the assumption that in calling the anarchism epistemological Feyerabend means to limit the arguments in its favor to consideration of what will benefit rational inquiry into the nature of things. But now, if we look more closely at what he has to say about human dignity, it will appear that the assumption is mistaken. Recall that (post-Enlightenment) political anarchism put its faith in science and natural reason. But now, as Feyerabend says, "this naïve and childlike acceptance of science" has been undermined, on the one hand by the transformation of science from philosophical inquiry into "a business enterprise," and on the other by "certain discoveries [mainly the result of the work of Mill, Mach, Boltzmann, Duhem and others] concerning the status of scientific facts and theories" (1975c: 177 and 1975b: 188; cf. 302):

> Unpleasant in appearance, untrustworthy in its results, science has ceased to be an ally for the anarchist. It has become a problem. Should he abandon it? Should he use it? What should he do with it? That is the question. Epistemological anarchism gives an answer. . . . It is in line with the remaining tenets of anarchism and it removes the last hardened [dogmatic] elements [of earlier forms of anarchism]. (1975c: 177 and 1975b: 188–189)

The answer epistemological anarchism gives is not that science be set aside in favor of some further *extra*-scientific "centrifugal" accomplishment, but that science cease to be treated as the rational product of universally valid rules. But clearly this answer is given to a question posed by some less naive heir to the aspirations of the political anarchist. In removing the remnants of dogmatism in the old anarchism the epistemological anarchist seems just as interested in throwing light on what the epistemological life, or the life of science, can contribute to the free association of individuals as in what is good for the epistemological life itself. Thus, likening the epistemological anarchist to the Dadaist in the range of what he is willing to attack or defend, Feyerabend writes: "Behind all this outrage lies the conviction that man will cease to be a slave and gain a dignity that is more than an exercise in cautious conformism, only when he becomes capable of stepping outside the most fundamental convictions, including those . . . which allegedly make him human" (1975c: 178; 1975b: 191). Isn't Feyerabend saying here that what the anarchist once naïvely thought was the exercise of a natural gift of reason is in fact uncritical obedience to arbitrary rules of "right" reason; that these are imposed by a clique which, precisely as a result of the turn to science, enjoys a position at the very center of society; and that forming as it does a significant bastion of authoritarianism which forces ordinary citizens into undignified acceptance of what they should be able to "step outside" and accept or reject at will, *this* institution is now the obvious target for the latter-day descendants of this self-same anarchist?

If this is indeed Feyerabend's epistemological anarchist, then we understand, as we would not otherwise, why he should be worried about human dignity. Epistemology is still the thing, in the sense that it is still within the realm of knowledge that we should expect to tap the centrifugal resources on which free and harmonious association will be built. Only now, unlike the political anarchist in the pre-critical era, we shall have uncovered the true centrifugal resource. And what is that? Feyerabend's answer is, "existential decision," the ability to "step outside," to hold up reach-me-down convictions for inspection and decide for oneself whether to put them on. In a more recent work Feyerabend also emphasizes the creative aspect of choice, the idea being that decisions in science are not mechanical selections of ready-made alternatives, run up according to cut-and-dried rules. "We may say," he writes,

> that any scientific decision is an *existential decision* that *creates* possibilities rather than *selecting them* from a pre-existing pool of alternatives (and the history of ideas does not contain the ideas it is the history of). Every stage of science, every stage of our lives is created by decisions which neither science nor life can justify. . . . The fact is, that we 'create' our lives by acting in and on conditions that constantly recreate us. (1982: 347; original emphasis)

Note, however, that even though parallels are drawn with "life," we are again talking in the first instance of science. We might read Feyerabend as saying that the kinds of convictions people have, when they accept them on their own responsibility rather than by appeal to authority, will increase their freedom and dignity as believers, and that *where relevant* they will also contribute to better science. In that case the political implication is unproblematic. We do not have to justify it as the product of good science, since good science is itself simply a product of one application of a general increase in dignity and freedom. However, this makes Feyerabend's references to dignity and freedom no more than expressions of a political view, the justification for which lies altogether outside the scope of the arguments presented in *Against Method* and its sequels. And if we do read *Against Method* as a political liberal's excursion (in this case a busman's holiday) into science, we simply meet our old problem again, though from the other end. For as soon as the political liberal looks for epistemological reasons for applying his liberal principles in science, he exposes himself to the possibility of having to decide "existentially" between upholding his political principle in science to the detriment of rational inquiry and upholding the cause of rational inquiry to the detriment of his political principle.

But we can read Feyerabend in yet another way. *Against Method* can be interpreted as a modern echo of the Enlightenment ideal of universal rationality, the faith that found expression in Descartes's earlier pronouncement that "good sense is of all things in the world the most equally distributed" (*Discourse*, Pt. I.). The need felt by the Enlightenment was to remove the burden of myth and dogma that deprived people of the right to form their own judgments about human goals. Feyerabend sees today a parallel need to remove the myth and dogma that deprive people of the right to form their own judgments on *truth*. Thus the epistemological anarchist is really a philosophical anarchist—intent on reducing authoritarianism in all areas of society—but that variety of philosophical anarchist that finds the individual's own cognitive encounter with the world of supreme value something to be protected politically (1978b: 84) even at the cost of a modicum of authoritarianism.[2] What is protected is not anarchistic science, but *Homo sciens* in all his diversity. Feyerabend's anarchist is thus a descendant of the Enlightenment, though, because he has a less puritanical and formalistic view of what *Homo* must be to be *sciens*, he is not altogether true to that tradition. Because this anarchist sees that society has been crippled by a pale intellectualist rationalism and a schoolmasterly concern for "correct" scientific behavior, he feels bound to "free society from the strangling hold of an ideologically petrified science, just as our ancestors freed *us* from the stranglehold of religion!" (1975c: 173), and to cut rationalism and science down to size: "Science or rationalism . . . are [merely] instruments put at the disposal of the people to be used by them as they see fit" (1980a: 15; emphasis removed). And then, finally, to show that far from being the option it genuinely is, rationalist science has been made to appear as some natural extension of people's brains and bodies, an indispensable organ of social survival. "Modern society is 'Copernican' not because Copernicanism . . . has been subjected to a democratic debate; it is 'Copernican' because the *scientists* are Copernicans, and because one accepts their cosmology as uncritically as one once accepted the cosmology of bishops and cardinals" (1975c: 168). Having proclaimed his freedom in this respect, the epistemologically philosophical anarchist then works on the newly enfranchised scientific electorate's self-confidence. He opens up a world of possibilities among which are some, discarded by rationalism, which stress the importance of individual experience and sensibility and of developing powers of discrimination in a particular (any particular) tradition. He takes us back to the origins of rationalism (Socrates), to that time long ago when "some extraordinary people preferred the results of intellectual games to what they could learn from their own senses and from tradition" (1975a: 3). He revives the rejected hypothesis of an Aristotelian harmony between man as such and nature, a harmony lost to rationalism but which "it is . . . possible to restore [by means of the right kind of] knowledge and moral impulse," a harmony in the sense that man's "natural powers (sense perception, language, *etc.*) do not deceive him about [the world's] basic structure" (1975a: 6). And he encourages the belief that

> [i]t is . . . *possible* that the *knowledge* and the *moral impulse* that are needed to restore *the harmony of man and nature* will be available only to those who again try to relate knowledge to man as a whole and not only to that small but ever-growing tumour some are pleased to call his reason. (1978a: 169; original emphasis)

In this, finally, he appeals to Mill's idea that there is "something like an instinct for right and wrong [and true and false?] which is developed by [the scientist's] interaction with the historical material," an instinct which "cannot be fully articulated" and so cannot be made into a set of rules (1975a: 14; cf. 10).

In short, this anarchist gives us a set of edifying suggestions, drawn from the discarded establishments of the past as well as the fringe traditions of the present, all directed at encouraging people to develop and trust their own powers of cognitive judgment in the face of authoritarian pronouncement.

The apparent advantage of this reading is that, unlike the first, it ties cognitive capacity in with the political principle of individual freedom.

Epistemology comes within the embrace of protectible human rights. Yet even here, in terms of justifying the right to exercise one's cognitive capacities as one thinks fit, we cannot relinquish without further ado the distinction between political and epistemological justification. Questions of the right to exercise one's power of cognitive judgment still differ from, and cannot be guaranteed to receive the same verdicts as, questions of the real extent of that power. Even where, as the relativist believes, there is no reason to doubt that the power is the best there is, the right to exercise it will remain subject to political interference. Or if the right is made basic and indefeasible, upholding it may still lead to epistemological losses, because the power of cognitive judgment in question is not the best there is, so that permitting its exercise implies a waste of epistemological resources.

We seem forced to conclude, then, that Feyerabend's epistemological anarchism is a hybrid. It is built on two heterogeneous, and only contingently compatible, foundations. There is the epistemological basis, on which the theory erected claims that, in time, if reality is exposed (by democratic relativism in its methodological role) to uncorrupted natural shrewdness on the widest possible front, the scientific theories selected will be nearer the truth than those that are discarded, as well as nearer the truth than if some less centrifugal approach had been adopted. And there is the political basis, on which the right of the individual to come to his own cognitive terms with the environment is recognized as essential to human dignity. The two bases will be complementary so long as the universal protection of this human right provides the most effective inquiry into nature. If not, there will have to be a political decision on whether to uphold the right or replace the methodology. Should considerations of truth prevail, the "right to know" will have proved defeasible and not basic, though there might still be ways of protecting some weaker version of the right, perhaps by putting it in the same bracket as freedom of worship, let us say, as a "right to believe," which, however, would be a severe curtailment of a right that was the right of the citizen *qua* citizen to take part in scientific decision-making.[3] Should considerations of truth not prevail, democratic procedures of selection will be approved for no other reason than that they do justice to human dignity.

In all this it is assumed that democratic relativism competes with other methodologies. But of course the relativist insists there is no objective measure of methodological performance. Does this mean that the democratic relativist sees his own position as self-guaranteeing? Or is it not rather that to be consistent the democratic relativist *qua* methodologist should allow a say to every competing methodology, including autocratic decisionism, and perhaps even allow autocratic decisionists to use bombs and tanks to gain the epistemological ascendancy, rather than the organs of democratic relativism? The implications of democratic relativism become obscure at this point. But whatever they are, the relativist must surely allow there are conceivable alternatives to democratic relativism, all of which, he claims, serve the interests of truth worse than democratic relativism. If what justifies him in making that claim is no conceivable test, his grounds must be *a priori.* Perhaps he will argue that if no scientific tradition can be objectively justified in its claims to scientific precedence, then all traditions must be pronounced equal. But note that however one interprets this argument, the conclusion is not that all traditions or theories should be allowed an equal *say.* That conclusion depends on the prior assumption that science and truth are to be given a say at all. Without such an assumption, science and truth can be relegated *in toto* to the political immunity of the ivory tower or subjected to strong, epistemologically arbitrary influences from the political center (see Alford 1985). In order to draw the politically liberal conclusion from epistemological relativism, the political acknowledgment of cognitive engagement has to be granted—either that or a general liberal policy of freedom to engage in socially harmless practices under which the exercise of cognitive judgment can be included on the further assumption that no significantly harmful consequences ensue.

The difference between these two assumptions is obscured by the Enlightenment's faith in science. If one believes that science provides the key to social harmony, one will not think of it as significantly harmful. But the epistemological anarchist doesn't have that faith. He believes that establishment science is cognitively as well as politically oppressive. Whatever his own faith in natural shrewdness, then, he should be immune to the belief that cognitive enterprises in general cannot be socially harmful. Therefore, he should be clear about the lack of any direct inference from epistemological relativism to the individual's right, under the name of human dignity, to count as knowledge what his intuitions tell him is true. It should also be clear to the anarchist that the more successful he is in "freeing" cognitive capacities from the control of central institutions, the weaker the defenses of the cognitive enterprise become against the influence of any remaining non-cognitive central institutions, or even of popular non-cognitive interests at the periphery. The prestige science currently enjoys depends in large measure on its having a portrayable personality and history, its own pantheon of heroes, a definite record of successes, and so forth. In the anarchistic situation, where the spotlight of fame has nothing in particular to shine on, it will be much harder to rally support for the cause of knowledge in the face of more clearly defined goals and interests. Why is it then that Feyerabend's anarchist appears to be blind to such risks to knowledge and blithely unaware that it can only be by a happy accident that the two legs he stands on go in one direction?

Away with the Subsystem?

Everything I have said so far assumes, however, that epistemology has some clearly defined area of operations, that there *is* some identifiable enterprise to be called "cognitive," that the word "epistemology" defines some recognizable political subsystem. I want to conclude by considering that from Feyerabend's point of view this may be a mistake. The belief that such a subsystem can be identified is precisely the illusion which the epistemological anarchist is bent on removing. If epistemology can be described as the search for canons of objective judgment (with philosophy of science as a special branch), then what the anarchist uncovers, if the arguments of *Against Method* are persuasive (without recourse to such canons, it must be assumed), is that epistemology is an absurdly impossible enterprise. This is the burden of the anarchist's attack on rationalism. Reason and objective judgment coincide in the tradition under attack, and that *is* the *rationalist* tradition. Reason, for the anarchist, "is no longer an agency that directs other traditions, it is a tradition in its own right with as much (or as little) claim to the centre of the stage as any other tradition. Being a tradition it is neither good nor bad, it simply is" (1978b: 8). The epistemological anarchist represents the system. He is now more clearly anti-Enlightenment, because he turns against his own subsystem to destroy the status it has enjoyed as society's special agency for truth. He demotes epistemology itself, understood as the search for canons of objective judgment, to the rank and file of traditions, and thereby dissolves those distinctions which he ascribes to the spurious elevation of this discipline, among them, distinctions, boundaries, and barriers between science, religion, ritual, magic, art, and so on. He demolishes the sacred hierarchy of compartmentalized disciplines which has grown on the Enlightenment belief that intellectual and social progress requires obedience to the canons of objective judgment in general and of scientific judgment in particular. No longer presiding over traditions— the belief that it does so now revealed as just one among them—epistemology in the anarchist era has the critical task of stating and restating the error of the assumption of a determinably objective truth in *any* sphere of life. Thus what applies to reason

> applies to all traditions. . . . They become good and bad (rational/irrational; pious/impious; advanced/'primitive'; humanitarian/vicious; etc.) only when looked at from the point of view of some other tradition. 'Objectively' there is not much to choose between anti-semitism and humanitarianism. But racism will appear vicious to a humanitarian while humanitarianism will appear vapid to a racist. (1978b: 8–9)

Thus choices between ethical and political alternatives are equally grist to this anarchist's mill.[4] It is interesting that a reviewer of *Science in a Free Society* points out that, unawares, Feyerabend seems to be extending Charles Stevenson's (1944) analysis of moral arguments to the evaluation of scientific beliefs and social traditions; i.e., "just as ethical disagreements can be analyzed into disagreements about facts and attitudes, with the latter predominating, so Feyerabend argues that evaluation of scientific arguments and traditions depends upon prior attitudes: 'arguments without attitudes achieve nothing' [Feyerabend 1978b: 61]" (Schlagel 1981: 384). Here we have Feyerabend represented as beginning with the assumption that there is no objective ground in ethical matters, a fairly conventional view since Hume, and extending it to science (recall his proposal that mankind "and even science" will "profit from everyone's doing his own thing"), where the doctrine of objective grounds still holds sway. The transition from epistemology to ethics and politics is no problem, simply because ethics and politics as well as art (cf. 1984) are where the anarchistic epistemologist begins. Incidentally, Hume would provide as good a precedent in respect of the analysis of moral arguments as Stevenson, though also, and more to the point, if Norman Kemp Smith (1941) is right, in respect of the extension to epistemology of a theory first applied to morals (by Francis Hutcheson).

Anarchism in this light may look more like a consistent theory with firm roots in Anglo-Saxon culture than the shockingly nihilistic position it is often presented as being—though we must recall that the politically conservative Hume was also thought to be shockingly nihilistic in his time. Its opponents are perhaps led to the belief that anarchism is a dangerous or destructive position by what the anarchist would regard as some lingering contamination of rationalism in their thought. They may be needlessly interpreting the fact that they have some unshakable intuition, say, that humanitarianism is always to be preferred to anti-Semitism, as implying some objective truth which this intuition reaches or grasps, and then perhaps confusing the thought of there being no such truth to back their rejection of anti-Semitism with the idea that their intuition has no epistemological value. In appealing to "ethical *critical* common sense" (original emphasis) as "the ultimate arbiter," a recent critic of Feyerabend says that if this authority "tells me that caring for life and minimizing pain is always better than dying and inflicting hurt on others even if it be in the name of an ideology that promises me and my clan the 'Tausendjährige Reich' if only I keep the blood clean . . . then any theory which fails to account for this ethical intuition simply must be wrong" (Gadol 1982: 26).

But of course the anarchist does not say that such intuitions have no epistemological value; on the contrary, for him this is the proper centrifugal location for anything to which it is worth attaching epistemological (or "epistemic") value; we are still allowed to know and to discover our own mistakes. As to whether the doctrine is a dangerous one, it could be argued that the contrary doctrine just expressed (not that caring for life is better than causing death, but that any view disputing this is *objectively* wrong) is the more harmful one. That is, that the less danger lies in the view that when we reject racism, war, and genocide it is not because we have hit upon or been vouchsafed an eternal moral truth but because we feel it in our bones and are willing to let our bones do the talking. After all, saying that one has come upon or been shown the truth in such matters can be to set a very bad example. Think of Jonestown[5] and other cases of the destructive effects of mass suggestion which critics of Feyerabend have sometimes cited as unhumanitarian consequences of the principle that "anything goes." But this 'principle' is surely not intended to guide our moral instincts (it couldn't, since it points in all directions at once), but is simply a concession to those who insist on being equipped with at least *some* principle. As Feyerabend says (1978b: 188, cf. 39), if you want a principle that always holds (though why should you?), then, this must be it. You *could* just as well do without one. Having no principle is of course a root sense of "anarchism," one side of the coin whose obverse reads "better for mankind and (even) science to trust and develop your own instincts than bow to authority."

The anarchist might say that rather than seeing anarchism as opposed to the pursuit of humanitarian goals simply because it opposes the cult of the belief in objective grounds for supporting them, it would be fairer to his position to ask such questions as whether it is worse, in terms of achieving humanitarian goals, to exclude traditions based on moral instincts or beliefs which we consider unhumanitarian than to let them continue in competition. Might not exclusion foster in the excluders the kind of instincts they want to exclude? Might it not impair rather than improve the chances that those who have these unhumanitarian instincts and beliefs will come to acquire others which our instincts tell us are more humanitarian? Might it not lessen rather than increase the chances of our improving our own instincts? Might it not even tend to make them worse?

The considerations here are similar to those that apply in the case of Popper's "principle of restricted tolerance," i.e., his attempt to close the doors of his open society to those who would close the society as well as its doors (see Dascal 1979). The questions that need answering here are largely questions of psychology, in the first instance the psychology of those to whom tolerance is to be extended. In the case of Feyerabend's proposal to incorporate laymen into the body scientific, for example, a lot depends on how far one may trust the judgment of the lay majority, either as enfranchised or as elected arbiters of theories and traditions (Feyerabend's civilian councillors). Feyerabend himself recognizes that a democracy must be an "assembly of mature people," and that "maturity is not found in the streets [but] must be learned" (1978b: 87). Not only is there the normal shortsightedness of human practical reasoning, and the natural proneness of even the shrewdest judgments to be dictated by immediate impressions rather than realistic assessment; even where the individual's judgments are mature and informed there is still the possibility that they will be rendered ineffective or irrelevant by obstruction in the chains of communication. And is it not perhaps utopian to suggest that democratic controls, implemented as they must be, on Feyerabend's view, by people whose powers of judgment, although no more than those of laymen, have nevertheless matured within the respective traditions (see 1980a: 14), will be effective filters against what some would claim was an imperialistic tendency latent in all scientific traditions (see Yates 1984)?

But human psychology also affects the attitudes of those who are invited to extend tolerance to anarchistic extremes. They may resist anarchism out of a sense of insecurity; already isolated at the outer edge of complex modern society, they may feel that anarchism promotes centrifugal tendencies they would rather see reversed. Instead of uniting mankind around (*faute de mieux*) the stable axis of Reason, anarchism would leave us alone to do our own "shrewd" thing. Perhaps there is a feeling that letting the pall of Weberian disenchantment spread to the very organon of modern "rational-ization" will plunge us all back into the spiritual darkness of closed, "organic" modes of social cohesion. The floodgates will open again to unreason and mass suggestion. Are these fears justified, or is the sense of insecurity false? Could democratic epistemological institutions filter out these tendencies? Whether they could or not, and apart from the question of how to preserve the democratic nature of these institutions, let alone anarchistically, Fey-erabend's fears are clearly on the other side. For him it is in any centralized stability imparted by Reason that the threat lies. The threat is to freedom: "a society based on rationality is not entirely free; one has to play the game of the intellectuals" (1978b: 29). One who thinks these fears unjustified can point out that societies with no games at all for intellectuals tend to be even less free. However, Feyerabend claims that his society will be dominated by normal shrewdness, open debate (1978b: 29–30), existential decision, and the natural evolution of standards of criticism (see 1978b: 7 and 16–31); that the protective structures in that society will mirror collaborative effort in the solution of particular problems rather than "objectively" drawn conclusions on what hazards we need protection from in general (1978b: 30). So the goal as he sees it is clearly progressive. Intellectuals *can* play, but they must be taught to play according to a variety of rules (standards) (1975b: 218). And if our reading has been right, far from involving a return to unreason and myth, disenchantment with science is represented as an opportunity for everyone to get on better in the enterprise in which science is engaged, but better also (untruistically) for mankind, because it involves the freedom to use and develop a natural human resource in the political business of establishing the structure of a free society, including the edu-cational (1981: 163ff.) and political means to protect that freedom. Certainly not a shocking point of view. An unrealistic one perhaps?

I don't see why. But it is hard to track down all the provisos. My shrewdness, for what it is worth to the non-anarchist, tells me that democratic relativism must be accompanied by a sense of science as a collective responsibility. Unless the multiplicity of traditions shares the sense of a common involvement in the search for a suitably multifarious truth, its members must surely remain competitive, not necessarily just for power, but in the first instance at least for the right to speak with authority on questions of truth. Each will seek a monopoly for its own version of reality, in spite of, though perhaps eventually by means of, the protective structures (see Yates 1984: 139). An alternative would be to give up the goal of truth altogether. Then the different traditions might sustain the tolerance or indifference one finds among different schools of artists. But that would be to give up the project of science along with its institutions, and I have argued that epistemological resignation is not a trait in Feyerabend's anarchist (see above and Hannay 1980: 217). There is truth to be found, and the epistemological anarchist holds that finding it in the way he proposes supports the good life. That being so, he must still be equipped with an ideal of knowledge, and should perhaps even drop his Dadaist façade now and then to proclaim the "universal idea" of Truth (see above the section "Civilian Involvement in Science"), if only to keep that dangerous notion out of less scrupulous hands.

So even if the search for canons of objective judgment has been abandoned, science persists; it is simply dispersed in native talent variably contextualized in a plurality of traditions. Questions of truth and freedom remain distinct; guaranteeing the universal right to "know" in order to enhance science can still have negative political consequences; while defending it on political grounds has no bearing at all on whether an anarchistic theory of knowledge is true. Nevertheless, given an ethos which links personal dignity essentially to the exercise of a right to make scientific judgments, a theory of knowledge which denies any one tradition a monopoly of access to truth and distributes this privilege to the masses certainly has consequences for the spread of self-respect. There is at least this connection between the arguments for epistemological anarchism and the welfare of society as a whole: if the theory is indeed true then the pursuit of knowledge will bring with it a more general satisfaction of a proposed criterion of human dignity.

Acknowledgments

This chapter was written in 1982 and is printed here with only slight revisions prompted by my own appreciation of its imperfections and by the helpful comments of the editors and referees.

Notes

1. Feyerabend also says, with what looks like a touch of uncharacteristic primness, that you will never catch an anarchist—even in his perverse, ready-to-say-anything guise—*defending* "universal standards, universal laws, universal ideas such as 'Truth', 'Justice', 'Honesty', 'Reason' and the behavior they engender" (1975c: 178).

2. For this as the "Achilles' heel" of democratic relativism, see Yates 1984.

3. This curtailment is not to be confused with the loss of power inevitably suffered by an enfranchised minority whose preferences—though *not*, it would usually be assumed, their basic rights—can be overruled by majority decision, as of course must be the case in democratic relativism too, which thus surely implies some constraint on how the "right to know," if basic, is to be defined.

4. Though not to his Mill, for Mill would subject such practical decisions to the objective measure of utility, thus not only overriding personal judgment, as Bernard Williams points out (1973: 116–117), but in the practical sphere working *against* that very proliferation applauded by Feyerabend in the theoretical sphere.

5. In Guyana, in 1978, an immigrant community (the People's Temple) recruited mainly from the poor black population of San Francisco, committed mass suicide at the instigation of its leader, Rev. Jim Jones, who feared investigation by the CIA and the Guyanese government. Over 900 persons (including about 260 children) died by poisoning or by gunshot.

References

Alford, C. Fred. 1985. Comment on Yates' "Feyerabend's Democratic Relativism." *Inquiry* 28(1): 113–118.

Brinton, Crane. 1967. Enlightenment. In Edwards (ed.), vol. 2, pp. 519–525.

Caldecott, Leonie. 1983. Sabotage of the species. *The Guardian*, London: 5 January.

Dascal, Marcelo. 1979. Closed society, open society, abstract society. In H. Berghel, A. Hübner, and E. Kohler (eds.), *Wittgenstein, the Vienna Circle and Critical Rationalism*. Vienna: Hölder-Pichler-Tempsky, pp. 253–257.

Dimbleby, Jonathan. 1982. Why a message of peace is filling East German churches. *The Guardian*, London: 15 November.

Edwards, Paul (ed.). 1967. *The Encyclopedia of Philosophy*. London: Collier-Macmillan, vols. 1–8.

Feyerabend, Paul K. 1975a. Imre Lakatos. *British Journal for the Philosophy of Science* 26(1): 1–18.

———. 1975b. *Against Method*. London: Verso.

———. 1975c. 'Science'. The myth and its role. *Inquiry* 18(2): 167–181.

———. 1977. Marxist fairytales from Australia. *Inquiry* 20(2/3): 372–397.

———. 1978a. In defence of Aristotle: comments on the condition of content increase. In G. Radnitzky and G. Andersson (eds.), *Progress and Rationality in Science*. Dordrecht: D. Reidel, pp. 143–180.

———. 1978b. *Science in a Free Society*. London: NLB.

———. 1980a. Democracy, elitism, and scientific method. *Inquiry* 23(1): 3–18.

———. 1980b. *Erkenntnis für freie Menschen*, Veränderte Ausgabe. Frankfurt am Main: Suhrkamp.

———. 1981. How to defend society against science. In I. Hacking (ed.), *Scientific Revolutions*. Oxford: Oxford University Press, pp. 156–167.

———. 1982. Science—political party or instrument of research? *Speculations in Science and Technology* 5(4): 343–352.

———. 1984. *Wissenschaft als Kunst*. Frankfurt am Main: Suhrkamp.

Gadol, Eugene T. 1982. Philosophy, ideology, common sense and murder—the Vienna Circle past and present. In E.T. Gadol (ed.), *Rationality and Science: A Memorial Volume for Moritz Schlick in Celebration of the Centennial of his Birth*. Vienna/New York: Springer Verlag, pp. 1–35.

Hannay, Alastair. 1980. Unvoreingenommen und radikal kritisch? In H.P. Düerr (ed.), *Versuchungen: Aufsätze zur Philosophie Paul Feyerabend*, vol. 1. Frankfurt am Main: Suhrkamp, pp. 200–224.

Quine, Willard V. O. 1969. *Ontological Relativity and Other Essays*. New York/London: Columbia University Press.

Schlagel, Richard H. 1981. Review of Feyerabend (1978b). *Review of Metaphysics* 35: 383–385.

Smith, Norman Kemp. 1941. *The Philosophy of David Hume*. London: Macmillan.

Stevenson, Charles L. 1944. *Ethics and Language*. New Haven: Yale University Press.

Williams, Bernard. 1973. A critique of utilitarianism. In J. J. C. Smart and B. Williams (eds.), *Utilitarianism: For and Against*. Cambridge: Cambridge University Press.

Woodcock, George. 1967. Anarchism. In Edwards (ed.), vol. 1, pp. 111–115.

Yates, Steven. 1984. Feyerabend's "democratic relativism." *Inquiry* 27(1): 137–142.

12
Participating in Enlightenment: Habermas's Cognitivist Interpretation of Democracy

James F. Bohman

From its beginnings in the modern period, democracy has been seen as the political form of the new principles of autonomy and reason. In Kant's "age of Enlightenment," democracy was to politics what the self-legislating rational will was to morality and what the transcendental subject was to epistemology. In each case, universal rules and reflective procedures of reason were founded in the subject itself. Because this innovative turn to the self-responsible subject entailed such a radical break, especially with regard to standards of justification, the proponents of modernity from Bacon to Kant understood themselves as standing at a threshold of human development that was roughly equivalent to a child's coming of age—to maturity, self-mastery, freedom and competence. Indeed, for a species ready to think and act on its own, democracy was the only appropriate political order. Now, some centuries later, the fate of democracy is still just as closely linked to the ideas of early modernity, or at least to the possibility of reinterpreting them. The Kantian confidence in the powers of reason has waned, so that it is no longer possible to think that publicity alone could bring about unending progress toward peace and justice.[1] Yet, as rationalism is now being challenged as never before, democracy, too, needs to be reexamined and perhaps defended in new and different ways. It had emerged as one piece with the justifications of rationality traditionally dependent on epistemology as a foundational discipline. This interpretation of epistemology, suspect since Hegel, has recently fallen on especially hard times.

One solution taken by some philosophers is to entirely abandon any hope of connecting political justification to justification in epistemic contexts. So interpreted, democracy then has to do with the expression of desire rather than knowledge, with the will rather than reason. Certainly, such a view would require changes not only in the intellectual foundations of political theory but also in institutional practice. Little would remain of the democracy we heirs of the Enlightenment have come to embrace.

Yet, difficult as it is, the Enlightenment is not without its defenders. It has long been one of the major endeavors of Jürgen Habermas's critical theory to establish a "minimal cognitivist ethics" and politics on which Enlightenment institutions and practices can be based. Both depend, he argues, on the truth of one central assertion, that "practical questions admit of truth" (Habermas 1984b: 176). For Habermas, this claim can only be defended and articulated today if we transform the two basic categories of the modern moral and epistemological tradition, autonomy and competence, in terms of a critical social theory. The political consequences of such a program are clearly in the direction of radical participatory democracy. Unfortunately, Habermas's discussion of democracy, scattered throughout his writings, is cast primarily in terms of the sociological concept of legitimation, rather than in terms of a political theory or philosophy. But because Habermas interprets legitimation in a normative and cognitivist manner, it should not be too hard to reconstruct the normative political theory and the relation of knowledge and politics, which underlie his sociological treatment of democracy. Indeed, this is the case because his concept of legitimation focuses precisely on the relation of reason and social organization, knowledge and politics.

While retaining many modern and Enlightenment institutions, the twentieth century has witnessed the rise of an often catastrophic counter-Enlightenment. The critics of modernity blame the Enlightenment itself; but for Habermas, Enlightenment should be criticized only when it is drained of its cognitive and normative content, when its institutions are no longer means of achieving the emancipatory goals of social learning and justice. Thus, Habermas sees an intimate relationship between knowledge and politics, as well as between epistemic justification and social criticism. But now, given the historical experiences of this century, these relationships can no longer be spelled out in terms of a naïve, eighteenth-century theory of progress, whether it be progress as the simple accumulation of knowledge as in Condorcet or progress by indirect and unintended means as in Kant's philosophy of history. Like his "reconstruction" of historical materialism, Habermas's cognitivist interpretation of democracy is an attempt to revise and improve the Enlightenment by means of critical social theory, in order to let it better fulfill its emancipatory intentions. The critique of progress is now incorporated within the theory of progress by expanding the notions of knowledge and reason beyond the narrow limits of science and technology. Habermas does this in a number of steps, represented in the sections of this chapter. First, Habermas transforms epistemology from a foundational discipline into a normative theory of social learning. Second, the concepts of reason and knowledge which emerge from this theory can then be applied to politics, in order to explicate the moral and cognitive presuppositions of a just, democratic order. Third, the normative force of these epistemic contents can become the basis for a critique of ideologies in the modern state. Thus, when both are normatively interpreted, knowledge and politics are interrelated: under certain general and specifiable conditions, politics can become a process of social learning directed to human emancipation.

Such a rich, multi-faceted concept of emancipation is the goal of Habermas's attempt to rescue, by means of a thoroughly cognitivist interpretation of democracy, the Enlightenment's connection of knowledge and politics.

Just as the consequences of one-sided conceptions of freedom and progress have become clear in this century, so too have the consequences of the non-cognitivist reactions against the Enlightenment. Shorn of the Enlightenment moral and epistemic commitments, democracy takes one of two forms: either it becomes a way of aggregating individual preferences or it becomes a mere legal procedure, reducible to something like the counting of votes in majority rule or the rule of law in liberalism. In either case, it can become irrational: on such impoverished interpretations, the theory of democracy typically ends up in the familiar paradoxes of the tyranny of the majority and the ambiguities of freedom as self-determination. These results lead some to reject democracy entirely as one more myth of the Enlightenment; for others it is to be restricted so as to eliminate its irrational tendencies, as in Riker's recent proposal (not unlike Schumpeter or Gehlen) to limit sovereignty of majorities to getting rid of ruling elites at periodic intervals.[2] While we can reject formal democracy in the same way that Bernard Williams rejects Kantian "morality"—because of its one-sided modern, overly formal interpretation—a more reasonable solution would be to give fuller content to the concept itself (Williams 1985: 55–70).

Given the obvious failures of concepts of the will and its preferences, only one option seems to remain open: democracy must once again be given an epistemic or cognitive dimension. Its results and institutional structures must be judged by epistemic, rational standards appropriate to its practical domain, similar to the role the concept of truth has in the sciences. This is precisely the task of Habermas's interpretation of democracy as a process of communication and social learning. At present, it is all the more necessary to develop such an analysis of democracy, Habermas writes, as "the institutionally secured forms of general and public communication that deal with the practical questions of how human beings can and must live under the objective conditions of their ever-expanding power and control" (Habermas 1971: 87). Democracy, then, must be defined as no less than an institutionalized form of communicative decision-making organized so as to achieve consensus based on free, uncoerced mutual understanding among equals about the ends of social life and how to attain them.

For Habermas, this emphasis on communication and collective deliberation points in the direction of a general cognitive solution. This sort of process presupposes certain abilities and capacities among the participants, so that the question for social theory becomes the following: how is it possible that members of complex societies can come to have and exercise the abilities necessary to make such decisions? The trouble with most theories of democracy is that they concern themselves one-sidedly with important, though not exhaustive, procedural questions about the formal structure of institutions. Against these merely formal approaches, Habermas's understanding of politics takes a cognitivist turn, as can be seen by the fact that he considers the recognition of the legitimacy of a political order to be a matter for epistemic judgment. He is, to use a phrase that Coleman and Ferejohn applied to Rousseau, an "epistemic populist," as evidenced by his cognitivist definition of a general will: on the cognitivist or epistemic view, a group must collectively manifest in its members' social relationships certain abilities of speaking and acting necessary in order to establish and reproduce a form of life with a democratic political order.[3] Of course, Habermas does not ignore formal aspects like procedures or the rule of law, but rather reinterprets them cognitively using the fruitful categories of his communicative conception of reason.

The connection between competences and abilities on the one hand and autonomy and emancipation on the other has a lot to do with what reaching a democratic decision actually entails. In a truly democratic order, participants must be able to determine the rules, values, ends, means and institutional procedures of their own association with each other, rather than accept as given those that have been handed down by tradition or convention. Because they deliberate about ends as well as means, they also have to supply their own interpretations of those same principles and values in reasoned public discussion, especially since the principles themselves may be publicly questioned. The exercise of this capacity preserves the autonomy of each, while resulting in something like a "general will" formed in the experience of one's own autonomy through the recognition of that of others.

Rousseau spoke of founding a democratic order on such recognition as a kind of moral transformation, making possible a higher, social level of freedom and moral identity. Contemporary populist theorists of democracy, inspired by Rousseau, continue this emphasis on self-governing moral abilities. As Cohen and Rodgers put it in their version of Rousseau's idea of autonomy: "Autonomy consists in the exercise of self-governing capacities of understanding, imagining, reasoning, valuing and desiring" (Cohen and Rodgers 1983: 151). In a democratic order such capacities become their own end, and the goal of collective deliberation is then to protect, enhance and cultivate them. But what are the "capacities for self-governing"? How are imagining and desiring related to collective, reasoned judgments? It seems that the cognitivist interpretation of democracy must go farther than Cohen and Rodgers do and specify which capacities and competences are presupposed in a democratic order. This specification is precisely Habermas's intention in appealing to theories of social development and learning. Democracy, we shall see, is based on abilities of social cognition, self-reflection and moral reasoning, the same cognitive abilities on which the social scientist depends as a virtual participant. Unlike the social scientist, whose abilities are manifested in adequate theories, the political achievement of these cognitive abilities is manifested in the participation and successful reproduction of a social structure and type of communication which Habermas calls "practical discourse." That is, democracy is the political expression of a set of general abilities required for complex interactions, including the ability to remove oneself from ongoing social life and to make public, shared judgments of epistemic adequacy based on a common set of norms and interests. The point of the cognitivist interpretation of democracy is to specify and to analyze the formal and epistemic conditions for the possibility of participating in such a practice of discourse.

Habermas's Transformation of Epistemology:
Social Evolution and the Reconstructive Sciences

Two avenues seem open to such an analysis: one is philosophical and transcendental, and the other is empirical and social scientific. Habermas began with the first, rejected it, and took up the second. Applied to democracy, a transcendental analysis might be given of the conditions of possibility of this type of communication. Habermas's main contribution, however, is the application of the second approach to modern politics, although in intention it is a continuation of the main idea of a critical theory of society begun by Marx and continued by the Frankfurt School. This way of dealing with the rational content of the modern philosophical tradition does not seek to abandon it, but to transform it into a form of critical social inquiry. The second type of analysis, it turns out, is also more appropriate to the political consequences Habermas wishes to draw.

In his first systematic works, culminating in *Knowledge and Human Interests*, Habermas attempted to follow the transcendental route, giving an analysis of the formal, universal and necessary conditions and structures of linguistic interaction. Such a transcendental analysis is supposed to reveal the basic universal norms underlying all possible speech. As Habermas put it, an a priori analysis of language use can give the ultimate principles of all understanding: "our first sentence expresses unequivocally the intention of universal and unconstrained consensus. Taken together, autonomy and responsibility constitute the only Ideas we possess a priori in the sense of the philosophical tradition" (Habermas 1971: 314). This analysis of universal and unavoidable conditions leads to the insight that speech is oriented to unconstrained consensus; as a norm, consensus functions both as a foundation and a regulative ideal, a basis and a goal, for actual acts of communication. It can become the moral and epistemic basis for "emancipatory interests" in autonomy, beyond "cognitive interests" in control.

As Habermas became increasingly skeptical of a purely transcendental justification of his claims about communication, although not about their content and political implications, he shifted to the second approach in order to transform the search for reflective-transcendental foundations into the social scientific search for certain empirically universal processes of learning. It became clear to Habermas that the Kantian epistemological turn to the subject as a self-transparent "mirror of nature" could not be coherently joined to the social and historical sciences. Thus, while the emphatic claim to reason made by Kant and the Enlightenment needs to be defended, the transcendental role for philosophy itself as the final tribunal of reason can not be. This stronger Kantian conception requires three main concepts, all of which Habermas thinks cannot be defended by epistemology done in the usual way. Even when applied to language rather than to self-consciousness, such epistemology requires too strong a notion of universal reason, too detached a conception of a universal subject, and too limited a view of knowledge as essentially representational. Historicism is correct, Habermas argues, to the extent that it rightly sees the inextricable ties of reason to action and language and to the domain of communication in everyday discourse within culturally variable forms of life, all of which reveal the contingency and conventionality of what often counts as the rules and criteria of rational speech and action. After the challenges of Freud, Marx, and Darwin, the subject, too, no longer seems to be as disembodied and sovereign over history, nature or the transparent inner domain. Finally, it has also become increasingly clear in this century that representation does not exhaust human knowledge, since the analysis of representation ignores the unarticulated background of our grasp of the world as agents already in it.[4]

Unlike those who see the end of epistemology as the end of philosophy itself, Habermas does not reject the tasks of epistemological reflection, but only the way in which it is carried out. Even in its post-Kantian form, philosophical thought remains epistemological, insofar as it "originates in reflection in reason as it is embodied in cognition, speech and action" (Habermas 1984a: 1). But the only way to approach each of these human capacities, whose performance manifests the basic competences of human reason, is through a new relationship to the human and social sciences. Epistemology can no longer be satisfied with second-order reflection, but must begin with first-order theoretical treatments of these abilities themselves, in the self-reflection of those sciences that try to understand and explain the products and structures of these abilities, as they are evidenced in their exercise and development in human societies. This attempt returns to the philosophical stance of early critical theory, in Horkheimer's idea of the unity of social science and philosophy, between which there is only a difference of degree of reflection and generality, not of kind (Horkheimer 1972: 34). While such a critical theory does surrender the historical metaphysical claim to formulate a "first philosophy" or the more epistemological claim to provide "ultimate foundations," the normative and universalist claims for reason can now be established, discovered and warranted in an empirical social inquiry.

Habermas focuses his attempt to retain the normative rather than the foundational status of epistemological notions like truth or reason in an empirical research program he calls "the reconstructive sciences." Their aim is to develop a modest, fallibilistic, empirical and yet universal account of the rationality manifested in human activities. This same sort of transformation of philosophy which Habermas envisions has already taken place to some degree, in the working relationships it has with the social sciences, adumbrated in the relation between the history and the philosophy of science, moral philosophy and developmental psychology, and the philosophy of language and empirical linguistics. What all these examples reveal is a basic attempt to answer philosophical questions by explaining and criticizing certain practices and abilities. Candidates for such "philosophical" human sciences also already exist in the works of Marx and Freud, Weber and Durkheim, Mead and Piaget. Habermas's own version emphasizes the attempt to render theoretically explicit, or to "reconstruct" in Habermas's sense, the intuitive and pretheoretical know-how underlying practices and performances of basic human competence; the reconstructive sciences generalize Chomsky's distinction of competence and performance to any species-wide ability, including speaking and acting, judging and understanding. Once the structure of these abilities is understood, their acquisition can be analyzed as a learning process on both individual and social levels. These reconstructions yield universal knowledge about human competence, but yet are hypothetical instead of necessary, empirical rather than a priori; they raise universal, though defeasible, normative claims to validity useful in social criticism of various practices.

The general result of Habermas's reconstructive sciences is a theory of social evolution, which organizes and shows the interrelationships of the sub-theories of various individual competences in a general theory of species-wide learning. Such a theory is guided by two hypotheses: first, that learning is the basic evolutionary mechanism in culture; and second, that homologous patterns exist on ontogenetic and phylogenetic levels for the cognitive development of individuals and of the species as a whole (Habermas 1979: 99, 205). Such development is not evolution in the Darwinian sense. It is the competences and not societies which develop, so that we may count as evolutionary any cumulative learning process which has a direction and becomes embodied in structures of communication in a society and in the personal identities of individual members. Both social institutions and individual personalities are related to the current stages in the acquisition of various competences of cognition, speaking and acting. These same cognitive abilities can be shown, on the level of social theory, to be precisely the mechanisms for the reproduction and integration of society. To avoid Spencerian misunderstandings, it should be kept in mind that this conception of social evolution was developed by Habermas precisely to "reconstruct" historical materialism, i.e., to rid it of its residual metaphysical commitment to the "fiction" of a collective subject of history still found in Hegel and Marx. Habermas's theory of social evolution is not about the teleological unfolding of a species subject, but rather about processes of "rationalization" leading in the direction of some epistemic achievement like formal law or cognitive disenchantment. However, Habermas's theory is multidimensional precisely in reaction to the one-sidedness of Weber's conception of rationality, so as to include a cognitive dimension (the development of worldviews), a moral dimension (moral and legal development), and a subjective dimension (the development of more complex personality structures and identities).

Habermas seeks a way between two extreme views of reason. On the one hand, he rejects the idea of the unity of reason which was operative in teleological philosophies of history such as in Hegel's idea of *Geist;* all the "aspects" and "dimensions" of reason neither advance in optimal, lock-step regularity nor do they adhere in a metaphysical collective subject. On the other hand, he equally opposes the positivist attempt to reduce reason to one or another dimension, such as the cognitive or the instrumental domains. Instead, given the argumentative-discursive nature of learning and self-reflection, Habermas proposes a weaker, "procedural unity" of reason, which permits the mediation and interplay between the domains of reason, while retaining their own specific integrity and standards. As against the particularity and irrationality of Weber's idea of separate "value spheres" rather than domains of reason, Habermas holds out the possibility that relationships may be established between each aspect in cultural achievements of self-reflective integration. Weber's more pessimistic view led him to disparage democracy and see the modern world as leading to "an iron cage" of rationality or to a polytheism of competing "gods and demons" (Habermas 1984a: 149–250). For Habermas, the basis of learning in all domains in higher order abilities of communication makes mediations between the separate domains not only possible but necessary if modern culture is to avoid the problems due to reification and overselective rationalization: the loss of freedom and meaning.

The significance of these reconstructive theories in political contexts is that they supply empirically controlled tests with which to evaluate arguments for the epistemic superiority of those norms and institutions which manifest basic cognitive abilities. In this way, normative social theory retains something of the fundamental task of epistemological reflection in supplying standards and criteria of rational adequacy and justifiability. For Habermas, the various competences represent aspects of an emerging form of reason in different, irreducible domains—what he calls "discursive rationality." As the highest exercise of the abilities which are only acquired socially in interaction and collective learning, it may be called communicative competence. Drawing upon Mead, Habermas argues that the abilities related to this form of rationality emerge on the social level in solving those problems which each form of social organization inevitably faces. For example, more abstract identities were required of subjects of the emerging state forms of ancient civilizations, and universal religions fulfilled this cognitive presupposition of a more complex social organization.

But this learning always begins with the needs and problems of people interacting with each other, particularly the cognitive requirement that they often must give an account of their actions by giving the reasons for them, even if it is only by way of an appeal to the traditional stock of knowledge. Our cognitive ability to do this takes us one step further: we can also discuss the reasons themselves, in what Habermas calls a "discourse." In acts of communication, reasons are typically connected to some claim considered to be valid; we make an utterance because it is true, normatively justified, or truthfully expresses our desires or intentions. Thus, any act of communication has an epistemic or cognitive component related to the claim it is making, which in turn can be made problematic in reflection on the level of metacommunication in discourse about these various reasons or claims. Theoretical discourse concerns the reasons related to the truth of our assertions as representations of the world; making assertions thus refers to a reflective social practice of giving reasons related to what counts as true or false, such as scientific discourse of different sorts. Aesthetic discourse is related to reasons given for expressive utterances, which are valid if they are truthful or authentic. Finally, and most importantly for our purposes, practical discourse relates directly to the normative contexts of action, in second-order reflection on the rightness of practices, norms, and patterns of interaction in a way independent of existing, particular relations of status and power.

In all these cases, the activity of giving reasons takes place in public argumentation of different types, which then may become institutionalized in a variety of ways. Arguments are social activities, in that speakers make different utterances in order to "rationally motivate" hearers to accept a claim according to public standards of rational acceptability. So accepted, reasons have "an intersubjectively binding force" (Habermas 1984a: 302). In practical discourse, arguments have the social function of coordinating plans for action and of repairing intersubjective bonds when consensus no longer occurs unproblematically. As these problems are solved, the learning process which actors undergo typically becomes institutionalized in various practices like science, jurisprudence, and as we shall see, democracy.

Criteria of epistemic superiority emerge as the capacity to make judgments based on discursive rationality is acquired; certainly whenever a learning process takes place, a set of arguments now becomes socially available which convincingly shows that certain reasons and claims, as well as the practices tied up with them, are no longer acceptable. Paradigm shifts in the sciences follow this pattern of learning. This process of rejecting old reasons also says something about the standards discovered in the reconstructive sciences. Their very formulation depends on the cognitive superiority of the theorist who has already successfully accomplished the learning process which he or she is observing, a fact that is especially apparent in the early stages of development where there is a strict separation of the theorist's reflective knowledge and the actor's prereflective, intuitive knowledge. Though less sharp, this distinction continues even later in the difference between the reflective but pre-theoretical competence of the actor and the explicit, theoretical knowledge of the reconstructive theorist. But it is learning itself which creates the criteria of epistemic superiority, and the role of the theorist is only to make them explicit as they have been achieved, rather than by projecting new stages.

This recognition of the superiority of a set or type of reasons over others has important social consequences. In significant periods of social learning, entire kinds of reasons are rejected, the consequences of which are enormous for the structures of social integration and reproduction so dependent on the acceptability of reasons according to actors' knowledge. Piaget calls this loss of belief the "devaluative effect" of learning; in it, previous types of reasons lose their justificatory and explanatory potential (Piaget 1950: 202). Once actors have experienced such a devaluative effect, typically prereflective and merely traditional reasons can no longer be convincing. In Western societies, according to Habermas, such learning effects have occurred at least twice.

> The caesurae between mythical, religious-metaphysical, and modern modes of thought are characterized by a change in the system of basic concepts. With the transition to a new stage, the interpretations of the superseded stage are, no matter what their content, *categorially devalued.* It is not this or that reason, but the *kind* of reason that is no longer convincing. (Habermas 1984a: 68)

Once a society has undergone one such devaluation in the domain of practical knowledge and moral norms, there emerges an important new dimension of social learning, leading to moral autonomy. Norms are no longer experienced as given, as what Durkheim called social facts (Durkheim 1933: 13). They lose their conventional character and sanctions, and their validity is no longer given as external, coercive or constraining. Without conventional reasons for acting, members themselves increasingly supply their own interpretations of cultural norms and knowledge and thereby gain enough reflective distance from their own practices to be able to put any reason at all up for discursive examination. This reflectiveness on reason giving and cognitive distance from existing social practices permit autonomy as a direct achievement of discursive abilities unavailable to prereflective actors' overwhelming experience of social facts and conventions.

A reconstructive account of social learning supplies the normative core of an epistemology with strongly anti-relativist moral implications in its standards of rationality. These standards are certainly revisable: that is one of the features of discursive rationality. Apart from these internal processes, there is always the possibility that a society could learn from other cultures, and their own sufficiently developed standards may require that they be ready to do so. Nonetheless, for Habermas, the social achievements of European societies have an undeniable universal significance, although in their general form and not their specific content. Given their empirical status, reconstructive theories still permit many developmental pathways to higher stages of social learning and become the basis for the recognition that the European path has been subject to deformities due to the baleful effects of various of its institutions, like capitalist markets, on processes of rationalization. But with regard to the reflective relation to social facts, modern societies mark the cognitive achievement of possible parity between theorist and participant. Participants and theorists become interchangeable, since both have available to them the same cognitive resources and abilities; they are equally disenchanted with the same types of reasons; and they are equally motivated by rational argumentation. This level of autonomy and competence leads to the need for those new social forms, reflective institutions, and types of rational justification, all of which began in the early modern period. Politics takes on a central role in modern societies as the self-conscious institutionalization of practical discourse so that problem solving and conflict resolution in democracy are not really possible in traditional societies. They may be more or less egalitarian in social structure, but actors lack the cognitive abilities to participate in democratic discourse or to form a "general will." Habermas recognizes that modern societies could regress back below the level of competence needed for these institutions, but the political consequences of such a denial of rationality would be the sort of violence exhibited in fascism, in which unspeakable force was necessary to violate many actors' judgments and to destroy already existing structures of communication.[5]

With regard to those changes in basic cognitive structures and patterns of interaction in a society, moral cognition is the true indicator of the level of social learning; it is the "pacemaker" of social evolution. For Habermas, as for Durkheim, society is a symbolically and normatively structured moral reality, so that each of its members must internalize this structure in his or her cognitive abilities. On the level of development of modern society, members can internalize these normative structures only by recognizing and affirming the epistemic basis of social institutions. This specifically modern demand for epistemic reflection and judgment is the basis of Habermas's strict, cognitivist interpretation of democracy. The moral reality of traditional societies is Durkheim's "collective conscience," a shared set of beliefs and attitudes externally given prior to interaction; only in modern societies is there an internalized, non-identical, and yet collective "general will." On the modern level of moral cognition and individuated identities, competence requires that politics itself becomes the activity of generating a common life by their own speaking and acting. Thus, democracy is the only instance and conceivable general form of a political institution consistent with moral autonomy.

The Moral-Cognitive Presuppositions of Democracy

How could such a fluid order be possible? The reconstructive sciences can help in discovering the internal structure of these higher order abilities and identities and how they may be acquired and exercised. However, democracy is not itself a particular competence, but a method of institutionalizing learning in such a way as to politically protect and enhance it. Democracy is therefore a practical hypothesis about how a collective will may be formed in public processes of deliberation. In its institutions, a collective will "ties the development of social systems to control through a politically effective institutionalization of discourse" (Habermas 1973b: 398). If this is the effect to be achieved, the proper goal is not merely to secure individual liberty, but to establish intersubjective social structures free from domination, violence and self-deception; for this to occur, the topic under discussion must be conscious, rational decisions about the moral structure of society itself. As evident in most modern constitutions, the structure of decision-making itself must be reflective and open-ended; the scope of the issues which this process considers cannot be limited a priori, but is itself an issue for revisable, public deliberation.

Habermas's discussions tend to be more on the level of practical discourse in general than of the political structure of democracy. He began his philosophical career with a book on the emergence of a new idea of the "public sphere" (*Öffentlichkeit*) in modernity. His *Structural Transformation of the Public Sphere* analyzed both the new forms of association, like salons, clubs, coffeehouses and even the public spaces of the modern city, and the new communication media, like newspapers, publishing houses, and even conversation, which were appropriate to the new level of moral autonomy. What unites all these diverse phenomena is that in them publicity itself takes on a normative rather than a merely functional significance; they permit the formation of "public opinion" in the normative sense of a "general interest" and not in the factual sense of the result of an opinion poll; they form those interests which then become the basis of collective decisions. Since Habermas continues his discussion of democracy beyond this point in terms of the sociological concept of legitimacy, it is necessary to find another concept out of which to infer further institutional and cognitive requirements of democracy. This concept is Habermas's basic idea of social identity in a modern, complex society, contained in "post-conventional" morality and its cognitive standards of justification.

Habermas identifies a number of basic features of post-conventional moral reasoning which must enter into a similar description of collective practical judgments in democracy. These features are the hallmarks of any modern cognitivist ethics, whose universal norms extend to the political sphere as to any other domain of action. Once these abilities for moral-practical reflection are described, they can be applied to democratic processes and political obligations in two crucial ways: first, Habermas's social reinterpretation of the categorical imperative supplies a distinct understanding of how universality is achieved in collective deliberation; and second, a comparison of the critical, reflective abilities which constitute the basis of both democratic participation and social scientific analysis shows how the independence of standards of rational consensus may be maintained through a self-reflective critique of ideology. Social scientific theoretical knowledge will have an important place in a democratic order. As both independent of and yet continuous with participants' knowledge of the social order, it can have a public, enlightening role in uncovering systematic self-deceptions and ideological and distorting influences on democratic structures of communication.

Unlike the early modern emphasis on science, Habermas finds "the rational content of modernity" in its new possibilities for moral and political identity. In modernity, moral and political reasons must have the following epistemic characteristics in order to motivate highly competent actors who have undergone a basic learning process that devalues all traditional moral and religious identities. Their abilities of moral reasoning extend to the following dimensions.

Reflexivity. The acceptability of reasons now requires discursive testing. This reflexivity begins to effect roles in interaction, which now are based on the mutual recognition of the validity of a norm. A sign of reflexivity is that second-order desires and expectations begin to predominate over first-order needs in structuring interaction.

Universality. By requiring that any norm be justified to all actors, post-conventional actors begin to adopt a stance that is independent of any one moral or social order. Their reasoning is "decentered," in Piaget's phrase; that is, it is no longer cognitively restrained by either egocentric or sociocentric limitations (Piaget 1950: 245–246). Under these conditions, purely conventional and particularistic reasons are simply cognitively inadequate and cannot motivate competent actors. Because of this requirement of strict universality, any content must be capable of being put up for discussion and possible revision, including one's needs and desires, and even the basic norms themselves, should that be warranted. Such a willingness to permit one's needs, desires, and norms to be formulated by the practical discourse itself is a necessary condition for full participation. Without this characteristic, democratic deliberations degenerate cognitively into little more than negotiation or bargaining, which do not establish a consensual social or political framework.

Differentiation and Abstraction. Fom universality, it follows that reasons for acting become increasingly abstract, complex and differentiated. (For example, considerations of justice become distinct from mere legality.) Actors, too, cease to identify themselves with their social roles, as they adopt multiple and sometimes unspecific roles and assume highly individuated identities. This is an empirical condition of democracy, since non-individuated political actors hardly need democratic procedures to mediate between them; they merely appeal to the never-questioned background of shared beliefs.

Temporal Generality. One of the more crucial features of this type of moral reasoning for political decision-making is the expansion of temporal horizons as a kind of generalization of moral motives that goes well beyond merely formal universality. In such a democratic order, post-conventional roles can only be established "if participants in interaction possess a temporal horizon that extends beyond the immediately actual consequences of action" (Habermas 1979: 137). Historical time consciousness extending both to the past and the future is thus one of the definite cognitive achievements evidenced in early modernity that became the basis for both the historical and social sciences and new types of collective deliberation. It, too, had "devaluating" and "decentering" effects, since certain types of conventional social reasons are only convincing to actors whose social cognition is temporally limited.

Taken together, these dimensions of post-conventional moral reasoning encompass the cognitive conditions of autonomy. As they are achieved in social learning, they progressively liberate the horizon of cognitive abilities of moral judgment from particularistic limitations of social structures and traditions. These changes often have been taken to mean the denial of morality as such, as evidenced by skeptical trends in modern moral theory.

But the devaluating effects are much more specific. All that is denied is a particular version of morality, one that is expressed in conventional, external social codes. Kohlberg has shown that such noncognitivist skepticism is typical of incomplete or stalled stages of moral development (Kohlberg 1981: 411). Thus, Habermas thinks that social criticism should be directed at particular versions of morality, as in the critique of ideology, not totalized to include all moralities; but this less totalizing criticism is based not merely on theoretical insight into social causation, but also on higher order moral capacities required for autonomy and reflection.

What is distinctive about these reflective cognitive abilities is that while motives become more differentiated, the distinction between the bases of moral and social cognition, or between the contents of the moral and the political domains of interaction, breaks down; both are governed by the same set of norms and rules. Post-conventional identities and abilities establish the basis for a new orientation in interaction and a cognitive standpoint for shared expectations. As Habermas puts it, "competent agents will— independently of accidental commonalities of social origins, traditions, basic attitudes and so on—be in agreement about such a fundamental point of view only if it arises from the very structure of interaction" (Habermas 1979: 88). This structure of reciprocity in interaction and orientation to consensus, Habermas insists, belongs *eo ipso* to the new styles and types of interaction which manifest post-conventional competence, viz., the universal reflective abilities of modern speaking and acting subjects.

The core of these abilities underlying the cognitive orientation to practical questions can best be understood in terms of Habermas's reinterpretation of Kant's categorical imperative, based on Mead's social psychology. For Mead, the categorical imperative can be seen as a way of conceptualizing certain requirements of post-conventional interaction (Mead 1934: 275). For Kant, competent actors merely perform a formal generalization and ask if what they are doing could be done by everyone. But from the perspective of social cognition, moral reflection does not attempt to say what some abstract person standing for all must do out of duty; rather, competent agents now use their reflective capacity to anticipate and create a perspective shared by others. Mead's reformulation of the Kantian test requires a reflective knowledge not just of one's own motives for acting but of the social process itself. The question that participants in interaction must now ask is how to coordinate the various perspectives of the participants in interaction; this requires asking not just what anyone must do but whether or not every participant in interaction could will that any of the other participants adopt a particular role.

The ability to provide an answer to such a question depends on at least two competences related to social cognition. It presupposes not only the cognitive ability to adopt the perspective of the concrete other in a reciprocal interaction; but also, in accepting the requirements of reciprocity and consensus, participants must be able to take the perspective of what Mead calls the "generalized other," that common perspective shareable by all competent participants. In the course of interaction, the morally and socially competent actor constantly shifts between these perspectives, i.e., between his own perspective, that of others, and that of the generalized other. Thus, such higher order cognition becomes the basis of ongoing interaction in complex societies. As Mead (1934: 268) puts it, complex societies present a cognitive challenge: "A highly developed and organized society is one in which the individual members are interrelated in a multiplicity of different intricate and interrelated ways." In such a society, complex social abilities are needed to avoid conflicts and disintegration, basic social problems whose solution now depends on collective and institutionalized discourse. Impersonal forms of organization can also be developed, although at the expense of reflective control and autonomy, as in the case of market mechanisms. But some institutions emerge on the basis of these abilities, such as democratic decision-making processes, all of which require complex abilities to shift between and to coordinate the perspective of the first person, those of others, and that of an impartial third person. The possession of each of these capacities of social cognition affects how interpersonal problems are solved, as has been verified in empirical, clinical and developmental studies of adolescents (Selmen 1980).

In those interactions presupposing these abilities, a new form of autonomy becomes available, one that is both a continuation and a revision of the basic Enlightenment perspective. It is not merely the autonomy of a detached, atomistic, observing self. The problem with Kant and most social scientific notions of objectivity is that they identify the universal perspective with simply the point of view of the generalized other. However, it cannot be said that an autonomous identity is abstractly universal and entirely independent of the identifications others make of us, nor can real individuation actually be achieved in a third-person perspective: identity is a product of mutuality in communication. It is achieved in the performance of competent acts of communication; therefore, "participants must reciprocally suppose that distinguishing oneself from others is recognized by those others" (Habermas 1979: 74). And because social interaction under post-conventional conditions is based on a plurality of perspectives, reciprocity and autonomy both increase proportionally in social institutions. Like error in science, individuation in social interaction is also a necessary condition for further institutional learning.

Once actors are individuated in new organizations and types of interaction and are equipped with developed capacities for social cognition, then they are able to form their beliefs, desires and identities through communication with others. Habermas calls this type of communication "discursive will formation," that is, a process of communication which forms an individual and a general will under the same conditions and in light of each other. A "rational will" may be formed by means of a mutual understanding and recognition of discursively redeemable validity claims made in utterances, but only on the condition that the procedures and norms of the discourse eliminate all non-discursive social factors which may influence the process of reaching an agreement. Thus, besides cognitive presuppositions, interaction within the discourse must be so formally structured as to control unreflective, non-rational influences, including material conditions unrelated to the discourse, such as violence and power. Discourses are institutionalized to the extent that a social setting is created that permits collective, post-conventional agreements which, in turn, create whatever shared structures such actors may have.

There are numerous necessary but not sufficient conditions for agreements with these epistemic and formal characteristics. Some are related to the formal conditions of the process of communication itself. To analyze these communicative conditions, Habermas has constructed a counterfactual model in which they are all fulfilled, the "ideal speech situation." The role of this model has been both misunderstood and overestimated in discussions of Habermas's view on politics. As entirely formal, it cannot exhaust all the conditions for democratic institutions; but it does serve the analytic purpose of thematizing issues of the structure of communication related to participation in the processes of reaching agreement. Formally and procedurally, all democratic institutions must more or less fulfill these conditions, or else the agreements reached could be problematized as forms of pseudo- or forced consensus. For example, if an agreement were reached under conditions in which all speakers are not given equal chances to speak, equal chances to utter any of the different types of utterances, or equal opportunities to adopt any role in interaction, then the consensus so reached could have been formed by extra-discursive means. Habermas's point, then, is to provide a counterfactual normative standard for the ideal conditions of reaching agreements in communication; such a standard serves as an independent test of any de facto agreement. These formal norms of communication and interaction in processes of reaching agreement are more inclusive and specific to the actual structure of democratic decisions than the usual interpretations of simple procedures, such as majority rule, or "one person, one vote." What is even more important is that they link formal structures to the cognitive presuppositions of this type of communication.

If these interdependent formal and cognitive conditions are met, then the result of the collective process of deliberation and argumentation will express a socially effective "rational will" based on a communicatively shared and established general interest. In some of his writings, Habermas seems to suppose that the formal conditions alone will be sufficient to guarantee the rationality of the will formed in discourse: "the discursively formed will can be called 'rational,' because the formal properties of discourse and of the deliberative situation sufficiently guarantee that a consensus can arise through appropriately interpreted, generalizable interests" (Habermas 1975a: 108). But if the interpretation developed here is correct, then the formal and procedural aspects of the communicative situation must be only necessary but not sufficient conditions of rational consensus, lest Habermas's theory of democracy slip back into the same dilemmas of proceduralism which his cognitivism seeks to avoid. Certainly, it is possible that all the formal conditions could be met, and yet the result still be a non-generalizable interest; but the same could not be true if we add the cognitive conditions to further restrict the scope of possible motives, reasons and interests to those consistent with post-conventional abilities. Only then has Habermas gone far enough to avoid the same old problems of formal theories of democracy, now transferred from voting to communicative procedures. Proceduralism in communicative terms is still paradoxical, unless these procedures become formal conditions for the political process of the formation of an epistemically defined general will.

That Habermas appreciates this need to delineate the cognitive as well as the formal dimensions of democracy can be seen in the attitudes that participants in practical discourses have not only to conventions and norms, but also to their needs and desires. Unlike Kant's view of moral reflection, in collective deliberation no needs are prima facie excluded until after collective deliberation is concluded and the generalizable interests are formed. But this general will cannot be determined in advance; it is only in interaction in institutionalized discourse that such interests are formed and discovered. If this were not so, no procedure could rescue democratic discussion from the intractable problems involved in ordering already fixed individual preferences. "Discursively redeemable norms or generalizable interests have a non-conventional core; they are neither merely empirically found nor simply posited; rather they are, in a non-contingent way, formed and discovered" (Habermas 1975b: 177). Democracy becomes the political form of this communicative process, where everyone affected by the decision must be party to the agreement, be able to recognize the validity of its judgments, and form this judgment and will in a collective process.

In a similar conception of democracy, Rousseau already recognized that not everything can be decided by "the general will," although he restricted the scope of issues to a greater extent than Habermas's interpretation would warrant. For Habermas, the question is not to distinguish the general will from the will of all; it is, rather, to determine what sorts of issues can or cannot be settled in a consensual manner. In this regard, Habermas recognizes that there are limitations to practical discourse that are not present in theoretical discourse. In political institutions, participants are actors as well as speakers, so in this sense science does not offer an apt analogy for democracy. Failing consensus, participants in communication must seek compromises; however, the judgment of their validity is still a reflective, cognitive affair. So long as they are democratically formed, compromises make cognitive claims; and because compromises are still arrived at communicatively, it is possible to distinguish genuine from de facto compromises, just as it is with regard to consensus. Habermas again develops cognitive and formal criteria. First, participants must be able to judge that the situation does not admit of consensus and that the interests involved are genuinely non-generalizable. Second, there must be a relative balance of power among the parties as a formal condition for reaching an outcome that could be collectively recognized as legitimate (Habermas 1975a: 112). Of course, the call for a compromise can often be a strategy in communication that attempts to remove an issue from the cognitive scrutiny necessary for consensus, as are attempts to appeal to certain given cultural standards to create a predemocratic consensus or to deny that practical questions make anything like claims resembling truth or falsity. Such phenomena show the place of the critique of ideology in the theory of democracy, and it is here that the reconstructive analysis of the necessary presuppositions of democracy provides a fruitful basis for the criticism of contemporary politics.

The Critique of Ideology and the Modern State

Until recently, Habermas has been reticent in applying the category of ideology to modern cultural phenomena, claiming that in modernity "culture loses the formal properties that made it capable of taking over ideological functions" (Habermas 1982: 292). However, given the communicative interpretation of democracy as a process of discursive will formation, we can locate a whole range of potentially effective ideologies that might restrict communication even in these relatively transparent and self-reflective institutional settings. It is certainly the case that modern ideologies of democracy are different from the old metaphysical-religious ideologies which employed a semantics of the sacred to cover over deficits in rationality. In the modern world, ideologies become primarily what Habermas calls "distorted communication"; that is, they need to be analyzed as barriers or structural restrictions on social processes of communication, which in modern conditions become significant primarily in discursive political contexts and in everyday interaction (Habermas 1982: 282).

In the critique of ideology, a new version of the epistemic superiority of the theorist reemerges, even when both theorist and participant are on the same post-conventional cognitive level: it is not the discrepancy between reflective and prereflective abilities, but between the undeceived and the self-deceived, where self-deception can inhibit the full exercise of existing rational abilities. Post-conventional cognitive abilities do not entirely rule out the possibility of socially caused, systematic self-deceptions, although they do make criticism that much more effective (since it is impossible for participants to believe in ideologies once they are pointed out). At this level, critics merely exercise the same set of reflective abilities necessary for democracy; but they use them in theoretical discourse which takes a third-person explanatory stance on interaction, in order to uncover existing shortcomings in the institutional and cognitive conditions of discursive will formation. By pointing out such restrictions on the possibility of reaching rational agreements, critics can have a "delegitimating" effect on post-conventional participants resulting from a greater self-awareness of restrictions on collective autonomy within the political discourse. Criticism of this sort should be institutionalized as part of the ongoing learning process of a society's attempt to arrange itself democratically, since a post-conventional political order must be constantly formed and re-formed by participants' acts of communication. Ideology can inhibit this learning even after the minimum levels necessary for social competence have been achieved. Given the description of the conditions for the formation of a rational will, three different ideological restrictions on democracy could be located, supplying a typology of different types of democractic ideologies: formal, material, and cognitive, each possibly related to and dependent on the others. Such a typology can demonstrate the critical uses of such a cognitive and normative conception of democracy.

The first sort of ideology has to do with the formal level of communication in the political process. Given Habermas's definition of democracy as an institutionalization of discourse, it can be inferred that the basic formal characteristics of democratic institutions and procedures, such as equality, must now be recast in communicative terms. All the basic formal conditions of communication related to processes of reaching agreement are contained in the counterfactual construction of the ideal speech situation, so that any violation of these conditions is inconsistent with the thoroughgoing democratic participation of all those affected. There may be different types of violations on this level. They may be internal to the process of communication itself, such as in the failure of the institution to create a framework sufficient for all to have an equal chance to be heard and to participate. External, material social conditions may also influence communication. For example, if participants enter the discourse with large-scale pre-existing inequalities of wealth and power, the difficulty in reaching a rational consensus will rise in the same proportion as the degree of inequality. Habermas thinks this is because such material conditions allow the privileged actors to act strategically; in any case they distort the formal requirements of the internal structure of communication in a process of consensus and create fundamentally conflicting aims between economic and political institutions. Capitalism, Habermas has always insisted, is inconsistent with democracy, since it organizes society non-democratically. Its structural inequalities delegitimize any existing democratic structures by having them take on functions with regard to economic conditions.

These same material conditions also may effect the cognitive conditions of participation for certain actors, since it is surely the case that the acquisition and exercise of certain politically significant competences requires access to social goods. The lack of development of these abilities leads to discrepancies in effective expression in interaction and to the further inhibition of the development of higher order communicative and cognitive abilities which are formed by participation in discourses. As Claus Offe points out, this cognitive-developmental fact leads to strongly strata- and class-based inequalities in the distribution of decision-making competences. Purely procedural conceptions of democracy, originally having the strictest egalitarian intentions, "privilege the members of those strata that 'know what they want'" (Offe 1985: 275). Habermas's own view faces the same danger, and it can be overcome only if the material conditions necessary for the development of cognitive abilities are thematized in practical discourses; in political theory, it shows a necessary connection between truth and justice in Habermas's cognitivism. Like Marx, Habermas criticizes purely "formal" democracy that does not take into account material and cognitive conditions of participation. In a "true" democracy, reflective of the causal effects of material conditions on social agreements, something like Marx's principle of justice in socialism must be applied to cognitive development: "the free development of each is dependent on the free development of all" (Marx 1977: 238). It particularly holds true for communicative abilities developed in interaction, and Habermas often neglects to recast the norms of justice in his discussion of democracy; justice, too, requires more than merely formal communicative structures; it requires equally strict egalitarian standards with regard to social goods.

Further critical analyses on the cognitive level thematize different ideologies on the basis of their cognitive presuppositions, which fall below the post-conventional level. For example, the quick production of collective decisions in advanced capitalist countries disrupts the temporal horizon of collective decision-making and the actual formation of a rational will in the process of interaction. Thus, speeding up a decision too much may disrupt the cognitive process by reducing collective decisions to the result of preferences instead of cognitive acts of interpretation (Offe 1985: 289).

The knowledge of the interrelatedness of these conditions saves the cognitivist interpretation of democracy from certain common ideological, short-sighted misinterpretations in the direction of elitism. One such popular interpretation, common in the "end of ideology" debate, tries to restrict decision-making to those who possess certain types of theoretical knowledge, rather than including all those affected by a decision. Democratic procedures can then be restricted to the selection of elites, who fall short of being tyrants only because they can periodically be taken out of office by plebiscites. But such theories ignore the formal requirements for rationality in a collective process of decision-making; indeed, even on the cognitive side, they depend on one-sided conceptions of rationality modeled on technologies of public administration and on a conception of truth, understood as a monological knower's relation to the world, which really has no place in politics. Such a view eliminates the rationality of the processes of communication and interaction themselves and violates the content of the norms which govern post-conventional interaction. Taken to its logical conclusion, the same set of arguments and standards of rationality may be used for other ideological purposes, in order to deny any cognitive content to democratic decisions. In this case, emotivism about political issues takes on an ideological form as well, since it eliminates the need for critical and discursive testing of democratic institutions and bases politics on no more than a non-rational commitment. But as the grotesqueness of Hobbes's absolute sovereign or Nietzsche's will to power should show, a politics with no relation to truth or validity cannot be democratic at all, nor can its results be anything more than strategic calculation or the exercise of force. Both the elitist and the noncognitivist interpretations remove political decisions from the domain of the exercise of cognitive abilities that modern actors are capable of as citizens and as social scientists. Both tend to be conservative and anti-egalitarian, in that they see political institutions as rational or moral enough as they are, and so inhibit any need for further learning in practical discourse on politics and institutions.

One other particularly contemporary ideological model of democracy can be analyzed using Habermas's cognitivist conception of collective practical reason. Conservatives and neoconservatives alike, especially neo-Aristotelians, see democracy as a means to restore the lost unity of communal forms of life, which were replaced in modernity by more complex forms of social organization. This nostalgia for the unity of the polis or *Gemeinschaft* typically requires that premodern forms of justification be defined in the genetic, rather than normative, terms of habits, customs, and traditions, none of which by themselves offer sufficient reasons for post-conventionally competent agents to act. But more importantly, it completely misunderstands the cultural potentials and purposes of modern forms of political organization, particularly the nation-state. The state cannot return to or create community; it is not now a community, nor can the means at its disposal—legal and administrative power—ever bring one about, except perhaps under extremely inegalitarian and authoritarian conditions and by extraordinarily violent means. As a form of organization, the state has taken over the political domain; as a highly complex, functional sub-system, its members require highly abstract identities. Under modern conditions and with the state monopoly on the means of violence, the conscious creation of community by force is particularly disastrous, as exhibited by the forced cognitive regressions of fascism. For all his hopes for democracy, Habermas does not think that the state creates social identity and integration; rather it presupposes them (Habermas 1979: 178).

In the opposite direction, the Enlightenment itself overly identified its conception of collective reason with the particular form of organization of the nation-state, and sometimes with that of the non-political market and its ideological "invisible hand" of unintended consequences. There were also political ideologies of the Enlightenment, and they were not originally democratic. As long as the "enlightened despot" held the means of violence, some thought, it might be possible to use force as a means to make people free. Against this oversimplification, a critical, cognitivist interpretation of democracy need not identify the state as the sole form of political order; indeed, as a form of political organization, it may even inhibit democratic processes when it begins to exhibit its own organizational imperatives independent of democracy itself. This is not to say that democratic will formation can occur under different political conditions; if it is to occur at all in the state, individuals will have to develop and to maintain the abstract and morally informed political identities of citizens so as to assure conditions of justice. It should remain possible for other democratic organizations with more particularistic orientations to exist within the framework of the state, so long as they do not conflict with the state's orientation to general and abstract conditions of autonomy. In such a complexly organized society, members of states can take on various roles, so long as one can consistently be a member of a secondary association, in Walzer's terms, and a citizen of the larger state (Walzer 1970: 227). Indeed, Habermas ought to have considered the insight of Walzer and Buber that participation in complex organizations concerned with the structure of society as a whole may often need to be mediated in such lower order intersubjective associations and social structures, or through various mechanisms of representation.

Instead of attempting to create community, such a state still has the basic function Rousseau set out in the *Social Contract* (Bk. II, ch. 12): it must promote freedom and equality, the general conditions of democracy. In promoting equality, the state can serve as an organizational means for overcoming the major obstacle to justice in cognitivist democratic institutions: the silence of the incompetent and the unheard, whose interests the state, as highest political organization, must serve and for whom social critics must advocate for the sake of the rationality of society. For Habermas, the critic can in such cases act as a hypothetical participant, expressing the supposed interests of the incompetent or oppressed group, as "if they were to enter into practical discourse" (Habermas 1975a: 114). Surely, the democratic critic, living in a post-conventional society, can do more. Only as theorists need we speak for someone, however hypothetically; as participants we can make sure, by use of our communicative abilities, that the incompetent and unheard come to express themselves. Here, too, Habermas thinks as a theorist and greatly underemphasizes the communicative role of the enlightened critic as a participant in existing democratic deliberation, as one who may seek to create greater democracy by realizing conditions of greater justice.

Besides understanding what the state can do, it is also important here to understand what Habermas's theory can or cannot do. Particular collective decisions cannot be deduced from the theory; its norms refer only to general conditions and structures. The role that it has for political practice is similar to the role a theory of truth has in guiding and criticizing scientific practice. While no one can deduce the true propositions of science from it, a theory of truth can still reconstruct the proper conditions under which the practice must take place if true propositions are to be discovered. The same holds true here, in that the cognitivist theory of democracy sets out general, formal material and cognitive conditions for the formation and discovery of collective and individual autonomy, which particular societies and political organizations may violate or fulfill. For Habermas, "the decentration of the understanding of the world and the rationalization of the life world" are necessary conditions of emancipation (Habermas 1984a: 74). To that extent, so is democracy, in whatever particular form it takes, so long as it realizes discursive rationality in the practical sphere. Indeed, if Habermas's discursive-argumentative view of reason is correct, we have every reason to believe that as a species we are and can become more rational as a collective-political body, rather than as an individual. This may even be borne out empirically to a certain extent by Condorcet's jury theorem, which shows the enormous gains of epistemic reliability which come from collective deliberations of competent agents.[6] Once generalized to apply to decisions of any collective body, such gains in competence provide a kind of indirect proof of Habermas's view of the epistemic superiority of collective reason. The results of the theorem show that given the minimal competence of a group of judges, its majority decision will have greater epistemic reliability than any of the decisions of the judges taken individually (Black 1958: 166). This result could well be used as a justification of elites. But while such elites could rightly be judged cognitively competent for particular decisions, their exclusive participation in collective decision-making would violate those formal conditions for rational communication which Habermas identifies as the reciprocal, egalitarian structure of practical discourse. If learning is indeed a social and discursive process, then the formation of elites also becomes a barrier to the institutionalization of those learning processes which are significant for democracy and for the widespread acquisition of higher level competences. Thus, Habermas sees more in the rationality of collective decision than the reliability of judgments; he does, however, judge any consensus by cognitive as well as formal standards, lest he fall back into the paradoxes of pure proceduralism which plague such formal-democratic rules like "one person, one vote." That is why, given his notion of reason and discourse, Habermas must have a "populist" and not a "proceduralist" interpretation of democracy, in that he emphasizes participation over the formal rule of how to be truly democratic. On this cognitivist interpretation of populism, discursive will formation must issue in a "general will," and not merely in a procedurally correct decision; Habermas's contribution is not only to understand the formation of the general will in communicative terms, but also to analyze the cognitive presuppositions for successful participation in processes of institutionalized discourses. The rule of law is but a formal condition of this cognitive process.

    For all of his attempts to rescue what is salvageable from the Enlightenment, viz., the ideal of rational autonomy as the "normative content of modernity," which has also to some extent already been achieved, Habermas has in recent writings become more and more pessimistic about the possibilities of achieving democracy in the full cognitivist sense. As politics reaches a certain threshold in the level of complexity, it becomes a relatively independent functional "sub-system" like the market. Once this independence becomes structural, the apparent discrepancy between "the (weak) capacity for autonomous self-understanding and the (missing) capacity for the self-organization of society as a whole" becomes accentuated (Habermas 1985: 418). Habermas rightly sees that under the conditions of the contemporary nation-state, the complexity of modern society and the functional imperatives which the political sphere has taken on constitute major new obstacles to the realization of democratic participation. In fact, Habermas has recently begun to speak of a "new obscurity" emanating from the exhaustion of the utopian energies connected to the Enlightenment hopes for the state and to modern social movements that demanded the emancipation of labor (Habermas 1986).

But whether or not there is hope for our weak cognitive abilities to overcome complexity, Habermas's interpretation of democracy brings into focus those general and formal conditions of communication in everyday life necessary for competent actors to realize their own future possibilities. That is all that the theory of democracy can, or should, do if it is to remain consistent. If Habermas is right that the complexity of the nation-state places it above the level of effective democratic participation and autonomy, then it is time that democratic political theory look elsewhere, to other institutions and forms of politics. The nation-state is a relatively recent evolutionary achievement; it should not be identified with politics as such, nor is it necessarily an entirely successful institutionalization of modern cognitive abilities. In the face of this new "obscurity," what must be changed is the conception of politics and political institutions, not democracy, as Marx pointed out long ago (Marx 1977: 93). It is not surprising that the state, which is primarily an institution of legal, administrative and often violent power rather than of discourse, cannot by itself create the conditions of social integration in an egalitarian society. The Enlightenment hope that the state could was always an inherently false expectation. The state could not do so even under the best of conditions. But now, to undertake this self-creative, learning process in a new way is what it means to bring about enlightenment, in which all or none are participants. It is the achievement of democracy, and nothing else, which is, in Habermas's phrase, the unfinished project of modernity.

Notes

1. In his writings on the philosophy of history, "What is Enlightenment?" and "Perpetual Peace," Kant tried to establish an intrinsic relationship between progress and publicity. Before this could be established, however, competition and self-interest drove human beings together in a political order based on the rule of law, a republican constitution, and the consent of free and equal citizens. Once established, the constitution could be perfected by public criticism, in the form of open debate and a free press. Thus, Kant saw this second stage of progress as a self-reflective learning process made possible by the constitutional framework itself, which protected the conditions necessary for public criticism and opinion. Publicity can then become both the goal and the basis of the process of the progressive realization of human freedom. Kant simply assumed that reason and social learning could make political institutions more and more transparent; he never doubted the power of reason to dominate and control inner and outer nature. Habermas wants to give a much more complex and differentiated account of progress through this process of self-reflective social learning, incorporating an essential moment of the critique of ideology as a check on public irrationality entirely absent in Kant.

2. Democracy now faces new charges of irrationality, in a debate sparked by William Riker's attempt to prove the rational superiority of the limited notion of democracy in an elitist version of liberalism; he uses the formal means of rational choice theory to show the irrational results of voting; see Riker (1982). Riker's views are not unlike those of the German theorists Carl Schmitt and Arnold Gehlen, who had very ambivalent political allegiances. For responses, see Coleman and Ferejohn (1986) and Cohen (1986).

3. Joshua Cohen provides an epistemic interpretation of voting, which in many ways approximates Habermas's view of democratic discourse. Such an epistemic view of voting has three elements, and where Cohen mentions voting we might substitute "democratic processes of communication and deliberation": "(1) an independent standard of correct decisions—that is an account of justice or of the common good that is independent of the current consensus and the outcomes of votes; (2) a cognitive account of voting—that is the view that voting expresses beliefs about what the correct policies are according to the independent standard, not personal preferences for the policies; and (3) an account of decision-making as a process of the adjustment of beliefs, adjustments that are undertaken in part in light of the evidence about the correct answer that is provided by the beliefs of others" (Cohen 1986: 34). Habermas gives an epistemic account of democratic participation more generally, according to a model of the egalitarian structure of communication and the collective character of discursive rationality; both supply standards which are independent of the current de facto consensus; they could enable reflective participants to judge the competence and the legitimacy of their agreements. Another way to put it, closer to Habermas's own concepts, is that he provides an epistemic account of legitimacy as the cognitive act of the recognition of the worthiness of belief in any political order; democracy is essentially the institutionalization of these general, normative conditions, which permit moral and collective autonomy.

4. These criticisms of Kant are developed at greater length in the editors' introduction to *After Philosophy* (Baynes et al. 1986: 3–5).

5. Klaus Eder (1985) uses Habermas's categories of social learning and rationality to analyze the political phenomenon of fascism.

6. The Enlightenment philosopher Condorcet, who saw all progress on the model of the accumulation of scientific knowledge, was one of the first to use the theory of probability to solve what is now called the "jury problem" (Black 1958).

References

Baynes, Kenneth, James Bohman and Thomas McCarthy (eds.). 1986. *After Philosophy.* Cambridge, Mass.: MIT Press.

Black, Duncan. 1958. *The Theory of Committees and Elections.* Cambridge: Cambridge University Press.

Cohen, Joshua. 1986. An epistemic conception of democracy. *Ethics* 97: 26–38.

Cohen, Joshua, and Joel Rodgers. 1983. *On Democracy.* New York: Penguin Press.

Coleman, Jules, and John Ferejohn. 1986. Democracy and social choice. *Ethics* 97: 26–38.

Durkheim, Emile. 1933. *Rules of Sociological Method.* New York: Free Press.

Eder, Klaus. 1985. *Geschichte als Lernprozess? Zur Pathogenese Politischer Modernität in Deutschland.* Frankfurt: Suhrkamp.

Habermas, Jürgen. 1962. *Strukturwandel der Öffentlichkeit.* Darmstadt: Luchterhand.

———. 1970. *Towards a Rational Society.* Boston: Beacon Press.

———. 1971. *Knowledge and Human Interests.* Boston: Beacon Press.

———. 1973a. *Theory and Practice.* Boston: Beacon Press.

———. 1973b. *Kultur und Kritik.* Frankfurt: Suhrkamp.

———. 1975a. *Legitimation Crisis.* Boston: Beacon Press.

———. 1975b. A Postscript to Knowledge and Human Interests. *Philosophy of the Social Sciences* 3: 157–189.

———. 1979. *Communication and the Evolution of Society.* Boston: Beacon Press.

———. 1982. *Theorie des kommunikativen Handelns,* Vol. 2. Frankfurt: Suhrkamp.

_____. 1984a. *Theory of Communicative Action,* Vol. 1. Boston: Beacon Press.

_____. 1984b. *Vorstudien und Ergänzungen zur Theorie des kommunikativen Handelns.* Frankfurt: Suhrkamp.

_____. 1985. *Philosophischer Diskurs der Moderne.* Frankfurt: Suhrkamp.

_____. 1986. The New Obscurity. *Philosophy and Social Criticism* 11: 1–18.

Horkheimer, Max. 1972. *Critical Theory.* New York: Continuum Press.

Kohlberg, Lawrence. 1981. *Essays on Moral Development.* Berkeley: University of California Press.

Marx, Karl. 1977. *Selected Writings,* ed. by D. McLellan. Oxford: Oxford University Press.

Mead, George Herbert. 1934. *On Social Psychology.* Chicago: University of Chicago Press.

Offe, Claus. 1985. *Disorganized Capitalism.* Cambridge, Mass.: MIT Press.

Piaget, Jean. 1950. *Introduction à l'Epistémologie Génétique.* Paris: Presses Universitaires de France.

Riker, William. 1982. *Liberalism Against Populism: A Confrontation Between the Theory of Democracy and the Theory of Social Choice.* San Francisco: Freeman.

Selmen, Robert. 1980. *The Growth of Interpersonal Understanding.* New York: Academic Publishers.

Walzer, Michael. 1970. *Obligations.* Cambridge, Mass.: Harvard University Press.

Williams, Bernard. 1985. *Ethics and the Limits of Philosophy.* Cambridge, Mass.: Harvard University Press.

13

The Infernal Recurrence of the Same: Nietzsche and Foucault on Knowledge and Power

Harry Redner

Incipit Zarathustra: reenter Nietzsche after a long eclipse. All the signs are there of a second coming of this anti-Christ. His resurrection has begun in France; his epiphany is being witnessed in America; now his native Germany is preparing itself for his return in power and might.

Why has Nietzsche chosen this particular historical moment to make a comeback? Or putting it more simply, what makes his philosophy so relevant to our time? Perhaps the French case is most instructive in this respect. The new French wave, the intellectual avant garde of the 1960s and 1970s, was not initiated by a revival of Nietzsche; Marx and Freud came first. But from its inception the recovery of Nietzsche was heralded by Deleuze's new interpretation published in 1962. Foucault himself taught Nietzsche extensively at that time, though little of this influence made itself felt in his early writings. The earlier exponents of the intellectual avant garde—Lacan, Althusser and Barthes—had little truck with Nietzsche, but for the later ones, the so-called post-structuralists, as Foucault said, "Nietzsche's contemporary presence is increasingly important." He went on to spell out the importance of Nietzsche:

> If I wanted to be pretentious, I would use 'the genealogy of morals' as the general title of what I am doing. It was Nietzsche who specified the power relation as the general focus, shall we say, of philosophical discourse—whereas for Marx it was the production relation. Nietzsche is the philosopher of power, a philosopher who managed to think of power without having to confine himself within a political theory to do so. (PK: 53)[1]

The theme of power beyond the confines of politics that Foucault invokes is above all that of power in relation to knowledge. This theme has also been raised by most of the other later-day disciples of Nietzsche. Habermas (1981), one of Nietzsche's contemporary opponents, has scornfully applied the term post-modernist to all these thinkers. Habermas perhaps does not fully realize to what extent these so-called post-modernists are really hyper-modernists, for they drive certain themes of modernity to their utmost; in Foucault's case it is the theme of the identity of knowledge and power. In this, Foucault and the others reach back to Nietzsche, for whom the reduction of knowledge to power was a cardinal principle. Bacon was the first to have said that knowledge is power but Nietzsche really meant it. With that move he inaugurated a radically modernist epistemology. Thus Nietzsche, one of the fathers of modernism, is now at the same time a forefather of post-modernism. As modernism recalls and repeats its origins it becomes post-modernism, a paradox which will become clearer as we proceed.

Foucault's main purpose in reasserting the identity of knowledge and power is once again to take up Nietzsche's attack on the modern epistemological view of knowledge as based on representation. In fact, the philosophy of representation in all its forms and wherever it is to be found, whether in science or politics or art, was one of Nietzsche's main targets and it has since become a central focus of criticism for the post-modernists. Representation was not named and addressed explicitly by Nietzsche, as it is by his followers today; it was there nevertheless in the background to many of his destructive endeavors. Nietzsche's devastating critique of the subject-object relation (the basic terms of the representative theory of knowledge), of democratic parliamentarism or political representation, and of representation as verisimilitude or realism and expression in art makes him the first and still the most potent of anti-representational thinkers. Marx and Freud were still largely situated within the representational mode of thought. This mode of thought typified all bourgeois symbolic forms, though its origins are earlier than the rise of the bourgeoisie and it culminated in revolutionary movements that were hostile to what they called bourgeois ideology.

To understand what it is that Nietzsche and the post-modernists are attacking we must go back to its origins. If we overlook the earliest sources and look for a fully formed general symbolic system of representation, we find it first of all in Hobbes. Hobbes was the first thinker explicitly to relate the new theory of scientific knowledge and the new politics of the State under one term, representation. Objective knowledge is secured by means of sensory representations, which Locke, following Hobbes, was later to call ideas of sense, just as a secure realm is achieved by means of the supreme political representative, the Sovereign. Thus knowledge and power are placed under the one representational paradigm. This paradigm, later taken up by Locke and the French *philosophes*, eventually became the dominant symbolic form of the Enlightenment and later still of all nineteenth-century bourgeois thought and culture. It entered German philosophy under the name of

Vorstellung, the leading term in Kant and Schopenhauer. Positivist philosophy was dominated by it from the Idéologues to Wittgenstein's *Tractatus*, which declared itself to be a new philosophy of representation. Thus representation continued to play a leading role even in the very modernisms that turned against nineteenth-century bourgeois modes of philosophy, politics and art.

This is the paradigm that the post-modernists are so intent on eradicating, going back to Nietzsche for a way of relating knowledge and power that does not depend on representation either in science, politics, or art. Foucault (DP: 127) castigates the "theatre of representation"—punning on the French word which has the secondary meaning of performance, a play on words which is utilized by all the other post-modernists. Deleuze declares peremptorily that "representation no longer exists; there is only action" (LCP: 211). He goes on to contrast the bourgeois representative intellectual to "a theorizing intellectual [who], for us, is no longer a subject, a representing or representative consciousness" (ibid.). Barthes (1966) had already denounced bourgeois representation as verisimilitude or verismo in art even before these latest attacks. Derrida (1972), Lyotard (1974), and Attali (1985) all are opposed to representational thought and art and its associated realism and expressivism. Attali writing on music—where the representational paradigm was predominant from the early operatic *stile rappresentativo* till the close of the harmonic order in atonality—speaks of the "end of representation": "representation is becoming an anachronistic form of musical expression incompatible with the requirements of the capitalist economy" (Attali 1985: 83). Though by representation he means predominantly performance and tends to miss its more important symbolic meanings, he sees clear links between representation in music and politics. Art and power are as closely linked as knowledge and power in the new post-modernist thought.

In what follows we shall concentrate solely on Nietzsche and Foucault, overlooking these other no less significant thinkers. Our comparison between the early modernist and the post-modernist will be structured like a mirror of time showing how the latter reflects on the former and reflects him. The main focus for our own reflections will be the theme of the subject, both as this figures in the representational epistemology of the subject-object relation and in representational politics of the subject-sovereign relation. The play of subjection and subjectivity is one that Foucault particularly emphasizes; it is part of the bad "theatre of representation" on which he seeks to bring down the final curtain. This is what he means by his celebrated dictum of the death of Man which is to follow Nietzsche's death of God. But Nietzsche himself had already sought to destroy subjectivity and the subject-object epistemology; he had already shown how the subject or Ego arises as a fiction to meet the needs of outer subjections and inner repressions.

The deconstruction of subjectivity in both Nietzsche and Foucault is based on the common theme of power. Foucault's *pouvoir* is not the same as Nietzsche's *Wille zur Macht*. However, at many points, especially as social power, they come close together. The differences between these concepts of power are not to be minimized but it is the similarities that will be stressed as will the likeness between the two thinkers in general. The differences might be briefly mentioned as a preparation and warning that the two are not to be identified in any simple-minded way as master and follower. There are many Nietzschean ideas that Foucault either ignores or deliberately departs from. There is nothing in Foucault to take the place of Nietzsche's concept of nihilism and no general conception or eschatological interpretation of the history of the West. The concept of value and its various versions, as devaluation and revaluation, is nowhere in evidence. Hence there is no parallel in Foucault to Nietzsche's master and slave morality distinction. Indeed Foucault seems generally indifferent to morality and justice, declaring in an interview that he seeks "to question the social and moral distinction between the innocent and guilty . . . to obliterate the deep division that lies between innocence and guilt" (LCP: 227). In general Foucault's social and political concerns contrast strongly with Nietzsche's: the latter's aristocratic elitism is antithetical to the former's involvement with the revolt of the outcasts and outsiders. However, even beneath this wide disparity we shall discover an underlying common predisposition to a politics that can only be called anarchistic for want of a better word.

With that warning in mind let us now proceed with the comparison by outlining some predispositions and themes common to both thinkers, beginning with what might be called a rhetoric of war which characterizes both the discourse and conception of the world found in their work. This will serve as an introduction to their epistemology and politics which are subsumed under the discipline of war.

Alogos Polemos

War is the father of all things, sage Herakleitus said. But Nietzsche went one better: war is all things and all things are war. Everything is struggle, conflict, overcoming, domination, incorporation, seizing and comprehension (*greifen* and *begreifen*). In short, everything is will to war which is the same as saying it is will to power. "War is indispensable" (HH s. 477); "war has always been the grand sagacity of every spirit" (TI: 21), said Nietzsche.

However, Herakleitus also said that throughout all the strife and flux there is a norm and order, a logos that binds and guides. This Nietzsche firmly denied, for the ebb and flow of the will to power that is the world follows no guidance, is bound by no norms or restraints, observes no limits. The world is a Dionysian world—will to power unlimited and unrestrained. It is an unregulated play of forces, endlessly changing and forever the same, altering and repeating itself, "out of a play of contradictions back to the joy of concord, still affirming itself in this uniformity of its courses and its years . . . this my Dionysian world of the eternally self-creating, the eternally self-destroying" (WP s. 550). Everything in this world is equally inherently unbounded and unconstrained, for all things strive to become more than they are by incorporating whatever they are not, by absorbing anything that does not resist. This is why all things are at war and are a war.

The Nietzschean discourse is suffused with a vocabulary of polemic full of military and political terms: overcoming, conquest, overturning, appropriation, absorption, struggle, discipline and strategy. This rhetoric of war is itself a crucial strategy in Nietzsche's battle against the traditions of Western metaphysics, epistemology, morals and politics. The strategy works by using the rhetoric of war to subvert and destroy all fundamental terms arising out of the ordering distinctions and categorial classifications of philosophic thought. Nietzsche sees "all events, all motion, all becoming, as a determination of degrees and relations of force, as a *struggle*" (WP s. 552). Thus there are no fundamental distinctions or identities since all is a matter of degree or quantity and no two such are ever exactly the same. Where other philosophers saw basic oppositions, Nietzsche sees only positions along a scale of power, varying quanta of will to power. Where other philosophers asserted basic identities, Nietzsche asserts only likenesses which it serves our purpose to treat as the same. Instead of the metaphysical opposition of Being and non-being there is only becoming; instead of reality and illusion there are only phenomena; instead of subject and object there are bodies; instead of truth and falsehood there are fictions; instead of right and wrong or good and evil there are values; instead of State and anarchy there is domination. And all of these Nietzschean positives—becoming, phenomena, bodies, fictions, values and domination—are only functions of will to power; none is autonomous or fundamental. And is will to power itself fundamental? Is it a substantive like the ether or energy of nineteenth-century physics, which clearly influenced Nietzsche's conception of will to power? Or is it merely a ground of differentiation as such contemporary interpreters as Deleuze make out? There is no need to press for an answer here or embark on fine points of Nietzsche disputation. It is enough simply to note the function this concept has in his discourse and what strategy of subversion it serves.

Nietzsche's philosophy—really a counter-metaphysics—is thus opposed to any past metaphysics in that it is neither monist nor dualist nor pluralist. It is a philosophy that sets up no oppositions; "there are no opposites: only from those of logic do we derive the concept of opposites—and falsely transfer it to things" (WP s. 552). Metaphysics arises out of "a faith in antithetical values" (BGE: 16). Instead of a metaphysics of antithesis Nietzsche develops a quasi-physics of quantification heavily influenced by the speculations of Boscovich—a quantum theory of power.

Following Boscovich, Nietzsche sees all bodies as centers of force and the whole "world may be thought of as a certain definite quantity of force and as a certain definite number of centers of force" (WP s. 1066). These centers of force are "quanta of power" which interact with each other, not as Boscovich would have it by a simple gravitational attraction and repulsion, but by means of a struggle utilizing all the strategies of war and politics. Each such quantum of power strives to become more than it is—this is its will to power—to grow and increase at the expense of other quanta of power. Where these entities are biological bodies exemplifying life, this will to power becomes a will to knowledge—a higher strategy of self-aggrandizement or self-enhancement.

Nietzsche's epistemology follows directly out of this quasi-physics or counter-metaphysics. Will to knowledge takes the form of perspectivism because "every center of force adopts a perspective toward the entire remainder, i.e., its own particular valuation, mode of action, and mode of resistance" (WP s. 567). Knowledge of this world is only "the viewpoint of utility in regard to the preservation and enhancement of the power of a certain species of animal" (ibid.). Such knowledge is always quantitative; qualitative differences are merely apparent, not real: "our 'knowing' limits itself to establishing quantities . . . quality is a perspective truth for *us;* not an 'in-itself'" (WP s. 563). And, furthermore, a perspectivism of knowledge is epistemology seen from the perspective of war and politics:

> Perspectivism is only a complex form of specificity. My idea is that every specific body strives to become master over all space and to extend its force (—its will to power:) and to thrust back all that resists its extension. But it continually encounters similar efforts on the part of other bodies and ends by coming to an arrangement ('union') with those of them that are sufficiently related to it: thus they then conspire together for power. And the process goes on. (WP s. 636)

So knowledge, too, is struggle and conciliation, or, in other words, it is politics by other means.

All the elements of Nietzsche's thought thus far outlined—the rhetoric of war, the denial of distinctions, quantification and perspectivism—are strategies for countering the opposed strategies of metaphysics in this psychomachia of Western thought. Here we shall concentrate especially on those that give rise to representation in knowledge and politics. The fundamental thought-strategy of Western metaphysics was always to postulate basic differences or antitheses and samenesses or identities and then set about mediating between them. In this way all philosophical systems developed. Nietzsche's counter-stroke is to deny any such fundamental differences or identities and thereby obviate the need for any mediation. This move blocks the possibility of erecting systems.

The two main traditional strategies of mediation can be called the mimetic and the representational. Mimetic mediation was the strategy utilized in the earlier metaphysical tradition prior to the Scientific Revolution and it best serves to mediate between identities, for it affirms the basic similitude or sameness of things. Mimesis or imitation and all its other variants, such as participation and emulation, were the mediating terms relating entities which were ultimately the same. As Morrison (1979) demonstrates, such strategies of mimetic mediation were prevalent in the work of Plato, Aristotle, and most subsequent metaphysics and theologies including those of the Renaissance virtuosi.

The reformers, especially Calvin, were among the first to break with mimesis and they began to form the opposed strategy of representation.

Between a fallen state of nature and humanity and the transcendent power of God as a *deus absconditus* there could be no mimetic relations of similitude or sharing; only symbolic representations could mediate between such diverse realms of being. From reformation theology the mediating strategy of representation entered epistemology, politics, and art. Between subject and object, the categorically diverse spheres of *res cogitans* and *res extensa*, mediation could only be by means of representations or sensations, ideas and volitions. Between the inner thoughts, passions and desires of one man and another there could be no direct access, only communication by means of mediating representations of signs and sounds or language, pictures and music. Between men in a state of nature and the same men in civil society there has to interpose a representative as sovereign. Thus piece by piece the whole representative paradigm was constituted as we find it in Hobbes and all later bourgeois thinkers.

Nietzsche implicitly destroyed this representational paradigm by denying the distinctions and categorial separations between which representations had to be inserted as mediators. According to Nietzsche the opposition of subject and object is a grammatical fiction or useful convention of language:

> It is not the antithesis of subject and object with which I am here concerned: I leave that distinction to the epistemologists who have remained entangled in the toils of grammar (popular metaphysics). It is still less the antithesis of 'thing in itself' and phenomenon, for we do not know enough to be entitled even *to make such a distinction*. (JW s. 354)

Hence there is no need to postulate representations (*Vorstellungen*) to make known objects or things in themselves to subjects. With that move the representative theory of knowledge and the correspondence theory of truth which is associated with it are dismissed as illusory projections of grammar into the nature of things. There are only perspectival phenomena, there is no objective reality to be represented; the phenomenal world is the only world, there is no true world behind it.

Side by side with the dismissal of representation in knowledge is the rejection of representation in politics. The State as supreme representative of the people and democracy and parliamentarism as representational institutions are shams that belie the real nature of ruling, that is, politics. Representation in politics is unnecessary because there is no need to mediate between an abstraction called the people or the will of all and an even higher abstraction called the sovereign or the general will, namely the State as conceived in representative theories of politics. Politics is a matter of ruling, which is a struggle for power, a social war to determine domination by the few and submission by the many. Groups and individuals that are politically active engage in this war utilizing all the strategies and tactics of battle; they seek alliances if too weak to dominate on their own, they practice policies of balance of power, they resort to ploys and stratagems. Thus both politics and epistemology resolve themselves into struggles for power which take the form of war at different levels of existence—knowledge is a war of perspectives, politics is a civil war.

Unlike the present post-modernists, Nietzsche did not directly address himself to representation or formulate an explicit critique of it. Nevertheless, it can be shown that this is implicit in what he was doing. Thus his epistemology is a denial of subjectivity and objectivity and so *ipso facto* of representation. There are no subjects or objects as understood in philosophy; there are only bodies, some more complexly organized and subtly adjusted to their environment than others. Biological bodies such as human animals come to conceive of themselves as subjects by postulating a coherent Ego or self-identical consciousness as standing behind the welter of phenomena that their bodies register, most of which necessarily remain unconscious. With the dissolution of the subject, the object goes as well:

> If we give up the effective subject, we also give up the object upon which effects are produced. Duration, identity with itself, being are inherent neither in that which is called subject nor in that which is called object: they are complexes of events apparently durable in comparison with other complexes— e.g., through the difference in tempo of the event (rest-motion, firm-loose: opposites that do not exist in themselves and that actually express only variations in degree that from a certain perspective appear to be opposites . . .)
>
> If we give up the concepts 'subject' and 'object,' then also the concept 'substance'—and as a consequence also the various modifications of it, e.g., 'matter,' 'spirit,' and other hypothetical entities, 'the eternity and immutability of matter,' etc., we have got rid of materiality. (WP s. 552)

If there are no subjects and no objects, if subjectivity and objectivity are unreal, then knowledge cannot be a matter of a subject coming to know an object by means of mediating representations. Epistemology as traditionally conceived is defunct. Instead Nietzsche proposes his view of knowledge as perspectivism and phenomenalism couched in the rhetoric of war. To know is to grasp or conceive, that is, to seize and appropriate. Anything known is comprehended by an interested party, ultimately a center of force, from its own limited point of view and for its own ends. Thus knowledge is a way of serving the needs and furthering the interests of the knower, whose being is enhanced and power expanded. For this purpose beings that pursue knowledge fashion tools and devices of knowledge of which the key ones are language, concepts and values, the rational norms of logic and eventually those of science. The Nietzschean epistemology is summarized by Foucault in a few steps which are worth quoting in full because they reveal the full extent to which these thinkers agree on the relation between knowledge and power:

> —knowledge is an 'invention' behind which lies something completely different from itself: the play of instincts, impulses, desires, fear, and the will to appropriate. Knowledge is produced on the stage where these elements struggle against each other; —its production is not the effect of their harmony or joyful equilibrium, but of their hatred, of their questionable and provisional com-

promise, and the fragile truce that they are always prepared to betray. It is not a faculty, but an event or, at the very least, a series of events; —knowledge is always in bondage, dependent and interested (not in itself, but to those things capable of involving an instinct or the instincts that dominate it); — and if it gives itself as the knowledge of truth, it is because it produces truth through the play of a primary and always reconstituted falsification, which erects the distinction between truth and falsehood. (LCP: 202–3)

Nietzsche and Foucault both adhere to what might be called an *epistémé polemike* which is inherently political in a larger sense. The epistemic credo to which they subscribe might be succinctly expressed as follows: there is no knowledge but power, and truth is its special kind of error.

Just as Nietzsche's epistemology is political so is his politics epistemic— these two spheres mirror each other. As in the anatomy of the world and our knowledge of it, so in politics and society there are no fundamental oppositions or antitheses, no absolute terms—all is supply, degree, position and relation. Social differences must be established through inculcating a "pathos of distance"; as the noble Kent puts it to the upstart Oswald: "I will teach thee differences." The social aim is to "establish distance, but create no antitheses. Dissolve the *intermediate forms* and reduce their influence" (WP s. 891). By "preserving distances" it will be possible to set up an order of rank which will be a natural social order. When antitheses do arise this is a sign of nihilism: "opposites replace natural degrees and ranks . . . [they] suit a plebeian age because [they are] easier to comprehend" (WP s. 37).

If there are no basic opposites or contrasts in society as in the world in general or in our knowledge of it, there is equally no need for "intermediate forms" or mediation through representation. The classical contrast between State and civil society disappears and with it the need for representatives and representative institutions. The latter are scorned as "parliamentarism, that is to say, the public permission to choose between five main political opinions" (JW s. 144); the former are mocked by reinvoking the generic theatrical sense of representation: "is it not necessary for him who wants to move the multitude to give a stage representation of himself? Has he not first to translate himself into the grotesquely obvious, and then *set forth* his whole personality and cause in that vulgarized and simplified fashion?" (JW s. 236). The State, Hobbes's Leviathan, that "coldest of all cold monsters" (Z: 75), is destined soon to be destroyed and disappear. The last stages have already been reached, "modern democracy is the historical form of the decay of the State" (HH: 472). The whole system of representative democracy, manhood suffrage, creeds of equality, party politics, liberalism, socialism and nationalism—all this is mere preparation for a new kind of tyranny.

However, Nietzsche welcomes the leveling effect of representative democracy and its associated doctrines, for it reduces all but the few exceptional natures to the common herd and prepares them for "a new slavery" (JW s. 377). On the leveled mass of the herd will strut the new masters, "men who like ourselves love danger, war and adventure . . . [we who] count ourselves among the conquerors" (ibid.). "The free man is a warrior" (TI: 38) who "needs the opposition of the masses, of the 'levelled,' a feeling of distance from them! He stands on them, he lives off them. This higher form of autocracy is that of the future" (WP s. 866). Politics will thus regain its primeval simplicity as a domination of the conquered by the conquerors. This is how the State arose in the first place: "it had begun with an act of violence, had to be brought to a conclusion by a series of violent acts, the earliest commonwealth constituted a terrible despotism, a ruthless, oppressive machinery for not only kneeding and suppling a brutish pop- ulation, but actually shaping it" (GM: 219). It was a matter of conquest, not contract, and it functioned by command, not consensus; and so it shall be again in the future when the wheel of history turns full circle.

Since a future "dominating race can grow up only out of terrible and violent beginnings" (WP s. 868), it is an unremitting age of wars that Nietzsche both prophesies and urges: "we have entered upon the *classical age of war*, war at the same time scientific and popular, on the grandest scale (as regards means, talents and discipline) to which all coming mil- lenniums will look back with envy and awe as a work of perfection" (JW s. 362). We have, indeed, had world wars but it is doubtful whether future millennia will look back with envy, and if there is another such war, future millennia might not look back at all. Nietzsche, however, was optimistic that a future barbarism of war was all to the good. "Where are the *barbarians* of the twentieth century?" (WP s. 868), he asked. History was not slow in answering; we have seen them and know that they do not constitute "a species with *classical* taste" (ibid.).

For Nietzsche all this—war, conquest, the rule of a master race, the future lords of the earth, supermen leaders and great legislators—is the stuff of Great Politics; the petty politics of representation and managing a State he leaves to scurvy politicians and demagogues. If one were to seek for a label to characterize this theory of politics, one could not find it among the classical terms of political discourse. Perhaps the paradoxical formula "au- thoritarian anarchism" captures something of its contradictory simplicity. Although Nietzsche was contemptuous of the anarchists of his day—"the anarchist as the mouthpiece of declining strata of society" (TI s. 34)—his views were the negative image of theirs. The abolition of the State, of representative institutions and delegated powers, of constitutionalism and law, or, in short, of politics as commonly practiced and understood constitutes a species of anarchism, though the authoritarianism of caste domination is foreign to the anarchistic tradition. As we shall soon see, Foucault shares with Nietzsche an anti-statist, antinomian outlook that is also anarchistic, yet in his case virulently anti-authoritarian and anti-elitist. Nevertheless, the basic epistemological premises from which Foucault's politics is derived are similar to Nietzsche's.

Epistémé Polemike

Foucault takes up Nietzsche's fallen standard of war but raises it to contest, not the mastery of the earth or the domination and interpretation of the world, but that of history and knowledge. "I believe one's point of reference should not be to the great model of language (*langue*) and signs but to that of war and battle. The history which bears and determines us has the form of war rather than that of language: relations of power, not relations of 'meaning'" (PK: 114). Thus for Foucault, as for Nietzsche, war is indispensable, apparently language is not. "From this follows a refusal of analyses couched in terms of the symbolic field or the domain of signifying structures, and a recourse to analyses in terms of the genealogy of relations of force, strategic developments and tactics" (ibid.). Power and war come before meaning and signification. "History has no 'meaning' . . . [but is] susceptible of analysis down to the smallest detail—but this in accordance with the intelligibility of struggles, of strategies, of tactics" (ibid.). In Foucault, as in Nietzsche, power is a *polemos* without a *logos*: "we should analyze [power] primarily in terms of *struggle, conflict* and *war* . . . power is war, a war continued by other means" (PK: 90).

Despite their common rhetoric of war it is not the case that Foucault's *pouvoir* is the same as Nietzsche's *Wille zur Macht*. Foucault did not generalize power as a world-power present in nature as much as in life and society. He left the development of the quasi-physical and counter-metaphysical dimensions of power to his colleague Deleuze, confining himself solely to power as a human and social manifestation. In his late work he deliberately distances his conception of power from Nietzsche's and even from Deleuze's. "Clearly it is necessary to be a nominalist: power is not an institution, a structure, or a certain force with which certain people are endowed; it is the name given to a complex strategic relation in a given society" (HS: 123). In an even later essay he tries to purge his conception of power as far as possible of any Nietzschean connotation:

> The exercise of power is not simply a relationship between partners, individual or collective; it is a way in which certain actions modify others. Which is to say, of course, that something called Power, with or without a capital letter, which is assumed to exist universally in a concentrated or diffused form, does not exist. Power exists only when it is put into action, even if, of course, it is integrated into a disparate field of possibilities brought to bear upon permanent structures. (SP: 219)

In a rather surprising recourse to a Habermasian tripartite distinction of three modes of social relations, power figures as distinct from relations of communication, or language, and objective capacities, or finalized activities. Insofar as he insists that power relations are not simply an aspect of the other modes, it seems to follow that the others are not aspects of power either. This irreducibility of communication and technical capacities to power is hardly in keeping with a Nietzschean standpoint. Nevertheless, in the rest of the article Foucault does retain a Nietzschean rhetoric of war with a strong emphasis on strategy and what he calls "agonism," or the constant persistence of struggle.

Despite this late theoretical departure from a Nietzschean standpoint, it is clear that his earlier middle-period work was much closer to a Nietzschean ubiquity of power. Especially in his work on prisons, discipline, and sexuality, he did try to analyze all social and psychological phenomena in terms of power. Not only knowledge and truth are functions of power, of a *volonté de savoir*, but so are subjectivity, sexuality, even individuality and all other human constants that masquerade as human nature or Man. As he puts it in an interview, "we have had sexuality since the eighteenth century, and sex since the nineteenth. What we had before that was no doubt the flesh" (PK: 211). Sexuality he refers to as an "apparatus" which has a "strategic function" in society. It is one of a number of apparatuses which constitute "an anatomo-politics of the human body" (HS: 139) and which he calls "disciplines" or "techniques of power." Those that arose in the seventeenth and eighteenth centuries, his so-called classical age, are of particular importance since they underpin the formal institutions of the State and of capitalism: "the rudiments of anatomo- and bio-politics, created in the eighteenth century as *techniques* of power present at every level of the social body and utilized by very diverse institutions (the family and the army, schools and police, individual medicine and the administration of collective bodies), operated in the sphere of economic processes, their development and the forces working to sustain them" (ibid.: 141). As he puts it in quasi-Freudian terms, "the investment of the body, its valorization and the distributive management of its forces were at the time indispensable" (ibid.).

Both Nietzsche and Foucault view the body in power terms and in terms of the bio-politics of discipline. In a thought-provoking recent article, so far the only one on Nietzsche and Foucault, Scott Lash explores the overlaps and divergencies of the two thinkers on the issue of the body. He states that "on a number of counts Nietzsche and Foucault are engaged on the same enterprise. For both of them discourse (values) exerts power over bodies. . . . For both, one important effect of such powers of discourse is to individuate, to 'invent subjects,' which are attached, so to speak, to bodies" (Lash 1984: 14). Lash focuses particularly on Foucault's extended treatment of Nietzsche in the essay "Nietzsche, Genealogy, History" (LCP: 134–164). Rather foolishly Lash accuses Foucault of falling in with Nietzsche's biologist and even racist ideas of bodily descent and so of offering a "genealogy of bodies" rather than a genealogy of morals (Lash 1984: 4). Clearly, Foucault is simply paraphrasing Nietzsche rather than expressing his own views. Foucault should be faulted for ascribing to Nietzsche the ideas of Deleuze, as in the following passage: "the body is the inscribed surface of events (traced by language and dissolved by ideas), the locus of a dissociated Self (adopting the illusion of a substantial unity), and a volume in perpetual disintegration" (LCP: 30). This is prose itself adopting the "deleusions" of insubstantial disunity that have little to do with Nietzsche. Although he avoids the more fanciful "derridadaisms," some of Foucault's treatment of Nietzsche is marred by an anachronistic grafting of the latest literary and somewhat flowery symbolist and *art nouveau* motifs onto the solider and sturdier stock of Nietzsche's original, largely biologically inspired, ideas.

Lash, proceeding from a basic Marxist point of view, lays the predictable charges that Foucault's treatment of the body leads to a "bodily passivity, a pessimistic vision of agency" and rather surprisingly asserts that in Foucault "resistances are rarely constructed, struggles are not engaged" (Lash 1984: 3). Nietzsche in turn is praised for an activist approach to the body and criticized for his biologism. Lash fails to consider the contrasting approaches that Nietzsche and Foucault take to discipline or how power acts on the body. Nietzsche is committed to a bio-politics of severity and even harshness— "from the military school of life" (TI: 23)—as he himself insists; Foucault is, by contrast, committed to the overthrow of all disciplines, and so by implication to the laxness of an unrestrained body pleasing itself as it wills. In this contrast lies the root source from which their political differences arise, as we shall see.

Foucault is at his most Nietzschean in relating knowledge and truth to power. He seeks to elicit the various struggles, techniques and mechanisms of discourse by which power constitutes knowledge held to be true, or what he calls a "regime of truth":

> 'Truth' is linked in a circular relation with systems of power which produce and sustain it, and to effects of power which it induces and which extend it. . . . It is not a matter of emancipating truth from every system of power (which would be a chimera, for truth is already power) but of detaching the power of truth from the forms of hegemony, social, economic and cultural, within which it operates at the present time. The political question, to sum up, is not error, illusion, alienated consciousness or ideology; it is truth itself. Hence the importance of Nietzsche. (PK: 133)

In thus reaching for Nietzsche, Foucault is deliberately letting go of Marx. He outrages the Marxian objectivist conception of scientific truth by speaking of the "political, economic, institutional regime of the production of truth" (ibid.). Despite this he resorts to Marxian economic metaphors to account for the production of truth. Truth is literally produced by "a system of ordered procedures for the production, regulation, distribution, circulation and operation of statements" (ibid.). Truth as the outcome of dialogue and debate, of discourse in the ordinary sense, is nowhere in evidence in Foucault.

These are formulations from the late period, but retrospectively Foucault also interprets his earlier work in neo-Nietzschean terms. "When I think back now, I ask myself what else it was that I was talking about, in *Madness and Civilization* or *The Birth of the Clinic*, but power? Yet I'm perfectly aware that I scarcely ever used the word and never had such a field of analyses at my disposal" (PK: 115). Indeed, not even his major work, *The Order of*

Things, contains any inkling of his later epistemology of power. The key terms in that work are *epistémé*, discourse, positivities and the historical *a priori*. Later he reinterprets these terms by reference to his power concept of the "apparatus": "strategies of relations of forces supporting, and supported by, types of knowledge" (PK: 196). He maintains that "an apparatus is a much more general case of the *epistémé*, or rather, that the *epistémé* is a specifically *discursive* apparatus, whereas the apparatus in general form is both discursive and non-discursive, its elements being much more hetero-geneous" (ibid.: 197).

However, as early as *The Order of Things* Foucault already began his critique of representation and subjectivity that would eventually bring him so much closer to Nietzsche and unfold one of the great thematics of post-modernist thought. In that work Foucault uses the term "representation" in a historically restricted sense, ascribing it merely to what he calls the classical *epistémé* from the seventeenth to the late eighteenth centuries. At the later date the limits of representation were reached as the classical *epistémé* dissolved to give way to the modern. Thus he mistakenly asserts that representation no longer functioned in modern knowledge after the later eighteenth century when "words, classes and wealth acquire a mode of being no longer compatible with that of representation" (OT: 221). In his latest writings he was to depart implicitly from this misconception and to realize that the theory of the subject and humanism in general is still bound up with representation; as he declares, "representation constitutes the subject" (LCP: 222).

Not only is Foucault's surmise about the conclusion of representation mistaken, so is his account of its origins. He completely fails to explore the historical sources of the classical idea of representation which in its political sense goes back to the Church councils of the late Roman period and in its epistemological sense is strongly influenced by Calvinist theology, espe-cially by his eucharistic doctrine of how the bread and wine represent the body of Christ. As other historians have noted, Foucault's procrustean bed of discrete *epistémés* cuts off the heads and feet of more extended bodies of cultural developments. Furthermore, by focusing solely on the classical theory of signs, according to which in order to signify, one idea must represent another, he completely overlooks the paradigmatic sense of rep-resentation according to which the representation mediates between subject and object. Without this representational epistemology there would be no ideas to represent other ideas; so in classical discourse representation as signification is always secondary to representation as knowledge or per-ception. It is not true that "classical philosophy, from Malebranche to the Idéologues, was through and through a philosophy of the sign" (OT: 66). It was primarily a philosophy of knowledge and only by extension a philosophy of the sign. Malebranche and Berkeley, on whom Foucault concentrates, are exceptional in that they treat the sensory idea as a sign from God, not as the impression of an object as do Hobbes, Locke, and Descartes.

Foucault comes closer to understanding the general paradigm of representation—in its relation to the subject and object and in its epistemological and political bearing at once—in his occasional remarks on Hobbes in sundry places. Hobbes, as we have shown, was the leading exponent of a general conception of representation, one which subsequently developed into the basic form of Enlightenment thought that underlay both bourgeois and revolutionary culture and practice in the nineteenth century. Foucault hints at but does not seriously explore the complexities of representation when in reference to Hobbes's *Leviathan* he speaks of "the myriad of bodies which are constituted as peripheral *subjects* as a result of the effects of power" (PK: 98). His own project to deconstitute subjectivity and show that it is the product of subjection is thus "the exact opposite of Hobbes's project in *Leviathan*" (ibid.: 97). Elsewhere he states that "the theory of the subject (in the double sense of the word) is at the heart of humanism" (LCP: 222). He sets about to attack this subject by a "desubjectification of the will to power (that is, through political struggle in the context of class warfare) or by the destruction of the subject as a pseudosovereign (that is, through an attack on 'culture': the suppression of taboos and the limitations and divisions imposed upon the sexes; the setting up of communes; the loosening of inhibitions with regard to drugs; the breaking of all the prohibitions that form and guide the development of the normal individual)" (ibid.). Thus the attack on the subject is partly in support of an anarchistic counter-cultural political movement which we shall further elaborate.

In speaking of "the subject as a pseudosovereign" Foucault seeks in a rather confused manner to link subjectivity and sovereignty via Hobbes's *Leviathan* and also via the contract and property provisions of Roman law. The identification of subject and sovereign was first suggested to him by his analysis of Velazquez's "Las Meninas" in *The Order of Things*. The king who is the invisible subject of representation in the picture figures as the absent subject-sovereign of the classical *epistémé* (OT: 308). Foucault extrapolates forward from this pictorial emblem to the rise of modern subjectivity—the emergence of the subject-king—and eventually also backward: "from the beginning of Roman law—the armature of our civilization that exists as a definition of individuality as subjected sovereignty" (LCP: 222). Since Roman law has neither any conception of representation nor sovereignty nor subjectivity, it follows that Foucault's anachronistic projection backwards of such notions is sheer fanciful word play. There is more justification in applying these ideas to Hobbes; so Foucault states, in countering the constitution of the sovereign-subject: "rather than ask ourselves how the sovereign appears to us in his lofty isolation, we should try to discover how it is that subjects are gradually, progressively, really and materially constituted through a multiplicity of organisms, forces, energies, materials, desires, thoughts, etc." (PK: 97). But this misidentification of the subject with the sovereign, suggested by the painting, is most unfortunate since in Hobbes and elsewhere in representational thought the sovereign is the representative, not the subject. The sovereign holds in politics an analogous place to ideas and thoughts in epistemology—corresponding to the representations, not to the subject that receives and apprehends these.

The demolition of subjectivity and the representational scheme that Foucault undertakes is not as easy as he imagines. His own thinking is fraught with all the errors to which we have averred: emblematic pictorial imaging, historical *allodoxia*, and anachronism and fanciful word play. He continues his skirmish with representation in *Discipline and Punish* but instead of an all-out undirected onslaught he takes aim on specific points with better accuracy. He seems at least to have implicitly realized that sovereignty and subjectivity are mutually supportive in the representational paradigm, not identical: "although, in a formal way, the representative regime makes it possible, directly or indirectly, with or without delays, for the will of all to form the fundamental authority of sovereignty, the disciplines provide, at the base, a guarantee of the submission of forces and bodies" (DP: 222), that is, subjectivity. The sovereign, as supreme representative, confronts the subject, as represented, just as ideas of sense confront the knowing subject; the place of the object or nature is taken in the political system by the state of nature or man prior to becoming the subject. Foucault shows convincingly that the legal and penal systems, as well as most other disciplines, were through and through determined by representation: "the art of punishing, then, must rest on a whole technology of representation" (DP: 104).

Where exactly did the penalty apply its pressure, gain control of the individual? Representations: the representations of his interests, the representations of his advantages and disadvantages, pleasure and displeasure; and if the punishment happens to seize the body, to apply techniques to it that are little short of torture, it is because it is—for the condemned man and for the spectators— an object of representation. By what instruments did one act on the representations? Other representations, or rather coupling of ideas. (DP: 128)

The political system of representation was the most crucial one because it made possible all the others: "historically, the process by which the bourgeoisie became in the course of the eighteenth century the politically dominant class was marked by the establishment of an explicit, coded and formally egalitarian juridical framework, made possible by the organization of a parliamentary, representative regime" (DP: 222).

It is this representative regime still in existence in Western democracies— formally almost unchanged, though largely evacuated of its original content— that Foucault seeks to undermine intellectually and eventually to overthrow by insurrection. That is the quasi-revolutionary political strategy of his attack on the State. This attack is motivated by the inverse concerns when compared to Nietzsche's analogous onslaught on the State, though the intent is the same. Nietzsche accused the liberal-democratic State of having become lax in allowing too much license to the herd and its mobs; Foucault, by contrast, sees it as too disciplined, too much given to surveillance and control of individuals. Foucault's disciplines are very different from Nietzsche's disciplines, yet at the same time both approaches to politics, the disciplinarian and undisciplined, have an underlying common basis in that they are both at some level anarchistic. Foucault uses this term explicitly for his own political campaigns, these "are anarchistic struggles" (SP: 211). Foucault's anarchism, as contrasted with Nietzsche's, is extremely libertarian, for all the causes Foucault espouses involve the lifting of prohibitions, mainly those conducive to the ultra-leftist counter-cultural "liberation movements," above all those of the sexual revolution. Bourdieu (1984: xii) draws an explicit parallel between French "ultra-leftism" and American "sixties camp." Hence it is not inappropriate to raise the question to what extent this most ruthless attempt at a critique of ideologies is itself the expression of a "camp culture." Though this is obviously an aspect of Foucault's thought that cannot be disregarded, to treat his work solely in this light is unduly dismissive, as it would be to regard it as the ideology of the lumpenproletariat which in fact Foucault also supported (PK: 23).

Foucault's counter-cultural prescription for doing as one pleases is the opposite of Nietzsche's harsh regime of severity in its attitude to law and morality. Foucault is antinomian and genuinely anti-moral, if not immoral: Nietzsche's immoralism only applies to exceptional individuals at a time of decadent slave morality; in a future society severe laws and moralities will be the means used to mould a new personality type. Foucault speaks out against any legal system and against justice of an organized kind: "re-employing a form like that of the court, with all that is implied in it—the third party place of the judge, reference to a law or to impartiality, effective sentencing—must also be subject to very rigorous criticism" (PK: 36). The only kind of court Foucault will countenance is a kangaroo court performing "acts of popular justice" (ibid.). He wishes to obliterate the distinction between innocence and guilt, good and evil, "to attack an institution at the point where it culminates and reveals itself in a simple and basic ideology, in the notions of good and evil, innocence and guilt" (LCP: 228). As against all existing social forms, "the rough outline of a future society is supplied by the recent experiences with drugs, sex, communes, other forms of consciousness, and other forms of individuality" (LCP: 231).

Thus Nietzsche's Great Politics of apocalyptic wars and master races is counterposed by Foucault's petty politics of the de-institutionalization of society—macro-power as contrasted to micro-power. However, both are anti-statist and in some fundamental sense anarchistic or anti-political. Neither has a grasp of the realities of political power despite their advocacy of a more grandiose conception of power. Nietzsche's actual political influence was disastrous; in Foucault's case, it is doubtful whether he will have any effect on politics for good or ill. Nietzsche's general intellectual, artistic, and cultural influence was profound; Foucault's thought, too, might have an impact in unusual places and in odd ways unforeseeable now. Just so, the present revival of Nietzsche's work has occurred in a surprising context and in ways that would have seemed incredible a few decades ago.

The Second Coming

Nietzsche has returned, thrown up by the new wave of French post-modernists. His second coming is at hand. Who is this rough beast slouching to Bethlehem to be born? What does its pitiless gaze and rhetoric of war presage? Is it anarchy or mere anarchism that is loosed upon the world? Why is it that the center cannot hold and de-centering is upon us? Is it that "man is to be erased, like a face drawn in sand at the edge of the sea"? Is the dawn of a new post-humanist thought about to light up? Or is it simply more of the same, another recurrence of the identical, an old familiar face returning from the past? Or worse still, is it the same infernal idea once again?

Putting it in less grandiloquent terms, so beloved of the post-modernists, the question is simply this: what is the intellectual and cultural meaning of the revival of one of the founding fathers of modernist thought? What is the significance of this historical moment when modernism begins to recall its own origins and to repeat itself? Being subject to such revivals, does this indicate that modernism is itself now merely historical? Is this the real meaning of post-modernism? Is this why post-modernism is also a kind of hyper-modernism, a modernism attempting to go one better than itself, to multiply itself by itself? Modernism squared equals post-modernism—is this the correct historical equation?

To answer some of the above questions let us once more briefly interrogate these ancestral voices prophesying war. To the extent that the rhetoric of war and discourse of power are not to be taken simply as modes of anthropomorphic thinking designed to promote a new mythology—and to some extent, as for example in Nietzsche's conception of "this my Dionysian world," they are certainly that—they are strategies of destruction directed against the traditional languages of Western philosophy. Nietzsche's and Foucault's main thrust is critical and negative and is intended to overthrow all fundamental entities and basic assumptions. They aim to tear down the pillars supporting traditional thought—the representational paradigm pre-eminently—so as to bring down the whole temple of God and Man or metaphysics and humanism. Are they, like Samson, eyeless in Gaza, out of rancor bringing ruination on their own heads as well? Or are they razing the old temple of representation so as to raise in its place a new temple of power? The answer to these questions depends on how crucial one considers the continuation of such classic Western thought forms as the representational paradigm; or alternatively, whether one believes the rhetoric of war and the discourse of power capable of creating new thought forms. In what follows it will be argued that the former cannot be any longer maintained in its traditional guise, but the latter is not capable of supplanting it and providing an alternative. We must seek for a thought form that goes beyond both of these mutually negating antagonists.

We shall first try to show that the rhetoric of war and discourse of power are self-defeating in their conception of knowledge. Knowledge conceived of as a weapon of war in a battle of discourses and ideologies is a sword that cuts both ways. If both sides to a dispute look on the knowledge they dispose of as weapons in the attack and defense of interests that lie outside knowledge, then the two forms of knowledge cancel each other out and what results is sheer oppugnancy, liable to move beyond knowledge, discourse and even speech into wordless violence and real war. The rhetoric of war and discourse of power insofar as they are intended as weapons to defend one kind of knowledge against another will inevitably be opposed by other intellectual weapons to attack the knowledge they defend. Hence, unless there is something more to knowledge than its use as an instrument of attack and defense, knowledge ceases to be able to function as knowledge. Paradoxically, it then becomes useless for attack or defense which it can only provide if it is granted its status as knowledge prior to its use as a weapon.

All knowledge entails discourse in more senses than Foucault is willing to entertain; discourse is also discussion, debate, and dialectic, namely, discourse as speech. Discourse and speech in general presuppose provisional areas of agreement without which the disagreements being contested would be unstatable. Without agreement as to the words used there could be no language; without agreement as to the presuppositions and assumptions according to which language is to be used there can be no discussion; without agreement as to the terms of the discussion there can be no debate; without agreement as to how a debate is to proceed and be resolved there can be no common knowledge; and without agreement about common knowledge there can be neither science nor politics, nor any other higher form of knowledge. Sheer difference without agreement in one form or another is impossible at any of these stages. Once there is agreement at some level unlimited difference becomes possible. Any such agreement is in itself never absolute; it is merely provisional, valid at least for the duration of the debate. It can always itself come into question as part of another debate or in the course of a debate that questions its own assumptions. Agreement as to the meaning of words might be indispensable as would agreement about the commonly accepted judgments or basic assumptions but it can always lapse as the meanings of words are disputed and altered, as judgments are revised and as assumptions are abandoned. But such revisionary discourse can itself only proceed on the basis of other agreements. For spoken or unspoken, explicit or tacit, in words or deeds, there must always be agreement in some sense for discourse to be possible.

In their rhetoric of war and discourse of power Nietzsche and Foucault do not allow for such provisional areas of agreement. As a result their view of knowledge is self-canceling and liable to reduce knowledge to something that is no longer knowledge and discourse, to something non-discursive— leading potentially beyond speech into the arena of violence. Other thinkers have stressed as crucial to knowledge this element of agreement, commonality, consensus or shared assumption, above all Wittgenstein, Collingwood, Arendt, Polanyi, and Habermas. There are other difficulties with their views of knowledge, but at least on this point they have proved themselves more perceptive than Nietzsche and Foucault.

Once the need for agreement is recognized most of the paradoxical consequences flowing from the rhetoric of war and discourse of power are also mitigated. Terms like truth and reality can return with something like their traditional force. For what is provisionally agreed on or adhered to is considered a truth and a truth pertains to something real. Of course, truth and reality are always themselves also provisional and subject to future revision and change; but at any one point in a discourse something must be accepted as true and real in order for the discourse to proceed. If everything were merely degrees of falsehood, as Nietzsche maintains, then everything would be in doubt and there would be no basis for an investigation to be undertaken to resolve the real doubts. For such an investigation to proceed, whether in ordinary practical matters or in science, it is essential that not everything be doubted at once and that some things be granted the status of truth.

Something analogous holds also for the main terms deriving from the representational paradigm: subject, object, and representation. These terms can no longer be given the original meaning that they held within the older epistemologies and the forms of thought which they upheld. Subjectivity can no longer mean the unquestionable presence of a pure self-certifying Ego, of a consciousness totally self-conscious and self-identical or of a *Geist* unfolding itself in self-determined stages; objectivity cannot mean a *res extensa*, sheer materiality or a thing-in-itself beyond the veil of phenomena; representation cannot be a perspicuous medium or "glassy essence," as Rorty dubs it, that brings the other two together without itself having any part in determining them. However, concepts of subjectivity, objectivity, and representation, provided they are given a sense different from that traditionally obtaining in the representational paradigm, are essential in any account of knowledge. To explain fully why this must be so is to give an account of knowledge which is beyond both the representational paradigm and the rhetoric of war and beyond the scope of this chapter. Nevertheless for the sake of argument the following brief sketch is offered.

Just as agreement in language is essential for discourse, so agreement in reference is required for knowledge. Without the possibility of asserting the identity of something perceived in different ways from different points of view, or referred to in different statements, or recognized by different aspects or features, there could be no knowledge. It can be shown that what is so identified must be an object or something objectively real such as a higher order object: for example, the battles and states of history, the electrons and galaxies of science and the phonemes and syntactical forms of linguistics. Any such real object is more than a so-called object of grammar or object of discourse or intentional object and it certainly cannot be considered a fiction or construct. For unlike artificial objects, real objects can never be exhausted by what we know of them, by the perceptions or statements or identifying criteria by which we recognize them. A real object is always capable of revealing new and unexpected facets of itself, some of which inevitably falsify what we have previously believed of it. The point of carrying out experiments is to elicit something from an object that cannot be deduced from its concept or established *a priori* in any other way; and the results of experiments are frequently surprising and unexpected. This is why knowledge of real objects is never complete but potentially unending and why only such objects can provide scientific knowledge. In this respect there is infinity in a grain of sand, eternity in an hour. Anything which is exhaustible and can be completely comprehended is by definition not a real object for it is not capable of eliciting new empirical knowledge, only the secondary knowledge we have of our own constructs.

A real object is not, however, totally independent of our mode of knowing it or describing it; it is not an absolutely autonomous external entity or thing-in-itself as the representational paradigm would have it. An object can only be identified, demarcated, described and so known within a certain mode of representation. Considered in itself apart from any such mode of apprehension, the object has no reality; it is literally nothing. Thus in that sense the mode of representation does enter into the constitution of objects but without constructing them solely by its own devices. The language in terms of which we conceive of objects is like the style of art in terms of which objects are drawn—the drawing could not exist without the lines, but the latter do not of themselves constitute the object depicted. Insofar as objects are facts, there are facts which are more than just interpretations, the inverse of Nietzsche's assertion is in fact true (WP s. 530). And insofar as knowledge is knowledge of objects, as is scientific knowledge, it follows that knowledge cannot be simply manufactured by processes of statement combination, rarification or condensation or any of the other mechanisms of knowledge production set out by Foucault in *The Archeology of Knowledge*. Depicted in this fashion the production of knowledge is like a factory operating without raw materials; the labor, machinery and power might be active but there is nothing to engage them in real work; it is a purely idle show.

What we have established of the object is in a parallel way true of the subject. Subjectivity is also a reference point enabling the identity of individuals and other higher order subjects to be established. The actions, perceptions, thoughts, passions, inclinations and other characteristics of people require to be identified in terms of an enduring and relatively self-consistent subject. This subject can be divided against itself in all the numerous ways that psychiatry has revealed in psychoses, but it cannot be so scattered that there is no way of establishing any personal identity whatever. The ways available of establishing individual identity are also the ways in which the subject is represented; hence the subject, like the object, is not totally independent of given modes of representation. However, the subject, like the object, is not exhausted by the representations made of it. There is always more to a person than what is known or described. Hence the subject cannot be merely the outcome of language, or some function of the use of the pronoun "I" in discourse. Even fictitious subjects, such as the characters in plays and novels, when they are realistic and not mere cyphers of the author's imagination, are always more than the author conceives them to be; they have an independent life outside the control of their creator and sometimes they can assert themselves against the authorial intention. *Pace* Foucault, the author has a presence in his or her work which is not just a function of the text and relates both to the whole opus and to its real world historical context.

In the context of a discussion of knowledge and power it is important to stress that the subject of the higher forms of knowledge, such as science, is not the mere individual but a socially organized complex of individuals constituting a scientific establishment, a research society and ultimately a historical tradition of research. Hence this complex epistemological subject is socially mediated and itself an academic-political entity. However, the kind of mediation which constitutes scientific knowledge is much more complicated and indirect than Hobbes as the exponent of the representational paradigm or Foucault as its critic assumes. There is no immediate and direct parallel between the individual subject and the political subject. The representational paradigm which views both in terms of the schema of subject, object and mediating representation is simply imposing the same set of formal terms on a very different relation. Foucault, who believes that the individual subject is somehow constituted through political subjection and subjectivization, seeks to make the relation historically and sociologically more telling but in the last resort can be seen to be simply playing on words. There is no such direct relation between the individual subject and the political subject—after all, the individual was there before the state which subjected him or her to its rule. Yet it is not altogether far-fetched to see the communal epistemological subject, the scientific society, and the political subject or citizenry of a developed state as historically related precisely because the representational paradigm provided, as it were, the symbolic system or ideological superstructure for constituting both. The rise of modern science and the modern state in its absolutist form were closely linked historical phenomena. But that does not mean that there is a simple relation between them. Science and politics or knowledge and power are linked, not in any reflective fashion, but through the social workings of both.

Society—working through culture and language, symbolic systems and discourses, institutions and practices of power—does provide the mediating relation between the knowledge of a given epoch and its politics but only in a very indirect fashion, different for each case considered. Yet short of such a specific and detailed historical consideration there is no other way of relating knowledge and power. Each major scientific dispensation, whether in the ancient world, in China, in post-Reformation Europe, or now in the contemporary world, has its own power features and a distinct way of integrating itself in the socio-political order. In *The Ends of Science* (1987) I sought to show how the contemporary relation of science and politics is essentially different from that of any previous epoch.

In an analogous way this is also the manner in which subject and object are related, for what mediates between them is the representation, understood not as a simple reflection, an impression or idea of sense, but as the whole system of symbolic rendering—such as a language, a cultural discourse or a scientific practice. The representation is not a single, separable, discrete atomistic item, as conceived by the philosophers of the representational paradigm, but always part of a complex symbolic system that is socially determined and maintained; it does not belong to the individual subject alone. This is why the sociologist of science Ludwik Fleck (1979: 158) asserts that "between subject and object there exists a third thing, the community. It is creative like the subject, refractory like the object, and dangerous like an elemental power." Even a single perception of an object by a subject entails a mediating representation that is the outcome of the social system which conditions perceptual abilities and determines how things are to be demarcated and identified.

It follows from this account that there are no absolute separations between subject, object, and representation. Each is a function of the others. Thus language as the primary system of representation plays a crucial part in constituting subjects and objects, which at a human level of knowledge acquisition could not be conceived apart from language. From this it does not follow that subject and object are language constructs or that there is nothing apart from power, interpretation and values. For language in turn cannot be conceived apart from subjects and objects; there is no such thing as an autonomous semantic and syntactic system, one that is indifferent to how individuals interact socially and jointly act on the objects that they identify in their environment. Wittgenstein's conception of the language game is meant to highlight just this aspect of language as a praxis. Subject, object, and mediating system of representation are three poles or inescapable aspects of any language game or any mode of human knowledge. They are three functions or analytically separable positions, which does not mean that they are absolutely distinct and substantially separate entities as the representational paradigm demands. Futhermore any item can alter its functional position so that what is subjective in relation to one kind of knowledge can be objective in the context of another and what is representational can also figure as either subjective or objective. But these are complexities that cannot be elaborated further.

Enough has been said in this brief concluding outline to suggest a need to get beyond the opposition of the traditional representational paradigm and the avant garde modernist and post-modernist attacks on it through the rhetoric of war and the discourse of power. Were such an alternative account to succeed, it would have consequences both for knowledge and power, for science and politics. It would offer a way of relating these that might be better suited to the needs of our time than either the now defunct representational conventions or the dangers of knowledge instrumentalism and political anarchism of Nietzsche and Foucault.

Notes

1. References to Foucault's and Nietzsche's standard works have been abbreviated as indicated in the reference list. Section numbers are prefixed by s.

References

Attali, Jacques. 1985. *Noise: the Political Economy of Music*, trans. by B. Massumi. Manchester: Manchester University Press.
Barthes, Roland. 1966. Introduction to the structural analysis of narratives. In S. Sontag (ed.), *A Barthes Reader*. New York: Hill and Wang [1982].
Bourdieu, Pierre. 1984. *Distinction: a Social Critique of the Judgement of Taste*, trans. by R. Nice. London: Routledge and Kegan Paul.
Deleuze, Giles. 1962. *Nietzsche et la Philosophie*. Paris: Presses Universitaires de France.
Derrida, Jacques. 1972. White Mythology. In *Margins of Philosophy*, trans. by A. Bass. Chicago: The University of Chicago Press [1982].
Fleck, Ludwik. 1979. *Genesis and Development of a Scientific Fact*, trans. by T. Bradley and T. J. Trenn. Chicago: The University of Chicago Press.
Foucault, Michel. [OT]. 1970. *The Order of Things*. London: Tavistock Publications.
――――. [LCP]. 1977. *Language, Counter-Memory, Practice*, ed. by Donald F. Bouchard. Ithaca: Cornell University Press.
――――. [DP]. 1979. *Discipline and Punish: The Birth of the Prison*, trans. by A. Sheridan. New York: Vintage Books.
――――. [HS]. 1980. *The History of Sexuality*, Vol. 1, trans. by R. Hurley. New York: Vintage Books.
――――. [PK]. 1980. *Power/Knowledge: Selected Interviews and Other Writings*, ed. by Colin Gordon. New York: Pantheon Books.
――――. [SP]. 1982. The subject and power. Afterword in H. L. Dreyfus and P. Rabinow, *Michel Foucault, Beyond Structuralism and Hermeneutics*. Brighton: Harvester Press.
Habermas, Jürgen. 1981. Modernity versus postmodernity. *New German Critique*, Winter [1981].
Lash, Scott. 1984. Genealogy and the body: Foucault/Deleuze/Nietzsche. *Theory, Culture and Society* 2(2).
Lyotard, Jean-François. 1974. Adorno as devil. *Telos*, Spring [1974].
Morrison, Karl. 1979. *The Mimetic Tradition of Reform in the West*. Princeton: Princeton University Press.
Nietzsche, Friedrich. [GM]. 1956. *The Genealogy of Morals*, trans. by F. Golffing. New York: Doubleday.
――――. [Z]. 1961. *Thus Spoke Zarathustra*, trans. by R. J. Hollingdale. Harmondsworth: Penguin.
――――. [TI]. 1968. *Twilight of the Idols*, trans. by R. J. Hollingdale. Harmondsworth: Penguin.
――――. [WP]. 1968. *The Will to Power*, ed. by Walter Kaufmann. New York: Vintage Books.
――――. [JW]. 1973. *Joyful Wisdom*, trans. by T. Common. New York: Ungar.
――――. [BGE]. 1973. *Beyond Good and Evil*, trans. by R. J. Hollingdale. Harmondsworth: Penguin.

_____. [HH]. 1986. *Human, All Too Human,* trans. by R. J. Hollingdale. Cambridge: Cambridge University Press.

Redner, Harry. 1982. *In The Beginning was the Deed.* Berkeley: University of California Press.

_____. 1987. *The Ends of Science: an Essay in Scientific Authority.* Boulder, Colo.: Westview Press.

14
Fundamental Ontology and Political Interlude: Heidegger as Rector of the University of Freiburg

István M. Fehér

In April 1933 Heidegger assumed the rectorate of the University of Freiburg. The months following constitute the only period of his life—one which did not abound in dramatic events or spectacular changes—which gave rise to vehement reactions and sharp criticisms for reasons other than the philosophical views which Heidegger put forward. A university professor's getting elected rector is, to be sure, not an event which requires special attention: it is well within the limits of a normal academic career. It was, however, at an extremely delicate moment, a few months after Hitler's appointment as chancellor, that Heidegger took over this office—and this, of course, is not without importance. What are the reasons which led Heidegger to assume this office, and what prior judgments about the era underlie his decision? And more akin to the concerns of this book, is this decision connected with his philosophy, and if so, how?

In what follows, an attempt will be made, first, to sketch Heidegger's basic philosophical outlook leading up to, and as elaborated in, *Being and Time*, concentrating on those tenets which can be shown to have some bearing upon his political involvement. This preliminary analysis will be followed by a reconstruction of Heidegger's conduct during his period as rector. I think that his activity as rector should be explored against the background of his philosophical outlook and of concrete historical circumstances, rather than stripped of (both philosophical and historical) context and judged by extrinsic criteria—that is, mainly by reference to what the social movement (national socialism) to which he temporarily committed himself subsequently became.

I. Heidegger's Philosophical Outlook by the End of the 1920s

I.1.

One might briefly characterize Heidegger's fundamental philosophical efforts leading up, after more than ten years' silence, to the publication of *Being and Time* in 1927—as found, e.g., in his lectures of the period, now gradually appearing in the *Gesamtausgabe*—as an attempt to unify the so-called irrationalistic or "existentialist" or "historicist" problematic which permeated post-war European culture (and was represented by thinkers like Kierkegaard, Nietzsche, Jaspers, Spengler, Dilthey, and Simmel) with the Husserlian ideal of "philosophy as strict science" (and, thereby, through Husserl, with the whole epistemological-metaphysical tradition going back to Aristotle and the Greeks).

Brought up in the scholastic tradition, but extremely responsive to the contemporary logical-epistemological ways of philosophizing represented by neo-Kantianism and phenomenology, Heidegger had as early as his doctoral dissertation and his *Habilitationsschrift* (published in 1914 and 1916, respectively) hoped to pose the Being-question, viz., to renew the metaphysical tradition.[1] His appropriation of the modern logical-epistemological tradition is conditioned from the very beginning by his endeavor to arrive at metaphysical conclusions; doing pure logic, epistemology or methodology, indispensable though it may be as a preparatory step, is seen by him as futile when conceived as an aim in itself.[2] His gradually deepening acquaintance with Husserl's phenomenological method provides him, in addition to theoretical insights, with a new access to classical philosophical texts, especially those of Aristotle and the Greeks.[3] His intense studies of the philosophical tradition as well as of modern philosophical trends thus become fused within a perspective which does not separate systematic and historical points of view. From this perspective, traditional doctrines no longer appear as mere relics worthy of only antiquarian interest, as opposed to the theoretical validity possessed by contemporary doctrines. Rather, traditional tenets are seen both as illuminating modern theories and as illuminated by them, and contemporary positions as proceeding from earlier ones.[4] Historical interest, in this sense, is strictly connected to systematic interest—indeed is at the service of it. Only if history is not "pure history"—that is, a heap of past and dead facts—will the history of philosophy regain its relevance for systematic thinking (cf. GA 1: 195ff., and later GA 61: 110f., GA 24: 31f.).

This point is important for our present purposes, not only because it sheds light on some of the presuppositions of Heidegger's first philosophical attempts, but because we need to realize that the *systematic* positing and working out of the Being-question proposed in *Being and Time* [5] rests upon a preliminary confrontation with the tradition. This point has become clearer since the publication of some of Heidegger's Marburg lectures. Further,

Heidegger's way of approaching the history of philosophy already contains a conception of history implicitly—one to be thematized explicitly in *Being and Time*, and particularly relevant to his engagement with politics. Studying modern logical or epistemological theories in order to use them for metaphysical purposes meant, for Heidegger, recognizing the fact that such theories are not exempt from metaphysical presuppositions.[6] Nor, inversely, can metaphysical or ontological theories be exempt from logical or epistemological presuppositions; that is, from more or less explicit assumptions concerning human thinking or knowing—in short, from a theory of man as a rational animal (see e.g., GA 20: 174). The insights into the metaphysic-ladenness of the logical-epistemological tradition and into the logic-ladenness of traditional ontology may be said to be the two basic, and reciprocal, results of Heidegger's early confrontation with, and appropriation of, Western philosophy. The necessity of positing the Being-question as the question to be asked first and foremost is derived, for Heidegger, from the highly paradoxical result of his confrontation with Husserl's phenomenology (the most advanced transcendentally oriented epistemology of the day). Indeed, Husserl, though claiming to suspend or bracket "assertions concerning being," cannot help committing himself to certain prior ontological distinctions, in particular, that between Being as consciousness and transcendent being—which Husserl himself called, symptomatically, "the most radical of all distinctions of Being" (Husserl 1976: 159). This prior commitment is left completely unthematized, having been antiphenomenologically (that is, dogmatically) assumed (see GA 20: 157f., 178). If the claim to dispense with the Being-question is thus shown to be a pure illusion, necessarily presupposing a dogmatic prior answer to it, exempt from and unsusceptible to any kind of critical examination (or, in other words, if dispensing with it turns out to be equivalent to answering it without first posing it), then the situation seems simple enough: what is needed is to explicitly pose or thematize this first and foremost question of all philosophy. In the light of the recognition, however, that traditional ontology is from its very beginning grounded in, or centered around, the doctrine of *logos*, i.e., logic,[7] an uncritical natural recourse to any kind of traditional ontological perspective must be out of the question. It even remains uncertain if the Being-question, lacking a prior ground in which to be embedded, can be posed at all.[8]

The way out of this impasse was suggested to Heidegger by his insight into the strict correlation between being and *logos* in Western philosophy—more concretely, by an ontological thematization of logic, of the theoretical-cognitive attitude or comportment [Einstellung] in the broadest sense. Heidegger's starting points were (1) the correlation of being and *logos* in the history of philosophy; (2) the functioning of the *logos* of the "subject" as the "ground" or "place" of the ontological problematic properly so-called; and (3) logic as the theoretical comportment *par excellence*. Thus he was able to thematize the *being* of the subject in a deeper way than that provided by the tradition—one capable of showing the very epistemological comportment as a derived mode of being. This offered a possible operative basis for the positing and working out of the Being-question. The metaphysical tradition from Aristotle onward had gained its access to Being from within the conceptual horizon provided by the theoretical attitude, giving thereby rise to theories of Being in terms of objective presence. That this comportment was far from being *the* original mode of being of human existence was, however, an insight which required the prior unification of the Husserlian perspective of philosophy "as strict science" with the "anti-metaphysical," "existentialist" tradition.[9] Contrary, however, to the tendency of thinkers like Pascal, Kierkegaard, Dilthey, and Nietzsche to combine a turning *to* factual-historical human existence with a turning *away from* metaphysics, and thus totally to reject systematic thinking, Heidegger's appropriation of the problematic of factual-historical life was conceived from the very beginning as a starting point *for* the renewal of metaphysics. The posing and working out of the Being-question pertains to what Heidegger calls fundamental ontology. As the above considerations suggest, this becomes embedded in, and begins with, a thematization of the *being* of the subject—a discipline named existential analytic.[10] The immanent critique and internal radicalization of phenomenology and epistemology, and the attempt at a radical re-examination of the whole metaphysical tradition through the assimilation of the "irrationalistic" problematic, are fused in Heidegger's effort to gain a new ground for the Being-question.[11]

I.2.

Man's[12] fundamental mode of being, Heidegger claims in *Being and Time*, is Being-in-the-world. His original relation to things emerging in his environment is one of using, handling, employing, arranging rather than "knowing" them. These are modes which presuppose antecedent acquaintance, familiarity, with the world. Even "knowing" things is one way of having to do with or caring about the world—a comportment which comes about as a modification of man's original relating himself to things. A phenomenological description of man's primary way of being should, therefore, suspend, i.e., "put into brackets," scientific or epistemological concepts and strategies of description. Only thus will it be sufficiently original, sufficiently unaffected by traditional theories concerning the issue, and able to *derive* scientific comportment from man's primordial way of relating himself to his world. If, apart from and prior to any kind of self-description such as "the totality of foundational connections of true statements,"[13] science is primarily one of man's modes of being—"not the only and not the first possible mode of being" at that (SZ 11)—then existential analytic must not resort to the conceptual framework provided by science. To do so would imply losing the possibility of gaining a perspective upon it.

Without going into the details of Heidegger's description of Being-in-the-world, it may be relevant to see how the epistemological problematic, with which Heidegger had first engaged himself on his way to *Being and Time* and whose insufficiencies led him to assume an explicit ontological standpoint, is treated within the framework of the new ontological perspective.

Given his thesis that man's primordial mode of being is Being-in-the-world, Heidegger's treatment of the epistemological tradition from Descartes on has two major aspects: a negative, or polemic, one and a positive, or "integrating," one. As to the first, he shows that the epistemological perspective properly so-called (with its typical questions concerning the relation of the subject to the object, of mind to the world, the way the knower can acquire knowledge about the object) is not meaningful without a prior ontological dualism such that knower and known, subjects and objects are assumed to be two separate entities, their relation being one of mutual exclusion (subject is what is not object and vice versa). However, if man and world are not two independent entities, and human *Dasein* is not the worldless [weltlos] "subject" characteristic of modern philosophy, but is in itself worldly [weltlich], having always already committed itself to the world, then the ontological ground underlying the epistemological perspective becomes untenable.[14] Heidegger's attitude is negative or polemic in that he elaborates his concept of *Dasein* and Being-in-the-world by opposing them to, and challenging, the traditional concepts of "subject" and "object." He insists that Being-in-the-world, as *Dasein*'s fundamental mode of being, must not be conceived of as an epistemological relation between subject and object.

Having developed his concept of Being-in-the-world through a contrast with the subject-object relation, he is in a position to show how, in virtue of what modifications of Being-in-the-world as an all-encompassing phenomenon, man's *knowing* relation to the world springs. This may be called the positive, or integrating, aspect. Heidegger shows, in a series of analyses, that in order for a thing to become an object of knowledge or scientific research, our preliminary access to it, that is, our way of having to do with it, must have undergone a specific modification. Only as a result of this will the thing as tool originally made use of, or handled, reveal itself as a neutral substance, simply "out there," susceptible of being determined by what traditional philosophical theories have come to call "qualities" and "properties."

Heidegger illustrates his point with critiques of Descartes's conception of the world and of Kant's refutation of idealism. He shows that Descartes's definition of world in terms of *res extensa*, that is, a neutral, indifferent space filled up with equally neutral, homogeneous substance, fails, in the light of Heidegger's own analyses of "world," to do justice to the genuine phenomenon of world met with in everyday experience—indeed, is based upon losing sight of and forgetting it. This is the negative aspect of his treatment of Descartes. However, that definition of world reflects a theoretical-intellectual comportment to the world (itself one way of Being-in-the-world), one which presupposes that what the glance characteristic of mathematical knowledge discovers in things constitutes their *real* being (see SZ 95f.). This is the positive, or integrating, aspect.

As far as Kant's refutation of idealism is concerned, Heidegger first shows some of the inconsistencies inherent in Kant's proof of the existence of the outer world. Then, more significantly, he proceeds to undercut the very bases of Kant's undertaking, insisting that the quest for a proof of this sort is not meaningful unless one assumes the Cartesian standpoint of the isolated subject. Indeed, once man is assumed to be basically Being-in-the-world, the question of how a knowing subject can get out of its interiority in order to ascertain the existence of, and establish a contact with, the outside world— the major epistemological problem of modern philosophy—loses its legitimacy. Attempts to demonstrate the "reality" of the outer world, or for lack of such a demonstration the mere "belief" in or presupposition of such a world (comportments which are themselves definite ways of Being-*in*-the-world), do not make sense without the prior assumption of a subject closed in itself—a subject which, uncertain about its world, should begin by acquiring certainty about it. The question of whether or not there is a world, and whether its being can be proven, Heidegger remarks significantly, is without sense for human *Dasein* conceived as Being-in-the-world—and who else could pose it (SZ 202)? If there is a legitimate question, it concerns rather the reasons why *Dasein* as Being-in-the-world tends to sink, *erkenntnistheoretisch*, the "reality" of the outer world into nothing in order to produce, after splitting up the unified phenomenon, infinite hopeless attempts to put together the two wrecks left: the isolated subject and the outer "world" (SZ 206).[15]

The aspects of Heidegger's existential analytic singled out thus far show how Heidegger's own ontological perspective enables him to make visible the implicit ontological framework latent in traditional epistemological-metaphysical thinking. Traditional ontologies are shown to be rooted in *Dasein*'s ways of relating itself to its world. The analytic of *Dasein*, by proposing to illuminate deeper and more original dimensions of *Dasein*'s being, both criticizes or dismisses *and* integrates or "justifies" them (in the specific sense of revealing their condition of possibility).

I.3.

What remains to be seen is the way in which the irrationalistic or existentialist or historicist problematic, accompanied by a strong anti-metaphysical bias in the thinkers who gave rise to and defended it, joins in, and becomes an integral part of, Heidegger's systematic ontological perspective.

The question of how Heidegger's ontological treatment of the epistemological perspective within a neutral analysis of *Dasein* relates to a Kierkegaardian problematic of authenticity is not easy to answer. Arguing along the lines elaborated by Richard Rorty (see Rorty 1979: Ch. 8, especially 360ff.), it might be claimed that knowing the world is just one among many human projects of edification (not the primary one, Heidegger would add). It might then be suggested that it is because the project of knowing the world has traditionally been assumed to be *the* proper path to authenticity (an assumption congruent with the prevailing conception of man as a rational animal[16]) that authenticity, for the epistemological-metaphysical tradition from Descartes on, was not, and could not be, a problem. (It became a problem, symptomatically, only for non-metaphysical thinkers like Kierkegaard.) Because Heidegger sets out to get behind the view of man as a rational animal, it is natural that the problem of authenticity will become an explicit problem for him, one distinct from the problematic concerned with knowing. We might also say, using the terms of our previous description of Heidegger's way to the Being-question, that the neglect of the question of authenticity by the epistemological-metaphysical tradition is a matter of answering it without first having posed it.

The question concerning *Dasein*'s inclination to dissolve the outer world into nothing is answered by Heidegger by reference to man's basic tendency to *Verfallen*. This is an encompassing concept of inauthenticity, characterizing a tendency inherent in everyday *Dasein* to interpret the world and itself within the horizon of what turns up *within* the world, thus taking itself to be one among the entities existing alongside others in the world (cf. SZ 58). The possibility of *Verfallen* lies in the fact that *Dasein* as Being-in-the-world is always already alongside [bei] beings in the world. Indeed, because, as early as the Greeks, Being was interpreted in terms of beings in the world (cf. SZ 44), the concept of inauthenticity provides what we have been calling an integrating aspect. It does so by accounting for the failure of traditional ontologies to seize upon the ontological problematic proper—a major reason why Heidegger names his investigation "fundamental ontology."

Considerations concerning authenticity emerge basically in connection with the concept of *Being-with* [Mitsein]. The "existence" of other human beings is for Heidegger as unquestionable as that of the "outer" world. *Dasein*'s way of relating itself to others is called (parallel with, and contrary to, man's *Besorgen* with the things of his environment) *Fürsorge*, care for. This has, apart from the deficient and negative modes characteristic of everyday Being-with, two positive modes: "leaping in" and "leaping ahead" [Einspringen, Vorausspringen]. The first is characterized by taking the "care" over and away from the other, "leaping in" for him in order to do what constitutes the other's concern *for* him. The other may thereby become dependent and dominated. The second, by contrast, does not refer to the other's *Besorgen* with things. One "leaps ahead," not in order to disburden the other, but rather to give him back his authentic and primordial care, that is, his existence, thereby helping the other to become conscious of it and free for it (cf. SZ 122; for a fuller analysis see Elliston, 1978: 66ff.). Everyday Being-with, however, is characterized by *Dasein*'s losing itself in the faceless amorphous anonymity of the "One" [das Man]. Only therefrom can it pass to the authentic way of existing.

The full concept of authenticity is developed in the second division of *Being and Time*. Living originally in an inauthentic way, *Dasein* can reach authenticity only in Being-toward-death [Sein zum Tode] and resoluteness [Entschlossenheit]. The concept of authentic existence is often explained very crudely as something denoting an aristocratic detachment from, and a scornful contempt of, everyday life. A closer examination of the Heideggerian texts lets one dismiss this reading as wholly unfounded. Deriving as it does from inauthenticity, authentic existence remains forever bound to it: it is but the constant transition or passage from the inauthentic existence to the authentic, and not a kind of independent realm opposed to it. Authenticity, to put it briefly, consists in consciously setting a limit to one's manifold possibilities— seeing them against the background of one's ultimate possibility, that is, death. This resolution, once taken, is capable of transforming one's life into a whole and giving oneself selfhood [Ganzheit, Selbstheit]. The authentic project of Being-toward-death is then confirmed, on the part of the factually existing *Dasein*, by the phenomenon of conscience. *Dasein*'s proper response to the call is, first, to make itself ready for it, that is, to-want-to-have-conscience [Gewissen-haben-wollen], and second, resoluteness. Rather than eluding death by escaping into the anonymity of everydayness, authentic *Dasein* anticipates it; rather than averting the call of conscience, thereby precluding becoming *itself* and being responsible for what it is, *Dasein* resolutely assumes it. Both ways enable *Dasein* to be authentic [eigentlich], that is, to appropriate the being it already is. On a closer look, resolution turns out to be not only compatible with, but even requires, authentic Being-toward-death. If resolution arbitrarily varied, without a view to death as *Dasein*'s ultimate possibility, there could be no question of resolution being authentic (SZ 302, 305ff.; see Gelven, 1970: 176; Demske, 1963: 48f.; Ugazio, 1976: 48). The unified concept of authenticity is therefore anticipatory resoluteness [vorlaufende Entschlossenheit]. Resoluteness in its turn gives rise to "situation." The latter does not mean a set of conditions given in advance, but rather being revealed and disclosed only by and in resolute *Dasein* (cf. SZ 299f.). Authentic *Dasein* should nevertheless not persist rigidly in any one situation; it has to leave itself open for the possible, and indeed necessary, re-appropriation of itself. Since the relapse into the existential irresolution of *das Man* remains a constant possibility, it is only in repeating, retrieving itself that resolution is what it is (SZ 307f.).

For the full concept of authenticity to be arrived at, however, a further addition is needed. The question of what should fill in the "content" of resolution is, Heidegger repeatedly claims, no part of the existential analytic. It may be answered only by resolution itself. However it is legitimate to ask whence such possibilities may arise (SZ 294, 383). This origin is history. Resolute *Dasein* opens up its possibilities by taking upon itself a given heritage of the past—a heritage in which it resolutely hands itself down. Grasping its innermost finitude in anticipating death, *Dasein* is driven back to itself. In handing itself resolutely down in a freely chosen tradition, it acquires destiny [Schicksal]. Seen from the perspective of Being-with, authentic historicity reveals itself as the common destiny of a community [Geschick]—a community in which the destinies of individuals are pre-liminarily assigned their role (SZ 384). It is not necessary, Heidegger remarks, that *Dasein* should explicitly be aware of the origins of the possibilities upon which it projects itself. But there lies in it the possibility to derive its project (the "content" of its resolution) explicitly from a tradition. Resoluteness, coming back upon itself from fallenness and handing itself down consciously,

becomes then the repetition, or retrieval [Wiederholung] of an inherited
possibility of existence.[17] To "repeat" in this sense does not amount to
"make a piece of the past actual again," "bringing it back," but rather
"retorting," "replying" to a past possibility of existence (SZ 385f.).

II. Heidegger the Rector and His Philosophy

This short sketch of Heidegger's philosophical development, together with
a quick survey of the basic philosophical outlook of *Being and Time*,[18] puts
us in a position to proceed to our proper theme. We can now set about
answering our initial questions—above all, the question of how Heidegger's
assuming the office of the rectorate can be connected to his philosophy. In
doing so, we shall return to and single out some of the themes previously
touched upon, and occasionally thematize them in more detail.

II.1.

Authentic existence, as we have seen, was explained in *Being and Time*
in terms of anticipatory resoluteness. Coming back upon itself from the
world of inauthenticity characterized by the anonymity of *das Man*, resolute
Dasein does not become detached from the world. This would be impossible,
for *Dasein* is and remains Being-in-the-world all along (cf. SZ 298). Resoluteness implies, on the contrary, entering fully into the world, opening up
and projecting oneself upon the (finite) possibilities which offer themselves
in a given situation. It is in anticipating death, in becoming aware of what
it means *not* to be, that the awareness of what it means to be becomes
accessible. Although in anticipation and conscience *Dasein* becomes isolated,
deprived of all its (inauthentic) links (that is, it becomes precisely its own
self), nevertheless, in choosing itself, *Dasein* not only chooses itself "out
of" the world (to use Kierkegaard's illuminating terms), but at the same
time and in the fullest sense, chooses itself "back into" it (cf. Kierkegaard
1957: 265; see Chiodi 1965: 107; Guignon 1984: 337f.). It is also resoluteness
that makes authentic Being-with possible, permitting *Dasein* to let the others
"be" in and for their own being. Once free for its own possibilities, *Dasein*
is both free of the danger (inherent in its tendency to fallenness) of losing
sight of or ignoring others' possibilities—possibilities which may supersede
its own—and of the temptation to reduce them to, and thus take them to
be identical with, its own.[19] "Leaping ahead," as the authentic positive form
of Being-with, gains its full concreteness only in and by resoluteness. As
opposed to inauthentic *Dasein*'s tendency to disburdening [Entlastung], only
the willingness-to-have-conscience, the assumption of one's own being, makes
responsibility for oneself and others possible. Only resolute *Dasein* can
become the "conscience" of others (cf. SZ 122, 127f., 288, 298; see also
Demske, 1963: 66). The thesis that *Dasein* is always its own, that it exists
for its own sake, Heidegger says, does not imply egoism; the concept of
Dasein is not equivalent to that of the isolated, egoistic subject. Because
only in relating to itself can *Dasein* understand something like "self" [selbst],

only thereby can it listen to a "you-self" [Du-selbst], and thus make something like human community [Gemeinschaft] possible (GA 26: 244f.).

Anticipatory resoluteness, therefore, points to something like social activity, or engagement. However, the analysis of authenticity is not yet complete. The concept of resoluteness, as we have seen, attains its ultimate form as a result of the analysis of historicity. If resoluteness, at an earlier level, meant keeping itself free to *retrieve* itself [Wiederholen], then authentic existence appears now, at the level of historicity, as the retrieval of a historical heritage that has been both handed down and freely assumed—a heritage in which *Dasein* hands itself over (SZ 308, 383ff.). By freely and resolutely taking over a historical heritage, authentic existence acquires its destiny [Schicksal]. Authentic Being-with thereby becomes, at the level of history, a common fate [Geschick], a community of authentic people (SZ 384f.). It may even be said that it is only in and by *Wiederholung* that its own history reveals itself to *Dasein* (SZ 386).

II.2.

If the existential analytic (moving, according to its hermeneutic character, in a circle) is guided by a "presupposed" idea of existence, and if philosophy, for Heidegger, must not deny its own "presuppositions," but rather elaborate them together with that for which they are presuppositions (SZ 310), then it seems legitimate to examine whether, and to what extent, such an idea may be brought to bear upon the author of *Being and Time* himself.

If authentic existence consists in retrieving a historical heritage, then the philosopher's activity as one possible human activity, one way among others to relate oneself to the world, is authentic insofar as it aims at retrieving his own historical heritage—that is, the tradition of philosophy itself. It is easy to see that *Being and Time* should be understood from its very first pages in terms of an explicit attempt at bringing back the most original of all the traditions of philosophy, that is, the Being-question. (This retrieval of ontology—the latter being at the time a "condemned term" (SD 47)—is also a retrieval of Kant's *Critique of Pure Reason*.)[20] *Being and Time* tries to retrieve, to revive, the Being-question (or since the question itself has long sunk into oblivion, "awaken" an understanding of its meaning [SZ 1]) by inquiring into the horizon of traditional philosophies' access to Being (time, presence), and by showing this access to be rooted in and dependent upon *Dasein*'s theoretical comportment. Authentic retrieval is, therefore, not a blind attachment to the tradition, but rather the unfolding of a horizon within which the re-appropriation of traditional concepts becomes possible; the ontological transformation of phenomenology claims to be nothing less than "the retrieval . . . of the origins of our scientific philosophy" (cf. GA 20: 184, 187f.). When the early Heidegger speaks of the oblivion of the Being-question, of the forgottenness of being, what he has in mind is not the claim that the history of philosophy has completely ignored this most original of all its questions, but rather the contention that the tradition blindly took over and tied itself to the Greeks, taking up their concepts and then building them into petrified systems. These concepts were conserved and dragged along through the centuries without any effort at an original re-appropriation or renewal—concepts whose roots in lived experience (from which they once emerged) have indeed long withered away. The "destruction" proclaimed by Heidegger does not propose to set the tradition aside, to rule it out, but rather to re-appropriate it into a conceptual framework able to respond to today's lived experience.[21]

A retrieval or revival of the tradition must go back as far as the Greeks because the perspective of modern philosophy appears, taken by itself, rootless. Heidegger does not see modern philosophy as having brought about a decisive change or development, for its basic concepts are wholly penetrated by the structural elements of the traditional Greek-Christian outlook—an outlook that itself had by then become rootless (see e.g., SZ 22, 93, 96; GA 20: 179; GA 21: 13; GA 29/30: 52f., 64). These "pre-suppositions" underlying Heidegger's access to the history of philosophy, and his fundamental problem, are hardly conceivable without resting upon his direct experience of the ever more intensifying crisis of European culture and civilization.[22] The initial contention of *Being and Time* that traditional metaphysical concepts of man like "subject," "ego," "reason," "spirit," and "person" are ontologically unthematized and thus obscure (SZ 22) implies that these concepts have become vacant for everyday life, worn out and empty. Indeed, the concept of an "ideal subject," characteristic of transcendentally oriented epistemologies, is, as Heidegger unequivocally says later in the book, a *"phantastically idealized* subject." Such a subject fails to do justice to nothing less than the "a priori" of the "'factual' subject," that is, *Dasein* (SZ 229).[23] We are not, to be sure, provided with anything that might properly be called Heidegger's "criticism of society." Nevertheless, his occasional remarks, in the course of lectures, about the culture and philosophy of the age—remarks often amounting to informal quips—are very effective. It is worthwhile to dwell upon them in some detail.[24]

II.3.

First of all, as far as developments in German culture and philosophy during the second half of the nineteenth century are concerned, Heidegger is highly critical of the epistemological-*wissenschaftstheoretisch* turn typified by neo-Kantianism, considering it to be a sign of going astray, of perplexity and, in a sense, even of decadence (see GA 20: 17f., 20f.). The same judgment is expressed in even stronger terms during his debate with Cassirer in Davos, when he remarks that the genesis of neo-Kantianism is to be sought only "in the perplexity of philosophy concerning the question of what it properly is that in the whole of knowledge has been left for it" (KPM 246). After the human and natural sciences, around 1850, had monopolized the totality of what can be known [die Allheit des Erkennbaren], all that was left for philosophy was knowledge of science, not of beings. Neo-Kantianism then re-interpreted Kant too, transforming him into an epistemologist of the mathematical-physical sciences, and "between 1900 and 1910 Husserl himself in a certain sense fell victim to Neo-Kantianism" (KPM 247). The breakdown of German Idealism is considered by Heidegger to be an undisputable fact; but, as he puts it in 1935, the very expression "breakdown" [Zusammenbruch] amounts to a kind of shield, behind which the rise of superficiality [die schon anbrechende Geistlosigkeit] and the dissolution of the original spiritual forces are taking shelter. For it is not so much German Idealism that broke down, but rather it was the age that was no more able to be equal to the greatness and originality of its predecessors' achievements (EM 34f.; see also GA 32: 57; SA 7).

The following excursus in Heidegger's 1925–1926 lectures is characteristic. When neo-Kantianism, taking up Lotze's obscure and incoherent notion of validity [Geltung],[25] became a philosophy of values [Wertphilosophie],

> it was soon discovered that Kant had written three Critiques, which were supposed to have discussed the theoretical, the practical, and the aesthetic attitudes, and to refer respectively to these three kinds of values. Kant had, of course, had something to say about religion too, but unfortunately not in the form of a Critique; nevertheless, religion must also be secured a place within the system, so the value of the 'sacred' was discovered. This, for Windelband, is of course no autonomous value; to put forward a claim of this sort *circa* 1900 would be too risky. As the world, however, has become very religious since the war, and as with international associations of chemists and meteorologists, even world congresses are being organized, one might now run the risk of claiming that religion is also a value. Or, since it is impossible to leave it at that (the insights presumably grow deeper and deeper), one must say that God is also a value, and, for that matter the highest one. The latter thesis is an obvious blasphemy, surely not mitigated by the fact that theologians assert it as an utmost truth. All this would be highly comical, were it not deeply sad, showing as it does that philosophy no longer reflects upon the things and problems themselves [man nicht mehr aus den Sachen philosophiert], but upon the books of colleagues.[26]

It is not difficult to see that this cultural decadence and shallowness affected Heidegger deeply. Someone committed to the appropriation and creative transformation of the problems of the philosophical tradition would naturally be repelled by the "self-conceited modernity, fallen into barbarity," which pretends that Plato's questions "are settled" once for all (GA 24: 157; see also GA 29/30: 48). Husserl had already complained about "the sort of pseudo-philosophical literature [philosophische Scheinliteratur] . . . which nowadays pullulates so abundantly" (Husserl 1965: 47). He had also described the extent to which the social changes taking place in the late nineteenth and the early twentieth century, and the consequent prevalence of positivistic culture, were transforming the framework of academic life:

> The natural science departments of the philosophical faculties—he wrote in 1910—are now very persistent in their efforts to acquire professorships in philosophy [philosophische Professur] for researchers who may perhaps be

very eminent in their own fields, but have no more sense of philosophy than,
say, chemists or physicists. (Husserl 1965: 47)

The idea of renewing philosophy emerged in connection with considerations pertaining to *Weltanschauung* as early as Heidegger's *Habilitationsschrift* (cf. GA 1: 406ff.). Although the term "Weltanschauung," because
of abuse made of it at that time, does not turn up in his vocabulary,[27] it
is clear that, from the 1920s onward, his retrieval and reformulation of the
Being-question acquired its specific outlines against the background of more
or less explicit expectations of a social-spiritual regeneration. Husserl's
observations had shown the extent to which the development of science
and philosophy cannot be viewed as a simple linear unfolding of their
allegedly intrinsic character and potentialities, but is, instead, dependent
upon extrinsic circumstances, rooted in the historical-intellectual climate of
the age. Heidegger, much more susceptible to the central importance of
historicity than Husserl, had already remarked in the 1920s: "each philosophy
and each science has its own destiny, and it would be petty-minded [kleinlich
und bürgerlich] to think that we can abstract from the conditions which
direct the questions . . . of philosophy" (GA 21: 53; see also 280 and GA
20: 182). Awakening the Being-question in an attempt to retrieve the
philosophical tradition and to clarify the meaning of the question itself was
however just a preparatory step, and Heidegger was very early aware of
its limited (finite) possibilities.

In the inaugural lecture at Freiburg in 1929 Heidegger explicitly formulated
his view of the situation of the sciences:

> The fields of the sciences lie far apart. Their ways of treating their objects are
> fundamentally different. This disintegrated multiplicity of disciplines is held
> together only by the technical organization of universities and faculties, and
> through the practical direction of the disciplines. . . . The roots of the sciences
> in their essential ground have, however, withered away. (WM in GA 9: 104)

II.4.

Heidegger's taking over the rectorate in 1933 must thus be seen as
connected to his hope of finding a way out of the spiritual decadence, the
deep crisis convulsing the whole country. (It may be sufficient to think of
the economic crisis between 1929 and 1932, and of the masses of unemployed
whose number increased from two to six million during these years.) He
hoped for a popular-national revival, perhaps giving rise to a philosophical
renewal, that of the Being-question. Such a renewal would open up a new
historical epoch, no longer characterized by the forgottenness of being. Was
not such a hope unfounded, and indeed illusory? This (slightly pedantic)
question—to adopt a Heideggerian phrase—arrives too late. That certain
features of the renewal were from the very beginning critically assessed by
Heidegger is, as will immediately be seen, beyond doubt. As soon as these
features gain momentum and prove to have the upper hand, Heidegger will
resign, and finally pass into opposition.[28]

For many different sorts of intellectuals who had been critical of developments in Germany during the nineteenth and twentieth centuries—such as the malignant growth of industrial-technological civilization, the springing into being of big cities with their slums, as well as the growing commercialization, fragmentation, and instrumentalization of science and culture—the idea of "national socialism" was pregnant with significance.[29] Since Germany's decadence could well be seen partly as a result of its being fitted into "international capitalism," the structure created in Europe by the Versailles pact (the source of a continuous sense of national humiliation in Germany), the attempt to find a national solution of the crisis was coupled, for good reasons, with strong anticapitalist feelings. "If Heidegger"—writes Bernard Willms—

> had made more public his political attitude before 1933 . . . he would sooner and more unambiguously have been considered as a representative of the kind of thinking which may be defined as that of the 'Conservative revolution.' . . . This reference to the 'Conservative revolution' is of course meaningful only if it is taken to mean something different from the 'preparation of National Socialism.' . . . It was no less typical of the 'Conservative revolution' that its representatives, for a short time and with hesitation, joined the National Socialists, than that the latter, simultaneously or very soon, pushed them aside, and finally even persecuted them. (Willms 1977: 17f.)[30]

II.5.

In April 1933, after holding office for less than one week, Rector Wilhelm von Möllendorf, professor of anatomy and a Social Democrat, resigned. Immediately after, he and other colleagues approached Heidegger, urging him to be a candidate in the new election. After some hesitation Heidegger gave his consent to his election—mainly because of the danger that otherwise a functionary would be named rector. One of his first measures as rector, taken a few days after having been elected by the university senate, was to prohibit the hanging of the so-called Jewish poster in the university—a prohibition which, in spite of repeated urgings put through from Berlin, he did not cancel later. He also forbade the book burning planned by Nazi students, seeing to it personally that the University Library remained untouched (cf. Fédier 1966: 899f.; Allemann 1969: 252f.; Palmier 1968: 74f.; Moehling 1981: 33; GR 193ff.; SUR 23, 31f.).

These were but defensive steps. As for his constructive ideas, Heidegger repeatedly pointed to the above-quoted passage of his inaugural lecture in 1929—namely, to his view of the situation of the sciences and the university (see GR 196; SUR 22). Heidegger's ideas about a cultural renewal, when reconstructed on the basis of his activity as a rector, may be summed up as having centered around the reciprocal coming together of the university (science) and the folk or nation [Volk]. On the level of concrete measures, as will be seen, they took the form of accommodating students' lives to that of the nation or folk, on the one hand, and attempting to raise the

Volk to science (university), on the other. But how is the awakening to take place? Who is to direct whom—should science lead the people or vice versa?

Given the premise that the decline of science and philosophy was but a reflection of a general social disintegration ensuing in the late nineteenth and the early twentieth century, and the idea that even science and philosophy have their own destinies, it is obvious that spiritual life could not be revived from and by itself. A comprehensive social renewal was required. Heidegger was well aware of this, as is shown by his quips connecting neo-Kantianism, and the state of German philosophy in general, to all-encompassing social developments. But there can be no question of the university and the sciences' being renewed from "outside," as it were. For the university would then run the risk of total subjection (a possibility that was to become painfully true later)—a risk that the renewal will *not* be a *spiritual* one. Heidegger's rectorial address treated the theme of the *self-assertion* of the university (a title no other rectorial address bore at the time) because he wanted to actively anticipate the possibility that the reshaping of the university would be determined by social transformations from "above." At the same time, he was attempting to re-define and give a new sense to the concept of learning and its role in social renewal (see GR 193, 196, 198; SUR 25f.; Moehling 1981: 33). Inconceivable as the renewal of the university may be without an over-all social awakening, still, the renewing of the university must nevertheless be carried through and achieved by the university itself—specifically, by way of a radical rethinking of its essence and tasks, a re-appropriation and a retrieval of the original meaning of science and of its vocation. Were *that* to come about, science would have been re-united with and accommodated to the nation's life, not by some external force, but by itself (for as we know from *Being and Time*, science is but one of man's modes of being, and not the primary one [cf. SZ 11; SU 7]). It is thus no mere accident—although it might well have seemed somewhat strange at the moment—that Heidegger should have begun his rectorial address in May with an analysis of the notion of science, and that, after tracing it back to the Greeks, should have linked it to the historical destiny of a people, claiming: "a spiritual world alone is the guarantee of the greatness of the people" (SU 13).[31]

A new aspect of the notion of retrieval thus comes to the fore. The Being-question, the original meaning of philosophy, Heidegger says at the beginning of his address, was rooted in the Greek people's historical-national existence [Dasein]; science was not for them a so-called cultural good, nor was it pure contemplation, that is, "theory" conceived in opposition to "praxis." On the contrary, it was "the highest realization of authentic praxis," a force encompassing the whole of their existence as a state and as a folk (cf. SU 9f.). If science was the Greeks' original mode of being, toward which all their efforts pointed, then it is very much a question of retrieving *that* world, of "*re-cuperating* [wieder-holen] the origin of our historical spiritual *Dasein*" (EM 29).[32]

But how is the relation between leaders and followers within the university to be reshaped, once the university re-appropriated its original essence?

What are the implications of the retrieval of the original notion of science? What difference will its rootedness in the historical-spiritual world of the people make for the task, mission, and internal life of the university? When we hear Heidegger saying at one point that "the much celebrated 'academic freedom' is driven out of the German university" (a statement that was to raise no little astonishment in decades to come), we should be aware of the precise context of this statement. The essence of the university, Heidegger says at the beginning of the address, is usually found in its "self-direction," but that is a purely formal way of putting the matter. If "self-direction" is taken to mean simply exemption from external influences and interventions, there will be a danger of increasing isolation, fragmentation, and disintegration. This would compromise the very notion of science, for, pushing this logic to its extremes, science is no longer science if any one university, faculty, or individual scholar can pursue, as it were, a science all its (or his) own. If one calls an arrangement for the interconnection of the various disciplines [Fachwissenschaften] a "university"—Heidegger says in 1935— then "university" becomes an empty name. "It no longer signifies a primordially unificatory and authoritative spiritual force" (EM 37). Such putative self-direction can be seen, in the light of Heidegger's diagnosis of Germany's spiritual decline, to be more than "the *Verkapselung* of the sciences into isolated branches [Fächer],"[33] "an unhindered and senseless dispersion" (SU 12), a boundless activity of research which—as he formulates it in another lecture—"hid its own uncertainty under [the mask of] the idea of an [alleged] international progress of sciences" (Schneeberger 1962: 74). If this "much celebrated 'academic freedom'" is now rejected by Heidegger, the reason is given by the words immediately following, namely, that "being merely negative, this freedom was inauthentic," because "it meant predominantly lack of concern, arbitrariness of aims and inclinations, licence [Ungebundenheit] in acting and not acting" (SU 15; see also GR 196).[34]

Heidegger, however, as we have seen, is concerned with retaining the idea of a university's self-direction, and with doing so precisely by attempting to explore its deeper dimensions. A closer reflection upon the idea of self-direction, that is, of autonomy, freedom, shows it to mean "giving the law to oneself"—a very Kantian view. The university is, accordingly, "the place of spiritual legislation" (SU 15, 21).[35] If self-direction is possible only on the basis of reflection upon or awareness of what one is [Selbstbesinnung, SU 6], and if science's gaining awareness of itself consists in retrieving its original sense, meaning, and roots, by committing itself to shaping and reshaping the spiritual world of a people, then the task of the university cannot be confined to a "dull and quick schooling [of the students] for an 'elegant' profession" (SU 16). Such a conception of the university's task is, in Heidegger's eyes, the correlate of an otherwise unconstrained academic freedom; both are interpretations of the university imposed upon it from "outside." The university may not aim at providing whatever specialized professional training may be asked for. Rather, it is because the different professions of "the statesman and the teacher, the physician and the judge, the priest and the architect lead and guard the existence of the people as a state [das volklich-staatliche Dasein]" that education in these professions is the task of the university. That the university is to shape the spiritual world of a people cannot imply domination over the nation, but rather that those educated and released by it will take care of and enrich the whole people's knowledge of its *Dasein* (SU 17).

The relation of leaders and followers is described by Heidegger in terms of *authentic existence*. Self-direction [Selbstverwaltung] based upon prior awareness of one's self [Selbstbesinnung] presupposes *resoluteness*, and the latter presupposes autonomy. What matters in leadership is not so much the will to lead the way [Vorangehen] as the strength to walk alone [Alleingehenkönnen] (SU 14). The leaders should concede autonomous initiatives to the followers, and, conversely, the latter should not blindly yield to the leaders. "Every following carries resistance with it. This essential tension inherent in leading and following must not be obscured, let alone eliminated" (SU 21; cf. De Waehlens 1947: 119; Harries 1976: 654; Guzzoni 1986: 76f.). Only thus will resolute self-awareness be turned by self-assertion into authentic self-direction (SU 21).

Autonomy, as giving the law to oneself, is for Heidegger not so much obedience to the authority of pure reason, unaffected by sensibility, as it is rootedness in an effort to retrieve a historical heritage freely and resolutely assumed. If science for the Greeks meant taking a stand in the midst of beings which are constantly hiding themselves, this persistence is nevertheless well aware of its powerlessness in face of destiny. Indeed, this amounts to what may be called the "creative powerlessness of knowledge" (SU 9f.).[36] For resoluteness, striving for the retrieval of the tradition, the future is open and indefinite. Taking over a heritage can never be compelled, but only free.[37] It is never unconditionally necessary that science as such should *be* at all, Heidegger says at the beginning of the address. In his conclusion he restates the same point. It is up to us, he says there, whether and how intensely we dedicate ourselves to the work of the renewal, whether we commit ourselves entirely to it, or merely change old rules and measures, replacing them by new ones. Nobody will prevent us from doing the latter. But neither will anybody ask about our approval or disapproval, if Western culture, well on its way to decline, ultimately collapses, thereby sweeping everything into confusion and madness. Whether that will come about or not is solely a question of whether we as a historical-spiritual people still want to be ourselves—but the young forces of our people have already taken their decision. "The greatness and splendor of the renewal," he says in the last words of the address, "will however be fully understood only if we assume that . . . soberness which the old Greek wisdom expressed this way: 'Every greatness stands in the storm'" (SU 21f.; Plato, *The Republic*, 497d, 9).[38]

II.6.

The rectorial address may, in the last analysis, be seen as a dramatic call for the rescue of a declining culture, for the building up of a new spiritual world. However, not only the concluding words, but also the remarks about the powerlessness of knowledge warned against an ardent zeal and excessive enthusiasm. The breakdown of a culture makes the building up of a new world no more than possible—and *that* requires long and patient work. If the Greeks needed three centuries—Heidegger significantly said—in order merely to formulate meaningfully the very question of what knowledge was, then we must not expect the complete clarification and realization of the German university to be carried out during the present or the following semester (SU 19f.). That Heidegger entertained few illusions about the tempo of the renewal becomes clear from a remark of his, made during the 1925/1926 semester. Aristotle's logic has but one single child of the same rank, Hegel's, Heidegger said. No other descendants are possible; what is required is a new species.

> When that species will come into existence cannot be known, but we, men of today, are certainly not of that species . . . our efforts may only be directed toward effecting the transition: what we can do [here Heidegger changes his tone] is no more than making the past alive for a future for which we yearn, but we shall not reach. (GA 21: 14)

In keeping with his claim that real progress in science and philosophy is brought about only in and by a revision of fundamental concepts, a change in our access to the object or area of research,[39] Heidegger envisaged the renewal of the metaphysical tradition, the new elaboration of the Being-question, as attainable only after a laborious and careful re-appropriation of the basic metaphysical concepts of Western philosophy. (The previous quotation may help explain why external pressure was needed to make Heidegger publish *Being and Time*.)[40] So it is no accident that he saw European culture and civilization, the development of which had underlain the unfolding of Western philosophy and which was now in a deep crisis, as something not to be renewed overnight.

Heidegger's recognition that the renewal, both of the philosophical tradition and of the social-national framework, is a long process requiring the re-foundation of the bases may shed new light upon a statement he made in his debate with Cassirer in Davos—a statement which has an odd ring: "philosophy has the task . . . to push man back into the hardness of his destiny" (KPM 263; see also GA 29/30: 248). And if in his lectures in 1935 Heidegger once more emphasizes that "philosophy, according to its essence, never makes things easier, but only harder" (EM 9), his underlying view is not a gloomy pessimism, but rather the conviction that the recovery from the decline, the creation of a new world, is dependent primarily upon a full and inexorable awareness of the extent, depth, and scope of the crisis. To suggest quick and random solutions is to mask the real character of the crisis. If the *Selbstbesinnung* remains blocked half-way, only pseudo-solutions will emerge, thus deepening the crisis even further.[41]

Given that his critical appraisal of *international* liberalism and its culture had left Heidegger susceptible to the idea of *national* socialism, does it follow that he remained insensitive to the condition of other nations, or that he thought Europe's spiritual reorganization should be performed under German hegemony? That Heidegger approved of Germany's withdrawal from the League of Nations in November 1933 cannot, in the light of what we have said above, be a surprise. But it is important that in the very address in which he defended this step he emphasized:

> Our will to the self-responsibility of the nation [völkische Selbstverantwortung] wills that each nation [Volk] shall find and guard the greatness and truth of its own determination. This will is the highest guarantee for peace among the nations, for it is tied to the fundamental law of manly respect and unconditional honor. (Schneeberger 1962: 150)

And in another address he put it even more clearly: "The will to build a genuine community of nations [Völkergemeinschaft] is equally far from the desire for a lame and unconcerned world-fraternity [Weltverbrüderung] and from the desire for a blind despotism. That will is operative at a higher level than this contrast" (Schneeberger 1962: 145).[42]

Further, in 1937, long after he had detached himself from political developments in Germany and had retreated from public activity into inner emigration and nearly complete silence, he once again took up this theme— presumably because of the ever more aggressive and military character which nazism had adopted. "A genuine reciprocal understanding between the nations," he wrote, "may be achieved only in that creative dialogue in which each nation commits itself to gaining full awareness of its historical endowments and of the possibilities that history assigns it." The rescue of European culture may be carried out only if each nation gathers itself unto a responsibility for its own historical traditions and heritage. Renewal must be effected by each nation one by one. "Understanding in the genuine sense is possible only . . . through acknowledgment of what belongs properly to the other from out of an all-encompassing necessity"—its traditions and tasks. "Genuine reciprocal understanding is not reciprocal reassurance [Beruhigung][43] which soon leads to mutual indifference, but rather a constant and intensive questioning of each other [die Unruhe des gegenseitigen Sich-in-die-Frage-Stellens]—a questioning that springs out of concern for common historical tasks. . . . One of the most German thinkers of all, Leibniz," Heidegger observes, "was inspired throughout his philosophical effort by a confrontation with Descartes." The renewal of the spiritual world has, from this point of view, two necessary conditions: "the persistent will to listen to or hear the other, and the resolute fidelity [der verhaltene Mut] to one's own determination" (WA in DE 15ff.). A creative historical commitment—he says in his lectures on Nietzsche in 1936/37—"cannot be limited either to particular groups, classes or sects, nor even to particular states and nations, but must be at least European in scope." The fact that this commitment must be accomplished by each nation separately does not imply "separation from the other nations or, still less, their oppression," but rather the rise of the nations through and in a confrontation in which they develop, each by itself, the strength of rising one above the other (N 1: 185). The question of who man really is (the main problem of Europe in the present and the next century) "may only find an answer in an exemplary . . . history-shaping [Geschichtsgestaltung] brought about by the nations competing with each other" (N 1: 361).

Heidegger's attempt at an original renewal of the essence of the university, or science, trying to tie these to and root them in a people's historical existence, was only one aspect of his activity. On the level of concrete measures, as we have said, there was the problem, not only of reconciling the students with, and making them participate in, the life and work of the people, but also, and of equal importance, of raising the people up to science. The program of national awakening included the project of procuring the unemployed not only work but also education. So we should look at the address that Heidegger gave to several hundred unemployed people who had been admitted to Freiburg University.

Heidegger spoke as rector in the assembly hall of the university. His speech starts out from the thesis that the end of unemployment should not be understood purely as the fact that one has now finally a job to do and is able to improve one's conditions of living. One should view it also as entering into the national community. Those given a job now belong to the whole of the nation, and are molding its future. It is from out of this lived experience that the formerly unemployed are supposed to recover their dignity *for themselves*, as well as appropriate security and resoluteness in relating themselves *to others*. Supplying with work is also supplying with knowledge [Arbeitsbeschaffung, Wissensbeschaffung]. If younger colleagues are ready now to transmit knowledge, Heidegger points out, it is not as "learned" men belonging to the "upper" classes, or as "educated" people over against a stratum (a "lower stratum") of the "uneducated." Rather, they do so as comrades, as members of the same national community (Schneeberger 1962: 200). The new common will is directed toward bridging the gap between manual and intellectual workers, and this bridge building [Brückenschlagen] is today no mere illusion.[44] For science is, he goes on to say, not the privileged property of the bourgeoisie to be utilized for the exploitation of the laboring people. Rather, it is a more rigorous and more responsible form of that knowledge which the whole German nation requires and seeks for its historical-national existence (assuming that this nation is to secure and guard its life and greatness at all). "Knowledge had by genuine science is essentially no different from knowledge had by peasants, woodmen, navvies, miners. . . . For to know means: *to know one's way* [sich auskennen] in the world, in which we all and each find ourselves"; to know means to master the situation, to be equal to it, to come up to the task. "We do not make a distinction between those 'educated' and those 'uneducated' . . . not because there is no difference, but because our evaluation does not depend upon this distinction. Genuine knowledge is possessed by the peasant and the manual worker, each in his own way and in his own field." A learned man may, for all his learning, go astray with his pseudo-knowledge

[Scheinwissen]. Not only the concept of science, but also that of labor is to be transformed. Spiritual labor is not exclusively that done by scholars: "every labor *as* labor is something spiritual," for it is based upon competence, freely appropriated skills, and an intelligent understanding of the rules to come by—that is, upon authentic knowledge. The performance of the navvy is fundamentally no less spiritual than the achievement of the scholar. There is no real contrast between the "workers" and those having knowledge peculiar to the sciences. "Every worker, each in his own way, is a knower, and it is as a knower that he can work at all" (Schneeberger 1962: 201f.). Such an understanding of knowledge and of labor is the condition of the possibility of a "bridge building" which is no longer extrinsic and artificial.[45]

II.7.

It was thus within the framework of a general spiritual awakening that the National Socialist revolution was meaningful for Heidegger. What mattered was not to "politicize" science and university but rather to lend spiritual content to society and politics—that is, to help shape an already existing movement, a movement born out of crisis, into a force capable of creating a genuine spiritual world.[46] Insofar as a renewal basing itself upon self-awareness presupposes resolute retrieval of and rootedness in one's own being, such a renewal is opposed to a radical subversion of factual conditions. (Philosophy, it may be remembered, has precisely the task of pushing men back into the hardness of their destiny.) The universities' gaining awareness of their original meaning and mission by bringing themselves back to the national-historical community does not, therefore, imply in the least that the universities should, as it were, "march into" the sphere of politics, taking over the role of the politicians. This mistake would lead, indirectly, to the same "politicizing" of the university against which its *self-assertion* had tried to defend it. Its own "political" function may be performed by the university only *as* university, that is, as a given, bounded domain within the national-historical community.[47] These considerations, which are in keeping with the main line of thought found in *Being and Time,* and with Heidegger's whole outlook, may account for the fact that Heidegger wanted to partake in the revival precisely from his own place. He did not desire to assume another, perhaps higher, position.

He might, however, have had a chance to do so. In September 1933, as the German press of the day reported in detail, Heidegger was offered the chair of philosophy at the University of Berlin, upon an initiative of the Prussian minister of culture. Scarcely one month later, the Bavarian minister of culture invited him to accept the premier chair of philosophy at the University of Munich. In neither of the cases did the newspapers leave much doubt that the calls carried no little political weight with them.[48] However, Heidegger refused both calls. The reasons for his refusal are made explicit, and put in a particular light, in a radio lecture Heidegger gave in the autumn of 1933—a lecture bearing the title "Why do we stay in the provinces?" It offers no plausible arguments, but, once again, a meditation.

On the steep slope of a wide mountain valley in the Southern Black Forest
[Heidegger begins the lecture] there stands a small ski hut; scattered throughout
the base of the valley lie farmhouses, higher up the slope the meadows lead
to woods with fir trees. This is my world. When the young farmboy drags
his heavy sledge up the slope and guides it, piled high with beech logs, down
to his house, when the herdsman drives his cattle up the slope, when the
farmer in his shed gets the shingles ready for his roof, my work is of the
same sort. A city-dweller thinks that in condescending to have a longer
conversation with a peasant, he has gone 'out among the people.' But when
in the evening during a work-break I sit with the peasants at the chimney-
corner, we mostly do not speak at all. We just smoke our pipes in silence.
City-dwellers are 'livened up' by a so-called 'outing in the country.' My work
is however sustained and guided by the world of the mountains and peasants—
a work of which I am not at all the master. City-dwellers are often amazed
by such long monotonous periods of loneliness. But in large cities one can
easily be lonelier than anywhere else. In the public world one can be made
a 'celebrity' overnight by the newspapers and journals. That is the surest way
to have one's intentions misinterpreted and quickly forgotten. In contrast, the
memory of the peasant has its simple fidelity which never forgets. Recently
an old peasant woman died up there. She used to chat with me frequently,
telling me many old stories of the village. Even in the past year, with her
eighty-three years, she would still come climbing up the slope to see whether
I was still there or whether 'someone' had stolen me off. The night of her
death, not long before the end, she sent one more greeting to the 'Professor.'
Such a memory is worth incomparably more than the most astute 'report' of
any international newspaper about my alleged philosophy.—Lately a very loud
and active obtrusiveness has been emerging, passing itself off as a concern
for the world of the peasant. Men of letters chatter about 'folk-character' and
'rootedness in the soil.' What the peasant wants is however no such citified
officiousness, but solely quiet reserve with regard to his own way of being.—
Recently I got a second invitation to teach at the University of Berlin. On that
occasion I left the city, and withdrew to the hut, where I listened to what the
mountains, the forests and the farmlands were saying. I went to see my old
friend, a seventy-five-year-old peasant. What would he say? He had read about
the call in the newspapers. Slowly he fixed the sure gaze of his eyes on mine.
Keeping his mouth tightly shut, he thoughtfully put his hand on my shoulder—
and ever so slightly shook his head. That means: inexorably no![49]

II.8.

The hope for a spiritual reorganization of the nation, for the university's
self-renewal and for its becoming rooted in an organic national community
was soon to become untenable, thanks to the ever faster and wilder
politicization of the society, the conversion of efforts to control the anarchy
into those making for a totalitarian system, and the consequent solidification
of a state-ideology, namely, racism. In the second half of 1933 Heidegger
was already facing increasing difficulties. His ideas concerning renewal met
pronounced resistance on the part of both "the old" and "the new." The
"new" was represented by the idea of "politicized" science—an idea that
Heidegger looked upon as a falsification of the essence of truth. The "old,"
by contrast, was the idea that everybody should be concerned with his own

discipline and its progress—thereby dismissing general philosophical reflection upon fundamentals as mere "abstraction," or admitting them as, at best, extrinsic ornaments (cf. SUR 22f.; GR 196).

In the winter semester of 1933/1934 Heidegger intended to nominate outstanding young scholars as deans of the faculties, without any regard to their relation to the Nazi party (cf. GR 201; SUR 35).[50] By Christmas it had become clear that his planned renewal could not be carried through. Within the university there emerged objections to his idea of introducing students into responsible positions in the administration of the university. At the "Todtnauberg camp," held by Heidegger to discuss impending tasks for the winter semester and to explain his ideas about science and about the university, some government functionaries, as well as some visitors from Heidelberg, introduced the theme of racial thought, thereby attempting to exercize pressure upon Heidegger and upon Freiburg University. In October 1933 the German rectors held a conference in Berlin to establish the new legal framework for subordinating the universities to the state. Freiburg University boycotted this conference: Heidegger did not go, nor did he send a representative. In February 1934 Heidegger was called to Karlsruhe by the minister, who demanded that he dismiss, and replace with colleagues more acceptable to the party, Wilhelm von Möllendorf, dean of the Faculty of Medicine, and Erik Wolf, dean of the Faculty of Law. Heidegger refused the request, and offered his resignation, should the minister persist in his demand. This is precisely what happened. At the end of the winter semester 1933/1934 Heidegger resigned. He tendered his resignation about a year after assuming office, and several months before the concentration of all power, subsequent to the death of President Hindenburg in August, in the hands of Hitler.[51]

In 1934 the orthodox Nazis started an open attack against the "Jacobinical," plebeian wing of national socialism. At the end of June Hitler destroyed the faction of the party which was demanding fulfillment of its social promises. There would be no more talk about the "spiritual revolution" of the workers, no more use of other ideas inspired by German Idealism. Their place would inexorably be taken over by a concept of the people defined in terms of race. By the time this new course prevailed, Heidegger had withdrawn from the movement.[52]

The certainty peculiar to resoluteness—we read in *Being and Time*—must open itself to what is disclosed in resolution. That means: it may not stiffen itself in the situation, but should rather keep itself open for the possible, and indeed from time to time necessary, re-appropriation of itself. Resoluteness as fidelity to one's self, as destiny, is freedom for the *giving up* of a particular resolution—a giving up required by the possible situation (SZ 307f., 391).

Acknowledgments

I am grateful to the editors for their comments and suggestions. I also wish to thank Richard Rorty for reading a first draft of this chapter, for commenting upon it, and—last but not least—for helping improve my style.

Notes

1. Cf. GA 1: 186f., 406, 410f. Heidegger's reading, at the age of eighteen, of Brentano's dissertation *Von der mannigfachen Bedeutung des Seienden nach Aristoteles* may be considered to be the first and decisive incitement to formulate the Being-question. Cf. his Preface to Richardson 1963: xi; and GA 1: 56.

2. "The constant sharpening of the knife," Heidegger quotes significantly Lotze in his *Habilitationsschrift*, "is boring if one has nothing to cut with it" (GA 1: 200). In a review written in 1912 on recent developments in logic, Heidegger even mentions Russell and Whitehead's *Principia Mathematica* (see GA 1: 42).

3. Cf. SD 87. For the presence of Aristotle in the formation of the young Heidegger's thought see Sheehan 1975, and Volpi 1984b, chapters 1–3.

4. An example may be the *Habilitationsschrift* itself, in which Husserlian phenomenology is utilized to illuminate, and thus show the theoretical significance of, Scotus's thought—an accomplishment which enables Heidegger, conversely, to situate Husserlian phenomenology historically as a continuation of a traditional problematic.

5. To pose and elaborate (work out) a question means for Heidegger primordially to clarify the prior ground or horizon which lends meaning to the terms in question. To put it out roughly, so as to be able to answer any question, we must have already understood its meaning (to the question, e.g., "What color is the table?" the answer: "Square" would fail to understand the *direction* of the question); that is, any question implies or carries with itself a pre-conceptual or—as Heidegger puts it—"pre-ontological" understanding of its meaning. We are able to *take up* the Being-question, J. Sallis comments upon the first paragraphs of *Sein und Zeit,* "only to the extent that we can *pose* it; to pose it appropriately . . . is to let the structure which belongs to the question unfold *from the question itself*" (Sallis 1978: 28f.). See SZ par. 232; Gadamer 1975: 250ff.; Herrmann 1987: 51ff.

6. The metaphysic-ladenness of epistemological or logical theories is, however, of a peculiar sort—one which those moving within the theory cannot become aware of. Incapable of being thematized, it is not susceptible of critical discussion or examination. See e.g., Heidegger's discussion of the latent, "dogmatic" metaphysical presuppositions inherent in Husserlian phenomenology (GA 20: 140ff., in particular 147, 155, 158, 178). Concerning Heidegger's confrontation with Husserl, see Volpi, 1984a; for the concept of phenomenology in Husserl and Heidegger see Herrmann 1981, in particular 37ff.

7. Cf. GA 20: 200f.; GA 24: 103f., 154f., 172, 444; GA 25: 167; GA 26: 19ff., 109; SZ 154, 183, 212; later e.g., EM 78. In Heidegger's perspective it is no mere accident that Hegel's ontology, as the offspring of a long development, is symptomatically called *Logic* (cf. GA 25: 167; see also GA 21: 311).

8. For Heidegger's discussion of the logic of questioning in his dissertation, see GA 1: 160.

9. I borrow the term "anti-metaphysical" from Otto Pöggeler (1963: 28).

10. Existential analytic might be seen as a polemic radicalization of Kant's replacement for traditional ontology, namely, a transcendental analytic of the pure intellect ("blosse Analytik des reinen Verstandes": *Critique of Pure Reason* A 304 = B 247). Heidegger, writes Richardson, "shifts the emphasis from an investigation of man's reason . . . to an investigation of man in his totality" (Richardson 1963: 31).

11. Existential analytic, so conceived, is not anthropology. For to elaborate a theory of man as one being among others already presupposes a prior clarification of the different domains of Being—a task not to be accomplished until after the Being-question is answered; cf. SZ 17, 45ff.; KPM 202ff., 227.

12. The term used by Heidegger for man is *Dasein*, which will be left untranslated in the text. The reason why Heidegger does not use the term "man" is, negatively, that this term is laden with traditional metaphysical presuppositions, suggesting as it does a "rational animal," a being "endowed with reason" (a conception Heidegger intends to criticize). The positive reason is that man, for Heidegger, has an intrinsic relation to *Sein*, and possesses a pre-conceptual understanding of Being. Man is indeed the very being which poses the Being-question. The term *Dasein* is apt to suggest all these connections with *Sein*. Concerning the term *Dasein* see King 1964: 65ff.; Richardson 1963: 44ff.; W. Marx 1961: 209ff.; Fell 1979: 31f.; Pöggeler 1983: 93; Biemel 1978: 111ff.

13. "Das Ganze eines Begründungszusammenhanges wahrer Sätze" (SZ 11). For the term "Begründungszusammenhang" see Husserl 1980. What Husserl means by this central term of his *Wissenschaftslehre* is that *Wissenschaft* (as opposed to mere *Wissen*) consists not only in one's *knowing* particular perceptions, or having isolated knowing acts. Rather, it requires, if it is to be worthy of its name, some "systematic connection in theoretical sense," that is, "the founding of knowledge" [Begründung des Wissens] (cf. Husserl 1980: 15, 230ff.).

14. Concerning parallels between Heidegger's ontological refutation of the epistemological standpoint and the perspective of German Idealism see Gadamer 1976: 140f.

15. Heidegger's argument may be seen as amounting to a kind of "refutation of skepticism." Insofar as it shows that some prior knowledge must by necessity precede or underlie all sorts of doubt, rendering doubt possible, his strategy is analogous to that of the later Wittgenstein (see Wittgenstein 1984: 141, 143 [pars. 105, 111]).

16. This may be one of the reasons why Heidegger rejects the application of traditional categories to man (e.g., "subject," "ego," "reason," "spirit," etc.; see SZ 22). One can say, Gadamer writes, that "it is *Dasein*'s inauthenticity from which metaphysics as the ontology of *Vorhandensein* developed itself" (Gadamer 1985: 19).

17. Cf. SZ 383f. For the variety of meanings and implications of the term *Wiederholung* see Caputo 1982: 343ff.

18. I should note that some basic issues—above all Heidegger's discussion of truth and time—have been neglected. Also the *vexata questio* of the incompleteness of *Sein und Zeit* cannot be discussed in the present context.

19. Cf. SZ 264, 298. Since finitude is the basic character of *Dasein*, gaining awareness of it by anticipating death helps it become conscious both of what possibilities are uniquely its own (that is, not the others'), and, vice versa, of those possibilities of others which are not—and perhaps necessarily cannot be—its own. Demske rightly speaks in this sense of a "social aspect" of the anticipation of death (Demske 1963: 38).

20. The term "Wiederholung" appears as early as the title of the first section ("Die Notwendigkeit einer ausdrücklichen Wiederholung der Frage nach dem Sein": SZ 2; see also KPM 232; Richardson 1963: 93). The notion of "retrieval" is thus present and operative long before the analyses of authenticity are provided (for this notion in the young Heidegger see GA 61: 80). From another perspective, Heidegger intended to "retrieve" the whole existential analytic from within the elaborated horizon of the Being-question. Because of the incompleteness of the work, this did not come about. But nevertheless the "second" Heidegger may pertinently be held to be a retrieval of the "first" Heidegger (cf. Richardson 1963: 625; Fehér 1984: 146).—All such attempts at retrieval must, however, be conscious of taking their starting points *from within* history (see SZ 20f.). So when Heidegger says in his lectures that his investigations too are determined by the historical situation, and

thereby conditioned by traditional philosophies' access [Zugang] to beings (cf. GA 24: 31), this situation both characterizes *extrinsically* the moment of his positing the Being-question and emerges *intrinsically* as one of the main tenets of *Being and Time:* namely, that authenticity is only an existential modification of inauthenticity, always preceded by the latter, and that *Dasein* can never remain unaffected by inherited everyday opinions [alltägliche Ausgelegtheit]. It is in these opinions, for them and against them, that all genuine understanding, interpretation, communication, discourse and re-appropriation take place. It is likewise in them, against them, and at the same time for them, that resolute *Dasein* projects itself upon the chosen possibility (cf. SZ 169, 383). This view helps us understand why and how the history of philosophy constitutes an integral part of systematic philosophy.

21. Cf. GA 61: 21; GA 20: 179, 188; GA 21: 13f.; GA 26: 101, 196f.; SZ 21ff.; GA 29/30: 53ff.; EM 10. As to "blind" traditionalism, see his critique of Husserl, his remarks upon Descartes's "dogmatism," present also in Kant, and his observations on Descartes's own inauthentic traditionalism: GA 20: 147; GA 21: 291; GA 29/30: 30, 64, 84; GA 32: 196.

22. The point that the cultural crisis in Europe was felt most intensively in Germany is made in a lively and convincing manner by Gadamer (see Gadamer 1983: 9f.).

23. I do not, of course, wish to claim that in his critique of traditional notions of man, Heidegger did not employ eminently *theoretical* arguments. (Indeed, I attempt to show some of these above.) What I do suggest is that, whatever the particular "psychology of discovery" may have been, the starting intuitions of such a critique must have been provided by factual experience of life. (We do know that one of his early lectures bore the title "Hermeneutik der Faktizität" [cf. Pöggeler 1963: 29 and the forthcoming GA 63; see also Gadamer 1986/87: 16].) Put in another way, the starting point of such a criticism must have been a prior dissatisfaction with commonly accepted notions of man.

24. We may refer first of all to his *Habilitationsschrift*, and in particular to those passages which offer critical reflections on the culture of the day (see GA 1: 200, 408f.).

25. Plato is claimed by Lotze to have remained captive to incoherence; however, Heidegger remarks, it is only in his interpreters that Plato turns out to be senseless (GA 21: 71).

26. GA 21: 83f. (The above passage is a close paraphrase rather than a translation.)— Not only has the Kant literature, he says on another occasion, become more important than Kant himself, but its effect will be that nobody will be able to get access to the thing [Sache] (GA 32: 41). To appropriate intentionality, he observes on yet another occasion, what one needs is not sharp intelligence [Scharfsinn], but only refraining from prejudice, concentration upon and disciplined description of what one has before one's eyes. Objectivity [Sachlichkeit] concerning what is evident, he adds, is nevertheless the most difficult thing one can achieve, for man is naturally at home in what is artificial, deceptive, what he picks up from idle talk with others (GA 20: 37). Finally, consider one last, interesting, series of observations, made in 1925: "Today people decide about metaphysics or even higher things at congresses. Nowadays there are conferences to decide every question—that is, people come together, and keep coming together, and everybody expects the other to tell him what to do. If he is not told, it is also of no importance, for what really matters is that one has spoken [hat sich ja nun ausgesprochen]. Though all the speakers may have little understanding of the thing in question, nevertheless it is believed that some understanding *will* finally be derived from the accumulation of non-understanding

[Unverstehen]. So there are people today who travel from one conference to the other, and get the feeling that something is really happening, as if they had been really doing something. But in fact they have just relieved themselves from work, and have tried to conceal their own helplessness under the cover of idle talk. . . . So finally people think that everything is all right, and one should be present at every congress" (GA 20: 376f.). "It is clear," he adds somewhat later, "that research and science are also *Dasein's* possibilities, and are, therefore, susceptible to the modifications of *Dasein's* being . . . , and in particular to fallenness . . . : so philosophy contains, always and necessarily, a bit of sophistry" (GA 20: 416f.; see also GA 32: 41).

27. For a critique of the philosophy of *Weltanschauung*, see Husserl 1965, and Heidegger's analogous considerations in GA 24: 5ff., especially 13, and GA 61: 44. For Heidegger, however, the insistence upon "scientific" philosophy in contrast to the philosophy of *Weltanschauung*, viz., rationalism in contrast to irrationalism, is simply beside the point. Cf. GA 1: 410; SZ 136; EM 136; N 2: 372, 531; BH in GA 9: 349; GA 32: 143; GA 52: 133; SD 79. See also Hogemann 1986/87: 56, 62; Kisiel 1986/87: 106f.; Rodi 1986/87: 168.

28. Heidegger, Karl A. Moehling writes, "was both attracted to and repelled by Nazism. He was put in what he called a 'middle position' of believing in the social and national ideas of the movement while rejecting the essential racism" (Moehling 1981: 36). At that time, Jaspers admits in his notes, "neither he nor any of us could know what was going to become of it all" (Jaspers 1978: 180). For Adorno's analogous misinterpretation of the situation, see Pöggeler (1985: 28).

29. The idea goes some decades back. The attempt to bring together the two major intellectual trends of the past century, nationalism and socialism, dates as far back as the 1890s. Friedrich Meinecke, the great German historian, shows this convincingly in his memoirs, written immediately after World War II (see Meinecke 1949: 33ff.). There was first of all Friedrich Naumann's attempt, in the early 1890s, to fuse the nationalistic and the socialist trends (the former supported mainly by the middle class, the latter by workers). Naumann tried to quell the hostility between the two classes so as to mitigate the extremely anti-nationalist (that is, internationalistic) faith of the socialists by attending to the workers' material and spiritual needs. Had Neumann's attempt succeeded (an attempt Meinecke calls "one of the noblest dreams of German history"), Meinecke thinks, Hitler could never have risen to power (Meinecke 1949: 34). It is significant that Naumann's name is mentioned by Heidegger in a positive sense in the *Spiegel*-Interview (GR 196; see also Pöggeler 1988: 27). As to differences between the forms of early national socialism and the subsequent totalitarian regime, see also Palmier 1968: 193; Pöggeler 1983: 392; Pöggeler 1984: 234.

30. Hermann Rauschning, a Conservative and one of the founding members of the Nazi party, who in 1934 went into exile and became a bitter enemy of the regime, spoke in 1938 about the "National Socialist usurpation" of the idea of the Third Reich. This was originally "a slogan of the Young Conservatives, the title of a book published in 1922 by Moeller van den Bruck,"—an idea which in its author's "original conception was not a German idea," but "a political idea of European scope." "In spite of its manifest defects," writes Rauschning, "National Socialism offered opportunities of pursuing initiatives in which the Young Conservatives were interested. . . . Many conservatives . . . found their way into the ranks of National Socialism from the very best of motives and in perfect good faith." " . . . ten years before the National Socialist seizure of power, the Young Conservatives of Germany had a home and foreign policy immeasurably superior to that of the present regime

of violence, and envisaged Germany's recovery only in connexion with a universal idea of right, with a 'European solution'. Nothing was more horrifying to the Conservatives than the gradual recognition that the 'national rising,' with which they had associated themselves to that end, was in reality a cynical nihilist revolution, the negation of their own ideals." (Rauschning 1939: 121, 119, 309; see Stern 1984: 12ff., 18). Heide Gerstenberger characterizes revolutionary Conservatives by the attempt "to revolutionize spiritually the society [Gesellschaft] by transforming it into a community of the people [Volksgemeinschaft]" (Gerstenberger 1972: 343). That conservative thinkers cannot be taken as simple precursors of nazism is also stressed by Palmier (1968: 172; see also Pöggeler 1974: 109). For a sense of the general historical atmosphere, Alan Bullock's analyses are useful: "1933, like other revolutionary years, produced great hopes, a sense of new possibilities, the end of frustration, the beginning of action, a feeling of exhilaration and anticipation after years of hopelessness. Hitler recognized this mood when he told the German people to hold up their heads and re-discover their old pride and self-confidence. Germany, united and strong, would end the crippling divisions which had held her back, and recover the place that was her due in the world. Many people believed this in 1933 and thought that a new era had begun. Hitler succeeded in releasing pent-up energies in the nation, and in creating a belief in the future of the German people. It is wrong to lay stress only on the element of coercion, and to ignore the degree to which Hitler commanded a genuine popular support in Germany" (Bullock 1952: 253; concerning the last statement, see also Picht's memoir of Felix Jacoby, quoted in note 46, *infra*).

31. It is not without significance that at this point Heidegger makes use of the term *Geist*, which he had primarily put in quotation marks and treated as an ontologically obscure concept. The fact that he takes it up now by re-defining it in terms of his own notion of authenticity ("Spirit is primordially attuned, knowing resolution towards the essence of being" [SU 14]) supports the assumption that retrieval of the philosophical tradition was for Heidegger not a merely intellectual project, and that his objections to traditional ontological concepts should be seen in the context of his dissatisfaction with lived experience which was linked to those concepts. "Heidegger's insistence on the autonomy of the university," writes Karsten Harries, "challenged those who wanted to make it into a tool of the movement and reduce it to a vocational school, while his emphasis on the spiritual opposed Rosenberg's subordination of spirit to race and biology." ("For Heidegger," writes Lucien Goldmann, "anti-semitism must have been but a serious and unfortunate error, for the biological has no place in ontology, and can, therefore, neither limit, nor increase *Dasein's* possibilities of choice between the authentic and the inauthentic.") "This is not to suggest," Harries goes on, "that Heidegger's commitment to the Nazis was less than genuine. He appears to have been convinced at the time that in spite of the threat posed by party functionaries and ideologues, the engagement of people like himself could help to shape the Nazi movement in such a way that it would become a force which could rescue Germany from crisis and confusion" (Harries 1976: 653; Goldmann 1973: 78; see also Palmier 1968: 63). "Fatal though the impression of some Heideggerian texts of the time may be upon us today," writes Hermann Mörchen, "it is equally remarkable that in those very texts no concessions to anti-semitism can be found" (Mörchen 1981: 254; see also to the same effect Ott 1984b: 122; Pöggeler 1985: 62, 44). Moehling rightly makes the point that the rectorial address "was a revolutionary appeal in that he argued that the time had come in German history when an examination of the relationship between the university and the nation was not only desirable but an absolute necessity. He urged the re-assertion of the university and learning in the life of the nation so that pressing and urgent spiritual issues could be confronted" (Moehling 1981: 33f.).

32. Heidegger, writes Harries, "calls for a thinking which, no longer content with the splintering of science into sciences, will help to establish the 'spiritual world' of the German people and thus help to overcome the disintegrating tendencies of the age" (Harries 1976: 654). "Clearly," writes Moehling, "Heidegger's thinking in 1933 on learning and the German university demonstrates a serious departure from the Nazis' understanding of the University as a place for training a racial elite subservient to the state" (Moehling 1981: 34; see also Richardson 1963: 257; the title of the rectorial address, as Michael E. Zimmermann points out, was "a daring title during the time when Hitler expected the universities to submit to what he asserted to be the demand of *das Volk*" [Zimmermann 1981: 171]). Seen in the context of other rectorial addresses of the time, writes Bernd Martin, Heidegger's was an exception; it was not at all in line with what the Nazis had expected (Martin 1986: 52; see also Schmidt 1986: 88). Obviously, this departure could not remain hidden. As Heidegger recorded in his recently published memoir, Minister Wacker immediately let him know his view of the rectorial address. In the minister's judgment, the address represented a sort of "private National Socialism," which circumvented the perspectives of the party program, failed to be based upon "racial thought," and rejected the idea of the "politicized science" (cf. SUR 30f.).

33. The expression "Verkapselung" is applied also technically by Heidegger to denote the "wordless" subject characteristic of modern philosophy (see SZ 62).

34. Heidegger's rejection of "academic freedom," writes Palmier, is not equivalent to the repudiation of the liberty of teaching or of the expression of thought (cf. Palmier 1968: 83). "In Heidegger's understanding," Moehling writes, "academic freedom in the modern age had come to mean academic specialization and the fragmentation of learning into distinct and isolated areas. It was the modern trend towards specialization, relativism, and irrelevancy which molded the university into a corporate entity which took pride in its autonomy but failed to recognize its isolation from the spiritual needs of the nation" (Moehling 1981: 34). That *Gebundenheit* in the positive sense is not synonymous with lack of freedom or subjection is a point made already in Heidegger's *Habilitationsschrift* (cf. GA 1: 199; see also SZ 122: "Authentic Verbundenheit alone renders proper objectivity [Sachlichkeit] possible;" and WW in GA 9: 189: "Freedom is not the *Ungebundenheit des Tun- and Nichttunkönnens"*).

35. Concerning the Kantian concept of freedom as *Selbstgesetzgebung* see GA 31: 24 (where it is called "the positive concept of freedom") and *passim*. The notion of the university as "the place of spiritual legislation" shows many parallels with similar views characteristic of German Idealism (see Moehling 1981: 35). The most relevant text in the writings of German Idealists is perhaps Schelling's *Vorlesungen über die Methode des akademischen Studiums* (1802). See Schelling 1977: 251, 254, 257 (Universities are defined here as "Verbindungen für die Wissenschaften," and Heidegger claims, in like manner, that the commitment to the essence of the university is the commitment to science [SU 7: 281f., 284, 299, 304f.]). Here we touch upon a further aspect of the concept of *Wiederholung*—namely, in the sense of a retrieval of German Idealism's understanding of the cultural role of philosophy in the national awakening, and in the nation's life in general (see also Hegel 1970: 402ff.). It must be added that one of Heidegger's constant philosophical concerns was the *essence of the university*; he repeatedly gave lecture courses on it, the first as early as 1919 (see Richardson 1963: 663, 666; Pöggeler 1988: 21f.; see also GA 61: 62ff.).

36. See also the remark, quoted in section II.3, on the destiny of science and philosophy.

37. For a Kantian parallel cf. Kant 1982: 704.

38. Werner Jäger, who was soon to leave Germany because of his Jewish wife, had the intention of publishing the rectorial address in the review *Die Antike,* for he held it to be an outstanding example of how the classical heritage was alive in the present (see Petzet 1983: 34). Karl Jaspers wrote to Heidegger on Sept. 23, 1983, that the rectorial address "is up to now the only document of a present academic will . . . that will be lasting [bisher einzige Dokument eines gegenwärtigen akademischen Willens . . ., das bleiben wird]" (Jaspers 1979: 13).

39. A view which has significant parallels with Kuhn's. See GA 1: 419; GA 20: 4; GA 21: 16f.; GA 25: 30ff.; SZ 9ff.; FD 50ff.

40. Cf. SD 87f. For the details of the publication of Heidegger's *magnum opus* see Sheehan 1981: 15; Sheehan 1984: 181ff.

41. Heidegger's critique of nazism from 1934 on will be based upon the insight that nazism, instead of offering a genuine solution to Europe's spiritual crisis, is, with its racial ideology, rather a continuation, and indeed a consummation, of the decline of the West, predicted by Spengler (see e.g., his critique of Rosenberg and Kolbenheyer in his lectures of 1934/1935 [GA 39: 27f.]; see also Schmidt 1986: 86). It is only too natural that those who were offering such pseudo-solutions were the first to accuse him of "pessimism" and "nihilism." "The meaning of this philosophy"— we can read in the journal *Volk im Werden* in 1934—"is outspoken atheism and metaphysical nihilism, as it formerly had been primarily represented by Jewish authors in Germany; therefore, a ferment of decay and dissolution for the German people. In *Being and Time* Heidegger philosophizes consciously and deliberately about 'everydayness'—there is nothing in it about nation, state, race, and all the values of our National Socialist world-view" (Krieck 1934: 247, reprinted in Schneeberger 1962: 225; see Moehling 1981: 36f., whose translation, with slight modifications, I adopted).

42. It is important to see that Heidegger's description of the passage from inauthenticity is now transposed to the level of history: just as *Dasein,* in effecting the passage, first becomes isolated by anticipating death and harkening to the call of conscience, in order to open itself newly and genuinely for the world, and to render authentic Being-with possible, a nation is now seen as stripping itself of the inauthentic international *Mitsein,* conceived of in terms of *das Man,* in order to set an example for other nations' possible retrieval of themselves, and to open up for them, in authentic "leaping ahead," their own and genuine care (the term Verbrüderung" is characteristically adopted in *Being and Time* to denote inauthentic *Mitsein* [SZ 298]).

43. The term "Beruhigung" also denotes inauthenticity; it is in fact a category of fallenness (see SZ 177).

44. It should be noted that the expression *Brückenschlagen* is also part of Heidegger's philosophical vocabulary, denoting as it does the (mostly hopeless) attempts made by modern philosophy to mediate between the subject-object dualism, viz., the self-autonomous egos (cf. SZ 124; GA 21: 91ff.). Heidegger's application of the term in a different context should not, I think, be taken as a mere extrinsic analogy. It should rather be seen as an aspect of the previously mentioned connection between the renewal of the Being-question, of the metaphysical tradition (of which the subject-object dualism is, after Descartes, an integral part), and the reshaping of the historical-factual grounds underlying the tradition. A new access to Being is, after all, not a purely intellectual operation. Heidegger may legitimately be said to have expected the national awakening to provide a new experience of Being (for hints to this effect see SU 10, 14; GA 26: 23).

45. The notion that labor is not equivalent to physical labor—a notion that goes back to Hegel and was elaborated in detail by Ernst Jünger in his *Der Arbeiter,*

published in 1932 (see Jünger 1959: 74, 84, 223, 283, *et passim*)—is stressed by Heidegger on other occasions too. He explains thereby why animals, properly speaking, cannot *work* (see Schneeberger 1962: 180; on Jünger's influence upon Heidegger cf. Petzet 1983: 37f.; concerning Jünger's rejection of racism see e.g., Jünger 1959: 160; on Jünger's becoming an opponent of the regime see Krockow 1958: 112, who mentions that Jünger's *Auf den Marmorklippen*, published in 1939, was generally understood as a *Widerstandsschrift*). Given this conception of labor and knowledge, the students' *Arbeitsdienst* can no longer be seen as "condescension" from a higher world to a lower one. "The so-called 'spiritual work' is not such because it concerns 'higher spiritual things,' but because *as work* it reaches deeper into the necessity of a people's historical *Dasein*" (Schneeberger 1962: 181; see Schwan 1965: 182).

46. Cf. SU 8, 14; GR 198; SUR 23; Schmidt 1986: 90. Concerning the way Heidegger conceived of the revival of the university, and particularly of what should *not* be part of the revival, Georg Picht relates an interesting story. To give the first lecture within the framework of "political education"—a measure introduced at the German universities by the Nazis—Heidegger invited a man, Victor von Weizsäcker, who was known to be not a Nazi. After interrupting abruptly the introductory words on national socialist revolution, pronounced by the leader of philosophy students, Heidegger let von Weizsäcker speak about Freud. Picht also relates the words with which Felix Jacoby opened his university lectures on Horace in Kiel, in 1933. It is perhaps worthwhile to quote them, to illustrate the general atmosphere of the day: "As a Jew, I find myself in a difficult position. But as a historian, I have learnt that historical events are not to be assessed from a personal perspective. From 1927 onwards I have made my option for Adolf Hitler, and consider it an honor to be able, in the year of the nation's rise, to lecture on Augustus' poet. For Augustus is the only figure of world history whom one can compare to Adolf Hitler." Jacoby, as Picht writes, later emigrated to Oxford (Picht 1977: 198ff.; see also Petzet 1983: 37; Stern 1984: 39f.).

47. Heidegger did not elaborate anything like a "political theory," for, as will have become clear by now, the "theoretical-practical" distinction was one of the traditional metaphysical distinctions he wanted to overcome (see e.g., SZ 193; SU 10). The elaboration of a "political theory" requires conceding some autonomy to the political sphere—a concession which, given his critical attitude toward the fragmentation characteristic of modern societies, Heidegger obviously could not make (see Pöggeler's objection to this effect in Pöggeler 1982: 50). Nevertheless, it may be said that Heidegger's philosophy, in a certain precise sense, is very political— namely, in a sense of the term associated with the Greek *polis* (cf. Palmier 1968: 159). The rejection of the autonomy of the "political," and the consequent lack of a "political philosophy" in his thought is explicit in his lectures in 1943. Commenting upon Heraclitus, Heidegger asks: "And what, if, thought in the manner of the Greeks, the concern for the emerging presence [Anwesenheit] of the Gods were the highest concern for the *polis?* . . . If such is the case, then . . . the thinker, in his concern for the essential proximity of the Gods, is the authentically 'political' man" (GA 55: 11f.).

48. Cf. Schneeberger 1962: 123, 132f. Heidegger received a previous call to Berlin in 1930 (Schneeberger 1962: 12).

49. "Warum bleiben wir in der Provinz?" *Der Alemanne,* 2 March 1934, reprinted in DE 9ff. English translation by Thomas Sheehan (see Sheehan 1981: 27ff.). I adopted this translation, with slight modifications, in the above paraphrase.

50. Heidegger himself was by then a member of the party. He entered on May 1, 1933, in order primarily to facilitate his relations with the ministry, and to be

thus in a better position to put his ideas through—that is, as he wrote in a letter to the de-Nazification committee at Freiburg University after the war, "to attempt from *within* National Socialism and while having a point of reference to it, to bring about a spiritual change in its development." But it caused no little astonishment in the ministry that none of the deans appointed by him in the autumn were party members (Heidegger's letter is quoted by Moehling (1981: 33); see also Fédier 1966: 900; Allemann 1969: 252; Palmier 1968: 9, 89; Pöggeler 1974: 18f.; SUR 33, 37). Erik Wolf, dean of the Faculty of Law, later to become a bitter enemy of the regime, wrote in 1945 that what he found fascinating in Heidegger's ideas was the hope in a "regeneration of the university" (see Hollerbach 1986: 39f.).

51. Cf. GR 201; SUR 37; Fédier 1966: 901; Allemann 1969: 253; Moehling 1981: 37; Palmier 1968: 159; Martin 1986: 67. His successor was appointed by the ministry, and Heidegger refused to be present at the public celebration of his successor's assumption of office (see also Wisser 1977: 264). The final events took place at the end of April (see Ott 1984a: 357). Although Ott is critical of Heidegger, he admits that "the accord between National Socialism and Heidegger could not last long, provided that Heidegger was to remain true to his own convictions, and the Nazis to theirs" (Ott 1984a: 353).

52. Cf. Youssef Ishaghpour's Introduction in Goldmann 1973: 44f. See also Picht 1977: 198. The tendency to overlook such changes in the concrete historical situation surrounding Heidegger's activities as rector is illustrated by Farias (1987), a book which appeared after the completion of this paper. A critic with strong anti-Heideggerian inclinations admitted that from Farias's book "nothing decisively new had come to light" (Augstein 1987: 215). It remains to be seen whether the German edition of this book, now in preparation, will contain substantive documentary support for its claims, as urged, among others, by Aubenque (1988) and Rorty (1988: 32).

References

Allemann, Beda. 1969. Martin Heidegger und die Politik. In O. Pöggeler (ed.), *Heidegger. Perspektiven zur Deutung seines Werks.* Köln/Berlin: Kiepenheuer & Witsch, pp. 246–260.

Aubenque, Pierre. 1988. Grobe Irrtümer über Heidegger. *Frankfurter Allgemeine Zeitung,* 25 January 1988.

Augstein, Rudolf. 1987. Aber bitte nicth philosophieren. *Der Spiegel,* 23 November 1987, pp. 212–220.

Biemel, Walter. 1978. Heidegger's concept of Dasein. In F. Elliston (ed.), *Heidegger's Existential Analytic.* The Hague: Mouton Publishers, pp. 111–131.

Bullock, Alan. 1952. *Hitler. A Study in Tyranny.* London: Odhams Press.

Caputo, John D. 1982. Hermeneutics as the recovery of man. *Man and World* 15: 343–367.

Chiodi, Pietro. 1965. *L'esistenzialismo di Heidegger,* 3rd ed. Torino: Taylor.

Demske, James M. 1963. *Sein, Mensch und Tod. Das Todesproblem bei Martin Heidegger.* Freiburg/München: Alber.

Elliston, Frederick. 1978. Heidegger's phenomenology of social existence. In F. Elliston (ed.), *Heidegger's Existential Analytic.* The Hague: Mouton, pp. 61–77.

Farias, Victor. 1987. *Heidegger et le nazisme.* Paris: Verdier.

Fédier, François. 1966. Trois attaques contre Heidegger. *Critique* 234: 883–904.

Fehér, István M. 1984. *Martin Heidegger.* Budapest: Kossuth.

Fell, Joseph P. 1979. *Heidegger and Sartre. An Essay on Being and Place.* New York: Columbia University Press.

Fichte, J. G. 1971. Deducirter Plan einer zu Berlin zu errichtenden höheren Lehranstalt. In *Fichtes Werke* (ed. by I. H. Fichte), reprint edition, vol. 8. Berlin: de Gruyter, pp. 95–204.

Gadamer, Hans-Georg. 1975. *Wahrheit und Methode. Grundzüge einer philosophischen Hermeneutik*, 4th ed. Tübingen: Mohr.

———. 1976. Die philosophischen Grundlagen des zwanzigsten Jahrhunderts. In H.G. Gadamer, *Kleine Schriften*, vol. 1, 2nd ed. Tübingen: Mohr, pp. 131–148.

———. 1983. *Heideggers Wege.* Tübingen: Mohr.

———. 1985. Gibt es auf Erden ein Mass? *Philosophische Rundschau* 32: 1–26.

———. 1986/1987. Erinnerungen an Heideggers Anfänge. *Dilthey-Jahrbuch für Philosophie und Geschichte der Geisteswissenschaften* (ed. by F. Rodi) 4: 13–26.

Gelven, Michael. 1970. *A Commentary on Heidegger's "Being and Time."* New York: Harper & Row.

Gerstenberger, Heide. 1972. Konservatismus in der Weimarer Republik. In G.K. Kaltenbrunner (ed.), *Rekonstruktion des Konservatismus.* Freiburg: Rombach, pp. 331–348.

Goldmann, Lucien. 1973. *Lukács et Heidegger* (ed. by Y. Ishaghpour). Paris: Denoël/ Gonthier.

Guignon, Charles B. 1984. Heidegger's "Authenticity" revisited. *The Review of Metaphysics* 38: 321–339.

Guzzoni, Ute. 1986. Bemerkungen zu Heidegger 1933. In B. Martin and G. Schramm (eds.), *Martin Heidegger. Ein Philosoph und die Politik. Freiburger Universitätsblätter* 25(92): 75–80.

Harries, Karsten. 1976. Heidegger as a political thinker. *The Review of Metaphysics* 29: 642–669.

Hegel, G. W. F. 1970. Konzept der Rede beim Antritt des philosophischen Lehramtes an der Universitt Berlin. 22. Okt. 1818. In G. W. F. Hegel, *Werke in zwanzig Bänden,* Theorie Werkausgabe, vol. 10. Frankfurt am Main: Suhrkamp, pp. 399–417.

Heidegger, Martin. [BH]. Brief über den Humanismus. In *Platons Lehre von der Wahrheit. Mit einem Brief über den "Humanismus."* Bern: Francke, 1947.

———. [DE]. *Denkerfahrungen* (ed. by H. Heidegger). Frankfurt am Main: Klostermann, 1983.

———. [EM]. *Einführung in die Metaphysik,* 4th ed. Tübingen: Niemeyer, 1976.

———. [FD]. *Die Frage nach dem Ding.* Tübingen: Niemeyer, 1962.

———. [GA]. *Gesamtausgabe.* Frankfurt am Main: Klostermann, 1975–. Quoted by volume and page numbers.

———. [GR]. "Nur noch ein Gott uns retten." Spiegel-Gespräch mit Martin Heidegger am 23 September 1966. *Der Spiegel,* 31 May 1976, pp. 293–219.

———. [KPM]. *Kant und das Problem der Metaphysik,* 4th ed. Frankfurt am Main: Klostermann, 1973.

———. [N 1, 2]. *Nietzsche,* Vol. 1–2. Pfullingen: Neske, 1961.

———. [SA]. *Schellings Abhandlung über das Wesen der menschlichen Freiheit* (ed. by H. Feick). Tübingen: Niemeyer, 1971.

———. [SD]. *Zur Sache des Denkens,* 2nd ed. Tübingen: Niemeyer, 1976.

———. [SU]. *Die Selbstbehauptung der deutschen Universität.* Breslau: Korn, 1933.

———. [SUR]. *Die Selbstbehauptung der deutschen Universität. Das Rektorat 1933/1934* (ed. by H. Heidegger). Frankfurt am Main: Klostermann, 1983. Also, translated with an introduction by Karsten Harries (*The Review of Metaphysics* 38: 467–502; 1985).

———. [SZ]. *Sein und Zeit,* 15th ed. Tübingen: Niemeyer, 1979.

———. [WA]. Wege zur Aussprache. *Jahrbuch der Stadt Freiburg*, vol. 1. Stuttgart, 1937, pp. 135–139 (reprinted in DE, pp. 15–21).

———. [WM]. *Was ist Metaphysik?* Bonn: Cohen, 1930.

———. [WW]. *Vom Wesen der Wahrheit.* Frankfurt am Main: Klostermann, 1943.

Herrmann, Friedrich-Wilhelm von. 1981. *Der Begriff der Phänomenologie bei Heidegger und Husserl.* Frankfurt am Main: Klostermann.

———. 1987. *Hermeneutische Phänomenologie des Daseins. Eine Erläuterung von "Sein und Zeit."* Band 1: *Einleitung: Die Exposition der Frage nach dem Sinn von Sein.* Frankfurt am Main: Klostermann.

Hogemann, Friedrich. 1986/1987. Heideggers Konzeption der Phänomenologie in den Vorlesungen aus dem Wintersemester 1919/20 und dem Sommersemester 1920. *Dilthey-Jahrbuch für Philosophie und Geschichte der Geisteswissenschaften* (ed. by F. Rodi) 4: 54–71.

Hollerbach, Alexander. 1986. Im Schatten des Jahres 1933: Erik Wolf und Martin Heidegger. In B. Martin and G. Schramm (eds.), *Martin Heidegger. Ein Philosoph und die Politik. Freiburger Universitätsblätter* 25(92): 33–47.

Husserl, Edmund. 1965. *Philosophie als strenge Wissenschaft* (ed. by W. Szilasi). Frankfurt am Main: Klostermann.

———. 1976. *Ideen zu einer reinen Phänomenologie und phänomenologischen Philosophie* (ed. by K. Schuhmann, Husserliana III/1). Den Haag: M. Nijhoff.

———. 1980. *Logische Untersuchungen*, vol. 1. *Prolegomena zur reinen Logik*, 6th ed. Tübingen: Niemeyer.

Jaspers, Karl. 1978. *Notizen zu Martin Heidegger* (ed. by H. Saner). München: Piper.

Jünger, Ernst. 1959. Der Arbeiter. In E. Jünger, *Werke*, vol. 6. Stuttgart: Ernst Klett Verlag, pp. 9–329.

Kant, Immanuel. 1982. *Die Religion innerhalb der Grenzen der blossen Vernunft.* In I. Kant, *Werkausgabe*, vol. 8 (ed. by W. Weischedel), 5th ed. Frankfurt am Main: Suhrkamp, pp. 645–879.

Kierkegaard, Søren. 1957. *Entweder/Oder*, Zweiter Teil. Düsseldorf: Diederichs Verlag.

King, Magda. 1964. *Heidegger's Philosophy.* New York: Macmillan.

Kisiel, Theodore. 1986/87. Das Entestehen des Begriffsfeldes 'Faktizität' im Frühwerk Heideggers. *Dilthey-Jahrbuch für Philosophie und Geschichte der Geisteswissenschaften* (ed. by F. Rodi) 4: 91–120.

Krieck, Ernst. 1934. Germanischer Mythos und Heideggersche Philosophie. *Volk im Werden* 2: 247–249 (reprinted in G. Schneeberger, *Nachlese zu Heidegger. Dokumente zu seinem Leben und Denken.* Bern, 1962, pp. 225–228).

Krockow, Christian Graf von. 1958. *Die Entscheidung. Eine Untersuchung über Ernst Jünger, Carl Schmitt, Martin Heidegger.* Stuttgart: F. Enke Verlag.

Martin, Bernd. 1986. Heidegger und die Reform der deutschen Universität 1933. In B. Martin and G. Schramm (eds.), *Martin Heidegger. Ein Philosoph und die Politik. Freiburger Universitätsblätter* 25(92): 49–69.

Marx, Werner. 1961. *Heidegger und die Tradition.* Stuttgart: Kohlhammer.

Meinecke, Friedrich. 1949. *Die Deutsche Katastrophe. Betrachtungen und Erinnerungen*, 4th ed. Wiesbaden: Brockhaus.

Moehling, Karl A. 1981. Heidegger and the Nazis. In T. Sheehan (ed.), *Heidegger. The Man and the Thinker.* Chicago: Precedent, pp. 31–43.

Mörchen, Hermann. 1981. *Adorno und Heidegger. Untersuchung einer philosophischen Kommunikationsverweigerung.* Stuttgart: Klett-Cotta.

Ott, Hugo. 1984a. Martin Heidegger als Rektor der Universität Freiburg 1933/34. *Zeitschrift für die Geschichte des Oberrheins* 132: 343–358.

————. 1984b. Martin Heidegger als Rektor der Universität Freiburg i. Br. 1933/34. II. Die Zeit des Rektorats von Martin Heidegger (23 April 1933 bis 23 April 1934). *Zeitschrift des Breisgau-Geschichtsvereins ("Schau-ins-Land")* 103: 107–130.

Palmier, Jean-Michel. 1968. *Les écrits politiques de Heidegger.* Paris: L'Herne.

Petzet, Heinrich Wiegand. 1983. *Auf einen Stern zugehen. Begegnungen und Gespräche mit Martin Heidegger 1929–1976.* Frankfurt am Main: Societäts Verlag.

Picht, Georg. 1977. Die Macht des Denkens. In G. Neske (ed.), *Erinnerung an Martin Heidegger.* Pfullingen: Neske, pp. 197–205.

Pöggeler, Otto. 1963. *Der Denkweg Martin Heideggers.* Pfullingen: Neske.

————. 1974. *Philosophie und Politik bei Heidegger,* 2nd ed. Freiburg/München: Alber.

————. 1982. Neue Wege mit Heidegger? *Philosophische Rundschau* 29: 39–71.

————. 1983. *Heidegger und die hermeneutische Philosophie.* Freiburg/München: Alber.

————. 1984. *Die Frage nach der Kunst. Von Hegel zu Heidegger.* Freiburg/München: Alber.

————. 1985. Den Führer führen? Heidegger und kein Ende. *Philosophische Rundschau* 32: 26–67.

————. 1988. Heideggers politisches Selbstverständnis. In A. Gethmann-Siefert and O. Pöggeler (eds.), *Heidegger und die praktische Philosophie.* Frankfurt am Main: Suhrkamp, pp. 17–63.

Rauschning, Hermann. 1939. *Germany's Revolution of Destruction.* London/Toronto: William Heinemann (German edition: *Die Revolution des Nihilismus.* Zürich/New York: Europa Verlag, 1938).

Richardson, William, J., S.J. 1963. *Heidegger. Through Phenomenology to Thought* (Preface by Martin Heidegger). The Hague: M. Nijhoff.

Rodi, Frithjof. 1986/87. Die Bedeutung Diltheys für die Konzeption von *Sein und Zeit.* Zum Umfeld von Heideggers Kasseler Vorträgen (1925). *Dilthey-Jahrbuch für Philosophie und Geschichte der Geisteswissenschaften* (ed. by F. Rodi) 4: 161–177.

Rorty, Richard. 1979. *Philosophy and the Mirror of Nature.* Princeton, N.J.: Princeton University Press.

————. 1988. Taking philosophy seriously: Heidegger et le Nazisme by Victor Farias. *New Republic,* 11 April 1988, pp. 31–34.

Sallis, John. 1978. Where does "Being and Time" begin? Commentary on section 1–4. In F. Elliston (ed.), *Heidegger's Existential Analytic.* The Hague: Mouton, pp. 21–43.

Schelling, F. W. J. 1977. *Vorlesungen über die Methode des akademischen Studiums. Schellings Werke* (ed. by M. Schröter), Dritter Hauptband, 3rd ed. München: C.H. Beck, pp. 229–374.

Schmidt, Gerhart. 1986. Heideggers philosophische Politik. In B. Martin and G. Schramm (eds.), *Martin Heidegger. Ein Philosoph und die Politik. Freiburger Universitätsblätter* 25(92): 83–90.

Schneeberger, Guido. 1962. *Nachlese zu Heidegger. Dokumente zu seinem Leben und Denken.* Bern: Author's edition.

Schwan, Alexander. 1965. *Politische Philosophie im Denken Heideggers.* Köln und Opladen: Westdeutscher Verlag.

Sheehan, Thomas J. 1975. Heidegger, Aristotle and Phenomenology. *Philosophy Today* (Summer): 87–94.

————. 1981. Heidegger's early years: fragments for a philosophical biography. In T. Sheehan (ed.), *Heidegger. The Man and the Thinker.* Chicago: Precedent, pp. 3–19.

————. 1984. "Time and Being" 1925–27. In R.W. Shahan and J.N. Mohanty (eds.), *Thinking About Being. Aspects of Heidegger's Thought.* Norman, Oklahoma: University of Oklahoma Press, pp. 177–219.

Stern, Fritz. 1984. Der Nationalsozialismus als Versuchung. In F. Stern and H. Jonas (eds.), *Reflexionen finsterer Zeit*. Tübingen: Mohr, pp. 3–59.

Ugazio, Ugo Maria. 1976. *Il Problema della Morte nella Filosofia di Heidegger*. Milano: Mursia.

Volpi, Franco. 1984a. Heidegger in Marburg. Die Auseinandersetzung mit Husserl. *Philosophischer Literaturanzeiger* 37: 48–69.

_____. 1984b. *Heidegger e Aristotele*. Padova: Daphne.

Waehlens, Alphonse de. 1947. La philosophie de Heidegger et le nazisme. *Les Temps Modernes* 2: 115–127.

Willms, Bernard. 1977. Politik als Geniestreich? Bemerkung zu Heideggers Politik-verständnis. *Martin Heidegger. Fragen an sein Werk*. Stuttgart: Reclam, pp. 16–20.

Wisser, Richard. 1977. Das Fernseh-Interview. In G. Neske (ed.), *Erinnerung an Martin Heidegger*. Pfullingen: Neske, pp. 257–287.

Wittgenstein, Ludwig. 1984. *Über Gewissheit. Werkausgabe*, vol. 8. Frankfurt am Main: Suhrkamp.

Zimmermann, Michael E. 1981. *Eclipse of the Self. The Development of Heidegger's Concept of Authenticity*. Athens, Ohio: Ohio University Press.

About the Contributors

Myriam Bienenstock is a lecturer in philosophy at the Hebrew University of Jerusalem. She was a Fulbright scholar at the Center for the History and Philosophy of Science at Boston University and Heinrich Herz scholar at the Hegel-Archiv in Bochum, West Germany. She has written on Hegel and Marx. Her book on the formation of Hegel's idealism is forthcoming.

James F. Bohman is assistant professor of philosophy at St. Louis University. He is the author of *New Philosophy of Social Science* and co-editor of *After Philosophy*. He has published articles on the theory of communication, social criticism, and Marxism, and has translated Offe, Gadamer, and Habermas.

Sergio Cremaschi teaches philosophy at the Università Cattolica, Milan, and has been a visiting professor at the New School for Social Research, New York. He is the author of *L'automa spirituale: la teoria della mente e delle passioni in Spinoza*. His second book, *Il sistema della ricchezza: economia politica e problema del metodo in Adam Smith*, will appear soon in English translation.

Marcelo Dascal is associate professor of philosophy at Tel Aviv University. He is the author of *La Sémiologie de Leibniz, Pragmatics and the Philosophy of Mind*, and *Leibniz: Language, Signs, and Thought*. He has edited *Dialogue: An Interdisciplinary Approach* and *The Just and the Unjust*, and co-edited *The Institution of Philosophy*, as well as several other volumes. He is the editor of the international journal of philosophy *Manuscrito*.

Jon Elster has taught at the Universities of Paris, Oslo, and California (Berkeley), and at Stanford University. He is currently professor of political science and philosophy at the University of Chicago. His books include *Logic and Society, Ulysses and the Sirens, Sour Grapes, Explaining Technical Change*, and *Making Sense of Marx*.

István M. Fehér is associate professor of philosophy at Budapest University. He has been a Humboldt Fellow at the Hegel-Archiv in Bochum, West Germany. He is the author of books on Sartre and Heidegger, and of articles on Lukács, Popper, Croce, phenomenology, hermeneutics, and German idealism. He is one of the editors of *Magyar Filozófiai Szemle* (Hungarian Philosophical Review).

Gideon Freudenthal is a lecturer at the Institute for the History and Philosophy of Science and Ideas, Tel Aviv University. He is the author of *Atom and Individual in the Age of Newton* and of the forthcoming book *The Conceptual Foundations of Mechanics in Descartes and Galileo.*

Ora Gruengard teaches philosophy at Tel Aviv University. She has published articles on the philosophy of social sciences and on the philosophy of action. In addition to philosophy, she has studied psychology and economics. Her current interests are the explanation of human cognition and action and the meta-philosophical issue of the philosophers' modes of cognition.

Jean Hampton is the author of *Hobbes and the Social Contract Tradition* and has written many articles on Hobbes and social contract theory. She has just finished a book with Jeffrie Murphy entitled *Forgiveness and Mercy.* She has taught at UCLA and the University of Pittsburgh and is now associate professor of philosophy at the University of California, Davis.

Alastair Hannay was professor of philosophy at the University of Trondheim, Norway, and is currently working for the Norwegian Research Council. He is the author of *Mental Images—A Defence* and *Kierkegaard.* He has translated works by Kierkegaard for the Penguin Classics. He is the editor of *Inquiry.*

Don Herzog teaches political theory at the University of Michigan, Ann Arbor. He is the author of *Without Foundations: Justification in Political Theory* and *Happy Slaves: A Critique of Consent Theory.*

Stephen Holmes is associate professor of political science at the University of Chicago. He is the author of *Benjamin Constant and the Making of Modern Liberalism.*

Jean-Louis Labarrière has taught philosophy at the École Normale d'Institutrices de St.-Germain-en-Laye and at the University of Paris (VII), and is currently a researcher at the Conseil National de la Recherche Scientifique. He is completing his *doctorat d'état* on Aristotle, and has published several articles on ancient and modern philosophy.

Richard H. Popkin is professor emeritus of philosophy at Washington University, St. Louis, and adjunct professor at UCLA. He is the author of *The History of Scepticism from Erasmus to Spinoza, The High Road to Pyrrhonism, Isaac la Peyrère,* and *Spinoza's Earliest Publication? The Hebrew Translation of Margaret Fell's Loving Salutation.* He has been the editor of the *Journal of the History of Philosophy.*

Harry Redner is a reader in the department of politics at Monash University, Australia. He is the author of *In the Beginning Was the Deed: Reflections on the Passage of Faust; The Ends of Philosophy;* and *The Ends of Science* (Westview, 1987) and co-author of *Anatomy of the World.*

Robert Paul Wolff is professor of philosophy at the University of Massachusetts, Amherst. He is the author of *The Idea of the University, In Defense of Anarchism, Kant's Theory of Mental Activity, The Poverty of Liberalism, Understanding Rawls,* and *Understanding Marx.* He has edited *1984 Revisited; Prospects for American Politics.*

Index

A priori
  historical, 304
  synthetic, 154
Absolute, the, 159, 176
Absolutism, 28, 56, 61, 63, 283, 312
Absorption, 295
Abstract (in the Hegelian sense), 23,
  148, 150–151, 153, 175, 185. *See
  also* Abstraction
Abstraction (in the Hegelian sense),
  147–150, 165, 177–179, 184, 209–
  210, 218, 222, 225, 229, 232, 235–
  236. *See also* Abstract
Academic-political entity, 312
Acceptability, 272, 276
Accidental (in the Hegelian sense), 149,
  175, 184
Accidental characteristics, 19
Action, 293, 296, 301, 311
  political, 21, 116
  practical, 269
  rational, 269
  technical, 163
  See also Collective, action
Activity, 227, 229, 234, 236, 301
  cognitive, 229. *See also* Cognition
  practical, 209. *See also* Practice; *Praxis*
  See also Scientific activity
Actual (in the Hegelian sense), 150,
  164, 168(n61)
Adler, M., 215
Administration, 228, 302
Adorno, Th., 342(n28)
Agency, 303
Agent, 269, 272, 275–279, 282, 284,
  286–287
Agonism, 302
Agreement, 309–310
  process of reaching, 279–283,
  288(n3)
Aisthēsis, 37, 42. *See also* Sense,
  perception

Alienation, 186, 189, 192–193, 199,
  202–203. *See also* Consciousness,
  alienated
Alliance, 297
Althusser, L., 291
Altruism, 16
Analytic-synthetic dichotomy, 71
Anarchism
  authoritarian, 300
  epistemological, 1, 6, 14, 26, 242–262
  philosophical, 245, 254–255
  political, 183, 241–262, 294, 300,
  305, 307–308, 313
Anarchy, 295, 308, 337
Ancient world, 312
Animal, man as, 225–228, 233, 298,
  340(n12). *See also* Political, animal;
  Rational, animal
Animal principle, 92
Anonymity, 324
Anthropology, 339(n11)
Anti-authoritarian, 300
Anti-authoritarianism, 132
Anti-capitalism, 329
Anti-democratic, 11
Anti-egalitarian, 284
Anti-elitist, 300
Anti-enlightenment, 258, 265–266
Anti-epistemology, 6, 12
Anti-essentialism, 15
Anti-foundationalism, 27
Anti-metaphysical, 339(n9)
Anti-metaphysical tradition, 214–215,
  318–319, 321
Anti-methodology, 241–262
Anti-moral, 307
Anti-nationalism, 342(n29)
Anti-political, 307
Anti-psychologism, 20
Anti-representationalism, 292
Anti-statist, 300, 307
Anticipation, 324–325
Antinomian, 300, 307
Antisemitism, 6, 258–259, 343(n31)

patterns of, 264–288
  social, 85, 271, 276–279, 281, 283
Interest
  common, 10, 44–45, 131, 196,
    239(n11), 268
  general, 275, 279
  generalizable, 279–280
  group, 99
  public, 223
Interested party, 298–299
Interests, 125, 130, 136, 234, 249, 251,
    257, 275, 279, 298, 306, 309
  of incompetent groups, 285
  of oppressed groups, 285
  See also Self-interest
Intermediate, 299
Internationalism, 342(n29), 345(n42)
Interpretation, 312–313, 341(n20). *See
    also* Marxist interpretation
Intersubjectivity, 230, 274, 285, 297
Intervention, 62–65, 95–96, 201
Intuition, 22, 130, 142(n6), 148–150,
    153–155, 157–162, 168(n11), 259
  intellectual, 5
Inversion, 23, 173–180, 182, 184–185
Invisible hand, 5, 140, 284. *See also*
    Heterogenesis of ends; Unintended
    results
Irrationalism, 317, 319, 321, 342(n27)
Irrationality, 287(n2)
  public, 287(n1)
Is-ought problem, 18, 70, 75–80, 116
Islam, 122
Itelson, G., 237(n5)

Jacobi, F. H., 159
Jacoby, F., 346(n46)
Jäger, W., 345(n38)
Jaspers, K., 317, 342(n28), 345(n38)
Jefferson, Th., 111, 116, 118–119
Jevons, W. S., 238(n8)
Jew, Jewish, 345(n41), 346(n46)
Johnson, M., 23
Jones, J., 262(n5)
Judaism, 122
Judge, 307
Judgment (in the Kantian sense), 153,
    166, 274–275, 280
Jünger, E., 345(n45)
Juridical system, 306–307
Jurisprudence, 272
  natural, 84–90, 92–93, 95, 99–105.
    See also Legislator, science of
Jury problem, the, 288(n6)
Jury Theorem, the, 286
Justice, 53, 57, 59, 75, 79, 90, 92–94,
    116–117, 119, 192, 200, 237(n3),

246, 262, 264–265, 283–285,
    287(n3), 294
  distributive, 11
  general rules of, 89
  natural, 89, 93, 95, 99, 101
  principle of, 283
  realm of, 25
  theory of, 7, 74, 84, 88–89, 93, 95,
    192
Justification, standards of, 264, 275,
    284. *See also* Rational, justification
Just price, 97

Kant, I., 5, 14–15, 24, 41, 55, 66(n6),
    69, 72, 153–156, 158–159, 161–162,
    166, 168(n11), 174, 184, 215t, 215,
    264–266, 268–278, 280, 287(n1),
    288(n4), 293, 320–321, 325–327,
    339(n10), 341(n21), 344(n35, n37)
Kantianism, 15, 214, 215t, 268, 331
Kantians, 54–55, 70
Kent, 299
Kepler, J., 54
Keynes, J. M., 97
Kierkegaard, S., 317, 319, 321–322, 324
Kingdom-of-Ends, 24
Knowing relation, 319
Knowledge
  a priori, 148–149
  authentic, 336
  causal explanation of, 155
  common, 309
  conceptual, 22
  empirical, 114, 311
  founding of (*Begründung des Wissens*),
    340(n13)
  growth of, 125, 128, 137
  mathematical, 114–115, 120, 320
  mechanisms of, 311
  metaphysical, 162
  moral, 9, 48–49, 57, 60–61, 64–65,
    115–116, 119–121. *See also* Ethics;
    Science, moral
  physical, 115, 120
  political, 35–38
  powerlessness of, 332–333
  practical, 22, 39–41, 43, 273
  pseudo-, 335
  reflective, 277
  reflective conception of, 156, 158
  religious, 61
  representational theory of, 297
  will to, 296, 302
Kohlberg, L., 277
Kolbenheyer, E. G., 345(n41)